From the Diaries of Felix Frankfurter

FROM THE DIARIES OF
FELIX
FRANKFURTER

With a Biographical Essay and Notes

 *BY Joseph P. Lash*

Assisted by Jonathan Lash, JD, Catholic University
Law School, 1974

W. W. NORTON & COMPANY, INC., NEW YORK

Copyright © 1975 by Joseph P. Lash. First Edition. All Rights Reserved. Published simultaneously in Canada by George J. McLeod Limited, Toronto

Library of Congress Cataloging in Publication Data

Frankfurter, Felix, 1882–1965.
From the diaries of Felix Frankfurter.

1. Frankfurter, Felix, 1882–1965. 2. Judges—United States—Correspondence, reminiscences, etc.
I. Lash, Joseph P., 1909–   II. Title.
KF8745.F7A33   347'.73'2634 [B]   75–8675
ISBN 0-393-07488-9

Printed in the United States of America
2 3 4 5 6 7 8 9 0

Grateful acknowledgment is made for permission to quote from the following: to William Morrow & Co, Inc., *Felix Frankfurter Reminisces*, talks with Dr. Harlan B. Phillips, and *Felix Frankfurter: A Tribute*, edited by Wallace Mendelson; to Harcourt Brace Jovanovich, Inc., *Portrait of a Philosopher* by Leonora Cohen Rosenfield; to the Harvard University Press, *The Holmes-Laski Letters*, edited by Mark DeWolfe Howe.

To Felix Frankfurter and his "Hot Dogs,"
who made New Deal Washington a
shining moment in the United States history

CONTENTS

PREFACE

I came upon these diaries at the Library of Congress in the course of research on another book. I found them so absorbing that I felt a larger public should have the pleasure of their company. They are what remain of what may have been a monumental record of half a century of American history, and of the complex, enigmatic character of the author. There is internal evidence in what we have that Justice Frankfurter, in deeding the Diaries to the American people, withheld and destroyed some parts. In this regard, although the biographer laments, he had distinguished company. Justice Holmes once wrote that though he was reconciled to having a biography written based on his personal papers, he had done his best to "destroy illuminating documents." In addition to Frankfurter's excisions from the Diaries, some sections were stolen after the Justice's papers were turned over to the Library of Congress. Some day the Federal Bureau of Investigation may recover them.

The substantial parts that survive are readable and illuminating. As Henry L. Stimson, Frankfurter's first chief, noted, his young aide had a talent "for keeping in touch with the center of things," and as a consequence there are in these pages revealing glimpses from the inside of the Taft Administration, of Roosevelt's Washington during World War II, and of the early years of the Truman presidency. There are also telling portrayals of the clash between Frankfurter and two other Roosevelt appointees to the Supreme Court, Hugo L. Black and William O. Douglas, over the nature of the judicial function. The emotional intensity with which Frankfurter invests these episodes gives the reader a sense that the great marble blocks of the Court must have shaken with the vigor of the battle.

Those who remember Frankfurter as a man of sweetness and vivacity, capable of intellectual detachment and impersonality, will be startled by some of the passages in these Diaries, passages that are full of wrath, contempt, superciliousness, and may ask why they are being published. "History also has its claims," as

Frankfurter often said. It may be, as has been suggested to the editor, that he used the Diaries as "a wastebasket" into which he poured his angers, resentments, and jealousies as a way of purging himself of them so that they would not affect the act of judgment. Others may conclude that a public posture of disinterestedness and restraint masked more elemental, darker drives that did affect his judgments. Diaries are often disappointing to contemporaries in what they reveal about the diarists. But for that reason they are the more enlightening and indispensable to our understanding of men and women and their role in history.

Frankfurter's references to some of his brethren positively "crackle," as Max Lerner once described his literary style, but there is every indication that he intended them to be published, along with the Diaries' record of how behind the scenes he had a hand in much of significance that went on in wartime Washington. In *Mr. Justice Holmes and the Supreme Court,* he observed that to understand the Court and its work it was indispensable "to understand what manner of men they were who sat on the Supreme Bench. Yet how meager is our insight into all but a very few. . . . On the whole we have a pitifully inadequate basis for understanding the psychological and cultural influences which may be the roots of judicial opinions." [1] In light of these comments it is a reasonable inference that Justice Frankfurter intended these Diaries to be published.

The biographical essay that introduces the Diaries is no more than a sketch of a remarkable life. It is not a preview of the Diaries. It seemed desirable to include it because there is no adequate biography of the Justice. He had selected Max Freedman, a newspaper columnist, for the task and spent many hours with him, dictating his version of what had happened. Freedman struggled with his assignment until his health collapsed and he had to abandon the task.

A word about keeping diaries. I came upon some notes on the subject that Justice Frankfurter made when his own *Reminiscences,* as recorded by Dr. Harlan B. Phillips, was published in 1960. [2] In his usual systematic way Frankfurter had surveyed some of the great American diaries—those of George Templeton Strong, John Adams, James K. Polk, Gideon Welles, Rutherford B. Hayes, and, in recent times, those of Stimson, James Forrestal, Harold L. Ickes. He noted that Strong's entries were those of a shy man who even in his own diary "concealed his own importance," while Adams's Diaries were impregnated with "self-absorption" and designed for "self-vindication." Polk, whose four volumes saw the light of day only in 1910, wanted a record of events and transactions during his presidency, while Welles, who "loved to write" and for whom writing was a form of communing with himself, nevertheless also had an eye cocked on posterity. Some diarists, he generalized, wrote primarily for writing's sake, and others played "for the verdict of history." Of Ickes, whose self-absorption he contrasted with Stimson's disciplined detachment, he noted that "it was his invariable habit to destroy the secretaries' shorthand notes and all preliminary drafts, usually burning them himself in the fireplace."

Frankfurter himself began his Diaries in 1911 for his own amusement and as an aid to the memory when he came to write of his life and times. They are clearly written with an eye to the historian and biographer, whether himself or someone else, and must be supplemented by other testimony. Nevertheless, discounting a certain bias that flows from the egocentric predicament, it is a pleasure to watch a powerful, civilized mind play over the events, personalities, and conflicts that are herein described.

I am greatly indebted to Dr. Paul T. Heffron, Assistant Chief, Manuscript Division at the Library of Congress, for his helpfulness and encouragement, and to Mr. Donald Hiss, the legal executor of Justice Frankfurter's estate. The following read all or part of the manuscript, but carry no responsibility for the book's point of view or errors: Victor Brudney, Chief Judge Frank M. Coffin, Benjamin V. Cohen, Associate Justice Benjamin Kaplan, Ida Klaus, Ralph Thompson, Herbert Wechsler, and Nancy F. Wechsler. They saved me from many errors and suggested answers to several problems.

In addition the following shared their memories of Frankfurter with me: Roger N. Baldwin, Hugo L. Black, Jr., Elsie Douglas, Paul A. Freund, Lloyd Garrison, Louis Henkin, Mrs. Mark DeWolfe Howe, David E. Lilienthal, Joseph L. Rauh, Jr. I spent four hours with Alexander M. Bickel talking about Frankfurter a few weeks before Professor Bickel's death. His mind was sharp, his memory precise, his spirit valorous. Several times, fearing that I was tiring him, I rose to go, only to be motioned back into my seat. "I haven't had such a good time in months," he said. "Usually I spend my days reading Trollope."

There was an especial pleasure for me in editing this book in the assistance I had from Jonathan Lash, a graduate of Catholic University Law School, in footnoting the legal material, and from Father Broderick, one of his professors, and an old friend from the political wars against Tammany. The manuscript was typed expertly by Mrs. Freda Weiner.

In my biographical essay, I have used many books, but I made particular use of the *Felix Frankfurter Reminisces* as recorded by Dr. Phillips, *Felix Frankfurter: A Tribute*, edited by Professor Wallace Mendelson,[3] and *Roosevelt and Frankfurter: Their Correspondence, 1928–1945*, annotated by Max Freedman.

I am again in debt to the Columbia Oral History Project, and to Yale University Library for permission to publish several letters from Henry L. Stimson, and to the Princeton University Library for the Frankfurter letter to Walter Millis of January 19, 1953.

From the Diaries of Felix Frankfurter

A BRAHMIN OF THE LAW:

A Biographical Essay by Joseph P. Lash

In 1905, in Felix Frankfurter's final year at Harvard Law School, he roomed with another brilliant young Jewish immigrant, Morris Raphael Cohen, who was working on his doctoral dissertation on Kant and "The Nature of Goodness." Both men were in their early twenties. Both, in Harvard's Golden Age, which in the Law School included such men as James Barr Ames, the dean, John Chipman Gray, Samuel Williston, and in the Department of Philosophy, such men as William James and Josiah Royce, had attracted the notice, indeed, enchanted their WASP mentors by their superior intellectual grasp, purposefulness, and industry.

Both had arrived at Ellis Island with their parents, Frankfurter from Vienna in 1894, Cohen from Minsk in the Russian Pale of Settlement in 1892. Both had strong mothers who were the backbones of their families and who pushed them toward the intellectual life. Both had lived on the Lower East Side, a teeming ghetto in which ideologies competed noisily with peddlers' cries. In the late 1890s Frankfurter read an essay on "The Dreyfus Case" before one club of East Side intellectuals, Cohen an "Essay in Bluffing" before another.[4] Both had attended the City College of New York. Such already were Frankfurter's forensic powers and mastery of English that the college literary and debating society set aside the rule that seniors only should represent it in the annual prize debate to permit him, only a junior, to do so. Short of stature—he was less than five feet, five inches—he needed eloquence and intellectual power to keep the world of taller men from overlooking him. He succeeded, graduating from City College at nineteen, third highest in his class. Cohen, too, was a phenomenon. He read everything, forgot nothing, won the Belden Medal in Mathematics, and was consumed by a Spinozistic passion for the truth.

Harvard awed them. "Nervous strain and poor health cut down my effectiveness," wrote Cohen. Runtyness added to Frankfurter's terrors. "The first day I was there I had one of the most intense frights of my life. I looked about me. Everybody was taller." He could not recall speaking up, he asserted fifty years later, "at all during the first year." [5] Shy and scared of speaking up he may have been, but in later years one of his professors would read to his first-year students a brilliant exposition of a case and then stun them with the announcement, "I have been reading to you, gentlemen, from the first-year blue book of Felix Frankfurter of the class of 1906." [6] He consistently led his class in the Law School, but, more activist and extroverted than Cohen, and of more robust health, Frankfurter was delighted to have his roommate write his *Harvard Law Review* notices of books dealing with jurisprudence and firmly resisted his friend's proddings that he, too, become a philosopher. His ambitions were more practical. His closest friend in the Law School was Emory Buckner, son of a Methodist preacher from Nebraska. "The two young men," wrote Buckner's biographer, "shared poverty and a brilliance immediately obvious to those around them because it came out in streams of verbal byplay; and both were unusually short." [7]

He did not want to be detached from the "actions and passions" of his times, as Oliver Wendell Holmes, one of his heroes, phrased it,* and the law seemed to provide the mixture of involvement and contemplative life that best suited his ardent temperament. So, preceded by glowing, almost lyrical recommendations from his Law School professors, especially Dean Ames, to several eminent lawyers in New York who themselves were products of the Harvard Law School, he returned to New York. The great law firms were still strongholds of the WASP elite, and there was no scramble to hire a young Jew, no matter how talented. He finally was employed by Hornblower, Byrne, Miller and Potter, distinguished and a Harvard bastion. "I'd heard that they had never taken a Jew and wouldn't take a Jew. I decided that was the office I wanted to get into. . . ." [8]

The partner who hired him was kindly disposed, gave him a starting salary of one thousand dollars, and suggested that this was a good time to change his name. Frankfurter was a religious agnostic, not a practicing Jew. More and more he moved in a non-Jewish world, but he had no wish to escape his Jewishness. "Hold yourself dear!" his mother advised him. The suggestion that he change his name went unheeded, and the welfare of the Jewish people would always be close to his heart.

Morris Cohen, incidentally, also armed with enthusiastic letters of recommendation—his were from James, Royce, and Perry—was less successful in obtaining a position teaching philosophy. He was obliged to teach mathematics; philosophy, which at City College had not wholly freed itself from its begin-

---

* Holmes also said that ". . . a man may live greatly in the law as elsewhere, that there as elsewhere he may wreak himself upon life, may drink the bitter cup of heroism, may wear his heart out after the unattainable."

nings as a branch of Christian theology, still shied away from employing a Jew as an instructor.

Frankfurter did not stay long with Hornblower. Henry L. Stimson, friend and disciple of Elihu Root, had just been appointed United States Attorney for the Southern District of New York by Theodore Roosevelt, whom Stimson found the "most commanding natural leader" he ever knew. In a break with the tradition of political jobbery in the U.S. Attorney's office, Stimson elected to surround himself with the best young men out of the great firms and law schools, especially his own Harvard Law School. Dean Ames advised him to get Felix Frankfurter. The offer stirred a wild conflict of feelings in Frankfurter. Public law appealed to him. But he had just joined Hornblower; would it not be disloyal to leave so swiftly? ". . . [F]ollow the dominant impulses of your nature," Dean Ames counseled him. A few weeks later, in the fall of 1906, he went over to Stimson's office, at a cut in salary. He was not interested in acquiring wealth and never would be; other types of power and influence stirred his spirit. He already was a recruiting agent for talent and promptly persuaded Stimson to bring in Emory Buckner. Not the least part of Stimson's appeal to the two young men was the opportunity it afforded them to fight under the banner of T. R. and reform.[9]

At first Frankfurter served as Stimson's personal assistant. He learned from the older man that "you must prepare the other fellow's case at least as well as your own" in order to guard against surprises. Frankfurter was good at that. In addition to great industry and a capacity for detail, he had the gift of seeing situations from "multiple perspectives." Within a year Stimson assigned him to try his own case before a jury, and when Frankfurter made his closing speech in behalf of the prosecution, Stimson slipped unobtrusively into a back row seat to listen to him.[10]

The U. S. Attorney's office in the Southern District, where America's new captains of giant combines had their headquarters and glittering mansions, was, apart from the Attorney General's Office in Washington, the chief federal law enforcement agency in the nation. Its cases ranged from the trial of smugglers to combat with the great railroads and industrial trusts. It was a splendid vantage point from which to see the realities of the American economy and what needed to be done to serve the public interest. New York also was the port of entry for a hundred thousand immigrants a month, with many detentions at Ellis Island and many *habeas corpus* efforts to get those detained out. Stimson assigned Frankfurter to handle the *habeas corpus* cases. "You are likely to have more understanding of their problems than some of the other lads in the office." [11]

The young staff Stimson had assembled included Thomas D. Thacher, later a judge in New York's chief court, with whom Frankfurter roomed; Winfred T. Denison, who all thought would go farthest but whose life was the briefest; and Goldthwaite H. Dorr, later a distinguished public servant. "We formed a little group," Dorr said of himself, Buckner, Frankfurter, and a few others in the U. S. Attorney's office. "We cared about books and art. We used to read mostly plays, assign parts. . . ." There was not much time for such diversions, but that did not matter, for work was even more exhilarating. Stimson was an exacting taskmaster and the office often worked evenings, even weekends, when all repaired to Highhold, the Stimson place near Huntington, Long Island, where among Stimson's memories was watching "a future Supreme Court Justice [Frankfurter] in a losing foot race around the fields of Highhold against a future judge in the New York Court of Appeals [Thacher]." [12]

In April 1909, coincident with the departure of Theodore Roosevelt from office, Stimson returned to private law practice. Public office had agreed with him immensely. ". . . [O]ne always feels better when he feels he is working in a good cause," he explained, and this, too, was a bond between him and the youthful Frankfurter, who said of his mentor, "I don't see how a young fellow coming to the bar could possibly have had a more desirable, more deepening, and altogether more precious influence during his formative years than to be junior to Henry L. Stimson." [13]

Frankfurter joined Stimson in private practice, and in 1910, when Stimson accepted the Republican nomination for Governor of New York, became his campaign assistant, serving as a one-man brain trust and speechwriter. Stimson was the reform candidate, nominated after a bruising fight with the Republican conservatives, and emerging as the handpicked choice of Theodore Roosevelt, who under the banner of the New Nationalism was heading toward his momentous split with President Taft. Roosevelt and Stimson covered the state between them with Frankfurter traveling on Stimson's special train, and on occasion also helping the Colonel with his speeches. But it was not a Republican year and Stimson was too austere a personality for the hustings. "Darn it, Harry," Frankfurter in later years recalled the Colonel in his high-pitched voice admonishing Stimson, "a campaign speech is a poster, not an etching!" Frankfurter's candidate lost but among the Democrats who came into office that year, as state senator from Dutchess County, was a Roosevelt who would prove to be the greatest campaigner in American history and whom both Stimson and Frankfurter would serve. He would amply satisfy the taste for politics that this campaign had aroused in Frankfurter. [14]

The 1910 election widened the breach between Roosevelt and Taft, and the latter, seeking to conciliate the Republican progressives, asked Stimson to become Secretary of War. Stimson accepted after ascertaining that it was agreeable to the Colonel. Frankfurter went back to the U. S. Attorney's office, hoping through Stimson to be appointed an Assistant Attorney General under Cornelius Wickersham. The position was unavailable, Stimson informed him, and while he could have the Assistant Attorney Generalship in charge of Customs, a job with a large salary attached to it, Stimson turned it down for him. He asked Frankfurter instead to come to Washington as Law Officer in the Bureau of Insular Affairs in the War Department. "The questions involved in the governing of our nine million people in our Insular possessions are most interesting, and involve many fundamentals and constitutional and international questions. . . . If you should accept it I would rely on you for a good deal more than that work alone, as you doubtless realize from your past experience with me. You would have to be my legal adviser on questions of general importance coming before the administration on which I may be consulted." [15]

Frankfurter's Diaries begin with his arrival in Washington in October 1911. The nation's capital before World War I was still a small town, more southern than *haut monde*, whose social and intellectual life, like its spacious avenues, radiated out from the White House and from Jackson Square, where an aging Henry Adams commented sourly but elegantly on the passing scene. The offices of State, War, and Navy were all lodged just west of the White House in one grey mass of a building whose outer dinginess was matched by the crepuscular quality of its high-ceilinged offices.

As Law Officer of the Bureau of Insular Affairs, Frankfurter was concerned with America's insular possessions—Puerto Rico, the Panama Canal, the Philippines, and San Domingo, Cuba, Haiti, where, as Frankfurter put it, "we had a kind of receivership." Neither in his *Reminiscences* nor in his Diaries is there much of the anti-imperialist perception that powerfully excited liberal thought at the turn of the century. By 1911 the establishment of American dominion in the Caribbean and the Far Pacific were settled facts, and Frankfurter already was a realist about power—where it was and who exercised it. His reforming impulses would always be bounded by a superb sensitivity to what was practically possible. "The whole push as you will read from this memorandum of mine on the Philippines," he said in his *Reminiscences*, "was more and more a push in the direction of autonomy." [16]

His stint with the War Department also freed him from the doctrinaire antimilitarism that was endemic in American liberalism. When he arrived from New York he could not distinguish between a captain and a colonel, and to be on the safe side called everyone "general." The generals soon turned into human beings, neither the heroes on white horses that some Americans saw, nor the tyrants incarnate of the radical, even the liberal, press. Frankfurter did have doubts about General Leonard Wood, a favorite of Theodore Roosevelt and Chief of Staff. He was, recalled Frankfurter, ". . . a powerful fellow . . . very unscrupulous . . . a dynamic personality. . . . Then he was sent out as Commissioner General of the Philippines where he messed up things." [17]

As Law Officer, Frankfurter argued his first cases before the Supreme Court, representing the Government; he was not quite thirty, "and of course that was very exciting for a youngster." A good deal of his work was with Stimson directly, helping him with speeches. Much of the Diary for 1911 deals with the ups and downs of a speech Stimson delivered on the central domestic issue of that and subsequent decades, the regulation of the great corporate trusts that had come to dominate the American economy. Frankfurter was also Stimson's confidant on the politics of the Taft Administration. He learned at first hand the difference between a strong and weak president and remembered all his life T. R.'s comment, "Oh, if only Taft knew the joys of leadership." [18]

A New York Jewish boy was not, as the Franklin Roosevelts who arrived

with the Wilson Administration were, welcomed into Washington society. But
he was no social outcast. He was often at the Stimsons. A letter of introduction
from Professor John Chipman Gray of the Harvard Law School to his old
friend Justice Oliver Wendell Holmes brought an invitation to call, and soon
Frankfurter was a regular visitor at his house, listening before the fire to "great
talk . . . a wonderful stream of exciting flow of ideas in words." [19]

His most intimate friends in Washington were his housemates in the
House of Truth, as Holmes dubbed the lodging house that was owned by Robert G. Valentine, at that time Commissioner of Indian Affairs. Frankfurter was
introduced to Valentine by another boarder, Winfred T. Denison, who had
gotten one of the Assistant Attorney Generalships that Frankfurter had wanted.
"We enjoy living together in this nice house very much," Denison wrote
Frankfurter's mother, whose photograph was on her son's desk, "and Felix
keeps us alive most of the time. The only trouble with him is that he wants to
sit up all night and sleep all day." [20] Others in the house were Denison's assistant, Loring C. Christie, a Canadian and graduate of the Harvard Law School,
where he had edited the *Law Review*, and Lord Eustace Percy. The latter was
one of the young men who were posted to the British Embassy after, as Henry
Adams had put it, "the sudden appearance of Germany as the grizzly terror"
had "frightened England into America's arms" and a century of Anglo-
American hostility had yielded to a recognition of an overriding community of
interests. It was a perception that was particularly shared by T. R. and his
friends.

This perception and the friendship with Percy, as well as with Arthur
Willert, the correspondent of the London *Times*, fed a budding Anglophilism
in Frankfurter which expressed itself in a study and admiration of English institutions that in later years sometimes made him seem more pro-English than his
English friends. It had its snobbish side. He yearned to be accepted by the
WASP establishment, but only on his own terms, it needs to be added, and
they included his Jewishness.

The loyalty that he felt toward the Jewish people from whom he had
sprung bound him to another shaping influence, the Boston "citizen lawyer,"
as Frankfurter called Louis D. Brandeis, perhaps the ablest man at the bar in
the United States. Brandeis combined a viselike grasp of economic and political
realities with a prophet's passion for justice. He was already emerging as one of
the leaders of a budding Zionist movement that was itself an act of filial piety
on the part of America's Jews toward the millions of their kinsmen in Eastern
Europe, especially in the Russia of ghettos and pogroms.

The Taft Administration in the last half of 1912 was buffeted and tossed
about by the waves from the Roosevelt insurgency. They were difficult months
for Stimson. He had debts both to Roosevelt, who had started him in public
life and with whose progressivism he was sympathetic by conviction, and to
Taft, who had brought him into the Cabinet, and, perhaps even more, to
Elihu Root, who was *his* father figure and who ranged himself firmly on the

side of party loyalty. According to Frankfurter, the Colonel had always understood that a necessary consequence of his approval of Stimson's joining the Taft Administration would be Stimson's support of Taft's reelection. If so, T. R. in the heat of the 1912 campaign forgot his acquiescence and, when Stimson publicly declared his support of Taft, angrily denounced him and did not speak to him for three years afterwards.

Frankfurter himself at the time was less charitable about Stimson's sticking with Taft than he was retrospectively. Stimson was as critical of Taft as he was, Frankfurter wrote Emory Buckner in New York, but his deep sense of personal loyalty "frequently lessens the acuteness of his judgments both in the appraisal of men and the significance of the personal elements to larger causes." That was in March 1912, and a month later he was so impatient with his chief that he informed "Buck," "I have stopped talking politics with him," and, indeed, Frankfurter wanted to resign and work for the Colonel. But the latter sent him a message to stay on the job, and "Mr. Brandeis the other night was strongly of the same opinion."

Buckner was surprised by his friend's self-flagellation over whether he should stay in Taft's administration when he was really for Roosevelt. Why cannot a minor federal official whose functions are nonpolitical favor a change in Chief Executive, he wickedly inquired. "You know, Sofy [Buckner's wife] charges both of us with too much strutting before the epistolary mirror." [21]

Stimson placed no obstacles in the way of Frankfurter's supporting the Colonel, but when his young aide wrote him ebulliently, "I'm Bull-Moosing and therefore resign," earnestly counseled him not to do so. "I have leaned on your judgment, and your character in the Department, as I have on almost no other man's. . . . If you think that you ought to go, the credit balance is heavily in your favor, and as you know, my blessing will go with you." But was such a step necessary or wise? "There is always a thrill in campaign time which is alluring to the fighting blood of any man, and particularly to the young man; I feel it strongly myself." But Frankfurter should not be "misled by the hurrah about you, into misjudgment of the comparative good which you can accomplish in the two paths that lie open before you. There is a great deal to be done during the coming winter in clinching the important but little understood reforms upon which you and I have been working during the past eighteen months." [22] Stimson wanted him to stay particularly to work on the water-power matters that Stimson, a conservationist, had assigned to him in an effort to slow down the alienation of the country's water-power resources. The War Department was in a position to do this by virtue of the responsibility of the Corps of Engineers for river and harbor improvements. Frankfurter heeded Stimson's advice. He supported T. R., but unobtrusively, and when the Wilson Administration came in he remained in the War Department to work on these first assertions of federal authority over water power in navigable streams. "You stay behind," Stimson charged him, "and get this new administration to put this thing you've been working on through. It's too important." [23]

Stimson hoped, however, that when the water-power work was finished Frankfurter would join him in private practice in New York. But other possibilities were germinating, in other minds, if not Frankfurter's. He had kept in touch with Harvard and with the men who perceived law as an intellectual enterprise concerned with social ends. "Every time Mac [James C. McReynolds, Attorney General, later Associate Justice of the Supreme Court] or I ask this fellow a question of law that is relevant to some aspect of our problem of the government of the dependencies," grumbled Stimson's successor, Secretary of War Garrison, "instead of getting an answer of what the law is, we usually get about 65 pages of what the law ought to be." [24] What the law ought to be— that was what excited him, the law as made by legislative bodies, the law as interpreted by the courts, especially the Supreme Court.

Frankfurter's friend Cohen, permitted finally to teach philosophy at the City College, was attracting the attention of jurists like Learned Hand and Roscoe Pound with his observations on jurisprudence as a philosophical and ethical discipline. He often tried out his ideas on Frankfurter and Buckner, and in April 1913 he organized a Conference on Legal and Social Philosophy where the speakers attacked "the central problem of determining what social welfare is, how changes in ideals of welfare bring about changes in conceptions of justice, and how law could be adjusted to these changes." Frankfurter did not take part in the conference, but he approved of Cohen's efforts. "You seem to me to be so admirably equipped to make philosophy and law a happy union," he wrote him, "and thereby to give more bite and content to philosophy and more reality and direction to law." [25]

Cohen named his first-born after Frankfurter and in later years Felix Cohen would speak of Frankfurter as "my father's best friend during his most creative years." There was little that Cohen wrote, especially in the field of legal philosophy, that he did not discuss with Frankfurter, but much as the latter respected Cohen's learning and analytical power, he also disagreed with him, as he did on the issue of the "case method" of teaching law. This method had been developed at the Harvard Law School in the great era of Langdell and Ames (1870–1910). Langdell had contended that the growth of legal principles and doctrines were "to be traced in the main through a series of cases; and much the shortest and best, if not the only way of mastering the doctrine effectually is by studying the cases in which it is embodied." He knew the virtues of the case system, Cohen wrote Pound, sending a copy to Frankfurter in Washington. "Nevertheless I think that the introduction of the case system in this country has been distinctly unfavorable to the growth of any philosophy of law, primarily because it has tended to emphasize precedent above social reasons. . . . As a layman I cannot but marvel at the learning and thoroughness of Professor Gray's Rule against Perpetuities. But there is not in it, so far as I can remember, any indication that this rule grew up in any definite economic environment or that in the history of its development it had any connection with social ends. So far as its method is concerned, one can imagine it to have been written in some monastery as a scholastic exercise."

Pound, the greatest legal scholar of the day, agreed with Cohen that "our Anglo-American judicial empiricism has neglected matters which the social-philosophical school is now compelling jurists to consider" but disputed that the case system of instruction had "anything to do with the status of the philosophy of law in Anglo-American countries." And Frankfurter, though acknowledging anew that he had learned all his jurisprudence from Cohen, vigorously defended the case system of instruction: "Legal instruction and legal thinking before the days of Langdell and Ames were arid and empty. It is the case system which has given to us the great storehouses of historical data, now availed of by man like Wigmore, Pound, and others, in gradually stimulating philosophic thinking in the profession and the evolution of a philosophic jurisprudence." [26]

Frankfurter appreciated the importance of Pound, indeed had had a small part in his coming to Harvard. In 1910 Buckner had written Professor Samuel Williston at the Law School that "Frankfurter and I on at least a dozen occasions have wondered why Pound was not brought to Cambridge. . . . He is too good a man to be anywhere except at Cambridge." (A certain chauvinism about the Harvard Law School is a characteristic of its graduates and faculty. There *were* other distinguished law schools.)

When the Pound campaign succeeded and the great scholar was snatched away from Northwestern University's Law School, Buckner and Frankfurter embarked on a new enterprise. "My intimate friend Frankfurter," Buckner wrote Pound, "is now Solicitor for the Bureau of Insular Affairs, War Department. He would like to see you on the Supreme Court, and you bet we all would. It will probably be impossible to pull it off with Taft and Wickersham, as you are not a metropolitan corporation practicing lawyer. He has . . . had Holmes' secretary mention it to him. Holmes thinks you are great. I wrote Frankfurter we ought to stir things up a little anyhow, because a little agitation might put you in the candidate class, and it would make it easier for us to pull it off with Wilson, LaFollette, or Roosevelt—who knows what's going to happen." A time came when a President did consult Frankfurter about appointments to the High Bench, but that was twenty years in the future. Now, with Stimson gone, government service as a minor official lost some of its appeal. Buckner, who had decided to go into private practice and make some money, had tried to get Frankfurter to join him. If he ever did practice law, he wanted to do it with "Buck," he had replied, but his interest in private practice was "pretty tepid." To teach law, above all to do so at Harvard as a colleague of Pound, was a very different matter. [27]

"It has just come to my ears," wrote Dean Thayer of the Harvard Law School to Stimson on June 24, 1913, "that Frankfurter might be persuaded to take up academic work. This interests Pound and me tremendously. Pound is a wonderful creature, and his advanced work is something from which I expect great results sometime, but he particularly needs to get the right sort of man with him, and I cannot think of anyone who would fit the place better than Frankfurter." There was a problem of financing a new chair, Thayer went on, but "with the spirit which is abroad nowadays it ought to be possible to find someone who is interested in the things that Frankfurter stands for to meet this difficulty. Pound has seen Brandeis who is very much interested and who, I understand, will try to interest Mr. [Jacob] Schiff. Mr. Brandeis suggested that you might be able to help with him." [28]

Two days later, Stimson received a letter from Frankfurter: [29]

Dear Mr. Stimson:

This question is put to me by Harvard Law School:

> "Suppose a new professorship is established for criminology or other or further subjects, largely in the control of Pound; suppose that the professorship were to become effective for the Academic Year 1914–1915, and were offered to you, would you accept it?"

If you can possibly snatch a minute I want very much a line from you as to your views. Probably no one knows better than you my potentialities and my aims of usefulness. Yet you may want to know my own attitude about this proposal. I am not a scholar, *qua* scholar. On the other hand, I do feel very deeply the need of organized scientific thinking in the modern state and, particularly, in a legalistic democracy like ours, the need of a definitely conceived jurisprudence coordinating sociology and economics. In other words I am struck with the big public aspect of what should be done by our law schools, and the kind of thing that surely is capable of being done with Pound at Cambridge. You know how much it means to me to have your thinking on any problem of mine.

Stimson, who had hoped to have Frankfurter as an associate, promptly replied in words that convey the impression Frankfurter had already made on governmental as well as legal circles: [30]

My dear Felix—

Your letter came yesterday and I had received one from Ezra Thayer a couple of days before on the same subject. I have been thinking it over and talking it over with Mrs. Stimson whose judgment of men is very good.

I have no doubt that you would do a very good and useful work and quite likely a uniquely useful work in such a chair in the Law School. You have certainly the ability and the exceptional experience. But I question whether it would afford you scope for some of your other abilities which to my mind are more exceptional than even your legal ability and practical experience in criminology. You have the greatest facility of acquaintance—for keeping in touch with the center of things,—for knowing sympathetically men who are doing and thinking, of almost all men—certainly all young men that I know. I query whether that most valuable faculty would not be to a great extent lost at the Law School. To me you seem a man whose place is at the center of the great liberal movement which (is) now going on in national and industrial life, and you have already had unusual opportunity for making a circle of acquaintance upon which your future work will be based. As Mrs. Stimson said "The law school will be a side track" and I am inclined to agree with her. That is the kind of work for a man like Pound but not for you. I should say, (altho' I have only met him once or twice) that you and he were of entirely different temperaments. I don't in the slightest degree depreciate the vital importance of and need for the organized correct scientific thinking that he is planning for, but that can be equally well done by a man or men who have not the tactful faculty of getting on with other men and the practical experience in administration which you have had.

Pretty soon you will have to be thinking of getting back to New York. Your life and work in Washington has been invaluable to you, but this is the big uncomfortable caldron in which American problems are brewing, and you must not lose touch with it. I have felt that very strongly since my return, and much as I hate New York I felt that in some respects my feet are on solider ground here than in Washington. . . .

Yours

Henry L. Stimson

Frankfurter consulted other friends. T. R. cautioned him that as a professor, "You'll have to adjust your wants. You'll have to have a wife who'll be content with a simple life. Your salary will substantially remain the same for the rest of your life." Holmes warned him against the academic life and the "irresponsibility," as Frankfurter paraphrased his advice, "of running the universe on paper." Brandeis, who urged him to do it and to whom Frankfurter suggested that he was not qualified to teach from the same rostrum as Langdell, Ames, and Thayer, counseled him: "I would let those who have the responsibilities for selecting you decide your qualifications and not have you decide that." [31]

He drew up a memorandum on the pros and cons of going to Harvard. [32] "All along the line we propose, determine, legislate—without knowing enough." What was required was "correlated, persistent, prophetic thinking" which could not be done in office but only from the outside. "There should be a constant source of thought for the guidance of public men and the education of public opinion, as well as a source of trained men for public life" and since lawyers were at the center of public affairs both "in the shaping of a jurisprudence to meet the social and industrial needs of the time" and in administration and legislation, the law schools must take the lead, and among the law schools Harvard was "the rightful leader." He was not a scholar but he did have the spirit of scholarship and the ability for "the mere book scholarship . . . needed to see what the past has to say in the work of tomorrow." There would be resistances and "respectabilities" at Harvard, but with Pound there "I think we could tug in a Trojan horse of what Hand calls our 'heretical thinking.' "

"The big thing, one of the big things, is that I would go in for about five years of thinking, not cloistered, but in the very current problems that are *the* national problems of greatest appeal to me." He allowed himself five years in Cambridge, at the end of which he would be only thirty-five, still "pretty much the same alive, contagious boy," and if at that time he found that he was going soft he could shift to some other forum. He knew he did not want to go into industrial relations, as housemate Bob Valentine was urging him; that he did not want to stay on in Washington where he found Wilson too doctrinaire, an unsympathetic figure, the atmosphere suddenly too "Southern-Democrat," and his new chief, Lindley Garrison, "a first-class mediocrity." T. R. and Stimson wanted him to stay in New York pursuing the career of a "citizen-lawyer, like Brandeis in Boston," including public office, but "I am not sure that Harvard isn't as good a ticket to draw in the lottery of chances for office as the other routes. . . ."

Above all, summed up Frankfurter, he was tired of "the intellectual hand-to-mouth" life that had been his lot since leaving the Law School. He wanted the stimulus of first-rate minds and he wanted time to sit back and think— "long and hard."

There were other attractions to settling down in Cambridge. He had fallen in love with Marion Denman, just out of Smith College, where she had been elected to Phi Beta Kappa and the presidency of the student body. The daughter of a Congregational minister in Longmeadow, Massachusetts, of old Yankee stock, she was neither stuffy nor conventional, indeed mildly shared Frankfurter's agnosticism, was intelligent enough to enjoy his stream of talk, and sufficiently independent to sometimes accuse him of "cant" and that, too, delighted him. She was a lovely girl whose oval face was framed in rich chestnut hair, whose hazel eyes sometimes seemed to turn green, and whose small mouth showed determination. She passed muster with Justice Holmes. He liked lovely ladies and thought Miss Denman so looked like a portrait of Luini that he always called her Luina. "A dignified serenity is the most marked characteristic" of Bernardino Luini's works, wrote Irma Richter in the *Encyclopedia Britannica.* "Their beauty depends as much upon the loving and dreamy expression in the faces as upon the refinement of form."

Serene she may have been, but Marion was "furious," reported Frankfurter, when he asked her advice whether to accept the invitation to Harvard. Frankfurter in telling of the incident left the impression that the unfairness consisted in his putting a question to her to which she could not give an informed reply. But Marion may also not have been ready to share in a decision that carried an implication of sharing in the life that would follow from it. In any case Frankfurter did not propose until 1918. What was a young lady, no matter how learned, to make of a young man who courted her in the language of philosophy and law? "Romance—oder nicht!" an early letter from Harvard began in which he noted that a mutual friend, a vagabond, unable to stand his loneliness, had gotten himself engaged to a widow with three children. Was one's choice, then, limited to vagrancy or settling down, Frankfurter asked. "I believe in ordered freedom and I terribly believe in dedication without trammels." To this he added a footnote: "One of the shrewdest observations that was ever made to me was to the effect that life must be dealt with like a pair of shears—there are *two* controlling principles, one always connects and supplements the other and the *two* form one effective instrument in action. You can't have freedom in riot, but *all* rules mean stagnation, etc." The letter ended on a more swainlike note: "O for a talk with you. . . . I'll be in N.Y. probably Sunday Oct. 25. Could you come in A.M. or afternoon sometime?" [33]

Unmentioned in Frankfurter's account of why he went to Cambridge was the powerful attraction that the Boston Brahmin lifestyle of gentleman-scholar-public citizen had for a boy from the ghettos. In a revealing simile, Frankfurter later said of the call to Harvard that he could not have been more overwhelmed had he been asked to become "a member of the House of Lords." Before he left the War Department he accepted a commission as major in the Army Reserves, a commission that he held until he went onto the Supreme Court. [34]

In the summer of 1914 Frankfurter began his remarkable career at Harvard. He began it in the library stacks in Cambridge catching up on the cases that had been reported since he left the Law School. The "correlated, persistent, prophetic thinking" that he had looked forward to amid Washington's busyness proved elusive as he began to outline his courses in public service companies and criminal law. He began to sense intellectual limitations, as he confided to Morris Cohen. Would Cohen not come up to Cambridge and spend a week with him during the summer? He was "scared stiff" as the semester began, but he was a born teacher. "I like it lots," he wrote Marion a few weeks after the term began, "and have some reflections on the environment that may gee with yours." [35]

His favorite course was Public Utilities. Francis Plimpton, who went on to become a distinguished lawyer and diplomat, caught its flavor in verse:

> You learn no law in Public U
> That is its fascination
> But Felix gives a point of view
> And pleasant conversation. [36]

He already was attracting the best and the brightest and making disciples of them. The casebook for his public utilities course was compiled with the help of one of his ablest students, Max Lowenthal, who later was one of the few men to challenge J. Edgar Hoover. Ethics and social policy were as much his subject matter as law. "We must show them [the young men] the law as an instrument, and not an end of organized humanity," he admonished the American Bar Association in 1915. "We make of them clever pleaders, but not lawyers, if they fail to catch the glorious vision of the law, not as a harsh Procrustean bed into which all persons and all societies must inexorably be fitted, but as a vital agency for human betterment."

Teaching came easily, hard systematic thought less so. His need to be at the center of things interfered. His friend Buckner, amazed at his dashes to New York and Washington, dubbed him a "human shuttle." Another friend, Harold J. Laski, the prodigiously intellectual young Englishman who in 1916 set Harvard * on its ears by the range, penetration, and elegance of his learning, wrote worriedly to Holmes, to whom Frankfurter had introduced him, about Felix's restlessness. "I don't find him able to sit down solidly to a single thing. He wastes the time that ought to be given to the permanent work that is in him in writing fine letters to antiquated New York lawyers with doubts about the Constitution. . . . To New York three times in one week is a drain I wonder whether even he can stand. I wonder what you think of this?" Holmes did query Frankfurter with results that Laski summarized in his next letter to the Justice: "The psychology ran thus—(a) Harold ought not to bother the Justice with these things, (b) anyhow it isn't true; (c) well, at least not as true as he makes out; (d) but perhaps I've been overdoing—oh, well! I'll draw in a little because I must not worry Holmes, J. (e) I do feel a bit tired and I'll rest—so we have got a good deal of happy play out of him this last ten days." It was not the last time, however, that Laski had to admonish his friend that he was getting too involved and leaving himself no time to turn what he had seen to good intellectual account.[37]

Even during his first year at the Law School his energies overflowed into other areas. He was in on the founding of *The New Republic* by Herbert Croly and Walter Weyl. Croly enlisted Walter Lippman, who had just published *A Preface to Politics*, and Francis Hackett, editor of the book page of the *Chicago Daily News*. He also wanted Frankfurter but the latter preferred the Law School, leading Croly to observe sourly that "the Lord meant me [Frankfurter] to be a journalist, but perversity took me into the law." Croly had a point, for Frankfurter frequently sat with the board of editors and wrote many of the magazine's editorials on constitutional matters.

It was with Croly and Weyl that Frankfurter in the summer of 1914 took time away from the Law School stacks to journey to Sagamore Hill to spend a day with Theodore Roosevelt, who wanted to deepen his understanding of the labor movement. The day was August 4, 1914, and the talk was of war, not industrial problems. Another guest was an Englishman, Charles Booth, author of

---

* In 1915 Frankfurter heard from crusading editor Norman Hapgood about a "most extraordinary young fellow" at McGill University and on a visit to Ottawa made a detour to meet Laski. He rushed back to Cambridge to tell the Dean of the Graduate School he had to have Laski. After inquiries and interviews, the invitation followed.

a pioneering welfare study, *The Poor of London*, and also the head of the Cunard Steamship Company. "You've got to go in! You've got to go in!" T. R. pounded away at Booth, gesticulating with his fists and doing what Frankfurter described as "a tomahawk war dance" around the impeccably courteous, delicately featured Englishman. On his way home from Oyster Bay, Frankfurter bumped into Stimson. "I wish you'd get your damned friend Lloyd George to be a patriot!" Stimson flung at his former aide. Although Frankfurter had never met Lloyd George, his sympathies were with the dynamic Welshman who was the leader of the left in Asquith's Liberal government. On that day, in fact, Britain did break relations with Germany, and Lloyd George was one of those in the Cabinet who voted to do so. Thirty months later the United States would be faced with the same decision. In the split in American liberalism that then took place over America's entry into the war, Frankfurter was ranged with those who supported Wilson's decision. So were the editors of *The New Republic*, not to mention T. R. and Stimson, who had raged at Wilson's caution on preparedness and at his declaration about being "too proud to fight." [38]

In addition to his extracurricular activities with *The New Republic*, Frankfurter was soon involved with Florence Kelley's National Consumers League. He took over several minimum wage and maximum hours cases from Brandeis when the latter went onto the Court. That involvement was also in the tradition of the Harvard Law School. Brandeis, who had graduated from the School in 1878, had been greatly influenced by the redoubtable Professor James Bradley Thayer. In 1893 Thayer had powerfully argued the thesis that the Constitution must tolerate economic reform and, indeed, had ample resources within itself to meet the changing needs of successive generations. For Frankfurter this article was "the great guide for judges." In 1909 Roscoe Pound, also a product of the Harvard Law School, had written his article "Liberty of Contract," which "deplored constitutional decisions on dogmatic grounds without regard to the practical effect of such decisions on daily life," and foreshadowed, wrote Harvard Law School historian Arthur E. Sutherland, "the rise of sociological jurisprudence." It was a significant factor in Harvard's invitation to Pound to come to Cambridge.

Sociological jurisprudence had already been given practical form in the famous "Brandeis brief" in 1908 in support of Oregon's ten-hour law for women. It consisted of two pages of argument and a hundred pages of supporting sociological data. Brandeis had avoided presentation of the case as a contest between abstract legal concepts. Instead, he had aked the Court to look at the facts of modern industry—the consequences of overwork, the nature of fatigue, the existence and effects of similar legislation in other countries. The Court had upheld the ten-hour law; nevertheless, its tendency in appraising the constitutionality of legislation was to equate "due process," a clause that was in the Constitution, with "freedom of contract," a clause not to be found in that document, and to strike down social legislation as encroaching on that freedom. [39]

The cases that Frankfurter as unpaid counsel took over from Brandeis included a minimum wage case for women and a maximum hours case for men. Brandeis had already argued the cases once; they were reargued by Frankfurter in January 1917. "Anyone who looked in at the Supreme Court chambers a few weeks ago," wrote a correspondent for The Nation, in March 1917, "while the two cases involving the constitutionality of the Oregon labor laws were undergoing reargument, saw that august tribunal listening intently to the plea of a small, dark, smooth-faced lawyer, mostly head, eyes and glasses, who looked as if he had stepped out of the sophomore classroom of a neighboring college. He lectured the Court quietly, but with a due sense of its indebtedness to him for setting it right where it had been wrong. . . . He was becomingly tolerant when the gray-haired learners asked questions which seemed to him unnecessary, and gentle when he had to correct a mistaken assumption." Not all were content to go to school with him. Justice McReynolds, the youngest member of the Court, heckled him harshly and sneeringly, and though the Court upheld the maximum hours for men statute, it divided four to four in the minimum wage case for women. That meant that a lower court judgment sustaining the statute was allowed to stand, but it was not an affirmation of the constitutionality of minimum wage legislation.[40]

In his Reminiscences Frankfurter connected his interest in social reform with the drive of organizations like Florence Kelley's National Consumers League for social legislation. He neglected to mention Rose Schneiderman of the Women's Trade Union League. She was a fiery socialist soapboxer whose speech after the Triangle fire in 1911, although heavy with an East Side accent, had brought emotion to a "snapping point," according to the New York Times. Cohen should tell his wife Mary, who was in close touch with the great women trade union organizers of that period, Frankfurter wrote him in 1914, "I found a new enthusiasm—Rose Schneiderman." "I attended a meeting the other night of the Women's Trade Union League on the Eight Hour Day for Women," he informed Walter Lippmann. "Three of the working girls spoke, and the way they spoke will make me feel for a a good many days to come that life is very much worth living."

Frankfurter's commitment to social reform long predated Mrs. Kelley's request that he take over from Brandeis, or his encounter with Rose Schneiderman and the Women's Trade Union League. In 1896, two years after arriving in the United States, he was making soapbox speeches on the Lower East Side for the populist idol of the day, William Jennings Bryan. The ghetto was itself, for the intellectually alive youngster, a forcing house of progressive thinking, especially if one lived, as Frankfurter did, in a coldwater flat and daily repaired to the Cooper Union reading room for warmth as well as free newspapers. He had been a Bull Mooser and the discussions in the House of Truth in Washington had focused on the reordering of society: "The air was rife with intellectual enterprise and eagerness, intellectual eagerness. After a preoccupation with more money-making, money-getting, money-keeping, opening up and despoiling the continent, the time had come for social movements, social reforms, putting an end to glaring and garish ruthlessness and inequalities. That's the kind of thing we talked about." [41]

But the impulse was reformist, not revolutionary, within the limits of the established structure, as befitted a student of the law and a graduate of the Harvard Law School. He was a practical man, not an ideologue; even Woodrow Wilson seemed to him too much of a dogmatist, too rigid a thinker. In his early years at the Law School Frankfurter occasionally addressed an open forum in Boston's South End, then a neighborhood peopled by recent immigrants. Once, after speaking on the need to subordinate private economic power to the public interest, he was heckled by the socialists who dominated the question period.

"Professor Frankfurter, since you believe these things, why aren't you a Socialist?"

"Because I cannot compress life into a formula," was the quick reply, which he followed up, recalled Herbert B. Ehrmann, then a young lawyer with the Boston Legal Aid Society, with a discussion of the "complexity of modern life, pointing out that difficulties in different industries required distinct remedies—some public ownership, some governmental control, some free competition, some various incentives, and so on. For me, at least, Felix in eight words had banished isms forever." But his commitment to social reform was solid. He argued with the always skeptical Holmes, the latter reported, that "to improve the conditions of life and the race is the main thing." Holmes sympathized, "but how the devil can I tell whether I'm not pulling it down in some other place?" [42]

In September 1911, Frankfurter had urged Stimson "to identify the Republican Party in the public mind as the liberal party." He had cited himself as an example of the young people who "in these transitional days of parties" were looking for a political anchor "and my gropings of hope for and loyalty to the Republican Party as the party that ought to be the liberal party and largely tends that way, are perhaps valuable as reflecting the rather troubled viewpoint of not a few of the younger generation." But after that letter he had become a Bull Mooser and by the close of the 1916 election between Wilson and Charles Evans Hughes he was prepared to cast his vote for Wilson, despite his misgivings about Wilson's intellectual inflexibility, especially his resistance to preparedness, "a resistance," as Frankfurter interpreted it, "to the thought that we might get into the war. . . ." [43]

In regard to preparedness he was closer to Hughes and Stimson than he was to Wilson. So the choice was a difficult one. It meant another divergence with Stimson, with whom he exchanged lengthy letters on the subject. When Cohen criticized Hughes, citing Holmes' low estimate of him, Frankfurter replied that the Republican candidate had a better nose for the operation of the peonage laws in the South than did Holmes. But Frankfurter was aware of the progressive legislation that had been enacted under Wilson. Then there was the appointment of Brandeis to the Court, a nomination that Wilson resolutely had sustained in the face of protests of "seven former Presidents of the American Bar Association, the petition of the Boston men of affairs, and the editorials in the financial papers." His decision to vote for Wilson was a reluctant one, he explained to Stimson. "I have no illusion about Wilson. I still have a feeling of insecurity about him, but I do think that Hughes and the Republican campaign have systematically underestimated the impressive achievements of Wilson, especially in the light of his difficulties." Nevertheless, even though Wilson's record "is truly impressive . . . I should have allowed my feeling of insecurity about him to govern if Hughes had given me a chance." But far from educating the country on the nature of the crisis that it confronted, "Hughes has 'played safe.' " Above all Frankfurter was disheartened by Hughes' conception of the presidency, "the statement in which he juxtaposes his notion of the President as the administrative head of the government, against Wilson's notion of the presidency as a political leader and law maker. It is a curious reversion to Hughes' notion when he first became Governor that he must not talk about legislation until it actually reached his desk for signature." [44]

Until the advent of the second Roosevelt, Frankfurter was in fact the archetypal mugwump. As he explained to Cohen, political allegiance for men like Stimson and Hughes was a matter of natural piety. Their fathers had fought in the Civil War. They had been brought up with the belief that the values of the Republic were best served by the Republican Party, which was a national, not a sectional party, which had saved the Union and abolished slavery. Men like Cohen and himself decided their relationship to parties on a "purely rational basis," he asserted. As far as party affiliation was concerned, he informed Stimson, "I have to be one of those who, by being outside of both camps, is going to pick and choose from election to election until one or the other is more predominantly governed by purposes which I share than either is now. I don't like the situation. It is not comfortable to be politically homeless, but I don't see my way clear to being other than a tenant at will until better days. . . ." [45]

In April 1917 the nation went to war. Before the election Frankfurter had criticized Wilson on failure to prepare; but he also thought the President "right not to bring this country, to the extent that the President does, which is a very great extent, into war until the country was educated." [46] Frankfurter, a major in the Reserves, was summoned to Washington by Secretary of War Newton D. Baker whom he had come to know sympathetically through their joint labors for the National Consumers League. "To Washington again," he wrote Marion, April 17, to make himself "an effective nuisance" in seeing that the United States on the industrial side profited by England's mistakes. He was afraid the war would be a long one. He hoped not, "for when I see these boys, as I now see them at Cambridge, in Khaki, and talk with them, the sense of all the dislocating force of war rushes in on me, the vast tragic irrelevance of it to all that should be life, and I have no patience at all with those who see in war a great moral purgative. At best I can't regard it as better than as a purely temporary process forced on us by living in a world with other people. I hope we may utilize the unselfish impulses it arouses for I do believe the President is right in saying that we went into it as a means of realizing a more decent opportunity for peaceful pursuits in an interdependent world. . . ." Baker wanted him to don a uniform, but he refused. "As a civilian I could get into the presence of a General without saluting, clicking my heels, and having a Colonel outside say, 'You wait. He's got a Colonel in there.' " With Felix in Washington, a youthful Harold Laski lamented to Holmes, "Cambridge has departed this life. He attracts everyone there, and none will come, far less stay, in this grave of youthful hopes." [47]

One of his first jobs for Baker was to prepare a memorandum on the law relating to the treatment of conscientious objectors. His exposition was hardheaded, but it emphasized that even those who refused alternative service and had, therefore, to be jailed, should be treated soberly and magnanimously—advice, unfortunately, that went unheeded the further down the chain of command that it traveled. His second assignment for Baker took him to Europe. He was asked to accompany Henry Morgenthau, "Uncle Henry" as he was known among the Wilson men, on a misssion to appraise the chances of detaching Turkey from the Central Powers. The State Department announcement presented the purpose a little differently: "In an effort to ameliorate the condition of the Jewish communities in Palestine," the announcement said, "the President has sent abroad Former Ambassador Henry Morgenthau and Professor Felix Frankfurter of the Harvard Law School, now serving as assistant to Secretary of War Baker. Mr. Morgenthau and Professsor Frankfurter will proceed to Egypt and from there conduct an investigation to ascertain the means of relieving the situation among the Jews in Palestine." A State Department spokesman added that the mission had no relation to the creation of an independent state in Palestine, which was then under Turkish rule. [48]

And yet, the selection of Frankfurter, a Zionist, for the mission, to accompany Morgenthau, an anti-Zionist, not to mention Chaim Weizmann's chairmanship of the British delegation, indicated that it was heavily enmeshed with Zionist hopes that out of the war would come the establishment of a Jewish national home in Palestine. Brandeis had taken hold of the Zionist movement in 1914, after the outbreak of the war, and his memos and directives, scrawled on yellow pads, were addressed to "JWM, SSW, RZ, FF"—Federal Judge Julian W. Mack, social reformer and second only to Brandeis as a lay leader of American Jewery; Rabbi Stephen S. Wise, the leader of the Free Synagogue and emerging as America's foremost rabbi; Robert Szold, Harvard Law Schoool, 1912, whom Frankfurter had sent to Puerto Rico to assist the Attorney General there, also a Harvard man. All of the Americans had been powerfully influenced by a remarkable Palestinian, Aaron Aaronsohn, an agronomist who had discovered wild wheat in the Galilee and who on his visit to the United States had done much to allay doubts about Palestine's absorptive capacities. Blue-eyed, fair-skinned, and outgoing, he won men's hearts and currently was heading up an anti-Turkish intelligence network in Palestine that was feeding information to T. E. Lawrence. Aaronsohn's Diary for March 15, 1913, recorded how he, Mack, and Frankfurter went to the Exhibit of the American Painters to look at the work of the Cubists and Futurists. Frankfurter, who had little patience for the *avant-garde*, left quickly and only rejoined the other two when they came to *Outlook* offices of Theodore Roosevelt. There Aaronsohn talked to the Colonel for almost two hours about the colonization movement in Palestine. "From now on my reputation will be: the man who made the Colonel shut up for 101 minutes . . ." [49]

Frankfurter's assignment brought him into contact with Herbert Hoover, in charge of American relief activities abroad. ". . . (A) truly great man," he wrote to Marion. "Belgium has smelted clean any alloy of self concern that Hoover ever had. Now he is an extraordinarily competent man completely devoted to keep life going in half the world—literally to keep life going. One hardly dares to put into words the feeling he arouses—intelligence supremely moved by the misery of the world." The admiration was evidently mutual, for three weeks later he again wrote Marion, "It's a queer world. Even I know what it is not to take a job that thrills you. After I came here Hoover said he 'had designs' on me—and I'd rather work with him than anyone I have seen in Government. He is the biggest thing here, unless it be Mrs. Hoover." Two weeks later, as he prepared to embark in the submarine-infested waters, he sent a farewell note to "Dearest Marion." He enclosed a copy of his passport photograph. "This forbidding face will somehow have to carry me around the world, even tho Mother misses what she calls my 'laughter' and my 'intelligenz.' The trip is getting perkier. It looks as tho it might carry us into France and even through Greece, to the unknown port of Alexandria. What an Aladdin's lamp my birth did rub! Yes, 'lucky man' says Mrs. Holmes, lucky the Fates give me so much stuff of life." [50]

The mission was not successful. In Gibraltar the U. S. group rendezvoused with British and French delegations but after six weeks of talk and inquiry concluded "the moment wasn't right." Frankfurter did not take to Morgenthau, "because my knowledge was critical and analytical, and his was just general, hot-air impressions." Not without reason Frankfurter sometimes conceded he might be an intellectual snob, and a public posture of bonhomie often concealed a private rancor. The politics and diplomacy of the Morgenthau mission were entangled in the conflicting attitudes of Zionist and anti-Zionist over the attitude to be taken toward a Turkish Government that was still sovereign over Palestine. For Frankfurter there was only one compensation in a journey that had removed him from the industrial front at a critical moment—the British mission was headed by Dr. Chaim Weizmann, whose impact on Frankfurter can be sensed in the latter's description of him forty-three years later: "quasi-messianic . . . electric . . . affectionate . . . radiated authority . . . fluent in German, French, Hebrew, Russian, and Italian," whom nothing interested "except the realization of a Jewish Palestine" and who pursued that objective with "an extreme intensity" of resolution and will. [51]

Frankfurter's work for Baker on his return thrust him into the field of industrial mediation, the job that Bob Valentine had urged him to make his life's work in 1913. In the autumn of 1917 when Wilson established a Mediation Commission to deal with an upsurge of strikes in defense-related industries in the West, he was named its Secretary and Counsel. In that capacity he traveled about the country, together with his assistant, Max Lowenthal, and the Secretary of Labor, William B. Wilson. In Arizona, where management, rather than deal with the real grievances of the striking copper miners, were accusing their men, many of whom were from southeastern Europe, of "pro-Germanism," the negotiations were protracted. He secured a settlement, with an assist from William Scarlett, a remarkable young Protestant rector, later a Bishop of the Protestant Episcopal Church, who had much of the copper-mine management in his parish.

From Arizona, where he and Max lived for months in a railway car, he journeyed to Southern California to settle a dispute in the oil fields, and then to San Francisco to deal with a strike against Bell Telephone. In the northwest there was a strike in the spruce industry to be ended, and on his way East a stoppage in the stockyards, where Armour and Swift's skillful lawyers, collaborating in their clients' shortsightedness, in his view, carried a large measure of the responsibility for society's failure to adopt industrial and economic reforms more expeditiously.

All the settlements bristled with difficulties, but no more than strike mediation generally. Two situations, however, not only generated lightning and thunder that reverberated throughout the United States, but earned for Frankfurter a reputation for radicalism that, assiduously kept alive by right-wing extremists, dogged him up to the time he assumed a seat on the Supreme Court. When President Wilson met with the Mediation Commission, he "gave us a cold, short, high-minded few minutes' talk," recalled Frankfurter, who in later years never could refer to Wilson except pejoratively, the scorn that the tough-minded have for the high-minded. At the end of his talk Wilson turned to Frankfurter to add: "There's one more matter I want this commission to look into and, as the lawyer of the commission, Mr. Frankfurter, this will be particularly your concern. That is the Mooney case which is greatly disturbing our Allies, Russia and Italy. When you get to California, I hope you will look into that and report to me about it." [52] Although it was a labor and radical *cause célèbre*, Frankfurter had not heard of the case until then.

Tom Mooney, a labor leader, had been sentenced to death for allegedly planting the bomb that killed many people in a Preparedness Day Parade in San Francisco on July 22, 1916. The Mediation Commission, after exhaustive inquiries, was persuaded that he had been convicted on perjured testimony, and in a report written by Frankfurter, urged the President to intercede with the Governor of California to obtain a suspension of the death sentence, "that a new trial may be had for Mooney whereby guilt or innocence may be put to the test of unquestionable justice." The President did as his Commission recommmended, but the Governor of California, turning down the suggestion of a new trial, simply commuted Mooney's sentence to life imprisonment, and he remained in jail, a labor and left-wing martyr, until pardoned by Governor Culbert L. Olsen in 1939.

The Mooney report scandalized American conservatives; so did Frankfurter's "Report on the Bisbee Deportations." A thousand I.W.W. miners in Bisbee, Arizona, had been routed out of bed by a force of vigilantes, shipped by train to New Mexico, and dumped on a desert town without adequate supplies of food or water. The vigilantes were led by Jack Greenway, a former "rough rider" and husband of Isabella Selmes, whose mother was an old family friend of Theodore Roosevelt, as Isabella herself was a favorite of T. R.'s daughter Alice and her cousin Eleanor. The "deportations" were justified as deeds of patriotism, "a matter of what we would now call 'security,' " said Frankfurter later. Theodore Roosevelt, appealed to by Greenway, in a public letter savagely lambasted Frankfurter for "taking on behalf of the•administration an attitude which seems to me to be fundamentally that of Trotsky and the other Bolshevik leaders in Russia; an attitude which may be fraught with mischief to this country." The letter, which was filled with references to the excesses of Robespierre and Danton, as well as those of the "Bolsheveki," was not among the Colonel's most distinguished utterances except as a period piece. Frankfurter answered firmly but gently: "Surely you must know what a great sadness it is for me to find disagreement between us on an important issue. . . . You are one of the few great sources of national leadership and inspiration for national endeavor. I do not want to see that asset made ill use of. . . ." [53]

There was applause from Learned Hand. "I am glad that you stood up to him as well as you did, and you certainly had him backed against the ropes. . . . Your Bisbee report was absolutely right and courageous. . . ." [54]

If Frankfurter's role as chief attorney for the Mediation Commission and its successor, the War Labor Policies Board, of which he was named Chairman, made him suspect among some conservatives, it also was the beginning of a working association with Franklin D. Roosevelt, then an Assistant Secretary of the Navy who represented that Department on the Board. In 1906 at the instigation of a Harvard classmate, Grenville Clark, Frankfurter had lunched with Roosevelt, when all three were beginning lawyers, and in the first year of the Wilson Administration they had worked on the same floor in the old State-War-Navy Department building, but it was during the war that they really became acquainted. There were only "two first-rate minds" on the War Labor Policies Board, Herbert B. Ehrmann, who served on it as a representative of the Shipping Board, wrote his wife; Roosevelt and Frankfurter. [55]

Once, Roosevelt brought Frankfurter home to lunch. "An interesting little man but very jew," Eleanor Roosevelt, still not freed from the anti-Semitism that was part of her social and cultural inheritance, wrote her mother-in-law. Anti-Semitism was a subject that Frankfurter rarely talked about as it affected him personally. He sometimes quoted his uncle's advice to him when he was a boy: "You'll encounter a great deal of anti-Semitism in your life, but don't go around sniffing anti-Semitism." His attitude was to be neither truculent nor subservient, but he knew that as a Jew he had to perform better than others; he had to achieve by merit and awareness what the Roosevelts and Stimsons and Grenville Clarks claimed as birthright. There were matters one never talked about but always thought about—one was your height; another was your Jewishness.[56]

In 1918 Frankfurter was back in Europe. "Felix flashed in yesterday on the way to England and I had news of you," Laski reported to Holmes. "*Entre nous* I gathered that he did not approve of the Secretary's organization of the war department and that when he returned from the West he found all his side of the work at sixes and sevens. I could almost envy Felix his glimpse of things if it weren't that he is so damned loveable one can't envy him anything. But I greatly wish he would spread himself less widely and learn to speak French." He was so busy that Laski jestingly spoke of Baker being but "the pale wraith that Felix casts before him in his progress."

He managed at the same time to press his case with Miss Denman with happy ardor and prolixity, a style that later came to be identified as "felixity." The young woman was having trouble finding a role. After Smith College she had served briefly as Secretary of the fashionable Miss Spence's school in New York City, but she did not like ministering to the rich and well-born. She returned to Smith for graduate work in economics and also became involved in suffrage activities. "I wish you could have seen me today," she wrote Frankfurter from Lyme, Connecticut, "peddling suffrage way out in a small hamlet miles from here." After she had been packed off to Saranac because of suspected tuberculosis, Frankfurter visited her and on his way back stopped over in Springfield to report to Mrs. Denman on her daughter's condition. The visit so upset Mrs. Denman she was unable to prepare dinner, and after Frankfurter left, she agitatedly told Marion's sister, Helen, "You know, I think he wants to marry Marion." A brief spell at the New York School for Social Work was followed by enlistment in the War Camp Activities Bureau, a Red Cross operation, and an assignment to France. The night before she sailed, Frankfurter hurried up to New York to see her off. They dined together and afterwards rode in a hansom cab around Central Park. Frankfurter proposed and she accepted and when she returned from Europe she greeted her sister at the gangplank with the announcement, "You know, I'm going to marry Felix."[57]

The war ended and now Frankfurter was off again to Europe, this time to hold a watching "brief" for the American Zionist movement at the Paris Peace Conference. He went at the request of Justice Brandeis and Federal Judge Julian Mack, both eminent jurists, both Harvard men, both leaders of American Zionism. It was a fateful moment in the affairs of Zion. The British Government had issued the Balfour Declaration, a policy, Frankfurter always carefully noted, concurred in by the United States, "that Palestine be established as a Jewish National Home." "It was issued," said Frankfurter, "after detailed consultation, even changes in the phrasing, between the Lloyd George Government and President Wilson in person," and it had the blessings of the French. But how was it to be carried out, how "formalized, institutionalized, internationalized?" What, in sum, would be the terms of the mandate under which Britain would serve as a trustee of Palestine? A mandate was a legal document, and that was why Brandeis and Mack wanted Frankfurter, a man of tough-minded legal competence, to be in Paris to backstop the dreamers like Weizmann. Mack was there, too, and one of his former law clerks, a favorite, Benjamin V. Cohen, already known as a superb legal draftsman, and there was Aaron Aaronsohn, fresh from his underground exploits in Palestine. He was, he told William Bullitt, the only man in Paris who would know whether a particular five-acre field should be given to the Zionists because "it contained a unique specimen of a wild plant, which should be preserved for the service of science and would be tended by the Jews, but might be neglected by the Arabs."

The Arabs also were in Paris. Their chief representative was Prince Feisal of Arabia, who was shepherded everywhere by T. E. Lawrence. One of the improbable meetings in history was between Feisal and Frankfurter. The Jews did not wish to restore Jewish civilization in Palestine at the expense of the Arab people and culture, the Harvard professor assured the desert chieftain. The Jews were not colonialists and the golden moment in the history of the two peoples and civilizations was when they had intermingled and coexisted. "We exchanged assurances, and it was agreed that each would put his remarks on paper. We went back to the Hotel Maurice where Lawrence was staying and I wrote my letter, and he wrote his and then they were duly signed."

The letter to Frankfurter, dated March 31, 1919, endorsed the Balfour Declaration:

> We Arabs, especially the educated among us, look with the deepest sympathy on the Zionist movement. Our deputation here in Paris is fully acquainted with the proposals submitted by the Zionist Organization to the Peace Conference, and we regard them as moderate and proper. We will do our best, insofar as we are concerned, to help them through; we will wish the Jews a most hearty welcome home.[58]

While in Paris Frankfurter went on a mission, again headed by Morgenthau, to newly reconstituted Poland, to investigate the miserable status of Polish Jewry. A year later he was back in Europe "enslaved by Zionist work," he wrote Morris Cohen, who considered Zionism a form of "tribalism." Frankfurter's involvement with the Zionist movement at this time was so extensive that he was a major figure at the crucial Cleveland convention of the American Zionist movement in 1921. There the hardheaded Brandeis-Mack leadership was rejected for that of Weizmann, despite a four-hour speech by Frankfurter, the floor leader of the Brandeis-Mack group, that brought the audience to its feet cheering. For a time there would be a diminution in his involvement with

Zionism, but later he was reconciled with Weizmann, who tried to persuade him to move to Palestine.

Jewish affairs were not his only concern in Paris. At the request of the State Department he helped in the drafting of the charter of the International Labor Organization, and, of course, like all the talented young men who had found a way of getting to Paris at that heady moment in world affairs, he gossiped, exchanged information, and deplored the doings of the Big Four. "It [Paris] is full beyond belief and one sees many celebrities and all one's friends," Eleanor Roosevelt, who was there with her husband, wrote her mother-in-law. Frankfurter had the same feeling. ". . . many of the younger people on our peace delegation were friends, associates, Harvard people" and he had good contacts on the British delegation—Sir Eustce Percy, Loring Christie, and Philip Kerr, later Lord Lothian, and at that time secretary to Lloyd George. "I know that he was happy to go," Laski commented on this foray to Paris, "which makes me pleased that he has gone. But I'm very anxious that he should settle down and gain the solid reputation which is the debt which he owes to his intelligence." [59]

When he returned from Poland, Philip Kerr asked him to lunch with the British Foreign Secretary, Arthur Balfour, "that wonderful charming creature." He also saw Balfour at a British weekend at Cliveden, where he had been invited as a result of a message from Lady Astor's sister, who was a friend. Winston Churchill, as so often was the case, was the focus of discussion with Lady Astor inveighing against him "on and on and on" until Balfour tenderly put his hand on hers and said, "Nancy, all you say about Winston may be true, but Winston has ideas, and to a statesman with ideas much shall be forgiven."

In the halcyon days of Lawrence's liberation of Arabia, when Britain's rulers were arranging the future of the Sultan's Near East domains with an eye to their own interests in the region, a homeland in Palestine for Western-oriented Jews seemed like an astute way of further underwriting long-time British paramountcy. "Weizmann seized the imagination and enlisted the will of people like Lloyd George, Balfour, Winston Churchill and Smuts," recalled Frankfurter. "Winston Churchill was devoted to him." No doubt the men of Britain's great houses were enthralled by Weizmann personally, but what he wanted also happened to coincide with the imperial dreams of Britain's rulers, and for the moment Frankfurter's love of England and love of Zion marched happily hand in hand. [60]

Frankfurter's stay in Paris did not enhance his feelings for Wilson. Ever the realist, he did not warm to Wilson's "idealistic rhetoric," and he was dismayed when he heard that Wilson in a talk with other delegations had said, "If I didn't feel that I was the personal instrument of God, I couldn't carry on." When later Frankfurter reviewed *The Americans in Paris* by Ray Stannard Baker, the biographer of Wilson, he focused on Baker's observation that "They all had something that they wanted to get out of the peace conference, and we didn't want anything." Such self-righteousness outraged him. "They were pushing their more or less limited objectives, and we just thought by announcing these noble principles they'd translate themselves into action." [61]

Frankfurter was no Sunday-morning quarterback. On July 11, 1919, he sent Lippmann from Paris his analysis of the reasons for the failure of Wilson, "Tommy" in the letter, an analysis illustrative of his tough-mindedness, respect for procedure, and meticulous preparation:

At least at bottom, if not *the* bottom fact is that neither the President nor the Colonel had any adequate conception of what the problem of peace making was. I do not mean the actual detailed question, but the technique of peace making, the processes which would come into play, the forces which they would encounter and the forces that they could rely upon. Without exception, the saddest day of the war for me was Labour Day of last year when the Colonel outlined to me the plan for the Peace Conference. I knew then (and I told L.D.B. [Brandeis] at the time) that they were the naivest children in the world and the President's efforts to achieve his principles were doomed to failure. To understand what has happened here one will have to analyze the President's theory of peace making and then the effect of our election and the British election. The latter, of course, was the fatal millstone around Lloyd George which made him utterly dishonest in regard especially to the reparation clause—and the reparation clauses are one of the axes of the Peace Conference. But when all that is said, when all those initial handicaps are taken into account (and not the least of which was the holding of the Conference in Paris) you will still have to analyze why it is that although in the Majestic and in the Crillon there was all the necessary knowledge and vision to approximate the world order that was obtainable these aims were frustrated. Of course there was lacking the directing will on top, but I wish you would explain—and I have asked Graham Wallas the same question—the causes that prevented two or three people from breaking through. If Smuts or Botha had shouted aloud months ago what they said in private, if there had been public courage on the part of two or three of our own people, this Treaty would never have been. Of course there were some brave people like Keynes (you may have met him, he was the financial adviser of the British) who resigned because of the utter breach of faith that the Treaty involved.

. . . I have not a particle of doubt that just one personality like L.D.B. would have made a world wide difference—and of course—it was of the essence of any consideration of Tommy's personality that he did not bring L.D.B. with him or ever realise the need of having him. . . .

You are the last person to be told that one might have a better time than to be in Paris all these months, but I shall be mightily glad to have been here. Not otherwise could I have known things that I ought to know and a little better understand. It will be great fun, though, to get back. Evidently, we are the most reactionary country in the world just now and I am going back to a great shindy at Harvard. Life *is* worth living these days! [62]

The "shindy" referred to the growing attacks on Frankfurter as in some way a subversive influence. "Men's minds moved with a freedom which is now incomprehensible," wrote Zechariah Chafee of Harvard's law faculty after the war of the period before America's entry, "for thinking had not yet been hardened into queer shapes by the emotions aroused by war and conflicting reactions to the Russian Revolution." Frankfurter came out of the war a controversial figure and his return to Harvard carried anxieties for Dean Roscoe Pound, a great scholar, but also under fire. Pound consulted Brandeis, who advised him not to worry, but men did worry. Rumors that Boston considered Frankfurter "dangerous" reached Holmes, who asked Laski about them. "Every once in a while, faintly and vaguely as to you, a little more distinctly as to Frankfurter, I hear that you are dangerous men. . . . What does it mean? They used to say in Boston that I was dangerous. . . ." There was under way "a real effort in Boston to make Frankfurter's position here untenable," Laski replied. "Anti-Semitism," he added, "might be a factor." Boston was prejudiced against Frankfurter, Holmes wrote his old friend Sir Frederick Pollock. "I think partly because he (as well as Laski) is a Jew. . . . It never occurs to me until after the event that a man I like is a Jew, nor do I care when I realize it." Holmes took Laski's warning sufficiently seriously to write President Lowell that he had the "very strong feeling that Pound and in his place Frankfurter have and impart the ferment which is more valuable than an endowment, and makes of a Law School a focus of life." This particular storm abated. "People meet him, and the adjective 'dangerous' melts as the snow before the sun," the faithful Laski reported to Holmes as the autumn 1919 semester unfolded. "He is very happy—the students, *bien entendu*, are wild about him." [63]

There was another cause for happiness, his impending marriage. "Nothing to tell," Holmes wrote Laski, "except the delightful visit of Felix and his joyful news—I think it will be a good thing for him as well as for her." In the portrait that Frankfurter drew of himself in his talks with Dr. Harlan B. Phillips, *Felix Frankfurter Reminisces*, he was reticent about his private life and feelings. We are indebted to playwright Garson Kanin, who with his wife Ruth Gordon were close friends of the Justice, for some engaging off-camera glimpses of him in his memoir "Trips to Felix." They include Frankfurter's account of the reaction of the Justice and Mrs. Holmes to his announcement:

Holmes jumped up and shouted for Fanny. "Dickie!" he called. "Dickie bird!" (F. F. gets up at this point to give a brilliant imitation of Mrs. Holmes coming into the room. She was old and infirm and moved without lifting her feet from the floor.) As she came in, Holmes said to F. F., "Tell her! Tell her!"

"I'm going to marry Miss Denman," said F. F.

Fanny said nothing, but turned and slipped out of the room. He and Holmes thought this behavior odd. Somewhat embarrassed they went on talking about other things. All at once, Fanny returned. She held out her fists and asked F. F., "Which do you think she would like? This?" She opened one fist, revealing a piece of jade. "Or this?" She opened another fist, which contained a piece of amber. F. F. pointed to the amber and said, "This I think." Fanny handed it to him, turned, shuffled out of the room, and was seen no more that day.[64]

Laski attended the marriage, which was performed by Judge Benjamin Cardozo of the New York Court of Appeals in Learned Hand's chambers, and reported to Holmes that it was a comfort to know that "Felix is safe. It couldn't have been better if I had deliberately arranged it. She's wise and grown-up and good to look upon—a real companion." They were back from their honeymoon at Southern Pines, "two cooing doves," Laski described them. "To see their anxiety for each other's proper protection against the snow etc. is charming. The Boy is very happy. The girl is still rather reticent and shy so that I can't expound her much, but she makes him sing an unceasing song and I therefore add my tribute."

Marion Frankfurter's withdrawn quality was more than a passing trait. That summer, 1920, when she and her husband were in London, Laski, who had returned home, wrote of how "Felix, in his whirlwind ways, sees everyone and everything; and his wife looks on in stately aloofness." She was reserved but not unfriendly. Dr. Henry A. Murray, the Harvard professor of psychiatry who became a close friend of the Frankfurters, would later speak of her "mysterious inwardness of spirit," which, he thought, provided a balance to Frankfurter's "expansive openness." He was a "door-hanger," she would reproach him mildly, when on speeding a parting guest from their Brattle Street home, he was unable to resist adding another paragraph. "Felix has two hundred best friends," she would observe. Did he have to read everything in print that fell under his eyes, was another amused complaint. "Felix has only two faults," a laughing Frankfurter quoted his wife when Garson Kanin admonished him on his rambling. "One, he *always* gets off the subject; two, he *always* gets back on to it again!" "Do you know what it's like to be married to a man who is never tired?" she would occasionally murmur, and mischievous tongues in Cambridge spoke of "the distinguished Mr. Frankfurter and the extinguished Mrs. Frankfurter," adding that for some reason she preferred it that way.

He was an urban, not a rural man, at home in the library, not the garden, and when his wife heard him advise his students to begin their practice in the small towns from which they came, she would bridle, saying "I was taking a lot of liberty with young lives, because the only small towns I ever knew anything about were Vienna, New York, and Boston." She was a better stylist than he, and in the prefatory note in his last book he thanked his wife "for improvingly editing some of these pieces . . . by means of her skillful pen and literary taste." He respected her judgment, and increasingly his letters to friends were dotted with the phrases "Marion says . . . ," "Marion thinks. . . ." It was an enduring relationship, but the marriage was childless, and there were friends who thought that the neurasthenia that put her intermittently under psychiatric care in the Twenties was rooted in some inner resistance to her marriage, as if she were never quite able to resolve her problems of living with a dynamo—a Jewish one at that—but he to the end of his days wooed her.[65]

Frankfurter was still young, thirty-seven, when he returned to Harvard. He was courageous. The knowledge that he was a marked man did not breed timidity. On the contrary, a normal inclination to intellectual pugnacity turned to militancy in the face of the postwar repression and unreason. He presided over a Faneuil Hall meeting that urged the United States Government to recognize Soviet Russia. "May would have been thrilled at the meeting last night for Soviet recognition," he wrote Morris Cohen. "Borah was the speaker and I presided." Without fee he headed the legal defense of the Amalgamated Clothing Workers of America against an action for an injunction that would have broken up the union as an "illegal conspiracy." Together with Chafee, he helped prevent the deportation of twenty aliens caught up in A. Mitchell Palmer's infamous "war on the Reds." In 1920 Chafee published *Freedom of Speech*, a devastating study of the Espionage Act generally and the *Abrams* case particularly, in which three men had been sentenced to twenty years imprisonment for publishing allegedly seditious leaflets. The *Abrams* case had been the occasion of Holmes's famous dissent in which he noted how time had "upset many fighting faiths" and that "the best test of truth is the power of the thought to get itself accepted in the competition of the market." Some of Chafee's colleagues—Pound, Frankfurter, and Wilson's son-in-law Francis B. Sayre—found his critique so compelling that they joined him in a petition for clemency for the *Abrams* prisoners. A little later, Frankfurter, Pound, and Chafee joined nine other distinguished men at the bar to publish a "Report upon the Illegal Practices of the United States Department of Justice," a report that led Charles Evans Hughes to wonder "whether constitutional government as heretofore maintained in this republic could survive another great war even victoriously waged." And when Roger Baldwin, Harvard '05, after serving his sentence as a conscientious objector, circularized the signatories of the Report of the Twelve to serve on the National Advisory Committee of the newly formed American Civil Liberties Union, Frankfurter was one of the few to respond affirmatively.[66]

By this time the cup of some distinguished but conservative alumni of the Law School, including Austin Fox, a member of the Harvard Board of Overseers, had brimmed over, and their pressure was sufficient to cause the Overseers to designate a committee to appraise Chafee's "fitness to teach" and the judgment of those of his colleagues who had joined him in the clemency petition. "The Trial at the Harvard Club," as it came to be known, turned into a battle between Austin Fox and Harvard's President A. Lawrence Lowell. And it was symptomatic of the mood of the times that the vote to acquit was a narrow one, six to five. Judge Cardozo cast the deciding vote.[67]

Undaunted and unabashed, Frankfurter, even though alumni were warning they would not give any money as long as he remained on the faculty, hewed to his militant liberalism. He regularly contributed unsigned editorials on constitutional issues to the New Republic, including a ringing denunciation, during the Senate's investigation of the Teapot Dome scandals, of "the preposterous assumption that an investigation into the conduct of public officials who are suspected of wrong-doing should be conducted under all the limitations of a criminal trial." [68] If he protested efforts to limit the investigatory powers of Congress, the survey that he and Pound directed of Criminal Justice in Cleveland underscored the need for assuring men and women charged with crimes all the protection and limitations to which they were entitled under federal and state laws.

In 1923 he again appeared on behalf of the National Consumers League before the Supreme Court [Adkins v. Children's Hospital 261 U. S. 525]. The issue was the constitutionality of a District of Columbia minimum wage law for women. Again he presented a "Brandeis brief," this one of a thousand pages, showing what actually happened when women had to work long hours for inadequate wages. The material had been researched by Molly Dewson, a spirited young woman who soon would enter politics and, as an ally of Eleanor Roosevelt, leave her mark on the Roosevelt era. The Court, speaking through Justice Sutherland, did not challenge the brief's accuracy. It called it irrelevant. It was pertinent to lawmaking by a legislature but not to judging a statute's validity by the Court, Justice Sutherland maintained. Brandeis did not participate, but Holmes did and dissented, as did Chief Justice Taft, and that was a comfort.

Frankfurter's experience with the War Labor Policies Board in the war had bred in him a realistic understanding of the weapons and tactics used by employers to keep labor in its place. He regretted Wilson's pell-mell abandonment of wartime controls; taking off the "harness" was opening a "Pandora's box," he wrote. "Industrial unrest is bound to continue just so long as the present state of mind and feeling of workers is generated by a growing disparity between their participation in politics and their exclusion from industrial direction." The right to organize and bargain collectively alone could equalize the parties in industrial conflicts and bring about a structuring of labor-management relations "where men produce primarily because they want to." It disserved the American democratic credo to ascribe strikes to "alien propaganda" rather than to deep-seated grievances, and to stigmatize them as "un-American" only delayed orderly clarification and correction. In an unsigned editorial in the New Republic, "Labor Injunction Must Go," which he wrote after a federal judge had issued a sweeping injunction against a railway shopmen's strike, Frankfurter disputed the efficacy of the injunction. "It neither mines coal, nor moves trains, nor makes clothing. As an adjustor of industrial conflict the injunction has been an utter failure." [69]

Although he had voted for Cox and Roosevelt in 1920, the unwillingness of the two parties to address themselves to the issues of industrial democracy turned Frankfurter again in 1924 to a third party, this time to Robert M. LaFollette. This was the period of his most militantly outspoken utterances. In April 1924, he wrote an unsigned editorial for the *New Republic*, "Why Mr. Davis Shouldn't Run," with an almost Marxist bite to it. He denounced Davis's association with the banking house of J. P. Morgan and Company. The "ideas with which one deals and the people with whom one mixes determine one's directions." They explained Davis's indifference to agrarian and industrial distress. To accumulate great wealth, as Davis had done, impaired one's ability to deal with the central issue of the times. "Our most vital political differences do now, and in days to come will still more, center around the human implications back of the vast differences in these very high and low income tax brackets."

Frankfurter was even more scathing about Davis's "cowardice" in the face of the postwar witch hunt. "Look at his record," he wrote Walter Lippmann, who had become the editor of *The World*:

(1) He returned from England in 1921 with great prestige at a time when the "Red hysteria" and all the nonsense about "Radicals" was in full swing. From that day to this, never a peep from Davis! Hughes, even, spoke out vigorously in 1920, while out of office; but not Davis in 1921, or '2, or '3.

(2) He was not merely resting under the duty to which a leading citizen is subjected at a time of nationwide hysteria. He was president of the American Bar Association when that Association was one of the leading encouragers of all the nonsense about "one hundred per cent Americanism." Never a peep from Davis! He was president of the American Bar Association when flagrant violations of the Constitution were perpetrated. Never a peep from Davis! On the contrary, read his presidential address before the American Bar Association in 1923 and you will find a regular stand-pat, hard-boiled enunciation of all the conventional bunkum in regard to the criticism of the courts, and all the conventional sophistication in defense of the invalidation by courts of social legislation. Apparently, some of the Supreme Court decisions are too liberal for him, particularly the decisions of that Court sustaining the rent laws, for he evidently has those in mind when he says, "Constitutional limitations have yielded to the police power under the pressure of real or supposed emergencies"—clearly a squint at the rent laws and, probably, also the Adamson law. A striking commentary on the conventional conservatism of Davis's outlook on these issues is to be found in the keen commentary of Lord Birkenhead who followed Davis at the Minneapolis meeting in 1923.

(3) After the hysteria of the war abated, vigorous effort was made, in which The World took the lead to secure pardons for the victims of mob convictions under the Espionage Act. I feel as you do about Senator Pepper's recent performance, but it will remain to his abiding credit that he made these convictions a charge upon his conscience and took the lead in securing pardons for unjustifiable convictions. Davis was approached as one of the leaders of the bar, but again not a peep from Davis! He was content to remain silent, and thus throw the weight of his authority by his silence against the rectification of wrong or miscarriage of justice.

(4) His attitude towards the Senatorial investigations has been one of criticism of the investigations instead of condemnation of what they disclosed. The World has asked in vain that names be named of those who suffered unjustly at the hands of the Walsh and Wheeler investigations. And yet Davis's contribution to the central issue of morality in this campaign was criticism of those who led the fight in this moral issue, together with an attempt by him to hobble the processes of future investigation, and to confuse the public mind in its judgment of the present investigations.

If The World deems John W. Davis a Liberal or a "progressive," then I wonder what its tests of liberalism or progressivism are. I don't want to bother you for a reply to me. But I submit that the questions which I raise are entitled to be dealt with editorially by The World while Davis is under consideration for the Democratic nomination.[70]

Yours,

But Lippmann was unpersuaded, and on July 11, 1924, Frankfurter ended the exchange. "You and I are taking very different roads in this campaign, and I shan't be bothering you any more, politically, till November, for controversial correspondence isn't one of your favorite sports, and you have the responsibility for guiding a Democratic newspaper." [71]

To Learned Hand at the beginning of October he unburdened himself in harsh terms:

And it is good neither for these lads that I see passing through this School from year to year, nor for this country, that at a time when we need the discouragement of material ambitions and the instilling of spiritual concerns that really matter and out of which alone will come the atmosphere of faith and understanding and confidence in one another, indispensable for the solutions of our greatest problems, that we should reward with the Presidency one to whom big money was the big thing, at a time when the country needed more than ever that a man of his ability should remain free to understand and to serve the common wants of men.[72]

He gave public expression to his dissatisfaction with *status quo* politics in his signed statement, "Why I Shall Vote for LaFollette." He characterized economic inequalities as "the most significant characteristic of our social-economic life," criticized the "economic imperialism" of the United States toward Latin America, and deplored the Democratic party's reliance on the "solid South," which he considered "the greatest immoral factor of American politics." The LaFollette candidacy alone "represents a determined effort to secure adequate attention for the great interests of the workers and of agriculture in those economic and social compromises which, in the last analysis, underlie all national action." To those who reproached him with wasting his vote, he replied, "If the clarification of American politics through the formation of a new party is required to make our politics more honest and more real, then all the talk of 'throwing one's vote away' is cowardly philosophy of the bandwagon." [73]

The Supreme Court was midcourse in a decade that would see it invalidate "more state legislation than during the fifty years preceding," and LaFollette's remedy was a constitutional amendment that would empower Congress by a two-thirds vote to override a Supreme Court veto over a legislative statute. Frankfurter did not endorse that proposal. He thought that perhaps the "due process clause," which was the sword the Court wielded to cut down state and congressional enactments, ought to go, but he was skeptical of any "mechanical device. The only reliance rests on the quality of the judges and the temper and training of the bar." "Against the fallibilities of the Court there is no simple panacea," he wrote in the *New Republic* in 1921 after the Court had upheld the power of the Postmaster General to suppress newspapers. "We must look to a broader and more conscious legal education." [74]

Absorbing though he found politics, involved as he was as a "public lawyer" in efforts to protect civil liberties and labor's right to organize, stimulating as he found political journalism, his real love was the Harvard Law School, where through research and teaching he could influence the direction of the law as well as "the temper and training of the bar." The standards of Harvard Law School were so severe that survivors said of themselves, "The cowards never started; the weak died on the way." Frankfurter's exactions from his students were even more demanding. "He could and did attract disciples who worked valiantly in his seminars, hoping for the reward of his approval" wrote the Law School's historian. "For brilliant men he was a strong stimulant." Mediocre students were ignored. He rejected the "romantic American political tradition that everyone is competent for everything," and he cited John Stuart Mill's observation that "Mediocrity ought not to be engaged in the affairs of state." [75]

He had time and patience only for the brilliant and the boys of old and wealthy families. He had his "favorites"—one, a youth of beetling brows and saturnine stare, was James M. Landis, who sat in Frankfurter's seminar on federal jurisdiction and procedure "with a kind of somber mastery," astonishing all with his phenomenal memory and sheer brilliance. His doctoral dissertation, "Constitutional Limitations on Congressional Powers of Investigation," reflected views similar to those expressed by Frankfurter in his *New Republic* editorials on the Teapot Dome scandals, and in 1927 he and Frankfurter published a book *The Business of the Supreme Court.* Original research, wrote Frankfurter, "means a very small number of rigorously selected graduate students. For no man can explore the unknown, track new knowledge, with more than a handful of students. Graduate work implies a personal relation between two students, one of whom is a professor." [76]

In 1924 he became Byrne Professor of Administrative Law, a chair that was intended for Frankfurter by its endower, James Byrne, member of the Harvard Corporation and of the firm that had given Frankfurter his first job. He taught "Public Utilities," "Jurisdiction and Procedure of Federal Courts," and "Administrative Law." But they said of Frankfurter, as he said of Ames, that with him "you took not courses but the man." He put on a theatrical performance before his classes, said David Lilienthal. He was a man "who could read the dictionary and make it exciting," as he bounced around, spending hours on one aspect of one case, so that his courses came to be known as "the case-of-the-month" clubs. Some students, Lloyd Garrison for one, found his lectures less than electrifying. He would begin with a question or two, rather perfunctory, it seemed to Garrison and his classmates, and from then on it was an uninterrupted monologue. "Rather dull," said Garrison. But his seminars, said Dean Pound, were Socratic think tanks. "Teacher and student were cooperating in juristic development of a branch of the law in the light of an assured grasp of the whole." [77]

In addition to collaboration, there was another accolade that Frankfurter bestowed on his ablest disciples. From the time that Holmes had gone on the Bench he had obtained his law secretaries from the Harvard Law School. Professor John Chipman Gray, who had served with Holmes in the Union Army, made the selection. "Gray knew the kind of boys Holmes wanted—they must be able to deal with *certiorari*, balance his checkbooks and listen to his tall talk," wrote Francis Biddle, who was Holmes's seventh clerk. [78] After Gray's death in 1915, Holmes asked Frankfurter to make the selection, as did Brandeis when he went to the Court in 1916. Landis clerked for Brandeis, as did Dean Acheson. Among the students Frankfurter sent to Holmes were Thomas Corcoran, Alger and Donald Hiss, Mark De Wolfe Howe, and James H. Rowe, Jr. He performed the same function for Justice Cardozo when he succeeded Holmes in 1932. Joseph Rauh, Jr., would serve as Cardozo's last clerk and Frankfurter's first.

"Why is he a Democrat, Mr. Laski?" some friends of Frankfurter to whom he was showing London inquired. "Because he is an aristocrat with an infinite sense of pity," Laski replied. "Why does he not want to make money?" "Because most people who have it are vulgar." "Why doesn't he collect books or pictures?" "Because he collects people." [79]

When Archibald MacLeish, poet, graduate of the Harvard Law School, and friend, wrote his introduction to *Law and Politics*, a collection of Felix Frankfurter's writing that appeared in 1939 just as Frankfurter went on to the

Supreme Court, he predicted that on the bench Frankfurter would be a fervent defender of the Bill of Rights against legislative erosion. In support of his prophecy, MacLeish noted Frankfurter's involvement in the Sacco-Vanzetti case, which, said MacLeish, showed "his peculiar sensitivity to attacks on civil rights and his deep and passionate devotion to their defense."

The Sacco-Vanzetti case, arising out of the arrest, conviction, and sentencing to death of a "good shoemaker" and "poor fish peddler" for the holdup and murder of a paymaster and his guard in Braintree, Massachusetts, engaged and polarized Brahmin Boston. Frankfurter in later years often quoted John F. Moors, Boston banker, Harvard Overseer, but a nonconformist: "It was characteristic of Harvard and in a way to the glory of Harvard that two Harvard men were the leaders of the opposing forces in the Sacco-Vanzetti affair. Here was A. Lawrence Lowell, the president of the school, and here was Professor Frankfurter of the Harvard Law School, who were the spearheads of those who expressed conflicting views." And Moors added of his Harvard classmate Lowell, that he "was incapable of seeing that two wops could be right and the Yankee judiciary could be wrong." There was an additional prejudice in the situation. Gardner Jackson, the young and pugnacious publicity man for the Sacco-Vanzetti Defense Committee, thought that Lowell's animus against Frankfurter seriously warped his judgment on the issues in the case. The hostility stemmed from a proposal by Lowell in 1923 to establish a "Jewish quota" at Harvard. That had occasioned a "vitriolic correspondence" between Lowell and Frankfurter, said Jackson. "Nobody but me has seen that exchange and it really was vitriolic. I am satisfied that the intensity of Lowell's animosity to Felix was a very large factor in what happened to his mind in the face of the evidence, since Felix had become the chief intellectual protagonist of the two Italians." [80]

The murders happened in 1920 while Frankfurter was abroad. It was at the height of the anti-Red hysteria, and Boston, as Frankfurter knew from his experience with the deportation orders, "was one of the worst centers of this lawlessness and hysteria." The prosecution's proof that Sacco and Vanzetti were the murderers was weak, and the district attorney played up to the jurors' aversion to radicalism and draft evasion which the defendants avowed. Frankfurter did not pay much attention to the case until his wife reported that Mrs. Glendower Evans, a Boston Gardiner and family intimate of Brandeis, whose children called her "Auntie Bee," as did the Frankfurters, was greatly exercised, "and wants to know what you think about the Sacco-Vanzetti case." He refused to give an opinion. "I haven't read the record and I don't know anything about it." But in 1925 William G. Thompson, a leading Boston trial and appellate lawyer, a great friend of Stimson and of Ezra Thayer, became counsel for the condemned men. When he moved for a new trial on the basis of an affidavit of Captain Proctor, one of the prosecutor's ballistic experts, Frankfurter suddenly began to pay attention. "Something happened to my insides," because Proctor in his affidavit asserted that the prosecutor, knowing that Proctor could not and would not testify that the mortal bullet passed through Sacco's pistol, cunningly phrased his question so as to leave the impression with the jury that he had so testified by eliciting the reply from Proctor that, "My opinion is that it is consistent with being fired from the pistol." Frankfurter felt it was reprehensible for a district attorney to get an expert to testify to something he had repeatedly told him he could not swear to.[81]

Frankfurter sent for the 6,000-page record, read it through, and the book "wrote itself." The passions aroused by the trial around the world have subsided, yet almost a half century later Frankfurter's study still compels reading. Incisive, logical, it peels away with cold fury the various layers of the prosecutorial case until it is revealed for what it is—an example of the lawlessness, prejudice, and hysteria of the times.

Frankfurter's analysis had an immediate impact. Men and women everywhere were soon citing its arguments. Feeling was so intense that when he entered a room or restaurant old friends would cut him dead. The article brought an answer from John H. Wigmore, Harvard Law School '87, Dean of Northwestern University Law School and author of the universally used *Treatise on Evidence*. Wigmore's purpose, he wrote in the *Boston Transcript*, was "to vindicate Massachusetts justice . . ." against the charges of "the plausible pundit of the leading law school." *The Boston Herald* held its presses for Frankfurter's reply, which appeared the next day. "I say without fear of contradiction that Dean Wigmore could not have read the record, could not have read with care the opinion of Judge Thayer, on which his own article is largely based, could not even have examined my little book. . . ." This was followed by another exchange two weeks later. "Felix," commented his colleague Professor Williston, a classmate of Wigmore, "I haven't read anything on the Sacco-Vanzetti case but I must say you pulverized him." "Wigmore is a fool! Wigmore is a fool!" Lowell is reported to have moaned. "He should have known that Frankfurter would be shrewd enough to be accurate." [82]

Lowell headed the commission that Governor Fuller appointed a few weeks later when he was petitioned for clemency. Its finding that the two men had been properly convicted ended the seven-year struggle to save them. The liberal New York *World*, which had staunchly upheld Sacco and Vazetti, editorialized that since the Lowell Committee had examined the facts in the case, the *World* must have been wrong. Frankfurter refused to admit defeat. "Pat, I'm catching the train to New York right away," he telephoned Gardner Jackson. "I've talked with Charlie Burlingham and he and I are going to have a session with Walter Lippmann. Don't lose hope just because the *World* has reversed itself." The Frankfurter-Burlingham meeting with Lippmann lasted several hours and the following day the *World* devoted its entire editorial page to the Lowell Committee report, "just tearing it apart, section by section. . . ." But nothing was changed. The Governor did not stay the sentence.[83] On the night of their execution Frankfurter and his wife, who had been as passionately gripped by the case as her husband, and would with Gardner Jackson publish the letters of Sacco and Vanzetti, wandered restlessly through the streets of Boston with a friend. At midnight a radio blared out: "Sacco gone, Vanzetti going." Mrs. Frankfurter collapsed and only was kept from falling to the ground by the two men. Learned Hand, who saw Frankfurter the following day, said he was "like a mad man. He was really beside himself." [84]

Physical courage, Brandeis observed to Herbert B. Ehrmann, who was associate defense counsel, was the commonest of human virtues, moral courage the rarest. He approved Frankfurter's involvement in the Sacco-Vanzetti case and toward the end of the Twenties said of him that he was "the most useful lawyer in the United States." But Holmes deprecated Frankfurter's "excursions and alarums," writing to Laski that he was "so good in his chosen business that I think he helps the world more in that way than he does by becoming a knight-errant or a martyr." * [85]

Shortly after the execution of the two men, Frankfurter heard that Jackson was collecting their letters with a view to publication. He came to Jackson and asked whether Marion could not be his collaborator. She was under psychiatric care, he confided, and both he and the psychiatrist thought such an enterprise would be good therapy. Jackson agreed readily and in the course of the co-editorship became Marion's "confidante and received from her expressions of the difficulties she had encountered in having married a Jew, and the social pressures to which she was subjected, and her inner struggle against this complex of circumstances. More than that, of course, Felix, being the kind of human being he is, or was and still is pretty much, made for difficulties. He is such a vital, dynamic, aggressive personality that that in itself was a difficulty, let alone the fact of being Jewish." [86]

The wound left in the American psyche by the Sacco-Vanzetti case was deep and lasting. Many Americans dated their turn to radicalism from the execution of the two men. But Frankfurter was of different mettle. Although he believed profoundly that as good a test as any of a civilization "is the degree to which justice is carried out, the degree to which men are sensitive to wrong-doing and desirous to right it," there were no shortcuts to judicial perfection. The remedy remained the training of the men who went into the law and the persistent and patient effort to elevate public opinion and feeling. The presidency especially set the moral standards of a nation, and in 1928 he supported the candidacy of Alfred E. Smith because, "In a democracy, politics is a process of popular education—the task of adjusting the conflicting interests of diverse groups in a community," and Smith was "a master" of such politics, whose

---

* In 1962 Francis Russell published *Tragedy in Dedham*, a careful and on the whole judicious re-examination of the Sacco-Vanzetti case, and came to the conclusion, "Sacco was guilty but Vanzetti was not." Russell did not, however, deal with the issues that engaged Frankfurter, the unfairness of the arraignment, prosecution, and trial procedures. Nor did Russell's "new evidence" shake the faith of men like Herbert B. Ehrmann and Judge Musmanno in the innocence of the two men. (See Ehrmann's *The Case that Will Not Die* [Boston, 1969]) If Frankfurter had second thoughts on the innocence of the two men, this writer has not come across them.

election, moreover, "will give decided momentum to the liberalizing tendencies in American Social economy." Holmes, incidentally, was persuaded by none of this. "I was glad that he [Hoover] beat Smith though there has been a sort of fad among the New York highbrows to blow Smith's horn, on what seemed to me very inadequate reasons." [87]

THE THIRTIES

"For you have as Smith has," Frankfurter wrote Franklin D. Roosevelt on November 8, 1928, after the latter had won the governorship and Smith, as much the victim of the electorate's prejudices as of Hoover's virtues, had crashed down to defeat, "the conception of government which seems to me indispensable to the vitality of a democratic government, namely the realization that the processes of government are essentially educational processes." It is the second letter in the voluminous Roosevelt-Frankfurter correspondence compiled by Max Freedman. Frankfurter's political dexterity was such that in the next few years he managed to keep on good terms with both Roosevelt and Smith, even as the latter, embittered by Roosevelt's success and his own decline, fought resentfully to keep his successor in Albany from getting the presidential nomination in 1932. Both men valued his judgment and technical abilities sufficiently to disregard his flirtations with the other camp. Roosevelt was not an effusive correspondent. He wrote a line for the other's page and rarely disclosed himself, yet so strong was his magnetism that his reticence rarely discouraged others from pouring their treasures at his feet. Within two weeks Frankfurter wrote again with the thought that Roosevelt stop off in Washington on his way to Warm Springs for a talk with Justice Brandeis. The governor-elect brushed him off: to stop in Washington would be viewed as "a bid for national leadership." [88]

That, however, did not keep him from turning to Frankfurter when he needed him. The New York Legislature in 1929 was Republican-controlled. Roosevelt quickly demonstrated his political talents by gaining and holding the initiative. In his combats with the Republicans over the regulation of public utilities and water power development, he sought Frankfurter's advice. The counsel was sufficiently sound so that at the end of the session Roosevelt wanted to know where he was going to be during the summer, for he wanted to talk with him. He also arranged for Frank P. Walsh, who was investigating the operations of the state Public Service Commission, to spend a day with Frankfurter in Cambridge. [89]

Roosevelt and Frankfurter were contemporaries, both having been born in 1882. Both had admired Theodore Roosevelt. Both had served in the Wilson Administration, and in their correspondence they were "Dear Frank" and "Dear Felix." Walter Lippmann had a low estimate of Roosevelt and was constantly needling him in the editorial columns of the World: "I am mighty glad to see that correspondence between Felix and you and Walter Lippmann," an exasperated Roosevelt wrote Professor James Bonbright, another of his appointees on the Public Service Investigation Commission. "Of course I have never been able to understand the editorial policy of the New York *World*. For instance it was the *World* which literally drove Al Smith into sending that fool telegram after the Houston convention telling how wet he was. Al had every wet vote in the country but he needed a good many millions of the middle of the road votes to elect him President. . . . If Walter would stick to the fundamentals, fewer people would feel that the *World* first blows hot and then blows cold. Perhaps you and Felix will have some effect. I hope so." [90]

Yet at the end of Roosevelt's first term as governor, Frankfurter to some extent shared Lippmann's reservations about Roosevelt. "I know his limitations. Most of them derive, I believe, from lack of an incisive intellect and a kind of optimism that sometimes makes him timid, as well as an ambition that leads to compromises with which we were familiar with Theodore Roosevelt and Wilson. But on the whole he has been a very good Governor." Frankfurter, however, did not say these things to Roosevelt, except by indirection, and after Roosevelt's landslide reelection when he performed the unprecedented feat for a Democrat of carrying upstate, rural, traditionally Republican New York, and immediately became the frontrunner for the presidential nomination in 1932, Frankfurter ended his congratulations, "And your friends rightly believe that the forthrightness and standards which made you a leader, overnight, in the fight against things that twenty years ago were symbolized by 'Blue-eyed' Billy Sheehan, guide you also today." [91]

As though politics, teaching, research, and writing did not sufficiently absorb his energies and sympathies, Frankfurter in 1930 was deeply involved again with the future of the Jewish settlements in Palestine. There had been an outbreak of Arab attacks on them in 1929, with many settlers killed, and this had led Britain, the mandatory power, to appoint a commission which in March 1930 recommended curtailment of Jewish immigration and acquisition of land in Palestine. Widespread Zionist protests led to the appointment of a new commission. "And much energy expended in preventing Felix from coming here to dip his fingers in the Zionist pie and create immense embarrassment," an exasperated Laski, who disliked Jewish nationalism, wrote Holmes. "It seems to be one of Brandeis' blind spots not to see that when the British government has a commission of inquiry in Palestine, not even Felix can get guarantees about policy until the commission has reported and that to send him here just now, instead of when there is a document to discuss, would injure his prestige and waste his time."

Ramsay MacDonald was Prime Minister and he persuaded Laski to mediate between the commission and the Zionists. "He [Brandeis] exercises a strange hold over Felix," Laski wrote Holmes, "for the latter who can usually be cool and independent is in these things simply an echo of L. D. B. He gives orders like an omnipotent Sultan and negotiations do not come to a success in that way." The crisis abated with a compromise solution, but the fate of the Jewish settlements would remain a constant preoccupation of Frankfurter. In 1931 he published in *Foreign Affairs* an article on "The Palestine Situation Restated" critical of the British for deviating from the principles of the Balfour Declaration. "I speak not only as a Jew," he wrote, "but as one who believes in the wisdom of the policy embodied in the Palestine Mandate for the establishment of a Jewish National Home in Palestine. But I am also one of those who believe that the excesses of nationalism led to the World war and who look to a realization of the interdependence of nations as the key to world peace. It is also pertinent to avow a strong Anglophilism. . . ." [92]

The congratulations that Frankfurter sent Roosevelt on his reelection brought from the Governor an invitation to spend the night "with us. I want to talk to you of many things—water power, .public utilities, New York City judges, deliberate editorial cads, and other choice subjects." Both men needed each other; both were old hands at the art of courtship. "Put your mighty mind to work on this," Roosevelt urged him at the end of a note about credit inflation. "I have left no opportunity unavailed out here," Frankfurter wrote him from Laguna Beach, California "to tell them about your work in detail— especially your knowing and aggressive leadership on Power and Unemployment." He should "stop off in Albany before you become a Professor again," Roosevelt asked him at the end of that summer. Yet both men held off from total commitment to each other. Frankfurter was a little vexed that Roosevelt had not acknowledged—he had—his little book *The Public and Its Government*, "especially the last essay on Expert Administration and Democracy," and when Roosevelt's persuasive powers evoked a reluctant agreement from Frankfurter to serve as chairman of a commission to reform New York's judicial system, he reversed himself after he returned to Cambridge, pleading other commitments. Nor was he invited in the period before the Democratic convention to join the group of Roosevelt's most intimate policy counselors, the Brain Trust. "I am wondering what will come out of Chicago," he wrote C. C. Burlingham, an elder statesman of the bar, just before the Democratic convention. "If F. D. R. is nominated, it will certainly prove there is no limit to the amount of fumbling one can do and still win a game." But Roosevelt, even if he suspected, as he must have, for his political antennae were the most acute in the country, that Frankfurter's heart still belonged to Smith, valued Frankfurter's counsel, and when it served his needs, he was an irresistible suitor. [93]

After his nomination, when his purpose was to conciliate the Smith forces, Roosevelt spoke at length over the telephone to Frankfurter, who pleaded with him to invite Governor Ely of Massachusetts, a Smith partisan, to see him. Roosevelt balked. Ely was one of the two men who had "overstepped the bounds of decency. . . . There is a limit to what a fellow will do to turn the other cheek." Frankfurter stuck to his guns. Roosevelt yielded slightly. He should talk to his son Jimmy, who was then living in Boston. "He will give you the picture." Frankfurter also wanted to talk to Roosevelt about the budget. "I wish you would see Colonel House," Roosevelt replied, "and ask him for a document on things economic that I mailed to him this morning. It was drawn up by Tugwell, Berle, and Moley." [94]

Some of their talk, according to Frankfurter's memorandum, related to Governor Ely's announcement, without advance notice to Frankfurter, that he was appointing him to the Supreme Judicial Court of Massachusetts. The reported appointment had been denounced by former Governor Fuller, the man who had refused clemency to Sacco and Vanzetti, as the appointment of "an open sympathizer of murderers," but respectable figures like Newton Baker had rallied to Frankfurter's support, and the appointment was his for the taking. He declined. It was "the most difficult decision of my professional life," he told Ely, but "as against the opportunities for immediate achievement on the bench, the long-term effects of legal education make their claim." For reasons of protocol, Frankfurter did not tell this to Roosevelt, who had opened the telephone conversation with congratulations on his judicial nomination, adding the fateful words, "I wish it were the Supreme Court of the United States— that's where you belong." It was a mistake to decline "the Massachusetts Supreme Judicial Court," Holmes felt, "but he and Brandeis know better than I do." [95]

Roosevelt's post-convention efforts to conciliate the disaffected in the Democratic party were complicated by the charges of the Seabury Legislative Committee against New York City's popular Mayor James J. Walker. The charges were a culmination of probings of Tammany that had revealed widespread, scandalous misgovernment. A mis-move might cost him the support not only of the New York City machine but engender suspicion of his regularity by machines everywhere. Yet not to move vigorously against Tammany and Walker would alienate the West and the South and independents generally and seem to confirm Walter Lippmann's harsh verdict voiced in January 1932 that Roosevelt was "a highly impressionable person, without a firm grasp of affairs and without strong convictions . . . not the dangerous enemy of anything. . . ." His handling of the Walker hearings, which ended with Walker's resignation, demonstrated how wrong those were who judged him as amiable, weak, opportunist.

Frankfurter's counsel in the Walker hearings was of inestimable help. "Since leaving Albany, I have thought a great deal about the Walker situation," he wrote Roosevelt on August 5. "If Seabury accurately represents the record . . . then it seems to me that the facts ineluctably compel removal of the Mayor. . . . To paraphrase Cardozo, there are many forms of official misconduct that do not amount to crimes but do call for removal. . . . The inescapable fact is that he was the beneficiary of sizable money favors from those who themselves had substantial money interests in having the Mayor as a friend, in being 'solid' with the Mayor who had enormous power in the dispensation of enormous public concessions of one sort or another."

"The Walker hearings drag on," Roosevelt wrote him a few weeks later, "but I am confident that it is best I should not give them any chance to say that I am railroading the case. When the hearing is over I hope much that you will run over here to talk with me in strict confidence about the ethics and the law involved." The trip was unnecessary. Walker resigned. "Resignation is concession and complete vindication of your firmness, skill, and fairness as chief executive," Frankfurter wired from Maine.[96]

Roosevelt found talk with Frankfurter a spur and excitement. "It was grand to see you both," he wrote Frankfurter and his wife after they had spent a day at Albany. "You stimulate me enormously. Repeat the dose again." He asked Frankfurter to help the Brain Trust group, and Frankfurter sent Max Lowenthal to represent him. But the Moley-Tugwell-Berle group, judging by Berle's reactions, was not hospitable to Frankfurter's participation. "Lowenthal came in because Felix Frankfurter wanted to bring him in on the proceedings," Berle noted in his Diary, "this over Moley's objection, with which all of us concurred." Berle considered Lowenthal an inflationist, "in touch with some of the Jewish financiers . . . ," a "typical liberal on the make" with "no loyalty except to Felix Frankfurter and the particular little group that revolves around him." Moley had his differences with Frankfurter but respected him. There was always an edge to Berle's opposition, a touch of resentment at having been excluded from Frankfurter's little elite group of student disciples at Harvard when he had been a student there in 1916.[97]

The Professor was no innocent when it came to palace politics. He knew how to bide his time. Moreover, he was one of the few Roosevelt advisers with technical expertise of a high order who genuinely functioned on the same political and policy wave-length as Roosevelt. A remarkable letter to Lippmann in April 1932, as the depression was moving toward its catastrophic nadir, indicated his social philosophy and how sympathetic its gradualism was to Roosevelt's: [98]

> Mine being a pragmatic temperament, all my scepticism and discontent with the present order and tendencies have not carried me over to a new comprehensive scheme of society, whether socialism or communism. Or, perhaps ten years in government, and as many more of intensive study of its problems, have made me also sceptical of any full-blown new scheme and left me most conscious of the extraordinary difficulties of the problems of the Great Society.

He agreed with a *Commonweal* observation that "greed is the witch," and it may be that at the end of the depression

> a greater percentage of the wealth of the country will be found to have come into the control of even a smaller percentage of the population than was the case before the depression. And if that be so, those of us who, by temperament or habit of conviction, believe that we do not have to make a sudden and drastic break with the past but by gradual, successive, al-

though large, modifications may slowly evolve out of this profit-making society, may find all our hopes and strivings indeed reduced to a house of cards.

And again in a letter to Lippmann, who had been pressing Roosevelt through Frankfurter to have the candidate declare himself against the soldiers' bonus, he showed considerable discernment of how Roosevelt operated politically. He advised Lippmann that Roosevelt could not be pushed: [99]

He has his own sense of timing and timeliness, as I have experienced on other matters. Had I been in his place, I would have disposed of the bonus business long ago—at least I think I would have, though God only knows what a candidature would do to a man. And so he may well be subject to criticism for biding his time in the way he does. But it has nothing to do with lack of decision or conviction. In fact, it is one form that his decisiveness takes. And what has struck me in the limited knowledge I have had of some of his campaign decisions is that he makes his own. . . . I was interested in the independence of his judgment and the confidence that he has in it, alongside of the eager accessibility of his mind. . . .

Yet he was still infected with some of Lippmann's doubts. "Your bonus treatment could not have been better done," he wired Roosevelt after his Pittsburgh speech, but to Lippmann he confided his disappointment. "If Roosevelt is elected, I think he will often do the right things, as it were, on inadequate and not wholly sturdy grounds. That's what I feel about his bonus statement. . . . I don't expect heroic action from him. . . ." His radio speech endorsing Roosevelt on November 5 was in the main an attack on Hoover with a few final paragraphs devoted to lackluster praise of Roosevelt whereas his endorsement of Smith in 1928 had dwelt enthusiastically on Smith's personal qualifications for the presidency. But his congratulations to Roosevelt upon his election were wholehearted: "No predecessor of yours, not even T.R., I believe, brought to the Presidency, so extensive and intimate a knowledge of his countrymen as you have." Holmes saw the matter differently. "As to the election if I had a vote it would have been for Hoover—without enthusiasm—Roosevelt when I knew him struck me as a good fellow with rather a soft edge, years ago." Of this judgment, one can only say that even Homer nodded.[100]

At the end of October Laski had written from London that he hoped Roosevelt would be elected "and that he makes Felix Solicitor-General." Frankfurter was "in the inner circle of Roosevelt advisers," Holmes advised Laski, at least so Brandeis had told him, but Brandeis did not believe Frankfurter would take the Solicitor-Generalship. So far as Holmes was concerned, "I think it would be queer to turn down a seat on the Massachusetts Supreme Judicial Bench for a Solicitor-Generalship." [101]

Roosevelt's election as President and his confidence in Frankfurter's judg-

ment meant that Frankfurter soon again would confront the decision whether
to participate in government or remain at Harvard. Roosevelt had grown genuinely fond of this irrepressible conversationalist who managed, even in the
most hectic moments of crisis, to come up with an unexpected answer to an
immediate problem. "Felix has more ideas per minute than any man of my acquaintance," Roosevelt told an associate. "He has a brilliant mind but it clicks
so fast it makes my head fairly spin. I find him tremendously interesting and
stimulating." [102]

In the four-month interregnum before Roosevelt assumed office, when
Roosevelt and his aides labored frantically to prepare for the takeover, Frankfurter was called on frequently for help. Some matters could not wait. Bankruptcy relief was one, Frankfurter and Berle "at loggerheads," Moley noted.
"Typically, F.F. comes in at the last moment with many ideas, some, very
good," Berle complained to Roosevelt in regard to the Railway Reorganization
Act, ". . . but will take no responsibility for getting anything done . . . with
considerable admiration of Felix Frankfurter's public career and an intense personal desire to see him shot." A few weeks after Roosevelt's inauguration Moley
called Frankfurter down to help draft a securities bill. He arrived in Washington with "two thin solemn young men," James Landis and Benjamin V.
Cohen.[103]

One of his most fateful services to the President-elect was recorded dra-
matically in the diary of Henry Stimson, Frankfurter's old mentor and Hoover's
Secretary of State. "Frankfurter called me up from Albany," Stimson noted in
his diary on December 22, 1932. "He was at the Executive Mansion spending
the night with Roosevelt. He said that in the middle of their conversation,
which lasted about two hours, Roosevelt suddenly out of a clear sky said, 'Why
doesn't Harry Stimson come up here and talk with me and settle this damn
thing that nobody else seems to be able to do?' " This referred to negotiations
between Roosevelt and Hoover in regard to the war debts and reparations.
When Stimson reported Frankfurter's message to Hoover the next day, "He was
against it I could see from the first." Frankfurter went down to Washington to
give Stimson his view of Roosevelt. "It was a much more attractive picture than
we have been getting from the other side." Stimson talked with Hoover again
and "he finally yielded and said that he was willing to have me go up there,
provided Roosevelt would ask him first." When Frankfurter communicated this
to Roosevelt, he said, " 'Tell me what to write—dictate right now the note you
think I ought to send him,' which I did, in substance repeating what Stimson
thought should be in the note."

On January 9 Stimson journeyed to Hyde Park and talked with Roosevelt
for six hours. Before the meeting Frankfurter had briefed Roosevelt on Stimson:
"I told him to remember that Stimson is rather slow-minded, methodical,
single-trackminded like Wilson and not quick and darting as he is, and that he
will therefore have to give Stimson ample time to lay out all that is in his
mind." A few days after the meeting Roosevelt, to the dismay of his neutrality-

minded advisers headed by Moley, Tugwell, and Berle, endorsed Stimson's policy of refusing to recognize political changes in the Far East achieved through aggression. Frankfurter saw the foreign situation differently than the Brain Trusters. "The impact of your support of Stimson on the 'Manchurian business,' " he wrote Roosevelt, "is of importance not merely on that specific issue, difficult as that is. It contributed and will continue to contribute much in making for coherence and common effort among the Western peoples generally." [104]

In and out of Washington, bringing Roosevelt messages from Brandeis and Justice Harlan Fiske Stone, understanding Roosevelt's methods and purposes better perhaps than anyone else around him, it was inevitable that Roosevelt would ask him to join the Administration. Even before Roosevelt took office, he had sounded out Senator Tom Walsh, who had headed the Senate inquiry into the Teapot Dome scandals and was to be his Attorney General, on Frankfurter's appointment as Solicitor General. According to Moley, Walsh opposed the appointment: he did not "want somebody in there who will lose cases in the grand manner." [105] But Homer Cummings, who succeeded Walsh after his sudden and tragic death, did not feel the same way.

On March 8 Frankfurter was in Washington to celebrate the ninety-second birthday of Justice Holmes. He was summoned to the White House where Roosevelt "took me completely off my feet" by offering him the Solicitor Generalship. Although surprised, he was ready with his reply: "It is my genuine conviction—I am sure it is so—that I can do much more to be of use to you by staying in Cambridge than by becoming Solicitor General. The fact of the matter is that I could not have anything to do on any of the matters on which you would want my help and do my job as Solicitor General—it just can't be done."

He really ought to be on the Supreme Court, Roosevelt pressed on, and he wanted to put him there, but "I can't put you on the Supreme Court from the Harvard Law School. But once you are Solicitor General, these various objections [that he was a professor, the Sacco-Vanzetti case, that he was a Jew] will be forgotten or disappear." But Frankfurter still resisted: "I do not think it is a wise way of life to take a job I don't want because it may lead to another, which also I'm not sure I'd want." He should sleep on it and talk it over with the "missus," Roosevelt urged him, but a few days later Frankfurter formally declined. "I have reflected much on all you said, and discussed the matter not only with my wife but also, very confidentially, with Holmes and Brandeis. They are clear that I can be of more use to the public and to you by not becoming Solicitor General." "I have not forgiven you," Roosevelt wrote almost a month later. "How can I find anybody else with just your qualifications to appear on behalf of the government before the Supreme Court?" Then he added a note of the wooer scorned, yet admiring: "You are an independent pig and that is one reason why I cannot blame you!" [106]

To keep a clear head, to think beyond the immediate moment and appraise the long-range implications of events and policies was not easy during the hundred days when the nation begged for leadership and action. Frankfurter did. He cautioned Lippmann against downgrading Congress in the need for speedy, remedial legislation. He should not urge the President to assume dictatorial powers. "I know your phrase has been concentration of authority, but the result is the same. We have not and ought not to have, government by Presidential decree—which is the essence of the theory and practice of continental dictatorship. . . . I strongly deplore the current tendency to assume that power as such generates wisdom and that the deliberative processes are drags upon wise action." Lippmann was not impressed! "Do you really think, for example, that I should have urged Congress to consider carefully and attempt to understand thoroughly the provisions of the banking bill before passing it, or was it right to call upon Congress to take the thing on faith, suspending debate, suspending the process of education, suspending the deliberative method?" Frankfurter yielded only slightly: "The actions of Congress at this session offend none of my prejudices regarding the appropriate scope for reason in government or the appropriate role of Congress in our scheme of things. What I object to—and it goes to the very root of my political convictions—is the building up of opinion hostile to the need for Congress, as a policy-making organ and as a critic of executive measures." He was not criticizing Roosevelt. He had no fear that Roosevelt himself would encourage the country to look to a "Great White Father . . . to pull rabbits out of a hat. . . . By temperament and experience he knows the importance of carrying the consent of the country—as far as may be—along with him, not merely generally and vaguely but by specific appeal on specific policies." [107]

The letters to Lippmann showed a remarkable independence and detachment, but the Harvard authorities—President Lowell and Dean Pound—did not, as Frankfurter's Diary indicates, look benignly on his role as a Roosevelt adviser. "He was summoned to Washington somewhat unexpectedly," wrote the Law School historian, "and so became a little unpredictable in his academic role. Pound, despite his own recent absence with the Wickersham Commission, allowed Frankfurter's absences to annoy him more than was wise or necessary. . . . Some of the older professors tended to take sides, became to some degree Pound men or Frankfurter men. . . ." Pound had once confided to Laski that he was prouder of Frankfurter as a colleague than of any other member of the university, but now he was his antagonist. "I think both of them had a little desire for power," commented James Landis, who succeeded Pound as Dean, "and Frankfurter had his clique and Pound had his." [108] Ironically it was Lippmann, an old friend and frequent beneficiary of Frankfurter's profound understanding of law and politics, who criticized Frankfurter most tellingly for his services to Roosevelt. He wrote in 1936 in connection with the Harvard Tercentenary that "members of the university faculties have a particular obligation not to tie themselves to, nor to involve themselves in, the ambitions and purposes of the politicians, the parties and the movements which are contending for power. . . . For once they engage themselves that way . . .

they cease to be scholars because they are no longer disinterested and having lost their own independence, they impair the independence of the university to which they belong."

"The article of Walter Lippmann's set me thinking," Judge Learned Hand wrote a friend, sending Frankfurter a copy. "I rather think that he had in mind among others Felix, and whether it was or not, it will not improve relations between the two distinguished gentlemen." Hand considered it "somewhat a large order to forbid professors in universities from taking part in current politics, and that is what it comes to, as I understand its purport." Max Freedman, the editor of the Roosevelt-Frankfurter correspondence, recorded that Frankfurter "never forgot and never forgave what Lippmann had written." [109]

The issue of involvement versus detachment as the proper posture for the scholar would vex the academic world again during the Vietnam War when the debate was even more ferocious. Frankfurter often said about such controversies there are no absolutes; it becomes a question of where to draw the line. Frankfurter's association with Roosevelt, especially as it turned into hero worship, carried with it some warping of judgment, as would become evident in the court "packing" battle in 1937. It was part of the Frankfurter credo of personal relations that men no differently from women "have to be told with great frequency that you love them," * yet the courtier-like expressions in some of his letters to Roosevelt are melancholy testimony to an eagerness to please that went beyond loyalty. But involvement with Roosevelt and participation in the New Deal also enriched his judgment as a scholar, gave his work at the Harvard Law School a unique relevance and meaningfulness. And looked at from the point of view of Roosevelt, and government officials generally, would they and the nation have been benefited by denying them the scholar's talents and expertise? The conclusion of Professor Louis Jaffee, one of Frankfurter's most brilliant students and like him Byrne Professor of Administrative Law at the Harvard Law School, after a perusal of the Roosevelt-Frankfurter correspondence, is persuasive: "Few persons, I believe, who read these letters, however much the defects and limitations of Frankfurter may irritate them, can escape the conclusion that in his role as presidential adviser Felix Frankfurter was a great and gifted public servant." [111]

Remaining at Harvard enabled Frankfurter to serve the law as scholar and

---

* In 1932–1933 Herbert Wechsler, fresh out of Columbia Law School, where he had edited the *Law Review*, was clerking for Justice Stone. He considered that what Stone needed was criticism "and that it was my responsibility to provide that criticism." His effort, he discovered, was being undone by a weekly Frankfurter missive to Stone in which he told the latter how wonderful his opinions were. "Stone fed on that pabulum." Frankfurter at that time regularly commuted to Washington from Cambridge, and he berated Wechsler for not appropriately sustaining Stone's morale. "My answer was 'what this man needs is criticism, not flattery.' I realized in later years that Frankfurter had been right and that I was overdoing it, which I later acknowledged. But Felix's total flattery wasn't good either." Frankfurter later changed his estimate of Stone. He wrote Wechsler after Stone's death in 1946, commenting on a Wechsler memorial essay that portrayed Stone favorably, "The short of it is that you might be shocked by the disparity of your 1932 picture of the Chief [Stone had become Chief Justice in 1941] and my present estimate." [110]

teacher. The weight that he attached to this service can only be measured by the reverence in which he held the law. "Why the need for law in a civilized society?" he would ask students in an introductory lecture and then use their answers as a springboard to demonstrate that law was a positive force for the liberation of individual and social energies. Law was not concerned exclusively with restraints upon the evil in men or with the material aspects of living. Laws, like the rules in literature, seek to liberate by imprisonment. Organization and discipline also contribute to making life worth living. In 1962 the Australian Ambassador to the United States, Sir Howard Beale, persuaded Frankfurter to go with him and his wife to see Robert Bolt's play about Sir Thomas More, A Man for All Seasons. In the play, More's son-in-law, Roper, at one point seeks to persuade him to arrest an enemy before he became dangerous, though he had not yet broken any law. When More refuses, saying he would give even the Devil the benefit of the law, Roper replies he'd "cut down every law in England" to get at the Devil. "Oh," counters More—

> And when the law was down, and the Devil turned round on you—where would you hide, Roper, the laws all being flat? This country's planted thick with laws from coast to coast—man's laws, not God's—and if you cut them down—and you're just the man to do it—d'you really think you could stand upright in the winds that would blow then?

Frankfurter could not contain himself, reported Beale. "That's the point," he kept whispering in the dark, "that's it, that's it!" [112]

The law, the bar, the judicial system were a majestic gleaming structure: the quality of a nation's justice was the measure of its worth. Politics and government were irresistible, but the law was his life. He was not yet on the Supreme Court, but he was the confidant of its two most distinguished members, Holmes and Brandeis, and a third, Justice Stone, sent messages to Roosevelt through him. In 1905 James, Royce, and Santayana had made Cambridge the intellectual hub of America; in the Thirties, for men concerned with the intellectual aspects of law and politics, a pilgrimage to Harvard to talk with Frankfurter and to be present at his weekly at-homes on Brattle Street, thronged as they were with Boston's brightest and best born, was obligatory.

There were two celebrated "at homes" in Cambridge in the late Thirties— those presided over by Mrs. Frankfurter and her rival over the teapot, Mrs. Alfred North Whitehead. Members of the "Establishment" thronged the latter; at Marion Frankfurter's, Boston Brahmins mingled with radicals and *avant-garde* types. "The Old Guard was terrified of Felix," recalled Mrs. Mark de Wolfe Howe, "but they respected him too." [113] Many of the young law school men worshiped at Marion Frankfurter's shrine, and she repaid them with quiet, cynical observations, often at the Professor's expense, but her "at homes" were dominated by him. Standing before the mantelpiece, a short, stocky man, cleft chin, blue-eyed, he would ask a question. "It was like a champagne cork going off," said Mrs. Howe. "Off he went and the conversation was marvelous." Marion alone was able to stop him in the midst of "a tirade. She had a great deal of breeding and style and put him in his place quite often." Even Brandeis was not sacrosanct. On one of Learned Hand's visits to Cambridge, he and Frankfurter were to visit the Brandeises at Chatham on Cape Cod. They were obliged to take a train, because "she wouldn't go down there. Neither of us could drive a car. We were sissies. And she wouldn't go down. She looked very handsome with her arms up. She said, 'He doesn't impress me at all. All his moral ideas don't impress me. He has nothing beautiful in his house. His food is awful too.' " Hand felt sorry for Frankfurter. "Poor Felix. He was jumpy. It was making him very unhappy not to have his god revered." [114] When the Frankfurters left the Law School and Cambridge, Mrs. Howe added, "many lamps went out and have never quite lighted up since."

The range of his scholarly activities during the Thirties covered more than his classes. He supervised a "Survey of Crime and Criminal Justice in Greater Boston" which resulted in three published volumes. He wrote the introduction to the first of them, Sheldon and Eleanor Glueck's pioneering study, *One Thousand Juvenile Delinquents,* [115] asserting that the undertaking "Above all . . . registered the responsibility of universities for research into the problems of human conduct and social policy." Together with Nathan Greene, he wrote a definitive book on the labor injunction which paved the way intellectually for the Norris-LaGuardia Anti-Injunction Act. For Holmes's ninetieth birthday, he collected a number of articles about the Justice, including essays by Cohen, Dewey, Learned Hand, Laski, Lippmann, and himself, and put them into a book "as symbols of our homage and affection." "You speak of my biography," Holmes wrote a friend about Silas Bent's *Justice Oliver Wendell Holmes* (1932). "I have not read it, but I should think it was harmless. I had nothing to do with it. Perhaps when I die my executors (John Palfrey and/or Felix Frankfurter) may do something, with more materials, but I have done my best to destroy illuminating documents." [116] In 1938 Frankfurter fulfilled this commission with his *Mr. Justice Holmes and the Supreme Court,* which was a muscular and superbly clear exposition of his own as well as Holmes's approach to the Court and the Constitution.

But Holmes as a personal model was too much of an original, too detached, too skeptical. When Holmes wanted to "twist the tale of the cosmos," as he characterized his thinking about ultimates, he did so with Morris Cohen, not Frankfurter. Brandeis was a more feasible model. For Brandeis's seventy-fifth birthday, as for Holmes ninetieth, he assembled a group of essayists, including Chief Justice Hughes, Max Lerner, Donald Richberg, and himself. He ended his own tribute with words descriptive of Brandeis that at the time seemed to represent his own private world of aspirations and standards: [117]

> In truth, Mr. Justice Brandeis is a moral teacher, who follows Socrates in the belief that virtue is the pursuit of enlightened purpose. His long years

of intimate connection with the history of the Harvard Law School symbolize his dominant impulse. Problems, for him, are never solved. Civilization is a sequence of new tasks. Hence his insistence on the extreme difficulty of government and its dependence on sustained interest and effort, on the need for constant alertness to the fact that the introduction of new forces is accompanied by new difficulties. This, in turn, makes him mindful of the limited range of human foresight, and leads him to practice humility in attempting to preclude the freedom of action of those who are to follow.

The Justice himself, while at the bar, disavowed allegiance to any general system of thought or hope. "I have no rigid social philosophy; I have been too intent on concrete problems of practical justice." Devotion to justice is widely professed. By Mr. Justice Brandeis it has been given concrete expression in a long effort toward making the life of the commonplace individual more significant.

Important as Frankfurter's role in the Thirties was as interpreter of the Court and the Constitution and as adviser to Roosevelt, his influence would have been less pervasive and enduring were it not for his "boys," the students, disciples, and protegés in whose hearts he kindled that "inextinguishable fire," which Holmes had described as the glorious purpose of the Harvard Law School. In June 1933, just before he sailed for England to spend a year at Oxford as George Eastman Professor, he sent a note to "Missy," Roosevelt's secretary, Marguerite LeHand, introducing "a very dear friend, Thomas G. Corcoran, and at present an assistant to the Secretary of the Treasury. . . . I commend him to you warmly. He is a person of entire dependability." [118]

"Tommy the Cork," as Roosevelt affectionately dubbed him, had abandoned a lucrative but dull New York law practice and on the recommendation of Frankfurter to Eugene Meyer, Hoover's head of the Reconstruction Finance Corporation, gone to work for that agency. He was an ebullient, entertaining Irishman, who played the accordion and sang zestfully, a first-rate intellect and a canny political operator. He teamed up with Benjamin V. Cohen, whose relations with Frankfurter went back to 1915 when he arrived at Harvard for a year of graduate study, described as the most brilliant man who had ever attended the University of Chicago Law School. Cohen was as austere, selfless, and shy as Corcoran was funloving and gregarious. He was also the best legal draftsman in New Deal Washington, a fine political strategist, and intimates said of him as Holmes did of Brandeis, "There goes a good man."

By the mid-Thirties, with the vast growth in presidential powers, Corcoran and Cohen were singlehandedly performing functions for the White House—speechwriting, bill drafting, Congressional liaison, politicking—that in subsequent decades required hundreds. Corcoran, wrote Moley, "achieved no small success in placing Harvard Law School graduates in strategic posts. . . ." The Administration's troubles, General Hugh Johnson, a master of invective, wrote in his column after he turned on the New Deal, were the fault of "the Harvard crowd," or, as he also dubbed them, Frankfurter's "Happy Hot Dogs." Another master of the epithet, Westbrook Pegler, blamed the New Deal philosophy on Frankfurter "through his contamination of mischievous cub lawyers. . . ." And even a Roosevelt stalwart like Berle grumbled about the influence of Frankfurter. There were three approaches to overhauling the economic system, he wrote in 1938—the radicals who favored "wholesale change," a group which believed "in making peace with business and letting matters run," in which he more or less included himself, and "the remnant of the Frankfurter group which is extremely powerful because it satisfies the President's desire for some personal villains. This group which includes Corcoran, Cohen, Ickes and a few others propose recreating the anti-trust laws in some fashion so as to create a thoroughly competitive machinery." [119]

The opposition portrayed Frankfurter as an Iago, a Svengali, an *éminence grise*, and it was true that he loved giving advice and exerting influence from behind the scenes. What is extraordinary is that he managed to exert that influence without being on the scene in Washington, whereas the conventional wisdom is that out of the President's sight means fading out of the President's mind. There was nothing sinister about Frankfurter's role. His basic positions were well known, better known perhaps than those of any other legal scholar, and his service as a one-man recruiting agency for the New Deal was a continuance of a function that he had been performing for Republicans as well as Democrats since 1906 when Stimson had asked him to become an Assistant United States Attorney and he had recruited the other assistants. "The key to [Harlan Fiske] Stone's problem," he wrote Lippmann when Stone in 1924 replaced Harry M. Daugherty as Attorney General, "is, of course, men. Everything is subordinate to personnel, for personnel determines the governing atmosphere and understanding from which all questions of administrative organization take shape." He was a great admirer of the British civil service and believed in experts as administrators and civil servants. As he wrote Stimson from Oxford:

> Of course there are some things we can no longer afford—above all we can no longer afford to do without a highly trained, disinterested governmental personnel. What this Administration has had to do is to create something like the English civil service over night. And few things have been more shocking to me than all the silly and partisan and unworthy prattling on the part of many a responsible public man about the 'brains trust.' The term is silly enough, but wickeder is the implication that somehow or other brains, the brains of men who have given their lives to the study of governmental and economic problems, are either dangerous or unworthy of service to the state. [120]

Frankfurter rallied to the defense of the young lawyers who flocked to Washington drawn by Roosevelt's forward-moving activism. Laws were implemented by men. "The esteem in which government work is held will determine whether men of parts are drawn to governmental posts. The attraction of such posts is not money but the opportunity for men of genuine ability to do really useful work and to try their mettle on problems worthy of their best powers." The nation's founders, he recalled, were mostly "youngish men" and that was natural. "Disinterested enthusiasm, freedom from imprisoning dogmatism, capacity for fresh insight, unflagging industry, ardor for difficulties—these are qualities that in the main youthful years must supply." Moreover a young man can be sweated. He "is freed from complicated ramifications of private life; he is diverted by a minimum of vanities and jealousies; he is more resilient, more cooperative in taking orders; and his technical preparation for his work is on the whole much better than the equipment of the generation that preceded him." [121]

"Dear F. F.," Corcoran and Cohen wrote him at the end of his year at Oxford,

> It's very difficult to map out just what you'd expect to do on getting home. The Skipper [Roosevelt] knows when you're coming back. . . . The most important consideration, however, is that (no matter whether you are in touch during the vacation) before the Skipper's return you have adequate time and be sufficiently reoriented in this peculiar atmosphere to be able to advise him concretely. Much has gone over the dam since you went away and affairs have proceeded pretty far toward concrete forks in the road. The Tugwell crowd has been pushed by its enemies—and its own loose talk—away over to the left. Ray [Moley] is vacillating considerably toward the right. Isaiah [Brandeis] is militant and impatient in the middle. You'll need, we should think, considerable detailed knowledge of what has gone on just to listen understandingly. [122]

The young served him as conduits of influence and as emanations of his spirit. Nor is there anything quite as satisfying as the discovery of youthful excellence and giving a talented young man a chance to develop his powers for the public good. That had been an especial pleasure of Frankfurter's from the days of law school on. Moreover the recognition and love were usually reciprocal. Holmes touched on that quality in his own relations with the young. When Frankfurter had brought Laski to him, Laski had read him a letter from Morley "that touched in such a pretty way the mixture of flattered vanity and real love for the young that makes meeting them so delightful. The young lawyers give me my share, and I respond with the same mixture." [123]

Holmes and Frankfurter were both childless, and some of the passion they lavished upon the young was in lieu of fatherhood. "He loved his protégés," Mrs. Howe observed, adding tartly, "but he also owned them. It was very bad for Mark." The latter had been one of Holmes's last secretaries and had been "ordered" by Frankfurter to undertake the definitive biography of Holmes that

Frankfurter did not have the time (and perhaps, also, the talent) to do himself. "It was wrong for Mark." When, inspired and advised by Frankfurter, Buffalo University established a law school, he ordered some of his "hot dogs," including Mark Howe and Louis Jaffee, to Buffalo. It was "like exile." Both ultimately got back to Cambridge. "From the first, I was subject to pressures from Justice Frankfurter to have Mark get on with his work on Holmes," Dean Erwin H. Griswold of the Harvard Law School recalled at Howe's memorial service in 1967.[124] "There was a sweet side to Felix's paternalism," Mrs. Howe acknowledged, "but he didn't care whether what he wanted was good for them."

During his year at Oxford Frankfurter had followed events in the United States closely and observed with wonderment how "the old crowd, now that they have gained their second wind and are out of the storm cellar," were making a concerted drive against Roosevelt. They were demanding that he forget reform and limit himself to recovery. But neither the President, nor Congress, nor the voters accepted the conservative view, and increasingly the business interests turned to the courts. "By the winter of 1935 the justices [of the Supreme Court] had become the last hope of the conservative interests in the United States," wrote Alsop and Catledge in their account of the great constitutional crisis of the Thirties that culminated in Roosevelt's effort to reform the court by enlarging or, as his opponents put it, "packing" it. In May 1933 Frankfurter, in a radio address defending the constitutionality of Roosevelt's program of the first hundred days, had reasserted the old Thayer doctrine that "if the Court aided by an alert and public-spirited bar has access to the facts and follows them, the Constitution is flexible enough to meet all the new needs of our society." But as the Court struck down one piece of New Deal legislation after another, Frankfurter's hopes for a Court hospitable to change seemed misplaced. His thinking on legal and political issues, Morris Cohen reproached him, was suffering from the intensity of his personal loyalties.

> I should be lacking in candor if I did not say frankly that the fundamental weakness of your position in this matter is due to your thinking in terms of personalities and neglecting ultimate issues. You think in terms of Holmes, Brandeis and Cardozo, and you think more men of that type would make the Supreme Court a good institution. In this you ignore the fact that it is only by accident that men of that type can get on the Supreme Court and that when they do they are more likely to be on the minority side. . . . But more important than that is the fact that the whole system is fundamentally dishonest in its pretensions (pretending to say what the Constitution lays down when they are in fact deciding what is good for the country). . . . I am persuaded that if we are to emerge from the present economic and social chaos without resort to a communist revolution or a fascist dictatorship, it can only be by easing up the restraints which the present idolatry of the Constitution and the Courts puts in the

way of national planning of production for use instead of for profit. It is because you ought to be with the forces of liberalism rather than against them that I hope you will devote a little more attention to these issues than your expression hitherto seems to indicate.[125]

There was "nothing in your letter I did not already know," Frankfurter replied with equal tartness and vigor. ". . . I have written predominantly against the Court's confusion between the majority's notion of policy and the requirements of the Constitution. But that is not the whole story of the Court's function and performance." He did not claim, he went on, that "the Supreme Court is in Washington and all's well with our world. You know I think no such thing. I do, however, deprecate these easy answers to very difficult questions—and the assumption that amending the Constitution, stripping the Supreme Court of its powers, making of us, in essence, a unitary state, are all a.b.c., so obvious that the implications and the cost need not be responsibly faced.

"Perhaps the difference between fellows like you and Lerner and me is that I have spent half of my life in the actual tasks of government and all of it in acquiring intimate knowledge of its practicalities. If I were you I would not be so cavalier!"[126]

In his thinking about the function of the Supreme Court, Frankfurter had never quite wholly reconciled two sets of views. As a historian of constitutional development and a realist, he often quoted Charles Evans Hughes's observation that "we are under a Constitution, but the Constitution is what the judges say it is." And it was desirable that "the stream of the Zeitgeist" should flood the sympathies and intelligence of our judges. Courts should reflect, in the felicitous phrase of Holmes, "the felt necessities of the time" and Presidents were right, as Theodore Roosevelt had been when he appointed Holmes, to assure themselves of the political and economic sympathies of their nominees. That was one way by which constitutional interpretation was made responsive to the changing needs of successive generations.[127]

But there was another line to his thought. The American democracy was founded on the separation of powers. The courts should be independent, immune from the pressures of the Executive and Congress, and the reverence in which the people held the Court was a principal safeguard of liberty. Separation of powers also required judges to guard against assuming that what upbringing and conscience urged, the Constitution commanded. By a policy of judicial restraint and rising above their private views the Justices would avoid usurpation of the powers of the Executive and Congress and becoming, as Brandeis had cautioned, "a super-legislature."

But what if judges refused to budge? What if they did inflate the powers of judicial review and usurped prerogatives belonging to the Executive and Legislature? How could this be changed without a political attack that inevitably weakened the independence of the judiciary? Frankfurter had never quite answered that question in an intellectually tidy way. In 1912 he had agreed with

T.R.'s criticism of judicial conservatism but recoiled from his proposal for the recall of judicial decisions by popular referendum. Similarly in 1924 he had endorsed LaFollette's attack on the judiciary, but not his remedy, which was to empower Congress by a two-thirds vote to override a judicial veto of a legislative enactment. What then was the remedy? T.R. once had observed, Frankfurter wrote in an unsigned *New Republic* editorial in 1924, that, "I may not know much about law, but I do know one can put the fear of God into judges." The "fear of God," Frankfurter had affirmed during the LaFollette campaign, "was needed to make itself felt on the bench in 1912. The 'fear of God' very much needs to make itself felt in 1924." But since "fear of God" was too capricious an instrument, he had also suggested that "the due process clause ought to go," by way of an amendment to the Constitution.[128]

Neither in 1912 nor in 1924 had the Court used the judicial veto on the scale that it did in the Thirties; nor did Frankfurter have the intimate and influential relationship with T. R. and LaFollette that he did with Roosevelt. And when the Court in May 1935 invalidated the National Recovery Act, plunging the nation into a major constitutional confrontation, Frankfurter, although no partisan of the N.R.A., as the nation's leading scholar of the Court and Roosevelt's intimate adviser, was at the storm's vortex, and it was not sufficient to deplore what the Court was doing without proposing a remedy and strategy.

"I am not defending the Court for this, that or the other thing," he protested to Morris Cohen, who had delivered another "affectionate castigation," as Frankfurter called his missives at this time: [129]

> and I should be much surprised if you and I differed about any particular case. . . . If you mean to imply, as Holmes did in his 1913 speech, that the Union would not come to an end if the power to pass on Congressional legislation were taken away from the Supreme Court, that is a different story, and there is a great deal to be said for it. Or if you were to suggest that the due process clause should be repealed, that is also a different story and a good deal is to be said for it; although I notice that some of my friends are keen about the due process clause when situations like the Scottsboro case come up. If you tell me that the due process clause should be restricted to its historical function, I can understand that, and again say there is much to be said for it. . . . I am also familiar with the practical difficulties of the various devices for dealing with these difficulties, and the evil ends to which gadgets like the 7–2 requirement, and judicial recall, etc. may be put. *Above all, I realize as I realize and speak as I speak, in the light of my convictions as to the state of intellectual unpreparedness of even informed Americans for dealing with these problems.*

This last was central in the advice he gave Roosevelt after the Court killed the N.R.A. Postpone fighting out the issue. Wait until decisions on other issues "accumulate popular grievances against the Court." Get measures "like the

Social Security bill, the Holding Company bill, the Wagner bill, the Guffey bill" through Congress. "Let the Court strike down any or all of them next winter or spring, especially by a divided Court. *Then* propose a Constitutional amendment giving the national government adequate power to cope with national economic and industrial problems." He cautioned Roosevelt that "a general attack on the Court, unlimited in the changes it *may* cause, would give opponents a chance to play on vague fears of a leap in the dark and upon the traditional loyalties the Court is still able to inspire." [130]

But the amendment route had its own difficulties. Apart from the time it would take to get an amendment adopted, there was no agreement on how it should be phrased. As Roosevelt later explained to C. C. Burlingham, "no two people agree both on the general method of amendment or on the language of an amendment." [131] It was also clear, as the 1936 presidential race neared, that Roosevelt's opponents, headed by the American Liberty League, wanted to make the Constitution and the Court rather than the objectives of the New Deal the paramount issues in the campaign. Although Frankfurter in general terms from time to time declared that it might be necessary to amend the Constitution, when it came to a specific amendment, he drew back. In addition to the political difficulties, he feared that an amendment to the Constitution would diminish the intrinsic character of a document that was intended to endure and that he profoundly believed had ample resources within its original terms to meet the changing needs of successive generations. When the Democratic platform was being drafted, Richberg, Tugwell, Moley, and others urged specific amendments. Frankfurter opposed all of them and he persuaded Roosevelt that the platform should maintain that under the Constitution the federal government has the power to deal with national problems requiring national action beyond the power of the several states. [132] The 3,500-word draft that he sent to Roosevelt on the eve of the convention was silent on the Court's blockade of New Deal legislation and the specific ways of ending it, but the semifinal paragraph of the draft articulated his deeply felt convictions:

> The Democratic Party pledges itself anew to the principles of constitutional government under our Federal System. The Fathers of the Constitution wisely contemplated that the States should have essential governmental powers in all matters of local concern and that the Federal Government should have all the necessary authority over all commerce among the States, with wise guarantees against arbitrary use of such power by either the Federal Government or the States. In the words of the great Mr. Justice Holmes, who fought the war caused by the Dred Scott decision, "It is not lightly to be assumed that, in matters requiring national action, 'a power which must belong to and somewhere reside in all civilized government' is not to be found." The Tenth Amendment was expressly intended to leave to the States the sovereign power of legislation in all matters not delegated to the Federal Government. It is inconceivable that

there is a No Man's Land where no government—not all the powers of the States and the Nation combined—can safeguard either liberty or property or protect the weak against exploitation and legitimate business against unfair competition.

The platform as adopted was deliberately discretional. If the problems of drought, flood relief, minimum wages and maximum hours, child labor and the like "cannot be solved by legislation within the Constitution," it read, "we shall seek such clarifying amendment as will assure to the Legislatures and the Congress . . . the power to enact those laws . . ."

A protesting letter from Morris Cohen dated October 29, 1936, gave some indication of Frankfurter's thinking as the 1936 campaign drew to a close:

> The common prejudice against "packing" the Supreme Court (like the House of Lords) as in any way unfair or 'indirect' rests on fictions and I am surprised that you should fall for it. Can you mention a single good reason in support of your preference? Of course, ultimately we must amend the Constitution, as I indicated; but you know that this is a long process and that it is silly to ignore the element of time in human affairs. An amendment can for a long time be blocked by a minority in Congress or in the States. Why should the majority not avail itself of the power to do what is necessary to get rid of the atrocious abuses of child labor, of exploiting men and women by wages below the minimum of decent subsistence? [133]

The Frankfurter letter that occasioned this reply, and his answer to Cohen, if he did answer, were not locatable by this writer, if, indeed, they any longer exist, but his general preference for the amendment route and his opposition to "packing" were well known. "There is no magic in the number nine," he wrote in 1934 in *The Encyclopedia of the Social Sciences*, "but there are limitations to effective judicial action. Deliberation by the Court is the very foundation of sound adjudication as is also a lively sense of responsibility by every member of the Court for its collective judgment. Experience is conclusive that to enlarge the size of the Court would be self-defeating." [134]

His general viewpoint was amendment if necessary, no packing. His operational policy, as has been indicated, was somewhat different. To Corcoran and Cohen he said, "no amendment—what we need is that the present Constitution be properly construed." [135] But how bring that about? At the back of Frankfurter's mind was the hope that systematic, scholarly exposure of the Court's abuse of its powers, coupled with a more careful drafting of statutes by the Administration, backed up by discussion and debate of amendment, "packing," and like remedies, would bring about a shift in the Court's viewpoint and enable the country to surmount the Constitutional crisis without drastic Constitutional surgery. "My formula to people like Charlie Burlingham is," he wrote Learned Hand after the Court battle was under way, " 'tell the truth about the

Court for a good stretch of time and then I don't care what remedy you propose or oppose.' " [136]

In 1924 he had not approved LaFollette's specific remedy for overcoming usurpation, but he thought discussion of it helped put the "fear of God" into the Brethren. Some such strategy appears to have been in his mind in the Thirties. A similar adroitness lay behind the suggestion to Roosevelt made by C. C. Burlingham, one of the Bar's most respected notables, but who felt as strongly about the Court's usurpations as Roosevelt and Frankfurter did. He proposed a Congressional joint resolution to amend the Constitution to make retirement at seventy-five obligatory. As soon as Congress passed such a resolution the Justices over seventy-five would retire, he predicted, without waiting for the adoption of the amendment to that effect.

But Roosevelt doubted the Justices would surrender so easily. "The reactionary members of the Court had apparently determined," he later wrote, "to remain on the bench as long as life continued—for the sole purpose of blocking any program of reform . . . Although it had become, on the average, the most aged Court in our history, although six justices had passed the age of seventy, not a single vacancy had occurred during my first term of office." "Produce their signatures and I will believe it," had been Molly Dewson's comment on Burlingham's prediction about the oldest Justices quitting and Roosevelt had agreed with her. [137]

In later years it was revealed that even Brandeis, in 1934 and again in 1935, when he thought that the aged Van Devanter was considering resignation because of his inability any longer to write his share of the Court's opinions, had implored him to remain because of the great value of his contribution in conference. Chief Justice Hughes evidently took the same view. The effect, of course, was to deny Roosevelt the opportunity to appoint a justice who might have shifted the balance in the Court.

Roosevelt doubted that "the fear of God" strategy would work. He was emboldened also by his landslide victory in the election, which he interpreted, with reason, as a mandate to end the Court's blockade of social and economic reform. So, without consulting Frankfurter, he instructed Attorney General Cummings and Solicitor General Reed to prepare a court reform bill in the utmost secrecy. Its rationale when the Justice officials finished their work of incubation was the more efficient administration of justice rather than the curbing of judicial abuse. Among its other features it would empower the President to add new Justices up to six for every Justice over seventy who did not retire.

The conference on January 30, 1937, at which Roosevelt finally decided to go ahead with the court "packing" bill consisted of Cummings, Reed, Donald Richberg, the former general counsel and head of the N.R.A., and Judge Rosenman. Roosevelt's failure to consult Frankfurter in the field of his special competence demonstrated what all those around the President understood—he used men and women for *his* purposes, not theirs, but for someone like Frankfurter who needed the feeling that Roosevelt's countenance was not turned away from him, the exclusion must have been dismaying, and, like courtiers usually, and there were elements of the courtier in Frankfurter's relationship to Roosevelt, the desire to be on the inside caused him to redouble his efforts to gain his principal's favor.

"Very confidentially, I may give you an awful shock in about two weeks," Roosevelt had written Frankfurter, January 15, 1937. "Even if you do not agree, suspend final judgment and I will tell you the whole story." ". . . and now you have blown me off the top of Vesuvius," Frankfurter acknowledged after Roosevelt announced his plan. His comment on it was carefully considered. He had consulted Corcoran and Cohen on what to say, and, in fact, took his cue from a suggestion made by Cohen:

> Dramatically and artistically you did "shock" me. But beyond that—well, the momentum of a long series of decisions not defensible in the realm of reason nor justified by settled principles of Constitutional interpretation had convinced me, as they had convinced you, that means had to be found to save the Constitution from the Court, and the Court from itself. . . . There was no perfect way out. . . . But I have, as you know, deep faith in your instinct to make the wise choice. . . .[138]

Roosevelt's relief and gratitude that Frankfurter would be a good soldier even if he did not approve the battle plan showed in his next letter, which contained a lengthy explanation of why he had rejected the amendment approach. It would have taken through 1940 to get an amendment adopted and the nation "cannot wait until 1940 or 1942. . . ." The letter ended with a plea that was unusual for Roosevelt, who was accustomed to having men volunteer: "Do you want to help me? . . . Do you want to send me a little elaboration of what you have mentioned in your letter and anything else you think I could use in a talk to the people themselves?" [139]

Frankfurter could have elected to sit the struggle out, but he was an intensely loyal man. He had come to love Roosevelt—and the influence that went with that love. Without ever approving of the bill—indeed, the disingenuous reasons that Roosevelt had given for enlarging the Court pained him acutely— he nevertheless soon was sending him material on the Court's misuse of its power, counseling him on tactics, sharing his anger when men like Herbert Lehman, who he thought just because of his relationship to Roosevelt should have remained publicly silent, spoke out against the plan, even quarreling with the revered Brandeis for joining Chief Justice Hughes in a letter to Senator Wheeler, the leader of the opposition, showing that the Court was abreast of its work. So completely did he identify with Roosevelt in this vast, furious struggle that when the Court began to reverse itself and minimum wage legislation, the Wagner Labor Relations Act, and the Social Security Bill were all unexpectedly and suddenly found to be constitutional, and Justice Van Devanter resigned, giving Roosevelt an opportunity to end the battle gracefully, he counseled the President, or, at any rate, agreed with him, not to accept a compromise. Professor Jaffee has called this "amazing," because the defeat of the plan and the change in the Court's attitude must have been a denouement agreeable to Frankfurter. Even Roosevelt writing about the Court battle later in the Introduction to his Public Papers took this view. In language that had been carefully reviewed by Frankfurter, he called the Court fight and its results "as among the most important domestic achievements of my first two terms in office. . . . The Court yielded. The Court changed. The Court began to interpret the Constitution instead of torturing it. It was still the same Court, with the same justices. No new appointments had been made. And yet, beginning shortly after the message of February 5, 1937, what a change!" Roosevelt was convinced, moreover, "that the change would never have come, unless this frontal attack had been made upon the philosophy of the majority of the Court." [140]

At the time of Van Devanter's resignation, however, it was not easy to see that the shift was permanent, especially as Roosevelt had promised the first opening on the Court to Senator Joseph Robinson, who, though a Roosevelt loyalist, was scarcely a liberal,* and as late as August 10 Frankfurter, in notes that he sent to Roosevelt for a radio chat, hammered on the theme that "for the present at least" a majority of the Court appeared to recognize that the legislative function belonged to the Congress. [141] Nor did Frankfurter, a man who tried to take the long view, see that the enhancement of the court's authority as a consequence of the "packing" plan's defeat would fortify it for the great civil liberties and racial discrimination decisions of the postwar period.

". . . [W]e must all pay dearly for our virtues," Morris Cohen had cautioned Frankfurter on the subject of personal loyalties, and loyalty to Roosevelt exacted a price in distortion of judgment and of the scholar's role. Frankfurter's position during the court struggle, although publicly ambiguous in that he allowed different men to read their conflicting wishes into his neutrality and silence, may not quite merit William O. Douglas's charge of "duplicitous," but it was less than explicit. Roosevelt had not consulted him on the merits of the "packing" plan; he had not approved of Roosevelt's approach; nor had he ever said that he did. He had been asked by the President, his friend, to help and he had, confining that help in the main to an elaboration of the thesis that the Constitution had to be saved from the Court and the Court from itself. But more needs to be said, even if in hindsight. Do Congress and the public not have a right to expect from the nation's foremost authority on Court and Constitution not silence but counsel? Learned Hand, who in 1936 had protested Lippmann's criticism of professors—meaning in the first place Frankfurter—who took part in politics, by 1939, Professor Jaffee noted, had swung over to Lippmann's view, declaring, "You may take Martin Luther or Erasmus for

* Robinson was stricken on July 14, and Roosevelt a few weeks later nominated Senator Hugo L. Black to the seat vacated by Van Devanter.

your model, but you cannot play both roles at once; you may not carry a sword beneath a scholar's gown or lead flaming causes from a cloister." And Jaffee asked, "Might the example of Frankfurter himself have made the difference between 1936 and 1939?" [142]

The Seat of Holmes and Cardozo

Eighteen months later Roosevelt repaid Frankfurter's loyalty when he nominated him to the Supreme Court seat left vacant by Cardozo's death. This is not to say that hope of a Court appointment motivated Frankfurter's position in the Court controversy. With two justices of the Jewish faith on the bench, the prospect that Roosevelt might appoint a third, or if Brandeis retired, a second, was slight, even if, as Freedman asserts, Roosevelt at some point told Frankfurter, "that he intended one day to put him on the Supreme Court, and he did not want him entangled in this particular controversy." [143] It is doubtful, however, that Roosevelt would have appointed him after Cardozo's unexpected death, had he not loyally kept his silence.

In Frankfurter's account of his appointment he went to great lengths to portray himself as a man who was happy at Harvard, who had no thought he might succeed Cardozo, and who, when Roosevelt in October regretfully informed him that he had promised the next appointment to the West, accepted it in good heart and objectively appraised for Roosevelt, as he had asked him to do, the qualifications of other men who were being proposed and "that was that." So that on the evening of January 4, 1939, when he was standing in his Brattle Street home in his underdrawers, while his wife exhorted him to hurry, and the phone rang and F. D. R. informed him, after a little teasing, that he was sending his name up to the Senate the next day, it was like a bolt from the blue, and all that a grateful Frankfurter, normally the most voluble of men, could muster in reply was, "All I can say is that I wish my mother were alive." And only as Frankfurter came to the end of this account of his appointment did he, as he put it, remember that Roosevelt also said, "I told you I can't name you, but wherever I turn, wherever I turn and to whomever I talk that matters to me, I am made to realize that you're the only person fit to succeed Holmes and Cardozo. Unless you can give me an unanswerable objection I'm going to send your name in for the Court tomorrow at twelve o'clock." [144]

The account was not wholly accurate. It reflected Frankfurter's self-protective need to deny that he wished to be at the summit of the law at the very moment that he was hoping fate's finger would point to him, a need to protest modesty in an account that breathed self-dramatization. The latter, Mrs. Howe pointed out to the author of this essay, is a characteristic of small-statured men, citing Napoleon, Keats, LaGuardia. It also explained the iron grip on the arm with which Frankfurter often compelled attention and the blue-eyed basilisk stare that he could fix on a listener. He had made himself a foremost authority on the Court and the Constitution. He wished to be on the bench. He knew that Tom Corcoran had set his heart on it.

Roosevelt, on his side, wanted to appoint Frankfurter. But he faced opposition, as he had told Frankfurter, from western Senators who insisted that the seat go to their region. In addition, Homer Cummings, his Attorney General, feared that Frankfurter's designation would open Roosevelt to charges of "Red" sympathies. And wealthy and influential Jews sent a delegation to Roosevelt to beg that he not appoint Frankfurter lest it stimulate the growth of the anti-Semitism that Hitler was doing his best to fan into a worldwide flame. On the other side, polls of the American bar showed an overwhelming preference even among lawyers opposed to Roosevelt for the appointment of Frankfurter; editorialists wrote that the seat of Story, Holmes, and Cardozo belonged to America's most distinguished legal scholar; and George Norris of Nebraska shattered the western senatorial front by declaring for Frankfurter. "Of course everywhere that Roosevelt went," a participant in the "conspiracy" once remarked, "people said to him, 'Why don't you appoint Felix Frankfurter?' We saw to it that they did." And Corcoran regularly called Frankfurter from the apartment that he shared with Cohen to report on the progress and prospects of the appointment.[145]

Roosevelt, in fact, had told Harry Hopkins that he intended to appoint Frankfurter to the seat held by Brandeis when Brandeis resigned. But Hopkins, and other New Dealers, notably Harold Ickes and Robert Jackson, who had been named Solicitor General, thought that such delay was too risky. He should go on the theory, Hopkins argued, that the Cardozo vacancy was the last one he would have the opportunity to fill. "If you appoint Felix," Ickes said to Roosevelt, "his ability and learning are such that he will dominate the Supreme Court for fifteen or twenty years to come. The result will be that probably after you are dead, it will still be your Supreme Court." Jackson wrote the President that ". . . what is urgently needed at this time is someone who can interpret the Constitution with scholarship and with sufficient assurance to face Chief Justice Hughes in conference and hold his own in discussion." Corcoran persuaded Norris to call on Roosevelt to urge Frankfurter's appointment, and another New Dealer, Irving Brant, the biographer of James Madison, advised Associate Justice Stone, a Frankfurter advocate, to go to the President. Stone, a Republican, particularly impressed Roosevelt with his advice that he disregard geography and that Frankfurter was the man to cope with Hughes's cleverness in splitting the liberals on the bench.[146]

The day that Roosevelt sent Frankfurter's commission to the Senate, Ickes organized a party in his office that included Hopkins, Attorney General Murphy, Bill Douglas, and "Missy" Le Hand. Tom Corcoran arrived bringing two magnums of champagne. "All of us regard this as the most significant and worthwhile thing the President has done," said Ickes. When "Missy" later told Roosevelt about the party, he commented, "I suspect[ed] that this was a little bunch of conspirators and I think, too, that if I had decided against them, they would have accepted my decision cheerfully and loyally." To which Ickes added, "My own guess is that until it was all over, the President did not realize that we had ganged up on him for Frankfurter." [147]

Before he went to bed the night of Roosevelt's momentous telephone call, Frankfurter sent him an appropriate note of thanks:

Dear Frank:

And now I have the highest authority in the land to prove that those much malign me to say that I'm a talker. You will testify that you found me tongue-tied. How could I have responded to your gracious message otherwise than to be moved to mumbling silence. When so much is involved of past and future it would shrivel great things into small to speak of "honor" and "confidence" and all that. Believe me that I am humbly aware of the consecrated task that you have laid upon me. And to have it at your hands—with all that you signify for my most precious devotion to the country—is to sanctify Law with its humanest significance.

With the affectionate devotion of old friendship.

Ever yours,
F. F.[148]

The hearings before the Senate Judiciary Committee presented few difficulties. A question that might have embarrassed him about his role during the Court fight did not come up. It was unnecessary to introduce the statement that he had prepared with the help of Dean Acheson, who was his counsel, that began boldly, "I have not expressed an opinion on the President's court proposals. . . ." A few fringe organizations turned up to oppose the nomination, ventilating once again T. R.'s attack on him for the Mooney case and Bisbee deportation reports and Dean Wigmore's criticism of his position in the Sacco-Vanzetti case. These right-wing zealots also charged him with radical sympathies because of his longtime membership in the American Civil Liberties Union. How deeply was Frankfurter involved? Acheson discreetly inquired of Roger Baldwin, the Union's Director. "A lot," Baldwin cheerfully replied, but it never became an issue at the hearings. Some asserted it was against the nation's interest to elevate a foreign-born Jew to the Bench. Most of the members of the Committee and the press dismissed these witnesses as crackpots and unrepresentative of anyone but themselves; but coiled, waiting for an opportunity to strike, was Senator Pat McCarran of Nevada. He pursued two lines of inquiry—that Frankfurter was not a citizen because his father allegedly had fraudulently obtained his citizenship by filing for his papers a year before he was eligible to do so, and when documents laid that canard to rest, he turned to Frankfurter's friendship with Harold Laski and tried to identify Frankfurter with the socialist views espoused by Laski in some of his books. "I trust you will not deem me boastful," Frankfurter countered, "if I say I have many friends who have written many books, and I shouldn't want to be charged with all the views in books by all my friends." When McCarran pressed for a more direct reply to whether he agreed with Laski's Marxism, Frankfurter responded with words that evoked applause in the crowded hearing room:

> Senator, I do not believe you have ever taken an oath to support the Constitution of the United States with fewer reservations than I have or would now, nor do I believe you are more attached to the theories and practices of Americanism than I am. I rest my answer on that statement.[149]

The nomination was promptly reported out to the Senate and unanimously confirmed. Afterwards, Frankfurter called on Ickes to express his thanks. Ickes wrote in his diary, "He was plainly delighted with his appointment, but I really think that this pleasure was not altogether personal. He feels that he is a symbol and that his appointment means much to the liberal cause." At the end of January Frankfurter took his seat among the brethren in front of the red velour drapes. Friends crowded the small, sedate chamber—Ickes and Hopkins, Murphy and Jackson, Corcoran and Cohen, Acheson and "Missy." He took his oath to "administer justice without respect to person," and back in his chambers, he immediately penned a note to Roosevelt, whose birthday it was, on his new Supreme Court stationery: ". . . And now, on your blessed birthday, I am given the opportunity for service to the Nation, which, in any circumstances would be owing, but which I would rather have at your hands than at those of any other President barring Lincoln." [150]

A gaffe in dress marred his first conference with his Brethren. He had the habit of wearing, unless in the classroom, "one of those little alpaca coats," when he was working, recalled Landis. So he came to the conference in an alpaca coat, only to discover the other justices fully dressed up. He was quite embarrassed, he later confided to Landis, and after the lunch break came back properly attired, only to see that Chief Justice Hughes had put on an alpaca coat.[151]

But would the Bench be able to contain this gregarious man of bursting energies whose irrepressible quality was caught by Matthew Josephson in *The New Yorker:* "Wherever Frankfurter is, there is no boredom. As soon as he bounces in—he never walks, he bounces—the talk and the laughter begin, and they never let up." David Lilienthal, the head of the T. V. A., breakfasted with him in the Georgetown house that he and Marion rented and was struck by the Justice's stress on the burdens of his new assignment. "There is a great pressure of briefs and record to read, and I want to have them read before the cases are argued. It is by far the most exacting work I have ever undertaken," he said. The work was the more demanding because of "the problem of adjusting the views and backgrounds of nine men. . . . And that adjustment of human beings he conceives to be a large part of the job, and one that takes precious hours that he finds too few. . . ." [152]

By the end of his second term Roosevelt had appointed five Justices to the high Court. In addition to Frankfurter, there were Hugo L. Black, Stanley Reed, William O. Douglas, and Frank Murphy. With Frankfurter's knowledge of the Court and the Constitution, his strong analytic powers, his energy and political savvy, he was expected, and he expected himself, to dominate the "Roosevelt Court." Even before he went onto the Bench, Court and President had turned to him to facilitate the initiation of Roosevelt's first appointee, Senator Black, into the Court's mysteries. Black had joined the Court in October 1937 amid great controversy over the press's disclosure of his membership, though brief, in the Ku Klux Klan, and even the liberal Brethren were unhappy to have as a colleague so political a man. Roosevelt had asked Frankfurter that he beseech a friendlier attitude toward the newcomer, a chore that Frankfurter performed tactfully, informing Roosevelt that Mrs. Black would be especially helpful, for she was "an altogether grand person, with a keen realization of the psychological aspects of the situation, and with unusual talents for mitigating difficulties and softening hard feelings." [153]

And it was to Frankfurter that some of the Court's members went for help when their newest Brother startled them by his revolutionary, tradition-disregarding dissents. "Do you know Black well?" Justice Stone inquired in early 1938, a year before Frankfurter himself went on the Court:

You might be able to render him great assistance. He needs guidance from someone who is more familiar with the workings of the judicial process than he is. With guidance, and a disposition to follow it until he is a little surer of himself, he might do great things. I am fearful though that he will not avoid the danger of frittering away his opportunity for judicial effectiveness by lack of good technique, and by the desire to express ideas which, however valuable they may be in themselves, are irrelevant or untimely. There are enough present-day battles to be won without wasting our efforts to remake the Constitution *ab initio*, or using the judicial opinion as a political tract. [154]

Frankfurter accepted the assignment. Judges, he wrote Justice Black,

cannot escape the responsibility of filling in gaps which the finitude of even the most imaginative legislation renders inevitable. . . . So the problem is not whether the judges make the law, but when and how much, Holmes put it in his highbrow way, that "they can do so only interstitially: they are confined from molar to molecular motions." I used to say to my students that legislatures make law wholesale, judges retail. In other words they cannot decide things by invoking a new major premise out of whole cloth; they must make the law that they do make out of the existing materials with due deference to the presuppositions of the legal system of which they have been made a part. Of course I know that these are not mechanical devices, and therefore not susceptible of producing automatic results. But they sufficiently indicate the limits within which judges move. . . .

For a brief period Frankfurter did lead his liberal colleagues, as he did, notably—and surprisingly—in the first flag-salute case. There the Court, in an opinion written by Frankfurter with Harlan Stone alone dissenting, ruled in June 1940 that the state could lawfully compel public school students to salute the flag even if it was a violation of their religious beliefs. This was in the case of the Gobitis children who came from a family adhering to the doctrines of Jehovah's Witnesses. The prescription of such a pledge was a proper exercise of legislative authority, Frankfurter wrote, although he acknowledged that in conflicts between "the liberty of conscience and the authority . . . to safeguard the nation's fellowship, judicial conscience is put to its severest test." Black, Douglas, and Murphy in this instance accepted the argument of a government interest that overrode what they later came to regard as the absolutism of First Amendment guarantees.[155]

It was the first wartime civil liberties case. The ruling was handed down as France fell, the British were completing their evacuation of Dunkirk, and reasonable men expected the destruction of the American democracy to be the next objective of the Axis. The war was for Frankfurter something special. He had an immigrant's feeling for American democracy, Archibald MacLeish wrote in 1939. "What other men inherited and therefore took for granted he discovered for himself and therefore earned. . . . What he said in April, 1938, he meant—'I can express with very limited adequacy the passionate devotion to this land that possesses millions of our people, born like myself under other skies, for the privilege this country has bestowed in allowing them to partake of its fellowship.' " Hitlerism threatened the American democratic fellowship. The "violence and madness now dominating Germany," he had written Roosevelt from Oxford in October 1933, ". . . make it abundantly clear that the significance of Hitlerism far transcends ferocious anti-semitism and fanatical racism." The onslaught against the Jews was an "index of the gospel of force and materialism" that threatened all civilized values and when the England which he loved—"he was genuine Anglomaniac," said Isaiah Berlin—because it so splendidly exemplified those values had declared war on Germany, he considered it his duty as an American, a Jew, a votary of the life of law and reason, to do what he could, within the limitations and restrictions imposed by membership on the Court, to accomplish Hitler's defeat.[156]

Frankfurter's reasoning in the Gobitis case, said Louis Henkin, a former law clerk and a distinguished scholar highly sympathetic with Frankfurter's positions, reduced itself to: "This is the flag of the United States. Is it wrong for the State to teach people patriotism, especially in wartime?" When Chief Justice Hughes assigned the case to Frankfurter, the latter and Justice Roberts put it to Hughes that he himself should write the opinion, "but he held to the assignment saying that he made it because of Frankfurter's moving statement at conference on the role of the public school in instilling love of country in our pluralist society." [157]

There was one dissenter in the *Gobitis* case, Associate Justice Stone. When he had indicated in conference that he would dissent, an agitated Frankfurter had sent him a five-page letter reflective of his dismay. He had only been following Stone's own admonitions about judicial self-restraint, he protested. But Stone was not swayed. "I am truly sorry not to go along with you. The case is peculiarly one of the relative weight of imponderables and I cannot overcome the feeling that the Constitution tips the scales in favor of religion." So strongly did Stone feel that he departed from practice to read his dissent in open Court. "History teaches us," he said, "that there have been but few infringements of personal liberty by the state which have not been justified, as they are here, in the name of righteousness and the public good, and few which have not been directed, as they are now, at politically helpless minorities. . . ." As for the advice of restraint, "This seems to me no less than the surrender of the constitutional protection of the liberty of small minorities to the popular will. . . ." [158]

Liberals were shocked by the Frankfurter opinion. They were looking to the Roosevelt Court, and to Frankfurter especially, to ensure that this war would not be accompanied by a repetition of the Espionage Act–Mitchell Palmer abominations. Were they unreasonable to have such expectations?

No jurist went on to the Bench with his views about the Court and the Constitution better known. As Frankfurter's namesake, Felix S. Cohen, reviewing *Law and Politics,* which appeared with his blessing just as he went on the Bench, wrote: "If future candidates for judicial office were compelled to follow Mr. Justice Frankfurter's wholesome example in opening to public view the padlocked premises of judicial reasoning, we might be able to extend to the judiciary the measure of democratic control that we have achieved in other branches of government." On the basis of Frankfurter's passionate, although scholarly, involvement in the Sacco-Vanzetti case, MacLeish in his introduction to *Law and Politics* predicted that on the Bench Frankfurter would be an influence for permitting "legislatures the widest latitude in framing economic measures altering property relations while sharply rejecting all attempts to curtail or restrict civil liberties." MacLeish buttressed this prediction by noting Frankfurter's emphasis in respect to Holmes that in the area of guaranteed rights and liberties Holmes was far more ready to declare acts of legislation unconstitutional because history had taught him that "since social development is a process of trial and error, the fullest possible opportunity for the free play of the mind was an indefeasible prerequisite." "It is difficult to avoid the conclusion," MacLeish went on, "that Mr. Frankfurter will take his stand upon the same distinction." [159]

His *Gobitis* opinion so jarred some of Frankfurter's closest friends that they felt a need to communicate with Stone. "How wrong I think Felix is," Laski wrote the Justice from an England that was waiting tensely for a Nazi invasion. "When a liberal judge holds out alone against his liberal brethren," the soft spoken Ben Cohen wrote him, "I think he ought to know when he has spoken not for himself lone, but superbly articulated the thoughts of his contemporaries who believe with him in an effective but tolerant democracy." [160]

"The flag, the flag," Justice Frankfurter murmured a few weeks later when President Roosevelt was mixing cocktails for him and Mrs. Frankfurter at Hyde Park, and the President was telling a story about a politician who made a set speech about the flag. The Justice having brought up the Court's ruling in the Jehovah's Witness case, Mrs. Roosevelt felt free to express her misgivings. She did not presume to question the Justice's legal scholarship and reasoning, but there seemed to be something wrong with an opinion that forced little children to salute a flag when such a ceremoney was repugnant to their conscience. She feared the decision would generate intolerance, especially in a period of rising hysteria.

For years, Justice Frankfurter answered her mildly, liberals had been complaining that the Court had exceeded its powers. He shared that view. His opinion had said in effect that it was not the business of the court to set itself up as a local school board or to overrule the judgment of the legislature. But the Court would certainly invalidate a local law that shut up a church, someone protested. It was a matter of degree, the Justice replied, a problem of reconciling two rights—the right of religious freedom and that of national unity. The President sided with the Justice. Suppose people desecrated the flag, he asked, or suppose religious custom involved being bit by rattlesnakes to obtain salvation; the local authorities would have to intervene. What the local authorities did in the *Gobitis* case was "stupid, unnecessary, and offensive," he went on, but it fell within their legal power. [161]

Even though Roosevelt agreed with him, the censure and reproaches of his friends and erstwhile allies rankled, and when some of the Roosevelt Justices on the Court began to express their misgivings about the ruling his chagrin was even greater. To Lilienthal, who saw him in October 1942, he suddenly seemed "quite gray. . . . I sense that Felix is not too happy about his own standing with his own younger contemporaries, including those on the bench with him." Much to his own surprise, Murphy's biographer has written, the Justice "found himself veering from the leadership of Felix Frankfurter, whom he had assumed would be his spiritual and intellectual knight, to that of Hugo L. Black." By 1942 Black, Douglas, and Murphy publicly acknowledged they had been wrong in the *Gobitis* case. Frankfurter was bitter about the reversal. His opinion in *Gobitis* was "okayed by those great libertarians until they heard from the people," he commented scornfully to Dr. Phillips. When historian Arthur M. Schlesinger wrote about the Roosevelt Court in 1946, the harsh echoes of the episode were still reverberating. "Then came the celebrated double-take of Black, Douglas and Murphy," wrote Schlesinger, "due, according to their friends to a revision of their blind faith in Frankfurter as a champion of civil liberties; according to their critics, to a recognition of the un-popularity of the *Gobitis* decision." [162]

In 1943, in a second flag-salute case, *West Virginia Board of Education v. Barnette*, 319 U. S. 624, the Court reversed itself, holding that the flag-salute ordinance infringed upon the free exercise of speech guaranteed by the First Amendment. Black and Douglas filed a special statement explaining their change in view. "Reluctance to make the Federal Constitution a rigid bar against state regulation of conduct thought inimical to the public welfare was the controlling influence which moved us to consent to the *Gobitis* decision," they wrote. The principle was sound but "its application in this particular case was wrong. . . . Neither our domestic tranquility in peace nor our martial ef-fort in war depend on compelling little children to participate in a ceremony which ends in nothing for them but a fear of spiritual condemnation."

The Court's reversal of his earlier opinion was galling enough; in addition the voice of the new majority was Justice Jackson, who as Solicitor General had argued so eloquently for Frankfurter's appointment to the Court in the interests of liberalism. He dismissed Frankfurter's argument that the legislative judgment must be allowed to prevail. First Amendment rights were specifically with-drawn from legislative reach and popular pressures. "They are susceptible of re-striction only to prevent grave and immediate danger to interests which the state may lawfully protect." The majority did not believe that "uniformity of sentiment," desirable as it was in wartime, can be produced by coercion. "Compulsory unification of opinion achieves only the unanimity of the grave-yard."

Frankfurter not only stood fast but his dissent opened with an unusual per-sonal statement which betrayed a depth of feeling that disturbed some of the Justices who pleaded with him unsuccessfully to omit it:

> One who belongs to the most vilified and persecuted minority in history is not likely to be insensible to the freedoms guaranteed by our Constitution. Were my purely personal attitude relevant, I should wholeheartedly asso-ciate myself with the general libertarian views in the Court's opinion, representing as they do the thought and action of a lifetime. But as judges we are neither Jew nor Gentile, neither Catholic nor agnostic. We owe equal attachment to the Constitution and are equally bound by our judi-cial obligations, whether we derive our citizenship from the earliest or the latest immigrants to these shores. As a member of this Court I am not jus-tified in writing my private notions of policy into the Constitution, no matter how deeply I may cherish them or how mischievous I may deem their disregard. The duty of a judge who must decide which of two claims before the Court shall prevail, that of a State to enact and enforce laws within its general competence or that of an individual to refuse obedience because of the demands of his conscience, is not that of the ordinary per-son. It can never be emphasized too much that one's own opinion about

the wisdom or evil of a law should be excluded altogether when one is doing one's duty on the bench. The only opinion of our own even looking in that direction that is material is our opinion whether legislators could in reason have enacted such a law. In the light of all the circumstances, including the history of this question in this Court, it would require more daring than I possess to deny that reasonable legislators could have taken the action which is before us for review. Most unwillingly, therefore, I must differ from my brethren with regard to legislation like this. I cannot bring myself to believe that the "liberty" secured by the Due Process Clause gives this Court authority to deny to the State of West Virginia the attainment of that which we all recognize as a legitimate legislative end, namely, the promotion of good citizenship, by employment of the means here chosen.

Not only should the Court defer to the legislative power, but it must adopt the same attitude toward alleged interferences with civil liberties as toward economic legislation. "The Constitution does not give us greater veto power when dealing with one phase of 'liberty' than with another. . . . In neither situation is our function comparable to that of a legislature or are we free to act as though we were a super-legislature. Judicial self-restraint is equally necessary whenever an exercise of political or legislative power is challenged." This had not been the position of Holmes, Brandeis, Cardozo, or Hughes, Professor Jaffee commented, and another student of the Court, Professor C. Herman Pritchett, observed with a trace of irony, "Thus the man who felt it necessary to deny that he was a Communist when he was appointed to the Supreme Court protests the inferior status to which the Court majority has relegated property rights." [163]

Frankfurter's argument, despite its passion, persuaded few of his old friends. Morris Cohen, living in Washington, partially disabled from a stroke but intellectually alert, asked a former student, Victor Brudney, who was clerking for Justice Rutledge, to take him on a visit to the Court. He wanted to meet Hugo Black, he said. He did not want to see Frankfurter. And Cohen's son, Felix, would say of his namesake's opinion in *Barnette* that he used "the same club" that Justice Sutherland had used against Professor Frankfurter in 1923 in *Adkins v. Children's Hospital*, 261 U. S. 525. In that ruling Sutherland, writing for the majority, had insisted that considerations which established the desirability or undesirability of legislation, and therefore properly the business of lawmaking bodies, threw "no legitimate light" on the constitutionality of such legislation. Frankfurter's warnings in his *Barnette* dissent that ". . . if the considerations governing constitutional construction are to be substantially those that underlie legislation then, indeed, judges should not have life tenure," and that through the majority's ruling "we unwarrantably enter social and political domains wholly outside our concern," Cohen pointed out, were "almost the very words of Justice Sutherland's opinion disposing of Mr. Frankfurter's brief in the *Adkins* case." [164]

To assert that the Court had no larger function in the protection of civil liberties than of property rights was a fateful refinement in Frankfurter's position, a departure from the view that he had appeared to endorse in his lectures, that some rights stood higher than others in the hierarchy of values to be protected by the Court.[165] In this writer's view this refinement uncoupled him from the locomotive of history. The power of state and federal governments to regulate social and economic affairs free of judicial veto was no longer in dispute. Instead issues of civil liberties and human rights were coming to the forefront of the Court's agenda, the issues and development so well delineated in Herbert Wechsler's paper, "The Nationalization of Civil Liberties and Civil Rights," precisely the issues on which Frankfurter might have been expected to lead the court. He did not. Invoking the hallowed name of Holmes he pushed the doctrine of judicial restraint to an extreme that violated the spirit of Holmes and separated him from the most innovative members of the Court. And we must ask why.

Frankfurter often said in later years that the most significant and moving aspect of Roosevelt's appointment of him to the Court in 1939 was its timing— that at the time that Hitler was propagandizing the doctrine of Jew as pariah, Roosevelt, the spokesman for the forces of humanity and freedom, had appointed a Jew to America's highest Court. But this awareness that he in some measure symbolized Western civilization's belief in equality and freedom carried a price. As a Jew, and a foreign-born one, Frankfurter felt he had to move circumspectly. From the time of the Sacco-Vanzetti case he had been stamped in the minds of many as a "Red," and campaign literature in three presidential campaigns, wrote Herbert B. Ehrmann, his associate in the case, "made Felix Frankfurter, rather than Franklin Roosevelt, the target of low political attack. The slander grew more vicious as the Goebbels-Coughlin anti-Semitic line was added to violent anti-Communism." [166]

Frankfurter knew, as the Diary entry for January 25, 1943 shows, that some of the "brass hats" regarded him as a "security risk," to use an expression of the postwar period. The studied off-handedness with which he always dismissed such attacks suggest the contrary; and a man who in many little ways betrayed his concern for what the world thought of him may well have found carrying the doctrine of restraint to Olympian extremes congenial for more than judicial reasons.

There was a revealing episode in 1944 that showed how sensitive the Brethren were to such considerations. Chief Justice Stone assigned Frankfurter to write the Court's opinion in *Smith v. Allwright*, 321 U. S. 649, which reversed a 1935 Court ruling that permitted the continuance of the white primary in the South. The selection of Frankfurter troubled Jackson, and though among the Justices appointed by Roosevelt he was closest to Frankfurter, he wrote Stone:

It is a delicate matter . . . . We deny the entire South the right to a white primary, which is one of its most cherished rights. It seems to me very important that the strength which an all but unanimous decision would have may be greatly weakened if the voice that utters it is one that may grate on Southern sensibilities. Mr. Justice Frankfurter unites in a rare degree factors which may unhappily excite prejudice. In the first place he is a Jew. In the second place he is from New England, the seat of the abolition movement. In the third place he has not been thought of as a person particularly sympathetic with the Democratic party in the past. I know that every one of these things is a consideration that to you is distasteful and they are things which I mention only with the greatest reluctance and frank fear of being misunderstood . . .[167]

Stone understood very well and at once reassigned the case to Stanley Reed. Frankfurter sometimes praised Brandeis for his disciplined ability to keep in mind a thousand considerations in exercising the judicial function. He was unlikely himself to be insensitive to his own infirmities.

There is also the paradox of his nonjudicial activities. At the very time that he was adopting on the Bench a position that carried with it a minimum expression of his own policy views, off the Bench he was more of an activist than ever. His elevation to the Bench had not diminished his assistance to Roosevelt. The chits, the memoranda, the letters and telephone calls continued. Increasingly they had dealt with the approach of the war that had finally begun on September 1, 1939, when Nazi Germany invaded Poland. MANY THANKS AND ESPECIALLY FOR NOT REQUIRING US TO BE NEUTRAL IN THOUGHTS, Frankfurter telegraphed Roosevelt after the fireside chat on September 3 in which he said, "Even a neutral cannot be asked to close his mind or his conscience." Roosevelt tried to keep the nation out of war, Frankfurter later said, but he never forgot that it might be beyond his control. He had to pursue a policy that on the surface appeared to be contradictory, "namely, with might and main to try to prevent from coming to pass the very situation in relation to which you're making preparation," and that was difficult and complex. It was a policy in which he had Frankfurter's help.[168]

"Although he had never heard a word of it from Frankfurter, Stimson believed that his own presence in Washington [during World War II] was in some degree the result of Frankfurter's close relationship to the President. In any event, he found Frankfurter always the most devoted of friends and the most zealous of private helpers, and the Justice's long and intimate knowledge of the Roosevelt administration was placed entirely at his disposal." [169] Thus Stimson and Bundy touched discreetly, for Frankfurter was still on the Bench when On Active Service was published, on Frankfurter's extraordinary behind-the-scenes involvement in the politics and administration of wartime Washington. As this Dairy abundantly illustrates, never had Frankfurter's "unimaginable gift of wiggling in wherever he wants to" been exercised more vigorously than during the War.

His full services to the nation in this greatest of wars await the documentation of a definitive biography. In the interests of winning the war he ruthlessly put aside personal sympathies and political preferences. In the late spring of 1941, when Hughes made his intention to retire as Chief Justice known he recommended Stone as his successor but urged Roosevelt to consult Frankfurter because "he knew more of the history of the Court and its needs than anyone else." According to Frankfurter's memorandum of his talk with Roosevelt, the latter asked him, "as between Stone and Bob Jackson whom would you make Chief Justice?" On "personal grounds," Frankfurter had replied, he would prefer Jackson

> But from the national interest I am bound to say there is no reason for preferring Bob to Stone—quite the contrary. Stone is senior and qualified professionally to be C.J. But for me the decisive consideration, considering the fact that Stone is qualified, is that Bob is of your political and personal family, as it were, while Stone is a Republican.
>
> Now it doesn't require prophetic powers to be sure that we shall, sooner or later, be in war—I think sooner. It is most important that when war does come, the country should feel that you are a national, the Nation's, President, and not a partisan President. Few things would contribute as much to confidence in you as a national and not a partisan President than for you to name a Republican, who has the profession's confidence, as Chief Justice.[170]

Grateful to Frankfurter Stone may have been, but this, according to A. A. Berle, did not deter him from expressing his uneasiness about Frankfurter's nonjudicial activities. Berle in the autumn of 1941 was worrying about an alleged Frankfurter move to get rid of Secretary of State Hull.[171] "Frankfurter is apparently getting a little out of scale," Berle wrote in his Diary, adding that "Stone is unhappy and wants to do something about it. If he wants the Supreme Court to be safe, he had better. . . ." A few weeks later Berle had "a quiet private dinner with Justice Stone. We talked of many things; I voiced my fear that Frankfurter's operations on so many fronts were beginning to imperil the Supreme Court's position; Stone indicated, with equal caution, that he felt the same way about it." It is not surprising that a man who was taking enormous risks, as Stone and Berle believed, with the Court's authority and independence, because he was seeking, to paraphrase Learned Hand, to lead a flaming cause from the cloister of the High Court's chamber, should have gravitated on the Bench to a philosophy of the judicial function that involved a minimum expression of his own policy views.

Frankfurter had come on the Court expecting that in time he would become its intellectual leader and that the authority he exercised in his seminar at Harvard would be replicated in the conferences of the Brethren. He had a yearning for disciples. At Harvard the best and the brightest had sat at his feet.

But the Brethren did not respond that way. By 1943 Chief Justice Stone, who himself had been dean of a law school, chafed under Frankfurter's tendency to turn courtroom and conference into classroom seminars, and Stone's biographer commented on his behalf, that "colleagues," meaning in the first instance Frankfurter, "who might have been expected to carry more than a proportionate amount of the work were hampered by their zeal for self-expression." "He's too discursive," was Learned Hand's explanation in 1957 of why his friend would not stand out in the Court's annals as did Brandeis. Brandeis had "infinite particularity," but he delivered his punches so that you were thrown "back on your heels." "If you're discursive, people get lost." [172]

Even more upsetting to Frankfurter than Stone's attitude was the failure of justices like Black, Douglas and Murphy to follow him. Black, as strong a personality as Frankfurter, far from deferring to Frankfurter's learning and procedural expertise, was forging his own judicial philosophy. Although the product of a two-year course at the Alabama Law School, he was every bit the intellectual equal of the other Brethren, with a moral passion that was unflagging. He was, said Paul Freund, "a Bentham with an unmistakably American accent." [173] Schooled in the politics of the county courthouse and the Senate, he was a more effective advocate of his viewpoint with the other Brethren than Frankfurter. By 1943 the latter was referring to the group that consisted of Black, Douglas, Murphy and Wiley Rutledge as "the Axis." Murphy, who had venerated Frankfurter, now dismissed his scholarship as "elegant bunk," and his campaigns for judicial self-restraint as masks for personal drives that he condemned in others. And though Murphy's legal competence is questioned, even by his biographer, Frankfurter valued his good opinion and constantly lobbied for his support. [174]

His vulnerability to the apostasy of disciples—or those he thought were or should be his disciples—was matched by an eagerness for praise and admiration that was the opposite of the monastic austerity and detachment that he constantly preached. Gardner Jackson had noted this trait during their work together in the Sacco-Vanzetti case. It was a flaw in his character, Jackson recorded, that "he wants so badly to be liked and thought wise and brilliant." Landis was disturbed by his "great friendliness with Justice Roberts," after he came on the Court. "I think he was always pleased by being recognized by the elite in our country." After the war some distinguished friends at the bar gave him a dinner at the Century Club. Learned and Augustus Hand were there, and so were C. C. Burlingham, Dean Acheson, Archibald MacLeish, Charles Curtis, Lloyd Garrison, and a few others. "We all got rather tight and got up one after the other and eulogized Felix, much of it very eloquent. Felix loved it all and he talked on at great length about his life, full of real sentimentality and enormous gratitude that all these great men were his friends. He liked to be praised—no doubt about that." "It's so easy in this life," commented Landis, explaining the consequence of too much vanity, "to associate with people who have prestige and money and so on, and you become a little loose in your thinking. The kind of things you sweated for when you were twenty and thirty, and forty, they get a little dim, and you start to compromise. . . . Now I don't think Hugo Black ever lost it." Neither did Brandeis, added Landis.[175]

There is another unsettling aspect to the paradox of Frankfurter's activism off the Bench and his restraint on it, and that was his constant invocation of Holmes. Frankfurter, wrote legal historian Pritchett, "undertakes to serve as the interpreter of Holmes to the present Court. . . ."[176] If any Justice served him as a model, Holmes did, and yet Frankfurter's espousal of Holmes's Olympian philosophy seems a little forced. Holmes was a genuine Olympian. He never read newspapers; Frankfurter devoured them, including, after the war, the daily airmail edition of the London *Times*. Holmes really was above politics. Frankfurter was deeply involved in the political struggles. For Holmes, law served as a jumping-off place for larger cosmic speculations; for Frankfurter, philosophy was of interest only if it helped to solve legal issues. Holmes never crusaded—at least after the Civil War, Frankfurter was always promoting many causes. Holmes was an ironist, Frankfurter an enthusiast. "Well, of course, he's got a very passionate nature," Learned Hand told Louis Henkin, who had been his as well as Frankfurter's law clerk, "and that is rather an initial handicap for a judge . . . not if he has the faculty of adding to it supreme self-restraint. But Frankfurter hasn't supreme self-restraint. He's learned a good deal of it. But he hasn't it."[177] If any "giant" of the Court should have served as his model, it was Brandeis, a man of intense moral feeling who, after he was on the Bench, continued to counsel Presidents, advise disciples on legislation and administration, and stay involved with the affairs of Zion.

What jolts one in the Diaries is that Frankfurter should have been so harshly critical of fellow Justices, William O. Douglas particularly, for their nonjudicial activities. Douglas's interest in elective office while on the Bench was not unique. "Lots of our judges have had the presidential bee," the revered Holmes had written Laski in 1930 when Hughes, who had left the Court in 1916 to run for President, was promoted to Chief Justiceship.[178] There was, to be sure, a difference between Douglas's political involvements and Frankfurter's in that Douglas was ambitious for office for himself and Frankfurter was not. We leave it to the reader to ponder how significant that difference is.

"Four Supreme Court Justices were frequent off-the-record White House callers," wrote Roosevelt's Secretary, Grace Tully, "these being Frankfurter, Douglas, Murphy, and Jackson. Their counsel was often of great help to the President. . . ." In June 1940, when Roosevelt finally decided to run for a third term, he had consulted Frankfurter and Douglas, each of whom later gave him papers detailing why such a decision was in the national interest. They cherished their closeness to Roosevelt. Between them some rivalry was humanly inevitable. That rivalry surely sharpened intellectual differences, differences that to some extent were a continuation on the Bench of the polemics between Harvard Law School's emphasis on the integrity of process and Yale's concern with the ends to be served by the legal system. "Just a Harvard-Yale argument," was the way the violent debates between the two men sometimes seemed to Hugo Black. "Had tea with Justice Frankfurter," Lilienthal recorded in February 1944. "Very sensitive about all the public comment concerning the Court, and particularly the rather vigorous remarks the Justices are making of each other in their opinions, which the newspapers are playing up. For some reason he seems much less impressive as a Supreme Court Justice than he did as a professor of law, to whom you traveled far for counsel. . . . Whatever ideas he had of welding the new Court into a unified body, speaking the voice of modern, enlightened law, have certainly never come off." [179]

Black more than Douglas emerged as the leader of one group in the Roosevelt Court with Frankfurter on the outside, the most articulate spokesman for the nonactivist viewpoint. The clashes between Frankfurter and Black were caustic and spirited, but personal relations never were broken as they were between Frankfurter and Douglas. These two in the end were scarcely on speaking terms, whereas Black, in 1957 on the spur of the moment during a conference slipped Frankfurter a note saying, "I strongly hope nothing will happen that causes you to leave the Court . . . ," and after Frankfurter retired from the Court, often dropped in on him and would say afterwards to his family, "Felix gave me a pretty good insight into this stuff." [180]

The differences within the Roosevelt Court expressed themselves as differences in judicial philosophy, and a part of the Diaries' interest is the glimpses they afford of these disputes and of the Court's workings as viewed from the inside. Although it is relevant to point to external factors of personality and politics that appear to have influenced Justice Frankfurter's conception of the judicial function, we also believe that he developed that conception with such scholarship, coherence, and intellectual power that the corpus of his opinions represents a shaping energy in legal thought and practice. The Court in the period after "the nine old men" was fortunate to have two such dominating men as Frankfurter and Black, one with his emphasis on "principled adjudication" and the other on the ends to be served by legal process. During his twenty-three years on the Bench Frankfurter produced 725 opinions, 263 writing for the Court, 171 concurring opinions, and 291 dissents. A systematic analysis of his contribution to the Court is beyond the scope of this essay except to note some of its characteristic features.

We revert first to civil liberties because in the postwar period the use of the judicial veto to protect First Amendment guaranties against legislative encroachments and popular tumults was the occasion of the sharpest split between Frankfurter and Black. The issue was how to reconcile the individual's claim to freedom with the state's claim to order and security. Frankfurter contended that the competing claims had to be weighed in each instance, and that in any case the legislative judgment had to be respected even if the Court might have reached a different conclusion with regard to the competing interests. Black maintained that the First Amendment safeguards of freedom were absolute and that they had been put into the Constitution precisely to give the judiciary a way of checking legislative encroachments. In the landmark *Dennis* decision in 1951, where the Court upheld the conviction of the Communist leaders under the Smith Act doctrine which made it unlawful to conspire "to advocate and teach" the violent overthrow of government, Black joined by Douglas contended the Smith Act abridged First Amendment guarantees. "I have always believed," wrote Black, "that the First Amendment is the keystone of our Government, that the freedoms it guarantees provide the best insurance against the destruction of all freedom. At least as to speech in the realm of public matters, I believe that the 'clear and present danger' test does not 'mark the furthermost boundaries of protected expression' but does 'no more than recognize a minimum compulsion of the Bill of Rights.' " Few will protest the conviction of the Communists, Black observed, "public opinion being what it is now. . . . There is hope, however, that in calmer times, when present pressures, passions and fears subside, this or some later Court will restore the First Amendment liberties to the high preferred place they belong to in a free society."

Frankfurter agreed that "the Smith Act and this conviction under it no doubt restrict the exercise of free speech and assembly." But he derided what he called "inflexible dogmas" that did not contribute to the solution of specific problems. Some speech had a far greater claim to protection than others. "Not every type of speech occupies the same position on the scale of values. There is no substantial public interest in permitting . . . the lewd and obscene, the profane, the libelous, and the insulting or 'fighting' words—those which by their very utterance inflict injury or tend to incite an immediate breach of peace. . . . We have frequently indicated that the interest in protecting speech depends on the circumstances of the occasion. It is pertinent to the decision before us to consider where on the scale of values we have in the past placed the type of speech now claiming constitutional immunity." Conspiratorial teaching and advocacy of violence, in his view, "ranks low . . . on any scale of values which we have hitherto recognized." On the other side of the scale were the interests which Congress had sought to safeguard, the preservation of the nation against the menace of communism. He could not say that Congress in enacting the Smith Act had acted unreasonably. ". . . there is ample justification for a legislative judgment that the conspiracy now before us is a substantial threat to national order and security." To press the matter further would be an intrusion into the legislative domain.[181]

It is difficult to remember, especially in a time of *"détente,"* when this essay is being written, that until the death of Stalin, reasonable men, not simply McCarthyites, feared and were preoccupied with the operations of the Communist movement, which operated internationally as an arm of a monolithic Soviet imperialism and domestically as disciplined "secret battalions" that were incompatible with an open, pluralist, democratic society.

"If you had raised the Holmes dissent in *Abrams*," which upheld First Amendment guarantees in the face of the hysteria that followed the first war, "against his views in *Dennis*, he might have said," surmised Professor Henkin, who was his law clerk in 1946–1947, "Holmes would have seen clearly the difference between the Communist conspiracy of the postwar period and the harmless doings of a few fellows like Abrams." The Founding Fathers did not foresee a technique, wrote Justice Jackson, who joined Frankfurter in upholding the Smith Act, by which Bill of Rights liberties "might be used to destroy themselves by immunizing a movement of a minority to impose upon the country an incompatible scheme of values which did not include political and civil liberties." He did not believe, he had said earlier, the Bill of Rights should be converted into "a suicide pact." [182]

There were, however, staunch anticommunists—Frankfurter's first law clerk, Joseph Rauh, for example—who, although he respected Frankfurter for his consistency, believed that democracy had better ways of coping with the subversive techniques of communism than the Smith Act, and that the latter reflected and contributed to the hysteria that culminated in McCarthyism.

Frankfurter, it needs to be added, was often allied with Black and other Court liberals in providing judicial protection against the popular and legislative fever for loyalty oaths and security checks that swept the country in the forties and fifties. He and Black joined forces in invalidating a Congressional rider to an appropriations act that barred from the federal payroll three officials accused of subversive connections. But Frankfurter's concurring opinion refused, on historical grounds, to call the rider "an unconstitutional bill of attainder," as the majority did. He wanted to avoid the constitutional question. The vindicated officials were entitled to their back pay, but not to the decision that Black gave them, that Congress did not have the power to block their employment. [183]

Frankfurter voted consistently to uphold the right of teachers charged with subversive affiliations to keep their jobs. But he did so, Helen Shirley Thomas has noted, on procedural and jurisdictional grounds, avoiding the substantive question whether subscription to and advocacy of a subversive doctrine disqualified one as a teacher. [184]

Frankfurter's concern with the integrity of judicial process cannot be overstressed. In retrospect, his interventions in such civil liberty *cause célèbres* as the Mooney case, the deportation cases after World War I, in the Sacco-Vanzetti case, his approval of the Court's overturning of the verdict against the Scottsboro boys, although they earned him a reputation for liberalism, even radicalism, can be seen to have had little to do with sympathy for the defendants, and nothing to do with approval of the doctrines they espoused. His outrage, Professor Freund has observed, had been over a miscarriage of justice, the perpetration of a gross abuse at some level of the judicial process. "The history of liberty, Mr. Justice Brandeis has reminded us," Frankfurter wrote in 1932 after the Court reversed Alabama's conviction of the Scottsboro boys, "cannot be dissociated from the history of procedural observances." [185]

This preoccupation with the fairness of procedure was also reflected in

Frankfurter's sensitivity to Fourth Amendment guarantees, the freedoms from unreasonable searches and seizures, from official brutality and coerced confessions, from unwarranted official intrusions such as wiretapping, and from what Frankfurter called "fruits of the poisonous tree"—evidence illegally secured. Black was considerably less concerned with Fourth Amendment rights; indeed, it was a term of scorn when he called someone a "search and seizure liberal," meaning a Justice like Frankfurter who went all out on search and seizure issues but did not support a Communist's claim of free speech.

Even when Frankfurter and Black agreed on results, Professor Bickel noted, they would not write together. Each went his own route—to the other's intense irritation. Frankfurter writing for the majority in *Rochin v. California*, 342 U.S. 165 (1952), reversed the conviction of a man held on a narcotics charge because the police had forced him to swallow a drug in order to make him vomit up two capsules which turned out to contain morphine and were admitted as evidence. Such methods offended "due process of law," Frankfurter wrote, because they shocked the civilized conscience. To escape Black's anticipated charge that such definitions of due process were subjective and capricious, and in the hope of persuading him to join the majority instead of penning a concurring opinion, Frankfurter wrote, "In each case 'due process of law' requires an evaluation based on disinterested inquiry pursued in the spirit of science, on a balanced order of facts exactly and fairly stated. . . ." To Black this was just "high-sounding rhetoric. . . . You may understand what this means; I do not. . . ." [186a]

Black's "due process of law standard" was essentially a case tried in accordance with the Bill of Rights. He not only stated Bill of Rights protections in absolutist terms, but he argued that "one of the chief objects" of the Fourteenth Amendment had been "to make the Bill of Rights applicable to the States." Frankfurter demolished this contention with his matchless scholarship and dialectical skill, and legal scholarship has sustained him in his reading of the Congressional intent in the adoption of the Fourteenth Amendment. But it was a pyrrhic victory; although the Court has never accepted Black's view that the Fourteenth Amendment incorporated all of the Bill of Rights, it has held, under the *Palko* principle enunciated by Justice Cardozo, that the provisions of the Bill of Rights essential to "the concept of ordered liberty" are made applicable to the states through the Fourteenth Amendment. Through the process of selective, one-at-a-time absorption, the Court has ruled, as Black pointed out in 1968, [186b] "that the Fourteenth Amendment guarantees against infringement by the states the liberties of the First Amendment, the Fourth Amendment, the Fifth Amendment's privilege against self-incrimination, the Sixth Amendment's right to notice, confrontation of witnesses, compulsory process for witnesses, and the assistance of counsel, and the Eighth Amendment's prohibition of cruel and unusual punishments,"—a judicial revolution that scholars have called "the nationalization of the Bill of Rights."

Black's "incorporation" argument was flawed, Ben Cohen has said, "but where should one look for guidance as to the meaning of the Fourteenth Amendment except in the Bill of Rights and that is the way the Court has moved. The idea of basic rights is historically implied in the expression 'due process' and it often happens in the field of human rights that one gain carries with it pointers to the next, to a step that was not originally envisaged."

It is a melancholy fact that in 1932 Frankfurter had anticipated and welcomed the process of selective absorption. In his comment on the Scottsboro case when the Court had reversed on grounds that denial of counsel meant that the defendants had been tried without due process of law, Frankfurter had anticipated the "incorporation" doctrine and had hailed the Court for having written "a notable chapter in the history of liberty."

> But upon the freedom of all state action,[he wrote in the New York Times,] the federal Constitution imposes a broad limitation, applicable to criminal as well as civil proceedings, to judicial as well as legislative acts. This is accomplished by the Fourteenth Amendment, which provides that no state shall "deprive any person of life, liberty, or property without due process of law." The assertion of that limitation is a study of the federal judiciary, and a right of defendants under the federal Constitution. In its application of this prohibition in the review of the conduct of a state criminal trial, the significance of the Scottsboro decision resides.

Had Frankfurter held to this original insight, he might have moderated Black's absolutisms and some of the Court's procedural excesses. "He would have rendered a much greater service," Professor Herbert Wechsler thought, "if instead of drawing the issues as frontally as he did, he had simply gone about adhering to his view rather than constantly attacking the 'incorporation' position." [186c]

"He is forever disposing of issues," wrote Professor Jaffee of Frankfurter, "by assigning their disposition to some other sphere of competence." That was "the really constructive part of his judging," said Professor Bickel, his law clerk in 1953–1954. "He devised all these jurisdictional ways of withdrawing from problems that were insoluble or that were overly difficult." Above all, wrote Jaffee, he was insistent on "reading the legislative power as setting limits to the judicial power." [187] But not always. Six years after *Dennis*, in *Sweezy v. New Hampshire*, 354 U. S. 234 (1957), he struck the balance a little differently between individual rights as protected by the Fourteenth Amendment and the right of a state to self-protection. He concurred in the Supreme Court's reversal of a New Hampshire court's conviction of a witness for refusing to answer questions about the Progressive Party and his affiliations to it. The witness had refused to answer questions put to him by the state's attorney general. The questions violated his rights to privacy in his political thoughts, actions, and associations, the defendant claimed. "For a citizen to be made to forego even a part of so basic a liberty as his political autonomy," wrote Frankfurter, "the subordinating interest of the State must be compelling." That, he held, had not been demonstrated in regard to the Progressive Party.

"In the end," Frankfurter acknowledged, "judgment cannot be escaped—the judgment of this court." The judgment involved drawing a line between contending principles and inevitably, even if safeguarded by historical scholarship and a regard for process, reflected an individual judge's preferences and values. In the fight against judicial supremacy in the 1930s Frankfurter had never wholly reconciled the need to make the Court responsive to the "felt necessities of the times" with the need of judicial independence. Now on the Bench he was unable to draw the line between a judge's duty to pass judgment and his duty to exercise self-restraint, in a serviceable way. "Judges may differ as to the point at which the line may be drawn," he said in his Cardozo lecture on "Reflections on Reading Statutes," [188] "but the only sure safeguard against crossing the line between adjudication and legislation is an alert recognition of the necessity not to cross it and instinctive, as well as trained, reluctance to do so." But this is a literary admonition, not a formula for adjudicating cases. Black's jurisprudence of "absolutes" has equal difficulties, not the least that absolutes tend to become a substitute for analysis and reliance upon them frees a judge from the necessity of discriminating among competing claims and setting forth his reasons for preferring one as against another. Nevertheless, where Black and Frankfurter diverged in regard to the Court's role as a guardian of individual rights and liberties, history has vindicated Black's absolutism and activism, for they served better to protect First Amendment liberties at a time when such protection was most needed, than did Frankfurter's doctrines of restraint and weighing of conflicting claims.

The difficulties of drawing the line between judicial restraint and judicial arrogation were shown in other cases. In the flag-salute rulings, Frankfurter had deferred to the legislative power, but in controversies involving public aid to parochial schools he did not hesitate to use the First Amendment's prohibitions to strike down such aid. That was equally the case in the historic *Brown v. Board of Education*, 347 U.S. 483 (1954), ruling which outlawed school segregation. It reversed the *Plessy v. Ferguson* (1896) "separate but equal" doctrine that had been in effect for fifty-eight years. Frankfurter played a pivotal role in bringing about a unanimous Court on the issue. The case had first been argued in December 1952. Fred M. Vinson of Kentucky was then the Chief Justice. Nine months later Vinson died. "I had lunch with Justice Frankfurter the day he was going to the funeral," recalled Alexander M. Bickel. "It was in his Chambers and he was putting on his striped pants. I can still see that barrel chest and the sleeveless undershirt. As he dressed he kept murmuring, 'an act of Providence, an act of Providence,' from which I concluded that he feared a splintered Court on *Brown* with himself in the role perhaps of casting the deciding vote."

Frankfurter had kept in close touch with Black during the discussions of *Brown*. He understood from the beginning that it was impossible to reaffirm

Plessy. Black's willingness to go along, both his reaching that result and his concern for taking it slowly, weighed a great deal with Frankfurter, Bickel felt. When President Eisenhower appointed Earl Warren to the Chief Justiceship, Frankfurter took him to school on the issues in the *Brown* case in lengthy talks out at his Dumbarton Avenue study. That was the teacher role that he loved. That was the period, too, of his greatest enthusiasm for Warren, an enthusiasm that later soured when Warren went down paths Frankfurther did not approve.[189] That, too, was an old story.

Although the Court was unanimous, the South was outraged when the *Brown* decision was handed down. James F. Byrnes, a former Associate Justice, dredged up the attacks that the New Dealers had used against the Court in the Thirties, accusing it of judicial usurpation and judicial lawmaking. He also coupled a denunciation of the Brethren for doing the work of the Communists with a demand for curbs on the Court's jurisdiction.[190] It was a ruling that Frankfurter, the critic of judicial activism, never regretted. How then square his hands-off position in the flag-salute cases with his activist attitude toward parochial school aid and segregated schools? The common thread, it has been argued, is his belief in the assimilationist, nationalizing function of the public schools.

That may well be, but the experience suggests that legal scholarship, a sense of history, the law viewed as process cannot in themselves settle the issue of what constitutes disinterested adjudication and what self-willed legislation. In the end the ultimate values of the individual Justice must enter. Frankfurter himself recognized this, for in other contexts he argued that a judge must be able to "pierce the curtain of the future . . . give shape and visage to mysteries still in the womb of time." He should "have antennae registering feeling and judgment beyond logical, let alone quantitative, proof." [191] The Black group in its anticipations of what the future required clearly was willing to take larger risks with the Court's authority than was Frankfurter, and history thus far has proved them right.

A misreading of the future coupled with his customary reluctance to interfere with the legislature, especially in a controversy that was heavily infused with politics, led Frankfurter to dissent from the Court's historic decision in 1962 in *Baker v. Carr*, 369 U. S. 186, to strike down malapportionment as unconstitutional. The Court must stay out of that "political thicket," Frankfurter had argued in 1946 in *Colegrove v. Green*, 328 U. S. 549, where he had written for the Court. He held to that view in 1962, when he was in the minority. "There is not under our Constitution a judicial remedy for every political mischief. In a democratic society like ours, relief must come through an aroused popular conscience that sears the conscience of the people's representatives." But relief had not come, and had Frankfurter's position remained the Court's, reapportionment would have been postponed indefinitely.

Wallace Mendelson in his meticulous study of the conflicts between Black and Frankfurter noted that the Black group consistently interpreted the Fair

Labor Standards Act and the Federal Employers Liability Act to favor the work-man. Frankfurter, who was invariably concerned with what Congress intended, sometimes favored the employee, sometimes the employer. For Black, com-mented Mendelson, "a generous 'New Deal' humanitarianism seems to be decisive. The other as judge is more concerned with the basic distinction be-tween legislative and judicial functions, lest the freedom of the people to gov-ern themselves, well or badly, be hampered by judicial legislation." Black and his group were much readier to reverse what a new majority considered to have been a wrong reading of the law, whereas Frankfurter contended that the Court's interpretation of a statute, once it had become established doctrine, should be left to Congress to alter. The tendency to disregard precedents in order to achieve a more liberal legislative result, he argued, shook confidence "in the consistency of decision" and left "the courts below on an uncharted sea of doubt and difficulty without any confidence that what was said yesterday will hold good tomorrow. . . ." Frankfurter and Black also treated the actions of administrative agencies such as the National Labor Relations Board and the In-terstate Commerce Commission differently. Black voted to sustain the "liberal" N.L.R.B. in twenty out of twenty-one instances, but the "conservative" I.C.C. in only two out of fifteen. Frankfurter, whose primary motivation was respect for the administrative process, voted to sustain the N.L.R.B. in sixteen out of twenty-one cases and the I.C.C. in thirteen out of sixteen.[192]

The function of judicial review whether of legislature or administrative agency seemed to Frankfurter essentially an "oligarchic process."

> The Court is not saved from being oligarchic because it professes to act in the service of humane ends. As history amply proves, the judiciary is prone to misconceive the public good by confounding private notions with constitutional requirements, and such misconceptions are not subject to legitimate displacement by the will of the people except at too slow a pace. Judges appointed for life whose decisions run counter to prevailing opinion cannot be voted out of office . . . their deliberations are in secret. . . . But a democracy need not rely on the courts to save it from its own unwis-dom. If it is alert—and without alertness by the people there can be no en-during democracy—unwise or unfair legislation can readily be removed from the statute books. It is by such vigilance over its representatives that democracy proves itself.[193]

He shunned judicial lawmaking. Having wielded the weapon of judicial restraint against the "old" Court's use of the veto to strike down government regulation of business and social welfare legislation, he had too much respect for consistency and regularity as the very essence of judicial interpretation, to turn around, once the Court majority consisted of Roosevelt appointees, and use the judicial power to "usurp," as he regarded it, a role in lawmaking, even if it was done on behalf of a progressive social policy. "Humanity is not the test of constitutionality," he had cautioned in 1922, and he remained true to that view to the very end. "Specifically, your biographers will have to face this question," he advised Justice Murphy, whose primary loyalties were to justice and compassion rather than to law, to results rather than to process, "which is the more courageous character—a sensitive humanitarian who has taken the oath as a judge, with the resulting confined freedom of a judge to give expression to his own compassion and therefore does not yield to his compassion, or the same person who thinks his compassion is the measure of law.

"What is the difference between you and Louis XIV, who said 'I am the law,' when you say 'I am the law, jurisdiction or no jurisdiction.' " [194] Consistency had another powerful motivation. A Court, shaken to its foundations by the battles of the Thirties that had been occasioned by its judicial activism on behalf of conservative interests, would further endanger its standing if the Court's foremost critic of that policy swung around and on the Bench asserted a judicial activism to protect liberal interests.

Justice Jackson, as close to Frankfurter as anyone on the Court, put the matter of the Court's consciousness of its own vulnerability with considerable candor: the Court "is subject to being stripped of jurisdiction or smothered with additional justices any time such a disposition exists and is supported strongly enough by public opinion. I think the Court can never quite escape consciousness of its own infirmities, a psychology which may explain its apparent yielding to expediency, especially during war time." [195]

The key to the Court's authority was public confidence in its independence and objectivity in reconciling conflicts "between the government and the individual, class and class, party and party" [196] and this, too, helps explain Frankfurter's unwillingness once on the Bench to switch to a philosophy of judicial activism. "The faith in judicial objectivity," Professor Jaffe wrote in "Mr. Justice Jackson,"

> is an ultimate source of personal security and social cohesion. But once it comes to be believed by one or another of the great social classes that the Court is an organ of another class, its function is impaired. This is peculiarly the case when the Court is a constitutional one and participates in the very creation of major social premises. To secure wholehearted and widespread acceptance of its pronouncements it has need of all the credit it can amass; to surrender it in schemes for social betterment is foolhardy.[197]

Frankfurter's emphasis on disinterestedness, impartiality, and restraint, his search for safeguards against excessively personal judgments were rooted in his conception of the role of law. Voting in 1947 to sustain a lower court's conviction of the United Mine Workers for criminal contempt because in striking the union had ignored the Court's temporary restraining order, Frankfurter said that he did so "upon the broad ground of vindicating the process of law . . .

the Founders knew that Law alone saves a society from being rent by inter-necine strife or ruled by mere brute power however disguised. . . . To that end they set apart a body of men, who were to be the depositories of law, who by their disciplined training and character and by withdrawal from the usual temp-tations of private interest may reasonably be expected to be 'as free, impartial, and independent as the lot of humanity will admit.' " [198]

We speak of a "master teacher" or a "writer's writer" to characterize men and women who exhibit a high degree of technical craftsmanship and concern with method and process. Frankfurter's preoccupation with procedure, wrote Paul Freund, had a deep justification in policy because issues and controversies are rendered "more tractable through the lawyer's contribution of a right struc-ture for their solution." The integrity and fitness of the legal process, Professor Freund wrote elsewhere, was "a kind of transcendent natural law, a law above laws, standing as the scientific process does to the mutable body of science it-self. . . ." [199] The young "tend to be impatient with what lawyers term proce-dural matters" he quoted Senator Paul H. Douglas:

> and to be far more interested instead in substantive issues. Only the latter seem to the young to have vitality. But as time passes and a man grows older, it dawns upon him that a great part of our progress has been made through transforming substantive issues of conflict into accepted matters of procedure. For it is in this way the society peacefully disposes of issues which, if not so handled, would tear it apart. May there not be a moral guide for action in this fact? [200]

Because of Frankfurter's view of the judge's role and of the Court as the guardian of legal structure and process, the great Learned Hand spoke of him in the late 1950s as "the most important figure in our whole judicial system." That view, practiced with a resolute consistency, and graced with learning, his-tory, and logic, assure his place in the history of American jurisprudence. In 1970 sixty-five law school deans and professors rated him along with eleven others as among the "great" Justices out of a total of ninety-six.[201]

Yet there are Frankfurter admirers who believe that Frankfurter's influence on constitutional law was greater before he went onto the Bench than after, and that the writings that culminated in *Mr. Justice Holmes and the Supreme Court* are of more lasting interest than the aggregate of his judicial opinions. He was not one of the giants of the Court. All instrumentalities must be judged in terms of larger purposes. The tool of judicial restraint, forged in a time when judicial activism obstructed the evolving purposes of the American people, became on the Bench a brake on his larger sympathies. In 1940 Eleanor Roosevelt, in her impulsive way, declared in the face of the Justice's learning and dialectical skill that there was something wrong with a ruling that forced little children to salute a flag when such a ceremony was repugnant to their conscience. Perhaps it was a tribute to a moral innocence and courage that enabled Eleanor Roosevelt to see through the structure of law and politics to the purposes they served, that caused Frankfurter, sick, crippled, and near death, to utter those strangely moving words: "Dear Eleanor, your life was full of beauty and achievement. In the words of Milton, there should be no tears, no wailing, for your life was not wasted. You were a vital part of Franklin's life, and he was a vital part of my life, and when you died, part of me died with you." [202]

With Roosevelt's death in April 1945, and the end of the war, Frankfurter's behind-the-scenes intervention in government affairs had largely ceased. Men still turned to him for advice, and the Diary has snatches of the talk that he and Dean Acheson engaged in on their daily walk to work. "For twenty years we walked downtown together every fair day," Acheson wrote in the *Harvard Law Review*. "My wife would speculate in amazement on what we could find to talk about for an hour every morning and during a telephone call or visit in the evening. Yet the talk never stopped or ceased to absorb us. . . ." [203]

At the Court his chambers continued to be thronged by the great and the gifted. Usually the law clerks were brought in for five or ten minutes to meet the panjandrum with Frankfurter "orchestrating" the ensuing discussion. The clerks hovered around his chambers. "If three law clerks gathered," said Bickel, "he would burst in and there would be an instant seminar." He was always prepared to talk with his own clerks, starting from the day's headlines and soon plunging back into his own rich experience. "We were not simply writers of memos on points but took part in the discussion and analysis of a case," said Bickel. "We were his confidants as well as his legal aides," said Henkin, to whom his clerkship was "the best year of my life. He was the most vital human being I ever knew. His antennae were always vibrating—to everyone and to everything." His clerks were sent to him by Professor Henry Hart, who took over his seminar on legislation and whose specialty was federal jurisdiction and procedure. Frankfurter was the first Justice to employ a black as law clerk, William T. Coleman. He made it a practice because of his fondness for his clerks to keep in touch with them after they left him. The year that Elliott Richardson clerked for him he broke his ankle skiing in Vermont. Three years later Frankfurter sent Richardson a letter to the editor that he had spotted in the London *Times* denouncing the perils of modern skiing.

He was much lionized in postwar Washington. Did he have to call on Alice Longworth, his wife chided him, when she learned that Mrs. Longworth had also received Senator McCarthy at her house. But he had a warm spot in his heart for Mrs. Longworth. She had spice and temperament; moreover, she had befriended him socially in World War I. Neither did his wife share his enthusiasm for Dean Acheson, but that, too, did not influence him. Sometimes Marion could be quite caustic when he waxed lyrical about a new friend or became the superpatriot. There was an annual dinner with his law clerks at which she usually spoke and often with amused affection poked fun at his current enthusiasm—whether it was a cause or a personality. In the early 1950s she began to suffer from arthritis and soon was totally bedridden. He could not have been more devotedly attentive. He read to her, reported to her. Often if a visitor told him something interesting, Frankfurter would stop him and go into Marion's room in order to tell her immediately.

At the end of 1958 there came the first tremors of the coronary afflictions that finally felled him. These were followed in April 1962 by a stroke which left him on the floor of his chambers, where his secretary, Mrs. Elsie Douglas, found him. John F. Kennedy was now President. Like Eleanor Roosevelt, Frankfurter regarded the son with suspicion because he considered the father a really evil man. But Dean Acheson arranged to bring the youthful President to call on him, as Frankfurter thirty years earlier had arranged Roosevelt's call on Holmes. Afterwards, Frankfurter confessed to Acheson that he had not realized it, but "that young man has grace." He hoped that Paul Freund would be appointed to his place on the Bench, but in August 1962 when after twenty-three years service with the Court, Frankfurter retired, Kennedy appointed his Secretary of Labor, Arthur Goldberg, to the seat.

Although his rate of speech had slowed "and the volume of his voice [had] dropped several decibels," and he was confined to a wheelchair, he was still an animated, interested conversationalist. Archibald MacLeish came to see him. What was he up to? Frankfurter asked. Another play, was the reply. "What sort of play?" "Well, I suppose it might be described as a patriotic play," MacLeish told him. "Good. You couldn't make it too patriotic for me." Frankfurter worked on his papers with Max Freedman, a scholarly newspaper columnist whom he had selected to write his biography. He became preoccupied with the arrangements for his funeral. He did not want a rabbi, he told Garson Kanin. He had left the synagogue at fifteen and never returned. The services should be in his apartment, and he listed those whom he wanted present and who should be the speakers. Finally, he listed Professor Louis Henkin as the last of those to speak.

"Do you know why I want *him?*" Frankfurter asked Kanin. "No," the playwright replied. "Because he is my only close personal friend who is also a practicing, orthodox Jew. He knows Hebrew perfectly and will know exactly what to say. I came into the world a Jew and although I did not live my life entirely as a Jew, I think it is fitting that I should leave as a Jew." [204]

"When he told me that," said Lou Henkin, "and when he added, 'you do what you want,' I decided to say *Kaddish.* You know that is not a lamentation but a *magnificat* which has bound generations of Jews to each other." Paul Freund, who was the other speaker at the simple services that were held in Frankfurter's apartment, spoke of other linkages: "F. F.'s" patriotism, his love of friends—"who of us will not continue to feel that iron grip on the arm, to hear the full-throated greeting, to be rocked with the explosive laughter, and to be moved by the solicitous inquiries about ourselves and our dear ones?"—his love of the law, and the courage it had taken to stand up for justice "not least in later years when he exercised the courage of judicial restraint and risked the misunderstanding and alienation of friends outside the law."

Then there was another linkage, unmentioned at the service. Two days before his death he had called in Freedman and asked him to stand beside his bed and hold his hand as they talked. He spoke of Freedman's work-in-progress. "Tell the whole story," he instructed Freedman solemnly. "Let people see how much I loved Roosevelt, how much I loved my country, and let them see how great a man Roosevelt really was." [205]

Footnotes to Preface and Biographical Essay

1. Felix Frankfurter, *Mr. Justice Holmes and the Supreme Court* (Cambridge, 1938), p. 13.

2. *Felix Frankfurter Reminisces*, as recorded by Dr. Harlan B. Phillips (New York, 1960), cited as *Phillips*. The Columbia Oral History interviews on which this book is based are cited as Frankfurter, COHP.

3. Cited as *Tribute*, (New York, 1964).

4. Frankfurter Papers, Library of Congress, hereinafter, FPLC; Leonora Cohen Rosenfield, *Portrait of A Philosopher: Morris Raphael Cohen in Life and Letters* (New York, 1962), p. 18.

5. Morris Raphael Cohen, *A Dreamer's Journey* (Boston, 1949), p. 131; Felix Frankfurter, *Of Law and Life and Other Things that Matter*, edited by Philip B. Kurland (Cambridge, 1965), p. 169; Frankfurter, COHP, p. 48.

6. Max Lowenthal in *Tribute*, p. 124.

7. Martin Mayer, *Emory Buckner* (New York, 1968), p. 4.

8. *Phillips*, p. 37.

9. Stimson, Henry L., *On Active Service in Peace and War* (New York, 1948), pp. 4, 6; hereinafter *Stimson: Phillips*, p. 39; *Mayer*, p. 29.

10. *Phillips*, p. 43.

11. *Ibid.*

12. *Mayer*, p. 29; *Stimson*, p. 70.

13. *Stimson*, pp. 16–17; *Phillips*, p. 48.

14. *Phillips*, p. 50; *Stimson*, p. 26.

15. FPLC, July 1, 1911.

16. *Phillips*, p. 64.

17. *Phillips*, p. 61.

18. *Phillips*, p. 54.

19. *Phillips*, p. 58.

20. FPLC, October 28, 1912.

21. FPLC, Felix Frankfurter to Emory Buckner, March 4, 1912 and April 20, 1912; Emory Buckner to Felix Frankfurter, undated, in *Mayer*, pp. 66–68.

22. FPLC, Henry L. Stimson to Felix Frankfurter, September 19, 1912.

23. *Stimson*, pp. 42–43; *Phillips*, pp. 54, 72–75.

24. Henry Breckinridge, COHP, pp. 94–95.

25. Cohen, *A Dreamer's Journey*, pp. 175–184; Felix Frankfurter to M. R. Cohen, July 23, 1914, in *Rosenfield*, p. 242.

26. Arthur E. Sutherland, *The Law at Harvard* (Cambridge, 1967), p. 174; M. R. Cohen to Roscoe Pound, March 7, 1912, in *Rosenfield*, pp. 297–299; R. Pound to M. R. Cohen, March 20, 1912, in *Rosenfield*, p. 209; F. Frankfurter to M. R. Cohen, March 9, 1912, in *Rosenfield*, p. 241.

27. Emory Buckner to Roscoe Pound, November 14, 1911; Felix Frankfurter to Emory Buckner, January 6, 1912, in *Mayer*, pp. 39 and 61.

28. FPLC.

29. FPLC, June 26, 1913.

30. FPLC, June 28, 1913.

31. *Phillips*, pp. 78–79.

32. July 5, 1913, cited in full in *Phillips*, pp. 80–84.

33. FPLC, Felix Frankfurter to Marion Denman, October 14, 1914.

34. *Phillips*, pp. 78, 79.

35. Felix Frankfurter to M. R. Cohen, July 23, 1914, in *Rosenfield*, p. 243; FPLC, Felix Frankfurter to Marion Denman, October 14, 1914.

36. Liva Baker, *Felix Frankfurter* (New York, 1969), p. 13, from Francis Plimpton's *Reunion Runes*.

37. *Holmes-Laski Letters*, edited by Mark DeWolfe Howe, 2 vols. (Cambridge, 1953), hereinafter *Holmes-Laski*; H. Laski to O. W. Holmes, November 17, 1916; December 1, 1916; March 30, 1918, pp. 35, 38, 39, 145.

38. *Phillips*, pp. 89–90; 92.

39. James Bradley Thayer, "The Origin and Scope of the American Doctrine of Constitutional Law," 7 *Harvard Law Review* 1893; Felix Frankfurter, *Mr. Justice Brandeis* (Yale, 1932), p. 53; *Phillips*, pp. 299–300; Sutherland, *op. cit.*, pp. 208, 238; *Muller v. Oregon*, 208 U.S. 412 (1908).

40. *Bunting v. Oregon*, 243 U.S. 246 (1917) was the maximum hours case; *Stettler v. O'Hara*, 243 U.S. 629 (1917) was the minimum wage case for women.

41. F. Frankfurter to M. R. Cohen, July 23, 1914, in *Rosenfield*, p. 242; F. Frankfurter to Walter Lippmann, October 16, 1916, FPLC; Garson Kanin in *Tribute*, pp. 37–38; *Phillips*, p. 107.

42. Herbert B. Ehrmann in *Tribute*, pp. 95–97; *Holmes-Laski*, August 12, 1916, p. 12.

43. FPLC, F. Frankfurter to H. L. Stimson, September 9, 1911; *Phillips*, p. 76.

44. F. Frankfurter to M. R. Cohen, October 13, 1916, in *Rosenfield*, p. 249; Max Lerner in *Mr. Justice Brandeis*, pp. 21–22; F. Frankfurter to H. L. Stimson, November 2, 1916, FPLC.

45. F. Frankfurter to M. R. Cohen, October 3, 1916, in *Rosenfield*, pp. 247–248; F. Frankfurter to H. L. Stimson, November 2, 1916, FPLC.

46. *Phillips*, pp. 113, 114.

47. FPLC, F. Frankfurter to Marion Denman, April 17, 1917; *Phillips*, p. 115; *Holmes-Laski*, June 1917, p. 98.

48. New York *Times*, June 20, 1917.

49. Interview with Robert Szold; Barnard, Harry, *The Life and Times of Judge Julian W. Mack* (New York, 1974), pp. 122, 123.

50. F. Frankfurter to Marion Denman, May 15, 1917; June 8, 1917; June 20, 1917; FPLC.

51. *Phillips*, pp. 178–184; 154–163.

52. *Phillips*, p. 130.

53. Theodore Roosevelt to Felix Frankfurter, December 19, 1917; Felix Frankfurter to Theodore Roosevelt, December 1917.

54. FPLC.

55. *Tribute*, pp. 100–101.

56. Eleanor Roosevelt to Sara Delano Roosevelt, May 12, 1918, Franklin D. Roosevelt Library; *Phillips*, p. 37.

57. *Holmes-Laski*, September 5, 1917, p. 98; January 31, 1918, p. 133; Marion Denman to F. Frankfurter, September 6, 1917, FPLC; Baker, *op. cit.*, pp. 50, 76.

58. *Phillips*, p. 56; Benjamin V. Cohen to Felix Frankfurter, October 6, 1964, FPLC; Barnard, *op. cit.*, pp. 245, 258.

59. Joseph P. Lash, *Eleanor and Franklin* (New York, 1971), p. 231; *Holmes-Laski*, February 23, 1919, p. 186.

60. *Phillips*, pp. 184, 186.

61. *Phillips*, pp. 161–162.

62. FPLC.

63. Chafee remark quoted in Sutherland, *op. cit.*, p. 251; *Holmes-Laski*, April 4, 1919, p. 193; April 20, 1919, p. 211; *Holmes-Pollock Letters*, edited by Mark DeWolfe Howe (Cambridge, 1941), April 5, 1919; *Holmes-Laski*, June 2, 1919, p. 211; November 3, 1919, p. 218.

64. *Holmes-Laski*, November 3, 1918, p. 218; Garson Kanin in *Tribute*, pp. 39–40.

65. *Holmes-Laski*, November 5, 1919, p. 219; January 14, 1920, p. 233; July 18, 1920, p. 271; Dr. Henry Murray in *Tribute*, p. 14; Garson Kanin in *Tribute*, pp. 52–54; interviews with Mrs. Mark DeWolfe Howe and the late Professor Alexander M. Bickel.

66. F. Frankfurter to M. R. Cohen, December 2, 1921 in *Rosenfield*, p. 252; Zechariah Chafee, *Freedom of Speech* (New York, 1920); Charles Beard, *Rise of American Civilization* (New York, 1927), Vol. II, p. 671.

67. Sutherland, *op. cit.*, p. 260.

68. *The New Republic*, April 23, 1924; also May 21, 1924.

69. *Felix Frankfurter: Law and Politics*, edited by Archibald MacLeish and E. F. Prichard, Jr. (New York, 1939), hereinafter *Law and Politics*, pp. 213–216; 219–220.

70. FPLC, F. Frankfurter to Walter Lippmann, July 1, 1924.

71. FPLC.

72. F. Frankfurter to Learned Hand, October 3, 1924, cited by Sanford V. Levinson, "The Democratic Faith of Felix Frankfurter," 25 *Stanford Law Review* 1973.

73. *Law and Politics*, p. 314.

74. *Ibid.*, pp. 27, 21, 129.

75. Sutherland, *op. cit.* p. 240; *Law and Politics*, p. 242.

76. Sutherland, *op. cit.* p. 301; *Law and Politics*, p. 297.

77. Roscoe Pound in *Tribute*, p. 148; interviews with David E. Lilienthal and Lloyd K. Garrison.

78. Francis Biddle, *Mr. Justice Holmes* (New York, 1942), p. 12.

79. *Holmes-Laski*, July 20, 1925, p. 766.

80. *Phillips*, p. 202; Gardner Jackson, COHP, p. 280.

81. Felix Frankfurter, *The Case of Sacco and Vanzetti* (Boston, 1927), p. 43; *Phillips*, pp. 209–212.

82. *The Boston Transcript*, April 25, 1927; *Phillips*, p. 216; Ehrmann in *Tribute*, p. 108.

83. *Holmes-Laski*, December 16, 1928, p. 1121; April 23, 1927, p. 999.

84. Gardner Jackson, COHP, pp. 295–296.

85. The "test of civilization" quotation is from Sir John MacDonnell's *Historical Trials* and was cited by Frankfurter in his introduction to a 1961 edition of his *The Case of Sacco and Vanzetti*; the Smith endorsement is reprinted in *Law and Politics*, pp. 320–328; *Holmes-Laski*, November 13, 1928, p. 1109.

86. Gardner Jackson, COHP, p. 230.

87. Learned Hand, COHP, p. 101.

88. *Roosevelt and Frankfurter: Their Correspondence, 1928–1945*, annotated by Max Freedman (Boston, 1967), hereinafter *Freedman*; F. Frankfurter to Franklin D. Roosevelt, November 21, 1928, p. 39; Franklin D. Roosevelt to Felix Frankfurter, November 24, 1928, p. 40.

89. *Freedman*, July 5, 1929, p. 41.

90. *Franklin D. Roosevelt, His Personal Letters*, edited by Elliott Roosevelt (New York, 1950) March 11, 1930, p. 109.

91. Felix Frankfurter to Walter Lippmann, October 23, 1930, in *Freedman*, p. 52; Felix Frankfurter to Franklin D. Roosevelt, November 11, 1930, in *Freedman*, p. 53.

92. *Holmes-Laski*, June 15, 1930, p. 1261; December 27, 1930, pp. 1301–1302; Felix Frankfurter, "The Palestine Situation," *Foreign Affairs*, April 1931.

93. Roosevelt *Letters*, December 1, 1930, p. 159; Franklin D. Roosevelt to Felix Frankfurter, November 4, 1931, in *Freedman*, p. 59; Felix Frankfurter to Franklin D. Roosevelt, August 28, 1931, in *Freedman*, p. 57; Franklin D. Roosevelt to Felix Frankfurter, September 7, 1931, in *Freedman*, p. 57; Felix Frankfurter to C. C. Burlingham, June 29, 1932, FPLC.

94. Felix Frankfurter Memorandum, July 3, 1932, in *Freedman*, pp. 74–77.

95. *Ibid.*; *Holmes-Laski*, September 1, 1932, p. 1406.

96. Felix Frankfurter to Franklin D. Roosevelt, August 5, 1932, in *Freedman*, pp. 80–81; Franklin D. Roosevelt to Felix Frankfurter, August 28, 1932, in *Freedman*, p. 85; Felix Frankfurter to Franklin D. Roosevelt, September 2, 1932, in *Freedman*, p. 85.

97. Franklin D. Roosevelt to Felix Frankfurter, August 7, 1932, in *Freedman*, p. 82; *Navigating the Rapids*, 1918–1971: *From the Papers of Adolf A. Berle* (New York, 1973), August 5, 1932 entry, p. 54.

98. April 12, 1932, in *Freedman*, pp. 64–68.

99. October 13, 1932, in *Freedman*, p. 89.

100. Felix Frankfurter to Franklin D. Roosevelt, October 20, 1932, in *Freedman*, p. 90; Felix Frankfurter to Walter Lippmann, October 26, 1932, in *Freedman*, p. 90; Felix Frankfurter to Franklin D. Roosevelt, November 7, 1932, in *Freedman*, p. 94; *Holmes-Laski*, November 23, 1932, p. 1420.

101. *Holmes-Laski*, October 30, 1932; November 7, 1932, pp. 1415–1416.

102. Grace Tully, *F.D.R. My Boss* (New York, 1949), p. 140.

103. Raymond Moley, *After Seven Years* (New York, 1939), pp. 106, 180–181; Berle, *op. cit.*, January 11, 1933, p. 83.

104. *Stimson*, p. 291; *Freedman*, p. 102; Moley, *op. cit.* p. 94; Felix Frankfurter to Franklin D. Roosevelt, Jan. 28, 1933, in *Freedman*, p. 106.

105. Moley, *op. cit.*, p. 123.

106. Frankfurter Memorandum, March 8, 1933, in *Freedman*, pp. 110–114; Felix Frankfurter to Franklin D. Roosevelt, March 14, 1933, in *Freedman*, pp. 120–121; Franklin D. Roosevelt to Felix Frankfurter, April 5, 1933, in *Freedman*, pp. 123–124.

107. Felix Frankfurter to Walter Lippmann, March 11, 1933; Walter Lippmann to Felix Frankfurter, March 14, 1933; Felix Frankfurter to Walter Lippmann, March 15, 1933, in *Freedman*, pp. 115–120.

108. Sutherland, *op. cit.*, pp. 288–289; Martin Kingsley, *Harold Laski* (New York, 1953), p. 23; James M. Landis, COHP, p. 151.

109. *Freedman*, pp. 330–331; Learned Hand letter, June 5, 1936, in *Freedman*, p. 331.

110. Felix Frankfurter to Franklin D. Roosevelt, November 15, 1935, in *Freedman*, p. 295; Louis L. Jaffee, "Professors and Judges as Advisors to Government: Reflections on the Roosevelt-Frankfurter Relationship," 83 *Harvard Law Review* 1969.

111. Interview with Herbert Wechsler.

112. *Tribute*, pp. 18–19.

113. Interview.

114. Learned Hand, COHP, pp. 81–82.

115. (Boston, 1934).

116. *The Holmes-Einstein Letters* (New York, 1964), September 30, 1932, p. 349.

117. *Mr. Justice Brandeis*, pp. 124–125.

118. Oliver Wendell Holmes, *Collected Legal Papers* (New York, 1920), p. 48; Felix Frankfurter to Marguerite LeHand, September 24, 1933, in *Freedman*, pp. 156–157.

119. Moley, *op. cit.*, p. 285; Berle, *op. cit.*, May 26, 1938, p. 176.

120. FPLC, Felix Frankfurter to H. L. Stimson, June 22, 1934; Mason, Alpheus T., *Harlan Fiske Stone* (New York, 1956), p. 148.

121. Felix Frankfurter, "The Young Men Go to Washington," *Fortune*, January 1936, reprinted in *Law and Politics*, pp. 238–249.

122. June 18, 1934, in *Freedman*, pp. 222–223.

123. *Holmes-Einstein*, July 11, 1916, pp. 132–133.

124. Interview with Mrs. Howe.

125. Felix Frankfurter to Franklin D. Roosevelt, April 23, 1934, in *Freedman*, p. 211; Joseph Alsop and Turner Catledge, *The 168 Days* (New York, 1938), p. 3; M. R. Cohen to F. Frankfurter, July 23, 1935, in *Rosenfield*, pp. 263–265; also M. R. Cohen to F. Frankfurter, January 27, 1936, in *Rosenfield*, p. 270.

126. F. Frankfurter to M. R. Cohen, August 8, 1935, in *Rosenfield*, pp. 265–267.

127. *Mr. Justice Brandeis*, Preface; *Mr. Justice Holmes and the Supreme Court*, pp. 23–24; *Law and Politics*, p. 7.

128. Felix Frankfurter, "The Red Terror of Judicial Reform," *New Republic*, October 1, 1924, reprinted in *Law and Politics*, pp. 10–16.

129. M. R. Cohen to F. Frankfurter, May 22, 1936; F. Frankfurter to M. R. Cohen, May 22, 1936; also, June 10, 1936, in *Rosenfield*, pp. 276–279.

130. Felix Frankfurter to Franklin D. Roosevelt, May 29, 1935, in *Freedman*, p. 272.

131. Franklin D. Roosevelt to C. C. Burlingham, May 23, 1937, in *Freedman*, p. 400.

132. Interview with Benjamin V. Cohen.

133. *Rosenfield*, p. 280.

134. Volume XIV, p. 478.

135. Interview with Benjamin V. Cohen.

136. Cited by Paul A. Freund, "Charles Evans Hughes as Chief Justice," 81 *Harvard Law Review* 1967.

137. Franklin D. Roosevelt, *Public Papers and Addresses*, Vol. VI, p. LXI; Franklin D. Roosevelt to C. C. Burlingham, May 23, 1937, in *Freedman*, p. 400.

138. Franklin D. Roosevelt to Felix Frankfurter, January 15, 1937; Felix Frankfurter to Franklin D. Roosevelt, February 7, 1937, in *Freedman*, p. 381; interview with Benjamin V. Cohen.

139. Franklin D. Roosevelt to Felix Frankfurter, February 9, 1937, in *Freedman*, pp. 381–382.

140. Jaffee, *op. cit.*; *Public Papers and Addresses*, Vol. VI, pp. XLVII, LXVI; Felix Frankfurter to C. C. Burlingham, June 9, 1937; Felix Frankfurter to Franklin D. Roosevelt, July 20, 1937, in *Freedman*, pp. 401–404.

141. *Freedman*, pp. 404–406.

142. William O. Douglas, *Go East Young Man* (New York, 1974), p. 322; Jaffee, *op. cit.*

143. *Freedman*, p. 372.

144. *Phillips*, pp. 279–283.

145. *Freedman*, pp. 481–482; interview with Joseph Rauh, Jr.

146. *The Secret Diary of Harold L. Ickes*, Vol. II (New York, 1954), pp. 539, 546, 550–552; *Harlan Fiske Stone*, p. 482.

147. *Ickes*, p. 559.

148. Felix Frankfurter to Franklin D. Roosevelt, January 4, 1939, in *Freedman*, p. 485.

149. *Nomination of Felix Frankfurter*, Hearings before a Subcommittee of the Commmittee on the Judiciary, United States Senate, 76th Congress, 1st session, January 7, 10, 11, 12, 1939; interview with Roger N. Baldwin.

150. Felix Frankfurter to Franklin D. Roosevelt, January 30, 1939, in *Freedman*, p. 485.

151. James M. Landis, COHP.

152. *The Journals of David E. Lilienthal*, Vol. I (New York, 1964), p. 103–104.

153. Felix Frankfurter to Franklin D. Roosevelt, May 18, 1938, in *Freedman*, p. 457.

154. *Harlan Fiske Stone*, pp. 469–470.

155. *Minersville School District v. Gobitis*, 310 U.S. 586 (1940).

156. *Law and Politics*, p. XVI; Felix Frankfurter to Franklin D. Roosevelt, October 17, 1933, in *Freedman*, p. 164.

157. Interview with Louis Henkin; Paul A. Freund, "Charles Evans Hughes as Chief Justice," 81 *Harvard Law Review* 1967.

158. *Harlan Fiske Stone*, pp. 526–527.

159. Review of *Law and Politics*, Felix S. Cohen, *New Republic*, November 22, 1939; *Law and Politics*, p. XXIII.

160. *Harlan Fiske Stone*, p. 531.

161. Joseph P. Lash, *A Friend's Memoir* (New York, 1964), p. 159; *Freedman*, pp. 699–701.

162. Lilienthal, *op. cit.*, p. 549; J. Woodford Howard, *Mr. Justice Murphy* (Princeton, 1968), p. 263; Felix Frankfurter, COHP, p. 309; Arthur M. Schlesinger, Jr., "The Supreme Court: 1947," *Fortune*, January 1947.

163. Louis L. Jaffee, "The Judicial Universe of Mr. Justice Frankfurter," 62 *Harvard Law Review* 1949. C. Herman Pritchett, *The Roosevelt Court* (New York, 1948), p. 135.

164. Felix S. Cohen, *The Legal Conscience* (Yale, 1960), pp. 169–170.

165. Pp. 49–50.

166. *Tribute*, pp. 110–111.

167. *Harlan Fiske Stone*, pp. 615–616.

168. Felix Frankfurter to Franklin D. Roosevelt, September 3, 1939, in *Freedman*, p. 499; *Phillips*, p. 76.

169. *Stimson*, p. 334.

170. *Harlan Fiske Stone*, pp. 165–166.

171. *Berle*, October 24, 1941; November 18, 1941, p. 377.

172. *Harlan Fiske Stone*, p. 503; Learned Hand, COHP, p. 130.

173. Paul A. Freund, *Of Law and Justice* (Cambridge, 1968), pp. 222–223.

174. *Mr. Justice Murphy*, p. 269.

175. Gardner Jackson, COHP, p. 396; James M. Landis, COHP, p. 96; interview with Lloyd K. Garrison.

176. Pritchett, *op. cit.*, p. 132.

177. COHP, p. 101.

178. *Holmes-Laski*, February 27, 1930, p. 1224.

179. Tully, *op. cit.*, p. 290; interview with Hugo L. Black, Jr., Lilienthal, *op. cit.*, pp. 625–626.

180. Interview with Hugo L. Black, Jr., FPLC.

181. *Dennis v. United States*, 391 U.S. 494, 521 (1951).

182. Interview with Louis Henkin; Robert Jackson, *The Supreme Court in the American System of Government* (Cambridge, 1955), p. 4; *Terminiello v. Chicago*, 337 U.S. 1, 37 (1949).

183. *United States v. Lovett*, 328 U.S. 303 (1946); interview with Hugo L. Black, Jr.

184. Helen S. Thomas, *Felix Frankfurter: Scholar on the Bench* (Johns Hopkins, 1960), p. 65.

185. *Law and Politics*, p. 192.

186[a]. Hugo L. Black, *A Constitutional Faith* (New York, 1968), p. 30.

186[b]. Hugo L. Black, *op. cit.*, p. 38.

186[c]. Scottsboro article in New York *Times*, November 13, 1932, reprinted in *Law and Politics*, interviews with Benjamin V. Cohen and Herbert Wechsler.

187. Louis L. Jaffee, "The Judicial Universe of Mr. Justice Frankfurter," 62 *Harvard Law Review* 1949; interview with Alexander M. Bickel.

188. Reprinted in *The Supreme Court: Views from the Inside*, edited by Alan F. Westin (New York, 1961), p. 82. The lecture was delivered November 18, 1947.

189. Interview with Alexander M. Bickel.

190. James F. Byrnes, "The Supreme Court Must Be Curbed," *U.S. News and World Report*, May 18, 1956.

191. Felix Frankfurter, *Of Law and Men*, edited by Philip Elman (New York, 1956), p. 39.

192. Wallace Mendelson, *Justice Black and Frankfurter: Conflict in the Court* (Chicago, 1961), pp. 30, 31, 40.

193. *American Federation of Labor v. American Sash and Door Company*, 335 U.S. 538 (1959).

194. *Mr. Justice Murphy*, p. 180.

195. Jackson, *op. cit.*, p. 25.

196. *Ibid.*, p. 2.

197. Louis L. Jaffee, "Mr. Justice Jackson," 68 *Harvard Law Review* 1955.

198. *United States v. United Mine Workers*, 330 U.S. 250, 308 (1947).

199. Paul A. Freund, *Harvard Law Review*, 1969, p. 1595.

200. Paul A. Freund, *"The Supreme Court and Civil Liberties,"* 4 *Vanderbilt Law Review* 1951.

201. Henry J. Abraham, *Justice and Presidents* (New York, 1974), pp. 289–290.

202. *Freedman*, p. 29.

203. *Harvard Law Review*, November 1962.

204. *Tribute*, pp. 57–58; interview with Louis Henkin.

205. *Freedman*, p. 744.

From the Diaries of Felix Frankfurter

((1911))

A YOUNG MAN GOES
TO WASHINGTON

The Diary opens with Frankfurter working in the Taft Administration for Henry L. Stimson, who had recently become Secretary of War. William Howard Taft, a rotund, lethargic man, was one of the more ineffective Presidents of the United States, whose faith, wrote Charles Beard, was "in the fixedness of the moral principles which he learned at his mother's knee." Other industrialized societies, such as the British, were responding under the leadership of Lloyd George and Winston Churchill to business fluctuations and working-class and agricultural unrest with the first increments of what later came to be known as the welfare state, but in the United States under Taft the doctrine of laissez faire reigned supreme, but not unchallenged. Senator LaFollette in Congress was the leader of a group of Senators who reflected agrarian revolt and who were trying to enact reform measures of the kind that had been instituted in some of the western states. Theodore Roosevelt, although he had hand-picked Taft as his successor, was moving under the banner of Progressivism toward his historic break. National unrest had been registered in the 1910 elections by a Democratic sweep that had included New York State, where Stimson, with Frankfurter as his one-man Brain Trust, had run for Governor as the ally of Theodore Roosevelt and had lost.

TRANSCRIPTION OF THE DIARY OF FELIX FRANKFURTER

Washington, October 20, 1911

I have always rebelled against diaries as expressive of dull and rather petty spirits. There is something dwarfing about the thought of daily bookkeeping of the daily routine. Of course unconsciously the necessity of system which is involved would be prohibitive to my leisurely and freedom-yearning habits. Yet I have felt from time to time that events out of the ordinary—that is out of the ordinary for ourselves—should be preserved for their own sakes and for the pleasure of reminiscence in whatever amber of permanence this halting pen of mine can give them. I am fortunate enough to meet men of rare spirit, of vaulting vision and fine deeds. Their talk, my experience in such encounters deserve to be embalmed for I cannot as hopefully as I once assumed rely on a faithful memory. To myself I must confess the dread secret of time's corrosive effect even on *my* retentive faculties. So I will sit me down, from time to time, as often as the spirit guides desire and the will is strong enough to give it expression, things that seem worth while—obiter dicta of intrinsic worth, whoever the utterer, illuminating gossip of men of real interest, things of permanent interest in the passing show, not the mere tittle tattle that passes current for conversation. For my own amusement I shall thus try to hold fast the fleeting sparks and preserve some of the bounties of animated spirits and wholesome souls.

Tonight is a good curtain raiser. I have had a good visit with Mrs. Stimson. She is a very genuine personality who always gives me a sense of human dignity and amplitude and faith in endeavor. Her bearing under the new honors and rank that have come to her additionally endear her to me. She doesn't care a farthing for straps and struts; she is unchanged by a hair's breadth from what she was after H. L. S.'s defeat for governor. She is a splendid type of the middle of the road woman who has a strong individuality, outside interests of her own and inside opinions but yet whose essential career is through her husband. But it is her downright, militant honesty that tremendously appeals to me. She not only can't be untruthful but she even has a hard job to keep her tongue when she is not really called upon to assert her faith. It is a most trying situation she is in therefore: intensely happy, in a rather objective way, that an opportunity for permanently useful public service should have come to Mr. S., she has her enthusiasm constantly checked by her complete lack of sympathy with the general trend of the Administration and her lack of faith in the President's capacity for leadership. She is a loyal woman, unusually so, for her loyalty is essentially to ideals, convictions, however vaguely she may have worked them out, rather than to men. And not an alloy of her own or her husband's selfish future enters into her viewpoints. And her political outlook is good. She has a good head, though not acutely intellectual, to which she joins the essential sympathetic attitude and the democratic faith and therefore she gets very far in her political thinking. There is indeed a fine and rare harmony between the two Stimsons in their devotion to things worth while, in their effective idealism and their warm-hearted but dignified humanity. I am fortunate in their almost paternal interest in me, an interest however without a touch of patronage so that I really feel myself a young companion of both of them.

Mrs. S. told me a recent talk she had with the Colonel about things political. He is still unforgiving for Pinchot's [1] tepid support of Stimson and Roose-

---

[1] Gifford Pinchot, leader of the conservation movement, had been removed by Taft as Chief Forester of the United States, and was goading Roosevelt toward the break with Taft.

velt in their last year's fight; he said knowing as he did T. R. and H. L. S., their years of joint labor, his attitude was nothing short of "mean." I felt so at the time, but, as I told Mrs. S., Pinchot could not swallow what he thought was a weak compromise in the platform in praising the national administration and the tariff and he had then gotten to such a state of religious exaltation in his opposition to Taft et al. that he was ready to sacrifice his lifelong possessions of rich friendships in behalf of his Cause. Mrs. S. had a fine glow for Pinchot's singlemindedness, his crusader's spirit and forgives him the consequent limitations. T. R. thought that Pinchot's Saturday Evening Post article was a strong statement of his position, didn't mind the publication of the letter P. wrote him in December 1909, but wished he had omitted the "Dear Theodore." I had the same feeling when I read the article though I realized that Pinchot never thought of such a detail.

T. R. thought Taft's speeches very poor, says he does not think out his ideas but on the whole he said T. was yet a better man than Harrison or McKinley, "for Taft has some convictions and they didn't have any." This rather surprises me as far as Harrison is concerned for the little I know of him tends the other way, but as to McK., the sainted martyr, it hits off the feeling I've always had except I always gave him credit for the conviction that our manufacturers should have all the tariff support at the hands of the government that the claims of infancy saw fit to make for them.[2]

Talked with Mrs. S. about the possibility of S.'s nomination for V.-P. She properly is dead set against it but fears the possibility of such a frame-up. I told her that it would be wicked and feared his election even more than his defeat. This must be blocked.

Lunched today with Brandeis and Denison.[3] Talked mostly about Sherman Law, B. pointing out that combinations of a monopolistic character have

[2] History's verdict on Benjamin Harrison sustains Roosevelt rather than Frankfurter. An Indiana lawyer, he campaigned in 1888 with a war chest filled by the nation's manufacturers, who feared tariff reduction, and defeated Grover Cleveland, the first Democratic President in twenty-four years, for reelection. He proceeded to raise the tariff and lost to Cleveland in 1892. In 1896 William McKinley, who had sired the high tariff bill of the Harrison Administration, defeated William Jennings Bryan, the spokesman of labor and agrarian discontent, for the presidency, defending the gold standards against Bryan's inflationary bimetallism. It was under McKinley that the United States went to war with Spain in 1898 and emerged an imperial power, responsible for Cuba, Puerto Rico, the Philippines, and the Hawaiian Islands. They were under the jurisdiction of the War Department's Bureau of Insular Affairs, of which Frankfurter was the Law Officer. In September 1901, McKinley was assassinated by an anarchist and was succeeded by Theodore Roosevelt of Rough Rider fame.

[3] Louis D. Brandeis (1856–1941) had achieved the highest grades ever recorded at the Harvard Law School and had made himself financially independent by thirty. He had become known as "the people's lawyer." He considered the Sherman Anti-Trust Act ineffective and in opposing an increase in railroad freight rates had spoken of the "curse of bigness." In early 1911 he supplied Senator "Fighting Bob" LaFollette with suggestions for strengthening the Sherman Act that had been embodied in the LaFollette-Stanley Anti-Trust bill. Winfred T. Denison had been in the United States Attorney's office with Frankfurter and had come to Washington as an Assistant Attorney General. He lived at the "House of Truth" along with Frankfurter.

not justified themselves in their alleged economies. Perfectly easy to get back to effective competition but he admitted there should be allowance for proper trade practices to be supervised by, say, Bureau of Corporations and that the time has arrived for particularity as to the indicia of monopoly such as is proposed by the La Follette bill. Brandeis has depth and an intellectual sweep that are tonical. He has great force; he has Lincoln's fundamental sympathies. I wish he had his patience, his magnanimity, his humor. Brandeis is a very big man, one of the most penetrating minds I know; I should like to see him Attorney General of the United States.

October 22, 1911

Ran into the Solicitor General, Mr. Lehmann,[1] and had good talk with him about the Supreme Court's vacancy, Taft and the Sherman Law. He expressed the rather commonplace objections to government service for lawyers, away from your home town, etc.; said he won't stay here long, to which I replied he'd be shelved before long on the Supreme Court. He retorted, "I have neither fears nor hope." To his mind, the President ought not to appoint another Democrat; he has appointed two—Lamar and Lurton—and promoted another to the Chief Justiceship. There has been a good deal of grumbling and there is no need to invite further criticism. "If the President asked me I would tell him not to appoint me or any other Democrat or Independent," was his fine bit of intellectual honesty of conviction, and he expressed it with vigor. As an abstract proposition it sounds well enough to say the Supreme Court is independent of partisan considerations, "but we are men of flesh and blood and not abstractions." The President, he thought, is facing a most difficult situation and there is no need of making additional enemies.[2]

I suggested that the President will be fortunate to get his views for he is badly in need of disinterested advisers. L. assented to this, adding "He is indeed in a most unfortunate situation." In a way he is the Van Buren of his party—despite Shepard's apologies for Van Buren. I thought this a most memorable comparison. "Like Van Buren he was the choice and nominee of his predecessor and hardly any man can satisfy such a role—on the one hand either avoid

---

[1] Frederick W. Lehmann, former President of the American Bar Association and a distinguished St. Louis attorney, was serving as Solicitor General.

[2] "The condition of the Supreme Court is pitiable and yet those old fools hold on with a tenacity that is most discouraging," Taft had complained in 1909 to his old associate, Circuit Judge Horace Lurton. In the intervening two years he had appointed Lurton and Joseph P. Lamar and elevated Edward D. White to the Chief Justiceship. All were conservatives from the South. With the appointment at the end of 1911 of Mahlon Pitney, a New Jersey Republican, Taft in his single term had appointed six men to the Court, and he felt, wrote his biographer Henry F. Pringle, that he had obtained a Court that "would protect the Constitution from attacks by Roosevelt and other progressives."

slavish devotion and thus loss of self-respect or condemnation through departure from his predecessor's policy." [3]

Then again there is a rift in the party with the Sherman Law situation to embarass it. L. disagrees with the President as to the Sherman Law. Law inadequate—legislation like other Sherman Act (silver purchase) "sop to Cerberus" and not careful legislation. Problem is how to deal with corporate organizations national in character. Prophesies much travail—his own mind tends toward administrative national regulation but hasn't deeply thought it out.

On the whole my talk confirms previous impressions I had of Lehmann: A very vigorous personality, of militant intellectual honesty and ample courage. A warm friend and delightful comrade, a strong, forceful advocate but much below Lloyd Bowers' [4] intellectual stature. Bowers was really a commanding intellect; Lehmann has a good mind, seasoned with much experience and study.

The Sherman Anti-Trust Act of 1890, wrote Charles Beard, "was vague in language and not enforced in practice." [1] *Theodore Roosevelt instituted more actions under its provisions than all of his predecessors, earning for himself the sobriquet "Theodore the meddler." Taft followed him in this, but the public was demanding a tougher, more precise antitrust law, and the experts were divided over whether the objective should be regulation or dissolution of the large trusts.*

Stimson as United States Attorney had prosecuted several antitrust actions and emerged from that experience "with a dual conviction—first, that effective federal regulation of large corporations in interstate commerce was absolutely essential, and second, that what Joseph H. Choate called 'government by indictment' was a most unsatisfactory method of arriving at his goal. . . . Both the public interest and the selfish interest of honorable businessmen required a more careful statement of the law governing competition and a more flexible instrument for federal supervision of business practice." [2]

Frankfurter in a letter to Stimson, September 9, 1911, [3] *had urged him to use the Kansas City speech "to identify the Republican Party in the public mind as the liberal party" and to do this by dealing with the central problem, "the changed industrial condition, the dependence or rather interdependence of peo-*

---

[3] Martin Van Buren of New York, a Democrat, was eighth President of the United States, serving from 1837 to 1841. His predecessor was Andrew Jackson, whose Secretary of State he had been. *Martin Van Buren* by E. M. Shepard (Boston, 1899).

[4] Lloyd Bowers had preceded F. W. Lehmann as Solicitor General.

[1] *Charles A. Beard,* The Rise of American Civilization *(New York, 1927), II, p. 569.*

[2] *Henry L. Stimson,* On Active Service in Peace and War *(New York, 1948), pp. 44–45.*

[3] *Library of Congress (hereinafter, L.C.).*

ple . . . a discarding of the old laissez-faire *philosophy, a frank recognition of the problems of modern capitalism and labor, and the growing need of a social program." He suggested various forms of government regulation and thought legislation based on careful ascertainment of the facts would meet the test of constitutionality and cited the success of the "Brandeis brief" in the* Muller *case in which the Court had upheld Oregon's ten-hour law for women.*

Frankfurter's approach was close to that outlined by Theodore Roosevelt in his 1910 Osawatomie speech that had been so terrifying to conservatives. "The way out," Roosevelt had declared, "lies, not in attempting to prevent such combinations, but in completely controlling them in the interests of the public welfare." He had suggested an increase in the powers both of the Federal Bureau of Corporations and the Interstate Commerce Commission. Brandeis, by contrast, was advocating a program that would restore competition. He felt that small, competing companies were more efficient than large corporations, even if supervised and regulated by the government.

October 23

Stimson returned today from his southwestern trip full of the zest and vigor that his western trips always give him, as tho he were nursed by the perennial thought of the mountains. Had a good hearty pow-wow with him about things in general, the ascertainable political condition, the President's trip. I confirmed his impression that the President in his speeches hadn't been able to "get across with it." Tho that very morning S. had a letter from Hilles [4] telling of the President's great satisfaction with his trip. I'm afraid that Taft makes the smile and applause of his audience go pretty far; he has the optimism of the nearsighted. Canvassed with S. at length the Trust situation and the great uncertainty caused by Taft's apparent reversal of his previous position in regard to the Sherman Law—the need of specific prohibitions supplemented by federal incorporation or the like—and his present sublime satisfaction with the lucidity which the Supreme Court has given that provoking statute. Told him he ought to try to correct situation in his Kansas City speech. Difficult, of course, because Taft apparently now committed to immutability of Sherman Law as last word on the subject, but felt still a chance to show that Taft has been a pioneer "constructive statesman" on the subject of efficient regulation versus strangulation, i.e., Butte and Columbus speeches. Read his utterances on this trip again and evident that T. has not entirely burnt his bridges behind him—real mischief his ambiguity as to his real purpose. In truth he hasn't thought the thing out or given it comprehensive consideration.

From other details and correspondence perfectly evident Taft has a happy-

---

[4] Charles D. Hilles, Secretary to the President and his political manager. He had served as intermediary between Taft and Stimson in offering the latter a spot in the Cabinet.

go-lucky mind—none of that intellectual campaigning, that look ahead as far as his head and that of his advisers or assistants will carry him that Stimson, for instance, brings to his work. What a delicious illustration a comparison of Taft and T. R. affords of the truth that people persist in easily acceptable assumptions totally belied by the facts. For Taft is supposed to have been the careful, judicial thinker, T. R. the rough rider, snapshot performer, while in truth T. R. thought profoundly or at least got all the available thinking of others but was denied the reasoning faculty simply because he acted expeditiously and pyrotechnically. You mustn't think too fast or having thought act so everyone could understand it if you would gain a reputation for judicialmindedness.

What a tonical presence Stimson is! He is full of clean, forceful thinking, an ardent public servant, thoroughly democratic but harnesses his ultimate aspirations to efficiency lest they run into sand. How much more effective his loyalty would have been as a member of T. R.'s cabinet, and the Colonel would have used him as an affirmative force; how much of S.'s time and talent are consumed in preventing breaks or minimizing those that have been made.

October 24

A wonderful morning gave me a rare joy of living on my morning ride. The morning air is crisp and the sky has an unspoiled freshness. Then too I seem to find more and more satisfaction in trees and foliage and the dancing leaves. Ran into the Attorney General [1] and rode with him. He was exceedingly cordial and genuinely friendly. Spoke very warmly of the outcome of the Heike case.[2] Then on it was a continuous, bubbling talk. He is kaleidoscopic and cinematographic, as Holmes, J.,[3] would say. Like Puck he girdles the globe. We talked of early morning exercise, Spanish jurisprudence, the German civil code and the comparative precision of definitions, American codifications versus the Sugar Cases, the increasing enforcement of law, Croly,[4]

---

[1] George W. Wickersham, Attorney General, a strong believer in the sufficiency of the Sherman Act if energetically enforced.

[2] *Heike v. United States*, 192 Fed. 83 (2nd Cir. 1911), affirmed, 227 U.S. 131 (1913). Heike, a sugar importer, appealed his conviction for fraudulent avoidance of the payment of duties on certain shipments of raw sugar. He argued that he was immune from prosecution as a result of his earlier testimony before a grand jury investigating possible antitrust violations by the sugar refining company of which he was an officer. A federal statute provided that an individual subpoenaed in such circumstances could not refuse to testify on Fifth Amendment grounds, but that having testified he could not be prosecuted for any matter about which he had testified. The Court of Appeals, in the case mentioned by Frankfurter, affirmed the conviction, finding the connection between Heike's testimony as a corporate officer on antitrust matters and his activities in evading import duties too attenuated to entitle him to immunity. Frankfurter as an Assistant U.S. Attorney had been involved in the original sugar case prosecutions.

[3] Associate Justice Oliver Wendell Holmes.

[4] Herbert Croly's *Promise of American Life*, called by Frankfurter "a notable, seminal book." Judge Learned Hand had brought Croly and Frankfurter together as kindred spirits.

Promise of American Life, and Oliver's Hamilton,[5] naturally leading into a discussion of Hamilton, according to him the ablest mind of America, Jefferson "the most baneful influence in American politics whose cult is the worship of ends," Jackson and his "blatant vulgarity," Hearst, Collier's—he couples the two—Lord Acton and Cromer's Egypt,[6] the Philippines, the lack of responsible newspapers with the possible return to pamphleteering—poor Lodge [7] told him he is much misunderstood in Massachusetts and can't get his side told—etc. etc. He talks glibly and attractively with all the outward indicia of omniscience. Wickersham has a vivid, fresh, agile, prehensile mind, but "I suspicion" pretty much as superficial as my own with considerable ability to mobilize effectively and quickly all his intellectual assets. He certainly is delightful and warmhearted, a whole souled man. But his statesmanship is of the aristocratic school—he is a thoroughly disinterested and fairly unconscious exponent of the school that the chosen should rule—and he's the chosen. I hear no little that he may go on the bench—can have it if he wants it. He certainly will stoutly "defend the Constitution" against "modern innovations." If we must have him in the service, I'd rather see him on the bench than in the Cabinet.

Wickersham illustrates the difficulty of correct contemporary appraisal. Those who don't know him and judge him merely by his performance have no conception of the humane, likable, generous-minded side of the man; those who see his attractive personal sides imperceptibly become blinded to his limitations in faith and intellect as a democratic statesman or delude themselves that so lovable a man must be a promoter of the public welfare.

Good talk with H. L. S. about his proposed speech. Wickersham tells him to write it and convince the President. Wick much disturbed by Taft's attitude. Said he had no consultation with the President about his speeches or his position twice announced. What an amazing light this casts on the President—tackling one of the overshadowing questions without consultations with his officers. W. said President knows nothing of business, has never had to advise business and hasn't thought problem out. The evidence is daily accumulating that Taft is not an able man at all. Crowder [8] is of that opinion as a result of having seen him closely for about a year when he first came to the Philip-

---

[5] *Alexander Hamilton* by Frederick S. Oliver (New York, 1908).

[6] Lord Acton, John E. E. D. Acton (1834–1902) English historian, Roman Catholic publicist, friend and political adviser of William E. Gladstone, a strong Liberal. He is remembered for his trenchant observations on the corrupting effects of power. Lord Cromer, Evelyn Baring Cromer, British agent in Egypt from 1883 to 1907. He believed in giving Egyptian authorities a wide freedom in administration under the umbrella of British rule. His policy was adopted by the Liberal government of Herbert Asquith. It was of interest to Frankfurter, who as Law Officer of the Bureau of Insular Affairs was struggling with similar problems in America's new dependencies.

[7] Henry Cabot Lodge, Senator from Massachusetts, for many years Theodore Roosevelt's closest friend.

[8] Enoch H. Crowder was the Judge Advocate General. Frankfurter, whose office was next to his, considered him "a first-class brain."

pines—an impression that Buck [9] and I had very decidedly when he was a candidate. But "if you get a reputation for early rising you can sleep all day" and "Bill Taft" has been deemed a big man too long for human inertia—that embalmer of good or bad, whether deserved or not—to have any other opinion. Stimson asked me to think along this line with a view of his drafting a speech to be submitted to Taft, "perhaps we can show him that he has been a constructive thinker on this question all along." Talked Taussig [10] to H. L. S. and gave him book to read. Suggested that Stimson in his speech can sound situation, giving President three weeks preliminary education in public opinion before message due. Stimson is impatient that President is swinging around instead of working here on hammering out his policy and message.

Talked Porto Rico citizenship with H. L. S.[11] He drafted letter to Dr. Borbosa (?) of Porto Rico asserting his belief in their fitness for citizenship but denying possible implication of statehood—ideal autonomous insular government under U. S. rather than state government by Washington. Suggested that qualifications unnecessary—will do no good, demand for citizenship and with feeler as first step to statehood and might do harm by "opening flood gates to academic discussion." Phrase seemed to tickle him and rather agreed with view.

Delightful evening with Dobbin Denison and his sister. Had good talk—he is a generous spirit, with plenty of self assurance for the good of others. Worries whether to become a judge or not—really thinks himself more fitted for higher secular leadership and I am not sure but that he is right. His sister is fresh and lovely, revelling in the richness of Washington life and absorbed in Winnie's future and greatness. How deeply women sink themselves in others—someone must be the object of their devotion, what a heap of generous thinking they bring to life and yet there are fools who prate about the danger of losing womanhood through too much masculinity! Most men ought to be cut off from these unearned, even unappreciated benefits of womanhood. Score one for Win Dennison as a really deserving one. I'll top off the night by reading LaFollette's autobiography [12] in the November American. As Denison, LaFollette's stock is going up with us.

---

[9] Emory R. Buckner, classmate at Harvard Law School and an Assistant U. S. Attorney with Frankfurter in Stimson's office.

[10] Frank W. Taussig was a professor of political economy at Harvard and a leading authority on the tariff.

[11] Puerto Rico was an American dependency under the jurisdiction of the War Department's Bureau of Insular Affairs.

[12] Robert M. LaFollette, Republican Senator from Wisconsin. Under his leadership Wisconsin had become the most progressive state in the Union, pioneering especially in electoral reform. His drumfire attacks in the Senate on the plutocracy produced walk-outs by his conservative colleagues, and until Theodore Roosevelt threw his hat into the ring, he was the leader of the "progressives" and their candidate for President in 1912. His *Autobiography* appeared in book form in 1913.

October 25

Spent a pleasant evening at the Edwardses,[1] together with Chandler Hale, Third Assistant Secretary of State, the rather flippantly bright—doncher know diplomatic type—son of the unlamented stand-pat and utter conservative Senator Hale of Maine. It's a truism that the company determines the character of conversation. As a result I maintained the cheap level of tittle tattle, superficial phrases of Edwards and his spouse. What an inordinate, childishly conceited person the general is. I have yet to hear a reference to an event or thought—big or little—that he hadn't had a hand in or analogously experienced. Crowder hit off one phase cleverly when he said Edwards "has to be inaccurate to keep up his volubility." He is extremely superficial, the most thoughtless kind of judgment and totally ignorant of the big forces that are at work in the country. In matters of economics and social needs he is a babe. And yet he writes to the President on the assumption of a master political adviser. How much stock the President takes in him I don't know. His home is full of evidence of Taft's personal affection. Edwards has force, volubility, and capacity to make superficial impression—all these go far. But he certainly is not an able man—utterly indiscreet and insufferably, no, amusingly vain—if you don't hear him too often. Very nice to me and helpfully friendly—regards me as "Stimson's man" and treats me as if I had status. This has more or less filtrated through and I enjoy the pleasantest feelings and relations with the War Department officials—other generals, service chiefs, etc. It makes me smile and at times sad, for it shows the necessity of having a status down here to have full opportunities for effective work and full utilization of the great opportunities of Washington life in the way of rare men worth while and contact with "the inside."

Mrs. Edwards is a lively, unattractive—though I am told even ten years ago she was really handsome—gossipy "live wire," the kind cheap novelists would call "a woman of the world"—with her approval. She has a rather racy tongue, concerned with the vital small talk of Society as viewed by Town Topics; and yet—Senator Root [2] is one of her "dearest friends" and the friend's picture dedicated with "affectionate regards" is prominently displayed on her walls. The Senator, incidentally, thinks highly of the general's ability. I wonder if it is the old confusion and he is thinking of the wife's attractions. Mrs. Edwards tells me Root has dinner with them—or would—once a week. I wonder how he can stand it or the basis of his selection.

---

[1] Major General Clarence R. Edwards was head of the Bureau of Insular Affairs.

[2] Elihu Root, Senator from New York, Secretary of State under Theodore Roosevelt. He gave Stimson his first job after Harvard Law School, and in 1897 the firm became Root, Howard, Winthrop and Stimson. A moderate Republican, he was Stimson's "great adviser, friend, senior partner and idol."

October 26

Spent the day on considerable insular business, educational and finance. Appeased Dexter, [Edward G.] the Commissioner of Education of Porto Rico who is being fired because he is following the academic tack with disregard of the industrial needs of the island. Accomplished plan of sending Meyer Bloomfield of Boston [1] to visit island with the view of formulating educational program appropriately adapted to needs of P. R. Dexter fell in with the scheme as soon as he was made to feel not in criticism of him; intimated he would be glad to invite Bloomfield, so before Dexter saw Stimson I slipped a note to Stimson to suggest to Dexter that in public statement about visit of Bloomfield it will be stated that visit of B. made at invitation of Governor [George R.] Colton of Porto Rico *and Dr. Dexter.* The latter's feelings and dignity will thus [be] preserved and I feel the better that the public object was accomplished without private hurt of a very faithful official. It seems to me in most cases some thoughts of others and little capacity for adjustment will go far to [one word illegible] and further reforms by preventing friction and even enlisting the support or at least avoiding opposition of possible victims of reform.

Had most interesting evening with E. B. Bruce, a prominent lawyer of Philippines. Enthusiastic about island's future, wouldn't think of returning to New York. The [one word illegible] of economic development of Philippine Islands and deflection of men's minds from angry political discussion seems to grip him. Speaks warmly of Governor [Cameron] Forbes [2] as only big mind over there in Govt's service. Told me of proposed Democratic effort at forthcoming session to put Taft in hole by passing independence resolution and efforts to [one word illegible] it, among others Martin Egan's work with Cardinal Gibbons and Bishops to bring force of Catholic Church to bear against actions for stable gov't of course desired by Church. I am more and more conscious of the powerful *political* pressure exerted by that institution. I am fearful only of the underground character of its operations—it is the one big force of modern society that successfully shuns the sunshine of publicity and frankness.

Bruce also spoke of the seething social forces at work in Japan. Evidently the patriotic enslavement in behalf of the state, the theory of self-immolation is challenged by the query "cui bono" and the pressures of economic troubles are beginning to tell. Says a strong Socialistic movement headed by sober and able leadership. The trend towards an economic and social readjustment towards a wider and deeper democracy is clearly worldwide.

Talked at length with H. L. S. over his trust speech and Taft's attitude on

[1] Meyer Bloomfield, associate of Brandeis, lawyer, social worker, specialist in vocational education and "the new profession of handling men." His assignment resulted in a report to Stimson, "A study of certain social, educational, and industrial problems in Porto Rico."

[2] Cameron Forbes was Governor General of the Philippines.

question. Referred to Taft's remark in a speech the day before, "save me from a candid friend" and wondered if he meant him for his plain speaking to him. Had recently written letter to Hilles, as result of my talk with him, advising President of state of unrest and recommending President to direct attention toward three vital questions—business and tariff, forgot to mention parcel post—and not indulge in unreadable, conventionally long message. Says President doesn't take kindly to criticism and doesn't like it. He thus clearly shows one great lack of leadership—ability to bear with and get different viewpoints. Have felt all along his friends are flatterers—like Edwards—and determines policies on a basis of personal good fellowship. Stimson says Taft is an enigma to him—he doesn't seem to be able to get up drive, doesn't think thoroughly and is stubborn. It's as clear as daylight that he totally lacks capacity for effective leadership in a modern democracy, and I think Brandeis is right that Taft doesn't care, he has no abiding convictions about the things that are the vital issues of the day.

October 27

Worked most of the day with H. L. S. on his Kansas City speech. What a great treat it is to be associated with a clearheaded thinker, who plows as deep as he can through an astounding ability to concentrate, doesn't fool himself about what he doesn't know and has a mind fresh and ready to meet suggestions or criticism. The speech will point out widespread uncertainty in business, need for greater definition in Sherman Law supplemented by constructive legislation to oversee operations of industrial corporations similar to national bank and Interstate Commerce Commission. Will make plea for spirit of moderation and intelligent thoughtfulness and necessary unpretentiousness of any reform in a problem so intricate and so much of an unknown social process. Effort to make Taft stand for it, despite his recent suggestion that Sherman Law is wholly adequate for situation by showing that he has been a pioneer constructive statesman for these reforms. The poor man won't realize what sound sense he talked years ago.

Excitement all over regard proceedings to dissolve steel trust.[1] H. L. S. told me that the A. G. told him he brought suit because "He was unwilling to assume responsibility of holding that steel trust was not a violation of Sherman Law." To my mind and to Stimson's (I think, though he didn't say so explic-

---

[1] Wickersham's suit to break up the steel trust was one of the factors that precipitated the final break between Taft and Roosevelt. The Government's suit claimed that Roosevelt in 1907 was tricked by the executives of the Steel Corporation into approving U. S. Steel's acquisition of the Tennessee Coal and Iron Company. An infuriated Roosevelt wrote that "the effort to restore competition as it was sixty years ago . . . is just as foolish as if we should go back to the flintlocks of Washington's Continentals as a substitute for modern weapons of precision." "Whatever the rights and wrongs of the situation," wrote Stimson, "it was certainly a most extraordinary charge for the lawyers of any administration to level without warning at an ex-President of their own party."

itly) this was a lack of courage on Wickersham's part. It seems to me he was not called upon to proceed unless affirmatively convinced there was a violation, if he did not think there was otherwise a large public interest to be subserved by suit.

Dinner tonight at Wickersham's, with Lehmann, Fowler, Denison, the other Assistant Attorneys General, [Charles] Earl of Commerce and Labor (a very nice fellow). On the whole these high law officers were a pretty ordinary lot. The A. G. however shines at a party—he is a fine host, brilliant at repartee, genial, effervescent. Really a warmhearted man but his great political limitations came out in sneers at T. R. Convicted the whole democratic movement as represented by them. He is a most likable man; I can see how social contact with such men gradually works an attrition of one's political estimate of their viewpoints. Verbum sap! [2] A fine big man is Lehmann. He sounded a courageous note when scoff was made about recall [3] by giving a fine outburst that crude, rude and ill-considered as such reform was there was good reason for its popularity, for the legal profession, next to the press, have been meanest, most selfish force in resisting just reforms and perpetuating public abuse in administration of laws. He has little patience with immunity of Courts from criticism and insists on their vigorous subjection to criticism. And yet for saying same thing as official leader of the U. S. bar, Roosevelt was reviled from Atlantic to Pacific as underminer of sacred Constitution. This sacrosanct notion of our judiciary must be hit whenever it can be effectively. There is a growing realization of this on the part of some wise judges but there is a natural tendency of self reverence by the members of an institution and it's up to the bar to keep alert eyes on our courts. They have failed and failed wretchedly because by training and selfish interests they are a conservative and timid body of the community. Thanks to T. R. there is live thought on the subject; the law schools too are showing signs of life. Few causes so appeal to me as the people's confirment [?] of the judges and their realization of the vital human rights that they are entrusted with. Had good time with Lehmann after dinner about all kinds of things—he is a broad, unusually well-read warmhearted man. "Beware," he says, of the man whose private habits are all perfect, and distrust "intellectual leadership," pointing to selfish leadership of Southern oligarchy before war—the worst intellectual leadership the country has had.

I could not help reflecting tonight, thinking of Taft and Wickersham, etc., the men who shape affairs now, how little of the magnanimity, the deep faith,

---

[2] *Verbum sap*, abbreviation for *verbum sat sapienti (est)*—"A word to the wise (is) sufficient."

[3] The recall of judges and of judicial decisions had been advocated by LaFollette and embraced by Theodore Roosevelt. The proposal to make it possible to recall judges was assailed as a threat to the independence of the judiciary and to the rights of property, but so great was the support for the movement that even President Taft was making speeches acknowledging that the judicial system was not working as it should. "Make your judges responsible," he said in St. Louis, September 23, 1911. "Impeach them. Impeachment of a Judge would be a very healthful thing in these times."

the humility of Lincoln they have. The more I see and hear of public affairs, the bigger he looms.

October 28

Continued with H. L. S. on speech. Bully good fun and all the intellectual stimulus that comes from contact with a more seasoned and wider mind on a basis of intellectual comradeship. He has the capacity to call forth the best there is in me and the intersection of our personalities is most vitalizing. He lacks Wick's brilliance but he is every inch a bigger, broader man, a much more useful counsellor of state, apart from the deeper democracy and finer faith.

October 29

Finished speech; trust it will go well. Stimson introduced me to Irving Fisher, the distinguished economist of Yale, a classmate of his, a simple modest man but of tremendous usefulness and public spirit.[1]

Had a good, cozy evening with Denisons. He and his sister still worrying whether he should be a judge. Since he is really disinclined he ought to dismiss it from his mind. I don't blame his sister for liking Washington—it makes the best appeal to the esthetic and social sides.

Had good talk with Christie [2] about line of our work. Shared experience that our friends think us damn fools but agreed that there is going to be increasing opportunity for public work and the ordinary practice is spiritless without real service and mainly impelled by money-making. If you like it, all right— but it doesn't begin to satisfy a fraction of the interest public work calls forth. Christie is an attractive fellow with a fine mind; still rather restless. He seems to have a deep emotional side which is not always administered to.

November 1

My daily prattle is crowded out by pressure of work. Life here is fascinatingly pleasant and insinuatingly distracting. Since I don't seem to discover any means of elongating the day, I'll have to get along with 24 hours by better utilization of time and necessary discrimination and sacrifice of secondary interests. President yesterday blurted out some more careless thinking about the

---

[1] Irving Fisher was currently arguing that the large corporations and trusts gave more thought and money to the conservation of human and natural resources than did small employers.

[2] Loring Christie, although a Canadian, was an assistant to Denison in the Attorney General's office. A graduate of the Harvard Law School, he roomed with Frankfurter in the House of Truth. In 1939 he was appointed Canadian Minister in Washington.

Sherman Law. It's pathetic the way he lets political fakers like Littleton [1] get away with a sound treatment of the question. Taft's latest talk necessitated recasting of some of Stimson's speech to avoid patent divergences of view. In speaking of the necessity for affirmative constructive legislation not overly negative prohibition I suggested the sentence, "In these days governmental activity must be productive not merely prohibitive." Stimson said, "I guess in view of Taft's talk about Socialism we can't use that," though he himself of course was in ready accord. It seems to me that illustrates the difficulty with the President as well as anything. He is certainly bucking the Zeitgeist tho I'm sure he doesn't know it. He lugs around with him a lot of untested assumptions, which he never puts to the test of facts or fitness to things; on the contrary he makes facts yield to them.

Had a wonderful evening with G. W. Kirchwey of Columbia who is all stirred up with his new Legislative Bureau group. [2] I think he has a great movement and with the right sort of devoted men much of his high hope will be realized. Spoke of my gradual connection with the group, working up from specific subjects. The thing appeals to me—one of my old hobbies—and wouldn't be surprised if one of these days I shall get into it. The temptation will be exceedingly enticing when I shall have to go back to private practice which appeals to me less and less.

November 3

The trust speech, after all, is to be stillborn! [1] H. L. S. called me in early this morning and told me rather startling changes in situation last two days. On

---

[1] Martin W. Littleton, Democratic Congressman from Queens, had attacked the Sherman Act as injurious to business before a Pittsburgh Chamber of Commerce meeting that was addressed the same evening by President Taft.

[2] George W. Kirchwey, Kent Professor of Law at Columbia Law School. His preoccupation was to demystify the law. It was not something of divine origin, he contended, and judges did not "find the law." Constitution and courts must reflect a nation's changing sense of right and wrong and of social justice.

[1] The trust speech was "stillborn," Stimson later wrote in On Active Service, because an indecisive Taft could not decide between men like Stimson, who argued T. R.'s case for regulation and not trust-busting, and Wickersham, who was content with the Sherman Act. In his annual message to Congress in December 1911, Taft adopted both positions, spending about eight to ten pages on a defense of the Sherman Law and the last two pages on Stimson's suggestions. Taft's straddle freed Stimson to deliver his Kansas City speech. It even included Frankfurter's line that Stimson feared Taft would consider socialistic, that the time had come for the government to exercise "its affirmative powers" to oversee and regulate corporate business engaged in interstate commerce. Frankfurter's deep involvement in the preparation of this speech is some corroboration of a letter that he wrote Arthur Schlesinger, Jr., in June 1963, stating that it was incorrect to assume, as Schlesinger had suggested, "that I saw completely eye to eye with Brandeis in socio-economic matters. . . ." The Clayton antitrust law of 1914, with its creation of a Federal Trade Commission to prevent unfair business practices, Stimson felt bore a "striking resemblance" to his own program.

Wednesday night, Oct. 1 [clearly meaning Nov.] saw Taft as he passed through here and outlined speech to him. The President told him to go ahead and deliver it—there is practically no divergence between them. Stimson told President to go slow, in view of possible misinterpretation and asked him to take speech with him to New York and read it. He, however, told President of insistence by Kansas City people for name of his subject and asked President whether he may announce his subject, and Taft said, "Go ahead and give them the subject." Stimson thereupon proceeded to wire that he was going to talk on "Sherman law and industrial problem." Last night President returned from New York, sent for S. and told him he read speech and considered matter carefully." Practically we are not at all apart," he said, "though I should amplify some things and differently emphasize," and after reflection, he said, he decided to treat the whole subject in his message and therefore thought Stimson perhaps better not anticipate the message. He was very apologetic about it and Stimson at midnight wired Kansas City that he'll speak on some problem connected with Panama instead of on Sherman law.

Stimson further told President need for crisp, telling message on four vital subjects—trusts, tariff, parcel post, arbitration and possibly currency and that he had taken it upon himself to give Chairman Emery [2] hell for not yet having wool report ready. President was startled when he heard the report was not *ready* and grateful to S. for putting on steam. President going to Hot Springs to map out "the circumference of his message" as Hilles phrases it.

The whole incident left a painful impression and a striking demonstration of Taft's lack of leadership and constructive thinking. Here he floats around the country talking on the industrial situation without having the thing at all thought out, without having formulated a definite policy after Cabinet consultation. In fact at least four members of his Cabinet felt the insufficiency of lack of his utterances on this subject. McVeagh, Wickersham, Nagel and Stimson. [3] With Taft as "coxswain," as Wickersham called him, the boat is just drifting. The tariff situation shows the same condition. He vetoes bills of reduction to await the full report and promises such report and then seems to take no telling measures that his Commission has such a report ready for the opening gun of Congress. Taft, amiable and well-intentioned, lacks vision and decision. He is indeed the tragedy of opportunities of greatness unrealized.

Stimson cheerfully said, "We'll have to find and solve some problem of the Panama Canal." Worked two days on matter and things seem fairly clear in big outlines. The need is for a definite centralized government, subordinating everything to running of Canal—the problem is the management of the great public work not the government of a republic. Secondly, general policy as to

[2] Henry C. Emery, Professor of Economics at Yale, was head of a three-man Tariff Board appointed by Taft to search out the facts relating to tariff revision.

[3] Franklin MacVeagh was Secretary of the Treasury. Charles Nagel was Secretary of Commerce and Labor; he was married to a sister of Brandeis.

tolls should be outlined so as to enable shipping world and merchants to adjust themselves to new trade routes. Details should be left in President's hands— need for flexibility, adjustment to varying facts, impossible to deal in Procrustean legislation. We're doing a great big job at Panama—will revolutionize trade movement of the world and add tremendously to military advantages of U. S. I haven't a particle of doubt that there still would be no Panama if T. R. hadn't been President at the time. The more I study his administration, the more detailed knowledge of the situation that confronted him, the more I contrast him with Taft, the more permanent his labors seem, the bigger his statesmanship. Boiled down, the points against him are aesthetic. He was a slugger—so is Lloyd George [4]—but there was need of slugging. And when his utterances are read as a whole they are marked by sobriety and remarkable consistency.

November 5

Sandwiched in during week miscellaneous things—industrial efficiency experiments in army are likely to encounter labor union opposition. Stimson saw point, shaped up statement and [rest of sentence illegible]. Difficult case of alleged discrimination against Jewish cadet at West Point—probably unduly suspicious but [two words illegible] articles bring out anew the deep causes for such susceptibility and suspicion—at my suggestion Stimson dispatched a Jewish officer of capability to West Point to investigate.

Saw something of Wood.[1] Fine blue [one word illegible] eyes—an intensely ambitious, aggrandizing man. Evidently jealous of his influence but a man of force, of decisive action, dynamic. He was very cordial—how they act reflects the attitude of the man at the top.

Had a delightful call with Señor Crespo, the Mexican Ambassador. He was formerly at Vienna, so we quickly found one another. A widely cultured Latin; with delightful Castillian disingenuousness, of simulated intensity of interest and friendship. A shrewd observer and a confirmed aristocrat. I found I could blarney a fact out as straight-facedly as he could—good conversational confetti.

---

[4] Lloyd George was Chancellor of the Exchequer in Asquith's Liberal Government. He represented the left wing of the Cabinet. Frankfurter frequently cited Lloyd George to Stimson.

[1] General Leonard Wood (1860–1927), Chief of Staff of the Army. He began his army career as a surgeon and as Colonel commanded the famous Rough Riders with T. R. as Lieutenant Colonel. Stimson considered him "the finest soldier of his acquaintance" until he dealt with General George C. Marshall. He was an advocate of preparedness in the face of Woodrow Wilson's opposition, a campaign in which he had the support of men like T. R. and Stimson and, within the Wilson Administration, of young Franklin D. Roosevelt. He was a candidate for the Republican nomination for President at the 1920 convention that chose Senator Warren G. Harding. In the 1920s he served as Governor-General of the Philippines.

November 6

Enjoyed again the subdued but stimulating company of General Crowder. He generates respect as few men do here—respect not unmixed with pity for his lonesomeness and his torturing neuralgia. He has a fine, clearcut mind, rather closely conservative—the military bent of obedience, excessive obedience to authority—but thoroughly honest and totally lacking in self-deception. He has driving ambition, a growing trait in him as I watch him, but ambition of a high intellectual order—to finish his career with some constructive work of statesmanship, preferably as governor of Cuba in case of another intervention, which is one of the probabilities of the not distant future. He'll never go down there again to hold the hand of "any nincompoop of a major general" that Wood might like to send down there.

Talk angled to Wood, whom Crowder thinks rather flighty and lawless. His thinking is too big and it runs to matters of persons and personal rule. Crowder rather confirmed my own impression thus far that Wood was a man of action and force but not of solid, far-seeing thinking. As Crowder put it, "He is apt, I doubt if he is able; he is quick-witted, but lacks a sense of proportion." I think he has T. R.'s speed without his stability, his vigor without his versatility. He is very attractive and superficially charms people.

Worked some more on Panama. H. L. S. hasn't got his heart in it as he had in trust speech. Telegram from Kansas City begging him to reconsider and talk on trust matter cut his emotional zest for his Panama speech—the little he had—[two words illegible] and led him to say, "I'd give $1,000 to make that trust speech." All of which and more leads me to wish I were down here while the surging, pervasive, dynamic personality of T. R. gave impetus and tone and passion to the government, and when he gathered about him the stout loyal band of able men, without ever a thought of *talking* loyalty. He was a motive force instead of ballast, a focuser and director. But the futility of waiting for the thing that is not; I can't keep thinking tho it will be amusing to read the "history" of the last ten years or so twenty years hence. As I read current comments even of a [one word illegible] character, I realize the universal significance of Lord Cromer's quiet observation—"I cannot say that what I have seen and [one word illegible] of contemporaneous events, with which I have been well acquainted, has inspired me with any degree of confidence in the accuracy of historical writing." Most of Cromer [1] I have still not yet had a chance to read—that and a dozen other books stare me in the countenance as charitable indictments of broken hopes. But the day, after repeated observations, does have only 24 hours. Outside of Lehmann I have yet to meet anyone here who does any reading to speak of—except Dr. Willmer [?],[2] during his three months vaca-

---

[1] Cromer's *Modern Egypt* in two volumes, 1908.

[2] "Dr. Willmer," if indeed that is the name written by Frankfurter in his almost illegible scrawl, could not be identified.

tion. Which reminds me that I haven't yet spoken of Willmer—the most tonical, rarest person I have yet met here. But I must reserve him for a word of real bubbling joy, of sunshine and the blue sky, when the sap of life runs fast and full of the worth of things.

November 21

Weeks have flown by since I have thrown the passing show on the screen of these pages. I've had a crowded, busy, loafing, variegated time of it. Seen much of Stimson, of Brandeis, had a fine talk in New York—Buck,[1] Sam,[2] Moskowitz,[3] Arthur Ludington,[4] Goodwin,[5] [name illegible]—and talks galore down here, with Senator Spooner,[6] Perry Osborne[?],[7] a man-to-man visit from Sanford, Freund.[8] The very competition of incidents scatters them all unless they are contemporaneously involved.

The work continues in variety and intensity and noninsularity. Just at present am wrestling with the exclusion of Christian Scientists from "practice" in the Canal Zone and the exclusion of Jews from Russia under our treaty. S. told me President much concerned over movement to abrogate treaty.[9] Fears

[1] Emory Buckner.

[2] Samuel J. Rosensohn had persuaded F. F. to go to Harvard Law School and F. F. shared his room the first two years there.

[3] Probably Henry Moskowitz, husband of Belle, friend and adviser of Alfred E. Smith, a leader of the Ethical Culture Society and a member of New York State's Factory Commission.

[4] Arthur C. Ludington, a leader of civic and political reform in New York and for a time an assistant to Woodrow Wilson when he was Governor of New Jersey.

[5] Russell P. Goodwin, an Assistant Attorney General.

[6] John C. Spooner of Wisconsin, an influential conservative Senator, later a leading New York attorney.

[7] Perry Osborne—not identifiable.

[8] Probably Ernst Freund, a distinguished legal scholar.

[9] Czarist Russia, as part of an anti-Semitism that was official policy, imposed crushing disabilities on Russian Jews. It restricted them to towns within the Pale of Settlement, prevented them from owning land, imposed a *numerus clausus*, and encouraged pogroms as a method of combating the revolutionary movement. United States Jews were in the forefront of the worldwide protests against these policies, and the Czarist Government in retaliation refused to recognize the passports of American citizens who were Jews. This violated the treaty of 1832 which provided for equality of treatment of the citizens of both countries. As a consequence a powerful movement had developed in Congress calling on the Administration to denounce the treaty.

The "Kishineff" massacre in 1903, in which some fifty Jews were slaughtered, six hundred injured, and hundreds of shops and homes pillaged, had produced universal revulsion with American leaders, governmental and private, in the forefront of the protest movement. In the trials that followed the massacre it had been shown that the reactionary Czarist government, hard pressed by liberalizing forces at home, had connived at the pogroms as a means of diverting the attention of the people from the agitation and activities of the reformers and revolutionaries.

In December 1911, after the House of Representatives had passed a resolution demanding abrogation of the 1832 treaty, President Taft informed Congress, without any reference to the House's

nothing will be accomplished except to induce further repressive measures against Russian Jews. President really friendly to Jewish viewpoint but has no program to meet situation. I think before abrogating treaty effort should be made to make moral demonstration and thus cow even Russia. Suggested to Stimson that President Eliot—now abroad—be commissioned as official ambassador to present America's position but *publicly* and thus get effect similar to Kishineff. He thought that hardly the dramatic material to which I replied that there is enough for the pens of Root and Eliot to generate moral fervor. Am communicating with Henry and Morris Cohen [10] for their ideas and information. Denison and [name illegible] Goodwin think the Eliot suggestion very effective way of handling it. The President seems to take seriously Russia's claim that public opinion prevents her desire to accord equal treatment to Jews. Told Stimson that President does not seem to be familiar with revelations that pogroms were induced by St. Petersburg whenever it wanted to deflect attention from local difficulties. "Get the material so I can show it to the President—the only way to get him to act is to get him mad!"

President now wrestling with trust problem. Working hard on material and Stimson says, "He is coming to our way of thinking." Stimson is nursing him along in his present determination to think over the situation—in the meantime T. R. has again the nation's ear by his Outlook article on trusts—right and sound.[11] Poor old Taft! Missed practically every chance of assertive leadership. He had it clearly on the trust question—now he is again a belated trailer.

Taft told Stimson he will stand firm against the Sulloway bill—the pension grab measure.[12] Stimson wisely told the President, "If you do, Mr. President, do it aggressively by vigorously giving your reasons, and full publicity." The President says he will stand firm no matter what happens to his political future. The poor man, according to all the talk I hear from the well-informed guessers, hasn't got any future!

Had a fine evening with Ray Stannard Baker [13] at Denison's. Baker talked

---

action, that he had directed the United States Ambassador in St. Petersburg to notify the Russian Government that the United States had denounced the treaty. The abrogation, diplomatic sources said, was acceptable to the Czarist Government because it avoided offensive language.

[10] Morris Raphael Cohen, Frankfurter's third-year roommate at Harvard, was then beginning a distinguished career in philosophy at the City College of New York. Henry Cohen, a lawyer, was his cousin.

[11] T. R.'s article in *The Outlook* of November 18, 1911, derided the Taft Administration's suits to break up the trusts. Roosevelt ridiculed the notion of treating the size of a corporation as a crime in itself. The article, wrote Pringle, regained for Roosevelt the support of the business community. Andrew Carnegie wrote George W. Perkins of International Harvester: "Steel and Oil and Tobacco are laughing at the government. Who isn't? Disbandment is futile."

[12] The Sulloway Bill was one of the dollar-a-day pension schemes for old soldiers that were afloat that year. Taft stood firm and none passed.

[13] Ray Stannard Baker, friend of Woodrow Wilson, later wrote the authorized biography of the wartime President, in eight volumes.

LaFollette to whom I am "cottoning" more and more. Said Senator Hale, the standpatter from Maine, who was on the extreme outs with LaFollette, called up the latter the other day and asked if it be agreeable if he'd call. LaFollette was pleased to have him. Hale said he came to pay a social call. "When you first came to Washington," he told LaFollette, "I thought you belonged on the political scrap heap and I determined to help place you there. But I have come to respect you and respect your viewpoints though I shall always differ with you." Short of a visit from Aldrich,[14] the high priest of the departing, fast-going, Toryism, no more significant tribute could be paid to LaFollette. The union between politics and the university, energizing organized knowledge in the interest of the state as LaFollette has done in Wisconsin is to me one of the most vital contributions he has made.[15] In fact all his concrete accomplishments are simply results of that viewpoint.

I could not fail to record my rich joy at the Irish Players.[16] I saw them twice—laughed boisterously at Blanco Posnet, with an undercurrent of its [one word illegible] wit, and guffawed uproariously at the Playboy. But the fine, perfect art was perhaps more thrillingly shown with a smaller piece by Yeats and Lady Gregory—whose vivid but serene face, her warm, spirited voice, reflecting the animation of a fighter that feels her day is come, has been ever since with me. The actors were exceptionally grouped, a cooperative harmony and rare intelligence in the roles—perfect art was realized for the simulation was complete.

I had almost forgotten to give to history my first appearance in the Supreme Court—Monday, November 20, at 12.13½, I arose and said, "May it please the Court: In No. 408, the People of Porto Rico against Rosaly, I beg to submit a consented motion to advance"—exactly 24 words but the road behind them, "the pain of ages and the hope of eternity." [17]

November 22

Good long talk with Stimson, covering department affairs, variety of insular problems and first army message. Had long and important Cabinet meeting

[14] Senator Nelson W. Aldrich was also the "high priest" of protectionism.

[15] This was known as "the Wisconsin Idea." LaFollette as Governor had used the state university "as a seedbed for its practical ideas" and he had made use of disinterested experts, many recruited from the University, as his advisers.

[16] The Irish Players had taken New York by storm—but not all New Yorkers. There were riots and demonstrations organized by Irish-Americans against *The Playboy of the Western World*, which they considered a travesty on the Irish character. George Bernard Shaw's *Showing Up of Blanco Posnet* was having its first performance in New York. It is not among Shaw's better known plays, but at the time it, too, stirred controversy, having been denied a license in London because of alleged blasphemies.

[17] *Porto Rico v. Rosaly*, 227 U. S. 270 (1913). F. F., along with Wolcott H. Pitkin, Jr., then the Attorney General of Puerto Rico, later argued and won this case, a land dispute in which the government successfully contended that the government of Puerto Rico was immune from suit.

yesterday. Water power was up for discussion. Stimson was loaded—we had spent the night before together and went into legal questions at length. He said with great joy, "We've got the President with us on water power, boots and baggage." Taft said that he always felt the "siren of federal power was attractive, but to claim the power was a sort of blackmail." "Hold on," said S., waving the controlling decision of the Supreme Court, *Green Bay* and *Canal Company*, 172 U.S.,[1] which he wisely brought with him, "Before you talk blackmail, consider how far the courts have gone." Taft, the judge, was here gently touched. He finally succumbed to Fisher [2] and Stimson, is ready to go the full hog on the federal power, only wants the thing to be exercised wisely and without delay. Speaking of the analogous power over interstate carrier, raised by S., Taft said he felt we have to come to Sanborn's view—the rate case which set the states rights governors by the ear—as to the interdependence of state with interstate rates so as to necessitate exclusive federal jurisdiction.[3] I haven't a doubt the Supreme Court if wisely led thereto will eventually go that far— White's concurring opinion in the Western Union and Pullman Company cases v. Kansas,[4] and the recent decision by Van Devanter [5] as to safety appliance law on a state used portion of an interstate carrier clearly foreshadow that

---

[1] *Green Bay & Mississippi Canal Co. v. Patten Paper Co.*, 172 U. S. 58 (1898). A conflict over the rights to the water power created when the federal government erected a dam to improve navigation on the Fox River in Wisconsin. One of the parties claimed rights to the power by way of a grant from the federal government. The Supreme Court held that the federal government's power over the navigable waterways extended to water power created in the improvement of waterways.

[2] W. L. Fisher, Secretary of the Interior.

[3] "Sanborn's view"—*Shepard v. Northern Pacific Railway Co.*, 184 Fed. 765 (8th Cir. 1911), affirmed in part, 230 U. S. 352 (1911). Minnesota sought to enforce regulations against the railroads that limited their rates to levels below those approved by the Interstate Commerce Commission. The Court of Appeals, in the opinion mentioned by F. F., held the rate regulations an unconstitutional entry by the state into an area reserved by the Commerce Clause to the federal government.

[4] *Western Union Telegraph Co. v. Kansas*, 216 U. S. 1 (1910), *Pullman Co. v. Kansas*, 216 U. S. 56 (1910). Kansas sought to impose a tax based on total stock value on out-of-state companies doing business in Kansas. The Court held the tax unconstitutional. It reasoned that the Constitution guaranteed the right to carry on interstate commerce, and that Congress alone had the power to regulate that commerce. States, the Court held, could neither prohibit nor impose conditions on the operation of interstate commerce.

Justice White accepted the majority's reasoning that the Kansas taxes violated the due process rights of the companies. He added, however, that the only argument made to sustain the tax—by Mr. Justice Holmes—was that by doing business in Kansas the companies had waived their rights. But the companies were doing business before the taxes were imposed, he argued.

[5] *Southern Railway Co. v. United States*, 222 U. S. 20 (1911). The railroads challenged the federal government's power to require the use of certain safety devices on railway cars used only within a single state, and thereby asserted not to be in interstate commerce and therefore outside of the scope of the Commerce Clause. The Court, in the opinion mentioned by F. F., written by Justice Willis Van Devanter, rejected the railroad's circumscribed view of the commerce power and held the federal regulation valid.

result. But again Taft slowly and with effort follows instead of leads—he is always behind, certainly never ahead of his problems. S. also with much glee said Taft in his trust message is now "with us" in recognizing that it is the era of big business—"Big business but not socialism." What a terror his inherited phrases have for him!

Went through a great deal of grist today—Porto Rico citizenship, civil service law and framed up public statement about Bloomfield's educational trip, discussing taxing reforms with McIntyre,[6] labor problems, etc.; took dip into Philippine litigation—what a mess poor [name illegible] left behind them and went further into Panama matter (toll legislation and the pesky question of Christian Science "practice"). What a *lot* of good time is consumed either stopping rat holes or most often undoing the rat's mischief. The tropics certainly don't tend to foster unduly patience and a sense of perspective on the part of the local administrators.

[This Diary kept in longhand in a ledger book breaks off here. The next consists of some entries for 1928.]

---

[6] Frank McIntyre, Deputy Chief of the Bureau of Insular Affairs; F. F. described him as "a very scholarly soldier . . . he devised the currency system for the Philippines. . . ."

((1928))

INCIDENT AT HARVARD I

Among the Diaries that were stolen but not returned were a substantial batch of entries for 1927. That was the year in which the Sacco-Vanzetti case reached its tragic end with the execution of the two men. The President of Harvard, A. Lawrence Lowell, a Boston Brahmin, headed the Governor's Commission whose report justifying the trial's proceedings doomed the two men. Since Frankfurter's own analysis of those proceedings had done much to persuade the public that they constituted an abuse of justice, he was asked whether he would resign from the Law School. "Why should I resign?" he answered brusquely. "Let Lowell resign." The strong feelings engendered by that case still smoldered in 1928 and undoubtedly accentuated the clash over faculty prerogatives described in the following entries.

June 14, 1928

Pound,[1] evidently distressed, told me that something very troublesome had arisen in connection with the appointment of Landis [2] to a professorship in legislation. From a letter to him by Lowell, it appeared that the place had been offered to Shattuck [Henry L.] [3] who has the offer under advisement. I asked

[1] Felix Frankfurter's initial enthusiasm for the Law School's Dean Roscoe Pound (see pp. 10, 11) had waned because of what he considered the Dean's timidity.

[2] James M. Landis had been a graduate student working under Frankfurter (see pp. 35, 36). In 1926 he had clerked for Brandeis; in 1927 he and Frankfurter had published *The Business of the Supreme Court*. He was appointed professor of legislation in 1928 and, in 1937, after having taken several leaves of absence in order to serve in the Roosevelt Administration, became Dean of the Law School.

[3] Henry L. Shattuck, prominent member of the Boston bar, a member of the Massachusetts

Pound what Lowell said in his letter, whereupon he said he would show it to me and went off to get the letter. Lowell wrote that he would submit to the Corporation [4] the names of Gardner [5] and Burns [6] for professorship and assistant professorship respectively and then went on to say, I am quoting with substantial accuracy, "Landis had better go over until Shattuck decides to take it. He is much attracted by it and, of course, in view of his experience would be a very good man." I asked Pound whether there had been prior talk about Shattuck and he said this came out of a clear sky, except that over a year ago occasionally Shattuck was mentioned, but he had heard nothing about it since. I then asked Pound whether Lowell had assented to the Landis matter and he said he assumed that he had. Pound was greatly distressed and said if this wasn't fixed up "it would disrupt the faculty." I assured him it would—that feeling would run very high, indeed. He seemed to blame Jerry Smith,[7] saying that Lowell is very amenable to stronger influences.

Pound was plainly laboring under the utmost anxiety and concern. He asked me not to talk to others about the Landis matter, saying that if it got out it would create the greatest possible disquietude among our faculty.

June 15

Saw Zech Chafee [1] and told him that a matter of critical importance in the life of the School is afoot which deeply distresses me; that I didn't want to

Legislature, director of many companies. In 1929 he became Treasurer of Harvard and a member of the Corporation.

[4] Harvard is governed by a self-perpetuating Corporation of seven Fellows elected for life and a Board of Overseers elected by the alumni.

[5] George K. Gardner became a professor at the Law School, teaching Insurance and Contracts.

[6] John Joseph Burns, appointed assistant professor of law in 1928; resigned in 1931 to accept appointment to the Massachusetts Superior Court.

[7] Jeremiah Smith, member of an old New England family with long associations with the bar. He was a member of the Committee appointed by the Board of Overseers in 1921 who conducted "The Trial at the Harvard Club" of Professors Chafee, Frankfurter, and others (see pp. 31, 32).

[1] Zechariah Chafee (see pp. 29, 31). Francis T. P. Plimpton at the 1924 Lincoln's Inn Christmas Dinner had read a celebrated poem, "In Personam," which included some equally celebrated verses on Chafee.

> And we've reached upon our lists
> Free speech's best Messiah,
> The bulwark of all Bolshevists,
> Our Chafee, Zechariah. . . . .

which among its many following stanzas included the Trial Committee's injunction.

> "Young man, if students hear you air
> Opinions any broader,
> Just think what will become of their
> Respect for Law and Order!"

tell him what it is about because I wanted him to be free to go to Pound and say that he had seen me and that I am deeply concerned about something affecting the School, to the end that Pound would draw him into consultation about the Landis matter.

Chafee told Pound that he had seen me and found me distressed about some School matter, the nature of which I would not reveal to him. He came to Pound to know if he could be of any use. Pound then told him about the Memorial appropriation * and said that he was straightening it out, but went on to say finally that there is some difficulty about appointments in that the Corporation wishes to select one of the research professors without consulting the faculty. Chafee said that such action might lead to resignations from the faculty, to which Pound replied that perhaps some would resign whom they would like to have resign. To which Chafee said, "I suppose they would like to have me resign because I would resign." Further talk between Chafee and me developed that R. P. in fact had not told him that the place offered to Landis and for which the faculty had voted to recommend him—the professorship of legislation—was the issue, and Chafee was much shocked when he heard of it. Prior to telling me of this talk with Pound, Chafee expressed great dissatisfaction with the trend of things at the School, particularly the consequences due to the large student body, etc., etc.

June 16

Maguire [1] came to me this morning and said that he had called up Pound last night to say that while in town he had heard talk about an offer of a place to Shattuck. Pound said that evidently there is talk going around and that it was important not to circulate any further talk. He told him briefly the circumstances of Lowell's communication to him, said he was hoping to straighten it out but we must use discretion in these matters; he said that Chafee had been to see him and had indulged in wild talk about resigning, to which Maguire replied that he did not know how wild it was, but that he, Maguire, would feel that he ought to resign if any such thing were consummated; whereupon Pound became quite "huffy" and said some members of the faculty were making it so difficult for him that he might resign himself. Maguire said that this makes it all the more important for those who are capable of calm thinking to think calmly. He said that Pound then expressed dissatisfaction with Shattuck's qualifications, perhaps even stronger than Maguire expressed himself, and Pound asked him his views regarding Shattuck. Pound further said that if Shat-

---

* When R. P. spoke to me about the Landis matter, he also said that Lowell was putting obstacles in the way of getting our money for Crime Survey and was trying to block Survey "for some good reason or other."

[1] John MacArthur Maguire, appointed professor in 1923; author of casebooks on taxation and evidence. He later wrote an influential essay on the poll tax, "Taxing the Exercise of Natural Rights."

tuck became professor of legislation, Landis might take the chair of judicial organization, to which Maguire replied that Jim might not like that, but Pound thought it is "better than the Pennsylvania job." Maguire came in to see Pound because the latter asked him to see him this morning.

Later in the morning Maguire told me of his talk with Pound. Apparently Pound did not communicate the faculty's recommendation of Landis until after Burns had accepted the appointment, which was several weeks after the faculty had taken action. Apparently also while Pound had told the President that Landis could be held by one of the research professorships, he did not specify which one until his letter of a few weeks ago (date not given to Maguire) making the formal recommendation.

Pound, in talking with me, said that if Shattuck is the conscientious fellow that he is supposed to be, he couldn't dream of accepting the chair of legislation. I told Pound that Loring Young [2] is a very close friend of Shattuck's and is the man to talk to. Pound said he didn't know Young, and asked me whether I did and whether I wouldn't talk with Young. I said the difficulties were that one could not talk to Young or anybody else, unless one could refer to facts of the offer to Shattuck, and he said he authorized me to speak as strongly as I could to Young, trusting entirely to my discretion. I told him I would think about it.

June 17

Chafee came to my house. Evidently he and Jack Maguire had been in conference and talked of seeing Williston [1] about the Landis matter, and asked whether I would go with him. I told him that in view of the restriction of confidence which Pound had placed upon me I had better not go with them. He went off and later returned together with Maguire to report their conference with Williston. In substance it was this: Williston said he had lived with the School for many years and hopes to die with it. He had seen some injustices in his days and was prepared to put up with more. He was impressed with the importance and the gravity of the situation, but said that Landis was young and had ample time to make his career. He thought it would be a great mistake to bring the matter up in the faculty meeting tomorrow, that he would arrange to see the President and talk to him about the matter.* Of course, the Corpora-

---

[2] Benjamin Loring Young, lawyer, financier, active in Massachusetts politics, and Harvard overseer.

[1] Samuel Williston, professor at the Law School from 1890 to 1938. He had written the standard treatises on the law of sales and on contracts. The Law School historian, Arthur Sutherland, described him as "poised, polished, his every question carefully calculated, knowingly directed to some pedagogical end. He was a master of the art of dialectical demonstration."

* Williston afterwards told either Maguire or Chafee that he could not get a chance at the President.

tion, he said, had the legal right to make these appointments and he got the impression that they wanted to appoint some "picture card" at least to one of the places. He thought Shattuck was a man more distinguished for his character than his intellect, but he might not be a bad man. Maguire put to him flatly the question of whether or not Landis ought to be told about it. Williston emphatically said that Landis should be informed, for it is very important he should know the circumstances that have arisen, and particularly the feelings of the faculty, of his colleagues, about him and about the new situation that had arisen. Williston thought that F. F. ought to tell Jim. Maguire said that the only difficulty about my telling Landis was the restriction which the Dean had placed upon me. We agreed, in any event, that nothing was to be said to Landis until after the talk between Williston and the President.

June 19

Agreeable to decision taken in conference with Maguire and Chafee, I saw Arthur Hill,[1] rather than Young, and told him the whole situation in regard to Landis and Shattuck. Hill said that, of course, the central difficulty is that Pound isn't candid in such matters as he himself has experienced. And his lack of candor grows out of his inability to deal decisively with issues when they come up. Hill thought the most effective way to deal with Shattuck is for Joe Warren[2] to talk with him. He was doubtful as to his own present relation with Shattuck. They had been very cordial, but he had reason to believe that Shattuck felt distinctly chilled toward him because of his participation in the S-V case last summer.

Chafee came to see me in the evening and I told him the substance of my talk with Hill, and he and Maguire were to put their heads together to see what was to be done about it.

June 25

Jim Landis came to me and asked me where his affairs stood and whether I had heard anything about his professorship. I then felt in duty bound to tell him the whole story. On the way to lunch we ran into Pound, who stopped the car, and then and there began to tell Jim, generally and without mentioning names, the snag he had struck and told him if the legislation doesn't come through, he would do something for him "just as good" and asked him to see him.

Zech Chafee, Jim and I lunched. We went over the whole story, includ-

---

[1] Arthur D. Hill was a prominent State Street lawyer, Boston Brahmin, and close friend of Frankfurter. He had been a Bull Mooser in 1912 and a supporter of Sacco and Vanzetti in 1927.

[2] Professor Joseph Warren gave a course in "future interests." He dressed in formal morning coat and a high stiff collar for his lectures and was known as "Gentleman Joe" because of his perfect courtesy.

ing the account of Zech Chafee's conversation with Mr. John F. Moors [1] that forenoon. Mr. Moors knew substantially nothing about the matter, except that he spoke highly of Jim and he said that he had heard that Shattuck was being considered for a professorship. Jim, at this luncheon, said definitely that the moving consideration for staying here was legislation and that he would not stay at another job. He also told us that, in view of Powell's [2] and Morgan's [3] advice to him not to give up Pennsylvania on any uncertainty here, he has asked R. P. very specifically whether the offer of legislation was approved by the President and R. P. assured him that it had Lowell's approval. Zech said he would see Pound and tell him definitely of Jim's feelings and his own feelings in case the matter were not adjusted. Pound had told Jim and me that he was to have seen Shattuck this morning but that Shattuck had phoned to say that he would not be able to come until the afternoon. Chafee hurried back to Cambridge in an effort to see Pound before the latter saw Shattuck.

June 27

Jim told me of his talk with Pound yesterday. Pound endeavored to rehearse the whole matter, first suggesting that Jim had not himself made up his mind which professorship he wanted, which Jim effectively repudiated, and then Pound said the trouble was that the Corporation did not know one professorship from another. Pound told him that he thought Shattuck would decline. If not, Jim was guaranteed a research professorship and that regardless of what name it had, he could follow in any professorship whatever work he wanted to do. Jim said he left himself entirely free to await the outcome of Pound's talk with Shattuck, which Pound said had not yet come off.

Jack Maguire told me of a talk he had with Joe Warren yesterday in the course of which Joe told him that he knew some months ago that Shattuck's name was under advisement but that he could not place the time of this conversation. Maguire reported Warren as saying that when Jim Landis was proposed for legislation, he had assumed the Shattuck matter was adjusted.

June 28

Jim Landis told of R. P.'s account to him of talk between R. P. and Shattuck. In sum: Shattuck does not intend to give up politics, had not realized that the chair in legislation was full time job and so will probably decline *that* job.

---

[1] John F. Moors, member of the Corporation, leading Boston banker, classmate of President Lowell, and a supporter of Sacco and Vanzetti.

[2] Professor Thomas Reed Powell taught Constitutional Law. Frankfurter said he had "an acute critical mind, a very questioning mind, and he was also witty."

[3] Edmund Morris Morgan, professor whose specialty was evidence. He would become acting dean in 1942 when Landis took another of his leaves-of-absence for wartime duty with the Government.

But R. P. suggested some part time arrangement with a new Institute of Legislation, with Jim as Director and Shattuck as a member of it. R. P. told Jim that the next move is Shattuck's or the Corporation's, but he expected Jim's appointment, as originally planned, to go through. Jim said that R. P. emphasized several times that his salary as professor would in any event begin in the fall.

I phoned to Maguire (having to leave town) the substance of Pound's report and pointed out to him the dangers of creating a new situation of commitments with Shattuck, whereby the Faculty would not have a free hand in acting on proposal of part time relation of Shattuck and its dangers not only as violation of full-time principle, but even more so of introducing a partisan public man into research field where above all, freedom from partisan entanglements is essential. I suggested to Jack that he might want to put it to R. P. on behalf of Zech and myself.

June 29, 1928

Professor Felix Frankfurter,
Duxbury,
Massachusetts.

Dear Felix:

After deliberation I concluded that it would be unwise to make any formal representations to the Dean. In this conclusion Jim concurred. But I made occasion for an informal talk. From this talk I emerged perfectly satisfied with the appointment of Shattuck in an advisory capacity. Jim himself will furnish any counter-poise which may be necessary. The Dean was undecided about referring to the Faculty the general make-up of the Institute. But finally he said that he would present the plan and insist upon early unanimity. If the matter dragged he would tell the Faculty that he could not wait, and would present his scheme direct to the Corporation.

Have you written Zech to keep his shirt on?

Sincerely yours,

John M. Maguire

Duxbury, Mass.
30 June 1928.

Dear Jack:

Frankly, I am saddened by your letter. You are far too readily "satisfied"—indeed, "perfectly satisfied." Apparently, past experience that is unpleasant is optimistically disregarded by you. Why should you be "perfectly satisfied" by a talk in which the Dean seriously is "undecided about referring to the Faculty the general make-up of the Institute" and as a concession says he "would present the plan and insist upon early unanimity" on threat of presenting "his scheme direct to the Corporation?" What is the Faculty—a deliberative body of scholars, or a lot of German privates *before the war?*—for since the war not even German privates are thus treated. Have we held up the Institute? Have we been lacking in responsible deliberation, that we are to be given the choice of "early unanimity" or the whip of the overlords? Not even of the United States Supreme Court is unanimity required, let alone "early unanimity."

What does an advisory capacity for Shattuck mean? And why have him on such ambiguous terms anyway—and why have him for scientific legislation, he who is a partisan political leader? Either we pursue juristic science or we don't. To say Jim will furnish a "counter-poise" is playing with words. Does it mean nothing to you to have a politician, however respectable, as a member of our Faculty within the field which it is most important to keep free from the taint of suspicion of partisan or political motives? Why Shattuck, I ask? Is there any doubt that any arrangement that is being proposed will be dictated not by the scientific needs of the School, but by considerations that are outside the scientific needs of the School? And is it not about time that we do not lend ourselves to such schemes? At least we don't have to be parties to these irrelevant and unworthy diplomacies.

I am sending Zech a statement of events since his departure and our correspondence.

Yours always,

P.S. You may have heard that four or five members of the Columbia Law Faculty have resigned following the appointment of Dean Smith without faculty consultation.

Professor J. M. Maguire,
Farncroft,
Wonalancet, N. H.

((1933))

INCIDENT AT HARVARD II

The 1933 group of entries, although small, give some indication of Frankfurter's involvement in the formative stages of the New Deal. His influence grew as the Roosevelt Administration settled in. This was all the more remarkable because until his appointment to the Supreme Court in 1939 he held no official position, and it is the conventional wisdom in Washington that to be out of sight is to be out of mind.

Tuesday, February 7, 1933

Harriman,[1] President of the Chamber of Commerce, in my office for over an hour's talk, mainly in regard to the proposal to write into the so-called Nye Bill [2] provisions authorizing the Federal Trade Commission to fine under-cutting as to hours and wages unfair methods of competition. I explained to him the legal situation, concluding that the proposal was worth trying; whether it would get by the Supreme Court in the light of the Child Labor decision [3] is

[1] Henry I. Harriman was a tireless advocate at this time of "industrial self-government." He favored an agency modeled on the War Industries Board to direct a planned national effort to get industry out of the depression. His ideas contributed to the National Industrial Recovery Act.

[2] Under the proposed Nye Bill the Federal Trade Commission would be empowered to give legally binding effect to trade practice agreements adopted by an industry. The bill was superseded by the National Industrial Recovery Act.

[3] This was a reference to *Hammer v. Dagenhart*, 247 U. S. 251 (1918), a notorious Supreme Court decision that ruled the federal statute which prohibited interstate transportation of the products of child labor to be unconstitutional because it exceeded the scope of the federal commerce power.

problematic—but it is worth trying. Then talked with him about other economic questions confronting the next Administration.

Faculty meeting. Proposal by Administrative Board for a new course in the second year, combining Agency and Partnership, as a preliminary to third year Corporation, a three-hour course. This would increase the third year schedule to 13 hours, and I briefly entered a caveat against what seemed to me a pernicious tendency. More hours I regarded as bad and said so. McLaughlin [4] strongly concurred.

After faculty meeting Pound said he wanted to talk with me a minute. He referred to the note I sent him two weeks ago, asking him to bring the McClellan [5] matter before the whole faculty. He said, "You remember the note you wrote me regarding the McClellan matter?" I recalled it. He then added, "Well, I think if we lie low, the matter will blow over and nothing will happen." I expressed gratification at that, and asked, "Is Judge McClellan a particular friend of Mr. Lowell's?" Pound said, "No, I don't think so. But you know there always is a man at the right hand of the throne, and now it's Murdoch, [6] and I think he is responsible for efforts at regimentation."

Wednesday, February 8

To Brunswick, Me., where I was met at Portland by Abrahams and Lockwood of the Bowdoin faculty. At my suggestion they phoned ex-Governor Brewster, who had tea with us, talking generally on expectations of realignment of parties and liberal directions to be expected from Roosevelt. [1]

Before delivering Cole Address, dined at President Sills' house with half a dozen faculty and their wives, including Burnet, Dwight Morrow's [2] great friend. After the lecture general discussion at Sills' house, attended by some of the students and Governor Brann of Maine and Judge Connelly and others.

---

[4] Professor James McLaughlin taught "Municipal Corporations" and "Labor Law."

[5] Hugh P. McClellan, a former judge and distinguished Boston lawyer.

[6] Harold Murdoch, Boston banker and Director of the Harvard University Press.

[1] Discussion of political realignment was much in the air at that time. In November Justice Brandeis, after a brief session with the President-elect, wrote Frankfurter: "He seems well versed about fundamental facts of the situation—declared his administration must be liberal and that he expected to lose part of his Conservative supporters. I told him 'I hoped so.'—that he must realign . . . part of the forces in each party."

[2] Dwight Morrow was one of the people to whom Frankfurter had a letter of introduction when he came down to New York from Harvard. Morrow was sympathetic and understanding but did not offer him a job. He was a Morgan partner, a sponsor of Calvin Coolidge, and United States Ambassador to Mexico.

Thursday, February 9

Lunched with Bob Proctor [1] and his friend Horatio Nelson Slater. Slater is heavily interested in textiles—the town of Brewster is practically a family town—and desirous of having an independent survey made of textile industry by someone who understands and also who would [have] influence with the next Administration. I suggested George Rublee [2] as filling the bill and an all-round man. I undertook to give him a note of introduction to Rublee, which I have done.

Abe Flexner phoned and asked me to write him an objective estimate of Mitrany's qualities from the point of view of his Institute. [3]

Friday, February 10

Moley [1] phoned and, in brief, dealt with the following: (1) he was greatly interested in the memorandum I sent him entitled "Notes on the Present Situation" by Eugene Meyer; [2] (2) he told me of his talk with the Governor regarding the conditions of his possible connection with the State Department, and one of them was the opportunity to select a satisfactory economic adviser. F. D. R. assented to this and Moley asked me whether I thought Feis [3] would fill the bill, in view of my remarks about Feis in my letter to Moley yesterday. I told him that I could recommend Feis 100 percent, and he replied that was good enough for him. I then went into details about Feis' qualities and Moley concluded, "It looks as though he is just the man I want"; (3) he said he had taken up the suggestions made by Brandeis that I had put to him in New York

[1] Robert Proctor, LL.B. Harvard, 1924, Boston attorney.

[2] George Rublee, Bull Mooser, friend and associate of Brandeis, one of the first Federal Trade Commissioners.

[3] Abraham Flexner was associated with the Rockefeller Foundation. He was the author of *Universities: American, English and German*, which had vigorously criticized American university practices. He was in the process of establishing the Institute of Advanced Study at Princeton. David Mitrany, Europe's leading scholar in the field of agrarian economics, author of a famous essay, "Marx versus the Peasant," did become a member of the Institute.

[1] Raymond Moley was the most prominent member of the Brains Trust at the time of the Brains Trust's greatest prominence. He was, except for Louis Howe, Roosevelt's most intimate adviser. Moley had known Frankfurter since 1920 when he had brought him to Cleveland to participate in a survey of criminal justice of which Moley was the director. "He infuriated me when he calmly told me that his primary task there was to educate my board of directors."

[2] Eugene Meyer, Governor of the Federal Reserve Board, resigned that position in May 1933, and a month later purchased the *Washington Post*.

[3] Herbert Feis, at the time economic adviser of the State Department. He was one of the people who helped set up the meeting between Secretary of State Stimson and President-elect Roosevelt. In the State Department he was considered a Stimson man.

but had not yet had a chance to read the memo in re public works but hoped to do so shortly and at the earliest moment would communicate with Brandeis; [4] he also wanted to have a session as early as possible in New York with Woodin,[5] Joe Kennedy [6] and Herbert Swope [7] (who he said was unemployed and ought to be put to work on problems) and myself. Told him I could do it next Thursday afternoon or evening; he said the Glass [8] situation was still unsettled and it might remain so until F. D. R. returns.

Monday, February 20

Corcoran [1] of the R. F. C. phoned as to the possibility of getting Fussell.[2] I talked with Macneil [3] and together we concocted a telegram to O'Melveny to get him to urge Fusell's acceptance.

Tuesday, February 21

Prof. Hermann Ranke, Egyptologist of Univ. of Heidelberg came to see me, with a letter of introduction from Philip LaFollette.[1] We had a most pleas-

---

[4] Frankfurter had been telling Moley he must see Brandeis and had sent him a memo outlining Brandeis' view: that Roosevelt at the opening of Congress had to promulgate "a comprehensive program" of public works, reforestation, and control of waters, including the Tennessee Valley project. On February 26, Frankfurter wrote Moley again: "It is most important that the very concrete, carefully thought out and strongly felt views of Brandeis reach F. D. R.'s mind, and I think by direct communication. . . ."

[5] William Woodin, president of the American Car and Foundry Company, Republican, a Trustee of the Warm Springs Foundation and a collector of funds for the Roosevelt campaign. He became Secretary of the Treasury. He was also an amateur composer.

[6] Joseph Kennedy, financier, was an early and heavy contributor to Roosevelt's campaign and Roosevelt's link with William Randolph Hearst.

[7] Herbert Bayard Swope, executive editor of the defunct New York *World*, a witty and gifted phrasemaker. He was close to Bernard M. Baruch.

[8] Carter Glass, Senator from Virginia, was one of the architects of the Federal Reserve System. Conservative opinion urged his appointment as Secretary of the Treasury. Roosevelt wanted him, but on his own terms. Glass declined the offer when he could not get the assurances that he wanted.

[1] Thomas Corcoran, one of Frankfurter's former students. While still a student he had written for Frankfurter "Petty Offenses and the Constitutional Guaranty of Trial by Jury," 39 *Harvard Law Review* 1926. He had clerked for Justice Holmes. (See pp. 52, 53).

[2] Paul Fussell was with the prestigious Los Angeles law firm of O'Melveny, Stevens and Millikin.

[3] Sayre MacNeil, Harvard professor of law. He taught property to first-year men and corporations to third-year students.

[1] Philip LaFollette had just finished a term as Governor of Wisconsin. Roosevelt considered offering him the Attorney Generalship when it appeared Senator Walsh might not accept.

ant chat. I sent him to Sarton [2] and gave him letters of introduction to Abe Flexner and Oswald Garrison Villard.[3]

Monday, March 20

Following Gardner Jackson's telegram of commendation, Svirsky [1] came to see me in my office.[2]

He mentioned the great shift in American opinion in regard to Russia as evidenced by the countless calls that came to him to speak on Russia from such organizations as womens' clubs, Rotary clubs, etc.; as evidenced also by Al Smith's statement on recognition and the favorable press notices it received, of which he showed me copies.

I said I had no doubt of this change in attitude. I asked him what men he knew in Washington, whether he knew Borah—which he did. I told him I thought Borah ought to make it his special contribution to induce the Administration to take action on Russian recognition, that the Administration is at present so preoccupied with immediate domestic problems that I know that Moley, for instance, had not looked at his mail for two weeks at a stretch. I suggested he have a talk with Moley, through a letter of introduction from Norman Hapgood or John Dewey [3] or both. I also suggested he get in touch with Ross of the Washington Post-Dispatch.[4]

We talked of recognition procedure, stressing the importance of the broad gesture: recognition first and then talk about the special items of complication between the two countries. There would be little dissent on this because of the awareness of trade possibilities between the two countries and the growing ridiculousness of trying to work on any world problems, especially disarmament and the Far East, with complete disregard of Russia, carried so far that Hugh Gibson [5] can never mention Russia nor Litinov by name.[6]

[2] George Sarton was Harvard's authority on the history of science.

[3] Oswald Garrison Villard was publisher of *The Nation*.

[1] Gardner Jackson, a free-wheeling, militant liberal who had handled public relations for the Sacco-Vanzetti defense. He became assistant to the Consumers' Counsel in the Agricultural Adjustment Administration.

[2] Boris Skvirsky was chief of Soviet Russia's Information Bureau in Washington and, as such, that government's informal representative. His large house on Massachusetts Avenue was a rendezvous of newspapermen, Senators, and Representatives. After the resumption of relations, Skvirsky became the Soviet Chargé d'Affaires.

[3] Norman Hapgood, liberal publicist, was a confidant of Brandeis. John Dewey, the American philosopher, was an early visitor to Soviet Russia.

[4] Charles Ross was head of the Washington Bureau of the St. Louis *Post-Dispatch*.

[5] Hugh Gibson, United States Ambassador to Belgium, was a career diplomat, and particularly close to Hoover. Roosevelt ordered him transferred to Brazil.

[6] Maxim Litvinov, Soviet Russia's Commissar of Foreign Affairs.

Monday, May 8

Grenny Clark [1] phoned me shortly after twelve to ask whether I could lunch with him. I picked him up at the faculty club at quarter to one and in order to have privacy took him to Gomatos in the Square. After some talk regarding Emory Buckner's condition—he told me of Emory's "miraculous" restoration—he said, with a kind of smile, "Well, I assume you're pretty unhappy about Conant's election." [2] I replied, "Well, Grenny, at the moment I feel like accepting that job that I declined in Washington." [3] To which he replied: "I thought you might feel that way. I can understand your feeling. I feel pretty badly myself." By that time we had reached Gomatos.

After the ordering was out of the way Grenny asked me, "Have you heard from Lowell?" "No, I have had no word from Lowell—what was I to hear from Lowell?" Grenny then told, in substance, the following:

About four or five days ago, each member of the Corporation received a letter from Lowell, enclosing a memorandum from Pound, in which Lowell asked us for our views regarding the situation set forth in Pound's memorandum. The substance of the business was an alleged disregard by you and Landis of the rule adopted by the Corporation some time ago for the government of the University regarding the keeping of teaching engagements or the notification of someone in authority—the President or the Dean—of inability to keep engagements. Pound, in his memorandum to the President, had stated that you had been in Washington and failed to attend to some lectures and disregarded altogether the requirement of notifying him; that Landis had failed to attend some classes and also failed to sit on some doctoral examinations. I wrote the President that I did not know what the facts were, but that I assumed you had been drafted for some work by the Government and that Landis had been associated with you, and that in any event, whatever the facts were, the matter should be dealt with with the utmost consideration. At the Corporation meeting today I was a little late and the matter was under discussion when I arrived and there was only a few minutes discussion. I repeated the substance of what I had written, adding that of course so far as Pound's state-

---

[1] Grenville Clark had been in the same class as Frankfurter at Harvard. "He was one of those deep but slow minds," Frankfurter said of him. He had started out as a young clerk in the firm of Carter, Ledyard and Milburn, the same firm that Franklin D. Roosevelt entered after Columbia Law School. He was one of the group of World War officers associated with the Plattsburg Training Camp movement, a volunteer preparedness effort smiled on by the War Department. At this time he was a leader of the New York bar and a member of the Corporation.

[2] What Frankfurter's objections were at that time to Conant could not be learned. James Bryant Conant was President of Harvard from 1933 to 1953.

[3] A reference to the Solicitor Generalship. (See p. 47).

ments were concerned, we all knew that no confidence could be placed in them, and that I was sure that what you and Landis did was in connection with Government work, and that in any event, whatever was done about it should be done with every possible consideration. My sentiments were expressed by Nelson Perkins [4] and some of the others, and I supposed that either Lowell or Pound would talk to you.

F. F.   Would you like to know what the facts are, Grenny?

G. C.   No, I don't care to know the facts (with a wave of impatience) no, I don't want to know the facts. I don't give a damn about the facts. I can about imagine what they were. I am telling you all this—I suppose it's a little irregular, but it's all right between us—because I was a little afraid if this were jumped on you suddenly by Lowell you might get so damned mad that you might tell him to go to hell. And it would be the most natural thing in the world for you to do. I know I would—I'd be as mad as hell and resent it, and probably tell him to go to hell. You have more patience and a calmer temper than I have. But even you might do it, and I didn't want you to do that and so I thought I would prepare you. If Lowell were on the job another year, it might be worthwhile having a real fight, but the old man is going to be on the job only two more months, so what's the use?

F. F.   Of course I am not staying here because of Lowell or Pound, and so I would not leave on their account. Of course it's an indignity.

G. C.   (with great heat) That's just what it is. Of course it's an indignity.

F. F.   But you needn't worry about me or the way in which I shall handle Lowell. I am concerned about Landis—not that he will do anything foolish, though he might be tempted to because he has the temper—but because of the discouragement that it will arouse in him. He's a moody temperament and very unhappy here as it is, under the present situation. But would you like to know the facts?

G. C.   (a little impatiently) Well, yes—I might as well, though I don't really give a damn about them—I am so damned sore about it.

F. F.   Well, these are the facts. Four weeks ago last Thursday I had a telephone message from Raymond Moley, saying that the original Securities Bill introduced on behalf of the Administration had encountered serious difficulties and the President wanted me to come down to help get it into proper shape. I realized that this was more of a job than a little tinkering here and there—for I had studied the Bill in question and was

---

[4] Thomas Nelson Perkins, member of the Corporation, "a good respectable Beacon Hill Yankee" who in the early Twenties had been an advocate of the recognition of the Soviet Union.

aware of the complicated particularities—and so I asked Jim Landis to come with me, and also arranged by telephone to have Ben Cohen of New York (perhaps one of the most brilliant doctors we ever had, afterwards Judge Mack's secretary and a man of very considerable financial-legal experience but wholly disinterested, and as you know it was essential to have people free from every possible entanglement) to join me in Washington. Friday morning I saw Moley, who went over the situation with me and then took me to the White House. It had already been arranged that I was to go before the House subcommittee of the Committee on Commerce to confer on the needs of the legislation. After talking with the President, I went before the House subcommittee and had a talk with Chairman Rayburn. He explained to me the unsatisfactoriness of the Bill then before the committee, the President's desire, as well as his, for my aid in working out an effective bill to carry out the President's message on securities regulation. I explained to Rayburn the time that that would take, and that I had brought with me Landis and Cohen—telling him who they were—and he then said it was essential, in view of the parliamentary situation, that I appear before the subcommittee with the general outline of the bill as I thought it ought to be. I was reluctant to stay over till Monday, but he said it was absolutely essential, that the President and he were depending on me to do so. I then consented and told him I would be back on Monday morning with the first draft of our bill. I thereupon returned to the Carlton—where our party was staying—told Landis and Cohen the arrangement that had been made and immediately telegraphed to Pound, telling him that at the President's request, I would have to stay over till Monday and asked him to make arrangements about my classes.

G. C.   In other words, you *did* take cognizance of the rule about notifying the Dean, and you did notify him?

F. F.   (nodding)

G. C.   (with a good deal of vehemence) In other words, you did take cognizance of the rule, which it is alleged you did not heed. The only possible point about the whole business is that of course it is necessary in running any organization to have some kind of orderliness and therefore it's proper enough to have some kind of rule whereby men won't just disregard engagements, just pay no attention to them, but provide some means to notify people in advance. And that's just what you did, and Pound never mentioned it in his memorandum. And the only possible excuse—it's miserable, silly, petty business at best—is that you paid no attention at all, when as a matter of fact you did.

F. F.   I returned to Cambridge Monday night and on Tuesday told Pound of the situation, explained to him the President's request of me in further detail and that Landis was being left behind and probably would not be back in time for the doctoral examination on Wednesday and asked Pound whether I could substitute for Landis. He replied, "Sure, that's all right. I am glad Landis is doing that—it's good for him." Later, probably Thursday, when it was clear that Landis would not be back to take his Friday seminar I again spoke to Pound and asked him whether I might take Landis' seminar. He again said, "Sure, that's all right," with entire cordiality and in a matter of course way. The hearings before the committee in Washington dragged on, as such things do—all sorts of interests had to be reconciled, and of course the legislation is very complicated and covers a wide range—and Landis stayed on into the week following. I again spoke to Pound—in the meantime had with Pound's permission substituted for Landis at another doctoral exam; incidentally, at both the doctoral exams at which I substituted for Landis, Pound was present as chairman of the committee so of course he knew that Landis was not there and I was—telling him that Landis was still detained on Government work at Washington and that with his permission I would take Landis' seminar. He assented eagerly and I took the seminar. And that's the story.

G. C.   Without knowing anything about [it], I just surmised that it was something like that.

Grenny then repeated his reasons for telling me about it—his desire to avert a natural resentment on my part of the offensive behavior of Pound and Lowell. He again repeated that the old man has only two more months to go and the thing to do is not to make a fuss about it. I forgot to mention that in the course of my remarks I said that having refused the request of the President for my services as Solicitor General, I could not possibly decline the President's request, these days, to do *ad hoc* jobs. Clark, with much impatience—and throughout he was the impatient and resentful one of the two and seemed to be under a good deal of suppressed anger against the whole incident—said, "Of course not. How could you? It's ridiculous, and I think it was very, very handsome of you to decline the Solicitor Generalship." He repeated that several times.

((1943))

JUDICIAL CONTROVERSIES
AND NONJUDICIAL
INVOLVEMENTS

Frankfurter when the Diaries resume in 1943 (the Diary for 1937 has not been recovered) has been on the Bench since 1939. The Court is now called "the Roosevelt Court," and the new alignments within it are primarily a reflection of the differences among Roosevelt's appointees. The Court's members in order of seniority are: Harlan F. Stone, Associate Justice, 1925; named Chief Justice in 1941 upon Hughes' retirement; Owen J. Roberts, 1930; Hugo L. Black, 1937; Stanley Reed, 1937; Felix Frankfurter, 1939; William O. Douglas, 1939; Frank Murphy, 1940; James F. Byrnes, 1941; Robert H. Jackson, 1941.

At the end of 1942 Byrnes resigned in order to become "Assistant President for Economic Affairs," and his place was filled in February 1943 by Wiley Rutledge.

The war is at a turning point. An Anglo-American expeditionary force successfully invaded North Africa in November, and Rommel's Afrika Korps, pressed by the victorious British Eighth Army on the east and Eisenhower's forces on the west, was organizing a final stand in Africa in Tunis. In Soviet Russia, the Red Army was on the eve of its decisive victory at Stalingrad. In the Pacific the Japanese had been turned back in the Solomons. Even though it was not so clear at the time that the fascist military tide was beginning to ebb, the debate over the political purposes to be served by the military successes was waxing more furious—what kind of governments should fill the vacuum in East Europe left by the withdrawing Nazi power? Should Britain and American have a common approach to Soviet ambitions? To DeGaulle's insistence that he represented France? What was to happen in India, in Palestine?

All these matters course through these pages because Frankfurter's mind was one of the best in Washington, and politicians, diplomats, and generals sought his counsel, and much of what he heard and said is recorded here.

Monday, January 4, 1943

At 10:30 we had the Conference [1] postponed from Saturday on three argued cases.

No. 171—*U.S. v. Oklahoma Gas & Electric Co.*, involving a construction of §4 of the Act of March 1901, giving the Sec. of the Interior power to grant rights of way on Indian Reservations or over allotted Indian lands held in severalty. Such a right of way had been granted to Oklahoma and she authorized delaying of distributing lines to the power company, and the question was whether a permit therefore must also be obtained from the Secretary of Interior under the earlier Act of February 1901 or a later Act of 1911. I had studied the matter a good deal and more particularly the status of lands held in severalty by the Kickapoo Indians. It fell to me to talk about it at some length. I concluded that the Kickapoo holdings were not a "reservation" and therefore as such not within the terms of the severalty 1901 and 1911 Acts, and though left with considerable doubt, I concluded that the right of way granted to the State left to state law, as a matter of national policy, the extent of the uses granted by the Secretary in granting a "right of way." That view, which involved affirmance of the

[1] The conference room is an oak-paneled chamber presided over by a portrait of Chief Justice Marshall. There are nine chairs around the rectangular conference table, each with a nameplate of a member of the Court. The Chief Justice sits at one end, the senior Associate Justice, Roberts, at the other. On the sides in order of seniority sit the remaining Justices. "Bookcases from floor to ceiling line the walls containing all the opinions of the Federal Courts. . . . Only the Justices are present at conference. There are no clerks, no secretaries, no stenographers, no pages. . . . Upon entering the conference room, each Justice shakes hands with those present, another custom dating generations back. We first take out our assignment sheets or lists for the day. . . . The Chief Justice starts the conference by calling the first case on the list and then discussing it. He then yields to the senior Associate Justice and on down the line seniority-wise until each Justice who wishes to be heard has spoken. The order is never interrupted nor is the speaker. . . . After discussion of a case a vote is taken. . . . After the vote is recorded in argued cases there remains the task of writing the opinion for the Court. At the conclusion of the conference the cases are assigned for writing. The Chief Justice assigns those in which he has voted with the majority and the senior Justice voting with the majority the remainder. . . ." The Court meets in conference at eleven A.M. "and rarely does it rise before 5:30 P.M." From an address by Associate Justice Tom C. Clark, reprinted in *The Supreme Court: Views from Inside*, edited by Alan F. Westin (New York, 1961), pp. 49–50.

United States v. Oklahoma Gas & Electric Co., 318 U. S. 206 (1943).
The Court disposed of the case in accordance with the views expressed by Justice Frankfurter. Justices Black, Douglas, and Jackson dissented without opinion.

Circuit Court of Appeals, prevailed with the Conference, Black, Reed, and Doublas dissenting.

No. 385—*Milk Producers Assn. v. San Francisco*, involving the validity of an ordinance giving a Milk Commission, designated by the San Francisco Medical Assn., the power to certify milk that could be sold though not pasteurized on the basis of standards formulated by a New York milk standards agency. There were numerous expressions of doubt about such delegation of authority to a non-state agency. While I had no doubt at all that such delegation did not offend the Due Process Clause, I was clear that the case had become moot on the basis of an affidavit by the Chairman of the San Francisco Commission, that, in view of a later city ordinance, allowing the sale of only pasteurized milk, the Commission had become *functus*, even though it was suggested that the Commission might, if the occasion arose, be subsequently revived. This view prevailed and the case is to be disposed of as moot by a *per curiam*.

No. 60—*Hendry v. Moore*, involving the power of a state court—that of California—to condemn a fishing net used in a navigable stream and thus raising the question whether this is a matter exclusively within Admiralty jurisdiction or one of the reserve common law remedies. The Chief had made a special study of the history of the matter, and concluded that there was ample grounds for holding this was within the jurisdiction of the common law courts and therefore within the concurring jurisdiction of the state courts. So the Conference voted, Black dissenting.

Heard Arguments.

Dined with Jean Monnets',[1] the others being Ben Cohen, Milton Katz, and Robert Nathan.[2] The talk concerned the need for recognizing the place of

---

Natural Milk Producers Association of California v. San Francisco, 317 U. S. 423 (1943).
The Court held the case moot (deprived of practical significance), as suggested by Justice Frankfurter. *Functus*—the Commission had no further legal efficacy. *Per curiam*—by the Court" without indication of individual authorship.

Hendry v. Moore, 318 U. S. 133 (1943).
The Court disposed of the matter in accordance with the views of Justice Frankfurter. Justice Black argued in dissent that if a state might seize a fishnet under its common law rules, then it might also seize a ship, and that the Judiciary Act was never intended to empower the states to deal thus with commerce.

[1] Jean Monnet as the head of the French procurement in Washington before France's collapse had impressed American and British officials with his level-headedness, competence, and ability to put first things first. He had stayed on in Washington, as an official of the British Supply mission and was consulted on the highest levels on Allied supply problems and those relating to relationships with France.

[2] Ben Cohen had returned from England, where he had been Counselor to Ambassador Winant, and was now serving as general counsel to former Associate Justice James Brynes, who in November at Roosevelt's request had stepped down from the Court to become Director of Economic

civilian supply and the inevitable pressures that will come from restriction upon civilian consuming availabilities in view of the enormous inroads upon our resources and potentialities by reason of the vastly expanded military needs. The upshot of the discussion was a recognition by all that there is now no central direction for the safeguarding of civilian supply needs, and the proper centralization of authority for the consumer interests regarding supplies. It was agreed that Nelson should be formally recognized for what he is as the responsible head of war supply production, that the Division of Civilian Supply within the War Production Board [3] does not fulfill the functions of its title, that there should be a coordinate head of civilian supply for ascertaining and safeguarding the consumers' needs with due regard to primary military necessities and the proper rationing and price fixing of such commodities and services, inevitably much reduced all along the line, that are ahead of us. There will then be needed the authority, probably of Byrnes,[4] to adjust whatever conflicts may arise among the various heads of the total war economy, i.e. war production, agriculture, manpower, and the new civilian supply. There was unanimity on the analysis of the problem and the need for the reorganization of the present economic effort as well as the organization of the effort there should be, as I have just outlined it. It was also agreed that this new head of civilian supply must be a person who has the quality above all of enlisting public support and identifying public feeling with him. In other words, it must be a man with a strong flair for begetting and holding confidence. At this point, the party , as it were, stopped. For when it came to considering specific names, it was easy to dispose of the inadequacy of the various suggestions that were made, but we broke up before anybody could think of anyone who could fill the bill. Nelson, Wallace, Milo Perkins, Jim Conant, Bernie Baruch (somewhat ironically proposed), all were tossed in the air.[5]

Stabilization. Milton Katz, another superb legal mind, was top assistant to John Lord O'Brian, the general counsel of the War Production Board. Robert Nathan, New Dealer, career economist, was head of the War Production Board's Planning Committee. Under fire from "brass hats" on one side who wanted to increase War Department controls over the domestic economy, and on the other from "dollar-a-year" men wedded to "business-as-usual" practices, he would soon resign and enlist as a buck private, only to be discharged a few months later because of his bad back.

[3] The War Production Board, headed by Donald M. Nelson, a former vice president of Sears Roebuck, had been established in 1942 to provide unified control over war production and end disputes and bickerings among the various agencies involved in economic mobilization.

[4] When Roosevelt asked Byrnes to take on the job, in Byrnes's words, of "assistant President" for domestic affairs, that in some measure reflected his feeling that Nelson had failed to establish himself as "czar" of war production.

[5] Henry A. Wallace, Vice President of the United States, head of the Board of Economic Warfare, had emerged as a major spokesman for liberalism in wartime Washington. Milo Perkins, an old friend and ally of Wallace, had been President of the Federal Surplus Commodities Corporation and was now director of the Board of Economic Warfare. Both the State Department and the Commerce Department, headed by Jesse Jones, feuded with Perkins and the B.E.W. In mid-1943

Tuesday, January 5

Sitting.

At Sir Girja Bajpai's (the Indian Agent General) suggestion, Kavalam Madhara Panikkar called. We talked for about an hour and a half on all the phases of the Indian situation.[1] Panikkar was once editor of the Hindustan Times—the leading organ of the Congress—and also a personal follower of Gandhi. He still is a profound respecter of Gandhi. He was Secretary of the Indian States Delegation at the Round Table Conference of 1930 and is now a constitutional advisor of the Princes. His view, in short, is that the central problem is the Hindu-Moslem conflict and that the conflict cannot be resolved either by the two communities themselves, or by the British. Nor can it be done by open intervention of the United States. His way out is private, non-official, exploration of the ground by some distinguished Canadian, for instance, and say the United States Minister at Delhi, who would formulate a solution which, in his judgment, neither side could reject. He surprised me by saying he was now against a United Federal India. He thinks that Pakistan is essential because otherwise there never will be a sufficient grant of central authority for dealing with the social problems in the Hindu provinces which the solution of those problems make indispensable. He thinks that Pakistan would not be opposed by the Congress which has, in fact, never declared itself formally against Pakistan. Of course, he would have an arrangement or treaty between Hindustan and Pakistan for those matters on which there must be a common control—matters of defense, currency, communications, etc. He is on his way to London to further his general ideas for which he thinks he can get British acceptance once the community problem is out of the way.

S. E. Morison, whom the President wisely made Naval Historian, with the rank of Lieutenant Commander, to dinner. During dinner, Stimson called and asked if we were alone, that he and Mrs. S. would like to come over because he felt rather low in his mind and needed some comfort. They came

---

Roosevelt abolished the latter. Bernard M. Baruch, on the basis of his production mobilization experiences in World War I, was often offering advice which was not as often taken. Roosevelt never admitted Baruch into his inner council. Conant was on leave from Harvard. He was a member of a committee headed by Baruch that was trying to find a substitute for natural rubber. He was chairman of the National Defense Research Committee and together with Dr. Vannevar Bush was involved in the atomic energy program.

[1] Churchill had specifically excluded India and Burma from the application of the Atlantic Charter. Gandhi in consequence had instructed his people to follow a policy of nonresistance to the Japanese and later ordered a campaign of civil disobedience to the British authorities. Gandhi, Nehru, and other Congress leaders were thrown into jail and Gandhi was on the eve of a hunger strike. The United States was greatly concerned. Although Roosevelt had found Churchill unbudgeable on this subject, he had just ordered William Phillips, a career diplomat and personal friend, to go to India to see whether some formula of accommodation could not be arranged.

and Sam, who, as one of the officers on the cruiser *Brooklyn* in the battle off Casablanca, had recently returned from North Africa, gave us many exciting details of the resourcefulness and unflinching behavior of various naval units under his own observation. He told, with some particularity, of the splendid collaboration between the two services, and generally an exhilarating and cheerful evening was had.[2]

Wednesday, January 6

Sitting.

My dissent in the *Monia* opinion, having been distributed the day before—turning on the proper construction of the immunity provisions under the Interstate Commerce and Sherman Laws and involving appropriate principles of statutory constructions—I got the expected rise out of Stone for citing *Boston Sand Co. v. United States*, 278 U. S. 24, in which Holmes from my point of view, dealt such a death blow to the so-called "plain meaning" construction, over the dissent of four, including Stone. The *Boston Sand* case is a bête noir to Stone and is the key to his habit of mechanical statutory construction except, of course, when there is a strong pull of policy in him the other way.[1]

Richard Casey, the Minister of State of the Middle East, came to the house about quarter past five, and we talked until nearly seven. After personal exchanges about himself and his wife and his children—the Caseys and ourselves became warm friends during his stay here as Minister for Australia—we talked of major war problems beginning with the Middle Eastern situation for which he gives a promising military outlook as soon as the weather breaks, to the personal conduct of the war (he left Cairo on December 7th and spent two and a half weeks in London), as to which he said that England is more than

---

[2] Professor (now Commander) Morison was regaling Washington with his accounts of the landings at Casablanca when the *Brooklyn* was in action for nine hours.

[1] *United States v. Monia*, 317 U. S. 424 (1943).

Monia was indicted for conspiracy to fix prices in violation of the Sherman Act. He protested that he was immune from prosecution by virtue of having testified before the grand jury with respect to matters involved in the indictment. The government replied that he had not asserted his right to immunity before testifying, and thus had waived it.

The Court, in an opinion by Justice Roberts, found persuasive the absence from the statutory language conferring immunity any mention of assertion by the witness of the right to immunity. Frankfurter, who always construed the privilege against self-incrimination strictly and narrowly, in a dissent joined by Douglas, argued that the intent of Congress was only to provide the minimal immunity necessary to save the Sherman Act from unconstitutionality under *Counselman v. Hitchcock*, 142 U. S. 547 (1892). The language of the statute, he contended, should be read in light of this intent, however clear it seemed on its face. Among the authorities that he cited to buttress his view was the opinion of Justice Holmes in *Boston Sand Co. v. United States*, 278 U. S. 41 (1928), a decision from which Justice Stone had dissented. F. F. wrote, "(T) he notion that because the words of a statute are plain, its meaning is also plain, is merely pernicious oversimplification. It is a wooden English doctrine of rather ancient vintage. . . ." 317 U. S. at 431.

ever a one man show, that Churchill after all is sixty-eight and it's that kind of a war, etc., so that there is the merest semblance of Cabinet government in London as there is the merest semblance of it here, until we got to what he regarded as the two dominating problems, to wit, Anglo-American relations and the relations of Great Britain and this country to Russia. He was deeply concerned about both, as I told him was I. I ventured to suggest that relations towards Russia are dependent on relations between Great Britain and ourselves. He assented, but said it was very important not to have the Russians feel that Britain and America are ganging up against them—the Russians are very difficult because they distrust us both, and so far as he sees their doings in his part of the world, they won't do more than make a day-to-day arrangement with us. I explained that I quite agreed that we neither must "gang up" nor give the appearance of it, but there certainly cannot be the making of good relations between ourselves and the Russians if Great Britain and ourselves are in feud rather than in determination to march together. From which the talk went on in some detail on Anglo-American relations which, he agreed, are at present very bad indeed. I then told him why I thought they are needlessly bad, and what materials there are for improving them, and how indispensable I believed it to be that Churchill be made to realize that Anglo-American relations are part of the war problem and indeed an indispensable part, and that nobody else but he can put in appropriate language and with historic detail the notion of the so-called British Empire, not as an exploiting force but as scattered members throughout the world of a cohesive whole expressing and making possible a democratic society. Casey said he agreed entirely, that he tried to talk to Churchill about it twice, but "he is, as you know, a man of temperament and of moods, and what I said didn't catch fire." I said that's precisely it—that Churchill must be ignited in order to put into words, after he himself has attained understanding of the problem, a picture of the British people and of British purposes very different from those which dominate the minds of so many Americans, namely, that Great Britain is an oppressor people and itself under the rule of fox-hunting, old school-tie, Buckingham Palace, George the Third, society. Casey started to take notes of what I was saying and asked me whether I could put on paper in a letter to him of a page or so the kind of thing I would say to Churchill if I were talking to him. I told him I would try my hand at it.

Casey told me he had a visit with Cordell Hull who rather bewildered him by a harangue of more than twenty minutes against DeGaulle [2] and the attacks

[2] The successful Allied landings in French North Africa had brought to the surface the intense conflict among several French factions for the right to represent the reviving French nation. On the one side the Vichy collaborationists were represented by Admiral Jean François Darlan, who suddenly appeared as the controlling authority in France's North African possessions. On the other side was General Charles DeGaulle, who had sustained France's honor at the moment that Darlan under Marshal Pétain had sullied it. In between was General Henri Giraud, who had been smuggled out of France and, arriving at Gibraltar, fell into violent argument with General Ei-

on him (Hull) for his Vichy policy which Africa has vindicated, and grievous complaints against Great Britain for being responsible, somehow or other, for DeGaulle. Casey said he didn't understand it for everybody he knew or had seen thought that Eisenhower's arrangement with Darlan was a military necessity, and that so far as DeGaulle was concerned to his knowledge Great Britain merely recognized the fact that when France collapsed DeGaulle did lift up the standard against Hitler and has maintained it since. I then explained to him Hull's excessive sensitiveness, to wit, preoccupation with criticism, that the State Department on the morrow of the North African landing, seized the opportunity to defend itself for its Vichy policy, that its premature crowing was quickly spoiled by the appearance of Darlan and the inability of most people to adjust themselves to Darlan as an ally from Darlan as an opponent, and the State Department instead of leaving the interpretation of the situation entirely to the military, was giving the appearance to the public, however unjustly, of sponsoring Darlan on his own account, or at the least sponsoring conditions that would enable Darlan to dig in for the future. I told Casey that what was plain to me was that all the political debate regarding the future of France by announcing impressively the principles of our French policy, namely, that the future of political France must be determined not by us but a future freed France; that that means the necessary steps for properly mobilizing and equipping as large a French Army as possible under a French Commander but subordinate to General Eisenhower, that the future Free France is, as it were, in suspense but under our trusteeship, and therefore we must allow nothing to be done to promote the interests of any contenders for political power once France is free to make her own choice; that of course there is need for local administration in Algiers, Morocco, etc., but within the confined scope of a civil administration in time of war—a very different thing from a provisional French Government. To which Casey gave hearty assent.

Isaiah Berlin [3] dined with us with his usual whimsical and wise comments on the universe. When we got around to the French problem, he told me that the feeling between the State Department and their Foreign Office on the French business was getting very troublesome. When I told him in substance my views on the French situation, as above summarized, he entirely agreed, adding, however, that that is not the policy that the State Department has been encouraging public opinion on either side of the ocean to understand.

---

senhower over who was to be in supreme command, and subsequently, especially after Darlan's timely assassination on Christmas eve, began to feud with DeGaulle. A. A. Berle wrote in his diary, January 4, 1943: "The DeGaulle-Giraud controversy reflects in large measure the desire of the British Foreign Office to have a public government of their own in North Africa, and there is an undercurrent of latent resentment that the United States appears in the area as a political factor at all."

[3] Isaiah Berlin was with the British Embassy. His analyses of American politics and personalities made such an impression on Churchill because of their style, wit, and clarity that Churchill directed that he see them immediately on arrival. Berlin had first come to know Frankfurter as a young tutor at Oxford, during Frankfurter's year there in 1933–1934 as Eastman Professor.

Thursday, January 7

Sitting.

We dined at the Tixiers'.[1] He is the head of the delegation of the Fighting French. Besides two other Frenchmen who are DeGaulle's representatives, Harold Butler, the British Minister, and his wife were there.

After dinner I had a rather full talk with Tixier about the North African situation. The sum of his position is contained in his statement that "We are fighting Fascists, including French Fascists." And his bitter grievance is that Mr. Hull over-simplifies the situation and really has not the slightest understanding of the French problem in North Africa. Tixier says that Hull tells them again and again that they should forget all their political differences—that is, the French—until after the war is over. Tixier says that is gross over-simplification. According to his view, Giraud is a prisoner of the Vichyites who surround him, and not until they are cleaned out will there be the effective incentive of Frenchmen to fight for Frenchmen do not want to fight for a Fascist France—the Frenchmen, that is, who were not collaborists after the collapse in '40, and who since then have become active men of resistance. Tixier thinks that once Giraud is "freed" from his imprisonment by the twenty or thirty-odd collaborists who surround him, there would be no trouble in working out an arrangement between DeGaulle and Giraud. He emphatically denied that he thought we ought to establish or recognize a provisional French government, but on the other hand, if arrangements for the peace among the United Nations are in process during the war, France must have a share in that process or it otherwise will not recognize any arrangements that may have been come to. When I asked Tixier who really is responsible for the French problem in the State Department—he replied "Everybody and nobody—Hull, Welles, Berle, Atherton." [2] But he indicated that nobody really knows anything about North Africa, that Murphy [3] is the great authority, and that Murphy's education and knowledge are derived from his relation with Weygand.[4]

---

[1] Adrien P. Tixier represented the Free French in Washington.

[2] Sumner Welles was Under Secretary of State, A. A. Berle an Assistant Secretary of State, and Ray Atherton, a career diplomat, was Chief of the European Affairs Division.

[3] Robert Murphy, wartime Chargé in Vichy, had been sent to North Africa in February 1941, to negotiate an economic agreement with General Maxime Weygand, who was then Vichy's "Delegate General of French Africa." In the course of these negotiations, which were protracted, Murphy became a major architect of U. S. policy in that area and was deeply involved in the political preparations connected with the Allied landings.

[4] Of General Weygand, who commanded the French armies at the time of France's surrender, Churchill wrote, "He had a profound, lifelong dislike of the parliamentary regime of the Third Republic. As an ardently religious Catholic, he saw in the ruin which had overwhelmed his country that chastisement of God for its abandonment of the Christian faith" (*Their Finest Hour*, p. 201).

Friday, January 8

Sitting.

Charlie Poletti [1] called after Court as arranged by phone earlier. He is now Special Assistant to the Secretary of War and is yet in the stage of becoming acquainted with the Department and finding himself. He told me that it was at first arranged he was to have the highest classification which carried with it a $8,000 salary, but he advised McCloy [2] that he thought it was undesirable to give him a higher salary than some of the others, say like Bundy, [3] because it might expose Secretary Stimson to the attacks of mischief makers who might try to make capital of what they would regard as a large salary to a Democratic politician; that since he is under financial sacrifice in any event in coming down here, and that Jean—his wife—will have to go back to her old profession and earn some money to keep the family going, $1,500 more or less would make no difference. But the real purpose of his call was to ask my advice regarding an incident about which the papers were apparently full but of which I had not become aware. It appears that among the Christmas pardons customarily made by the Governor of New York, Charlie included somebody named Hoffman, a minor labor leader, who had served eight months of a from four to eight years sentence. The Hearst press and Pegler and the World-Telegram have violently opened up on Charlie because of the discovery that Hoffman had once taken part in a Communist May Day parade or something like that, that therefore Hoffman was a Communist, that Charlie was the stooge of Communists, was flooding the country with subversive criminals etc., etc. The fact is that he pardoned Hoffman on the representations made by Sidney Hillman as well as the Employers Association and the impartial chairman and one of the lawyers for Archbishop Spellman, all of whom urged on Governor Poletti the past record of the man and the doubts about the justice of his conviction, tried as he was before a judge named Downs who is notoriously unjudicial in his performances. Charlie wanted to know whether he should take any note of the vicious campaign against him, his concern being more particularly that Stimson and McCloy might feel embarrassed by this turn of some of the press against him. I told him that that is not the kind of a man Stimson is.

[1] Charles Poletti, *cum laude* Harvard Law School, 1928, elected lieutenant governor of New York on a ticket headed by Herbert Lehman, had served briefly as governor after Lehman had resigned in late 1942 to become Director of Foreign Relief and Rehabilitation. Although Poletti went to Washington to serve as civilian adviser, he was commissioned as a lieutenant colonel, having declined the rank of colonel, and was assigned to the Civil Affairs Division, the section dealing with the military government of occupied countries. Of Italian descent, he later became military governor of Italy.

[2] John J. McCloy was Assistant Secretary of War and Stimson's troubleshooter.

[3] Harvey H. Bundy, one-time Assistant Secretary of State, was Secretary of War Stimson's closest personal assistant.

Of course such an attack is not pleasant, but that he should pay no attention whatever and not allow himself to be betrayed into any kind of comment, otherwise he will be spending his time answering back and forth. The thing to do is to let the vicious press campaign eventually spend itself and if and when this is trotted out against him, in some future years, quote the documents on the basis of which he acted. He said he could not talk now without involving all the other people on whose recommendations he acted which, I said, is an added reason not to answer.

(Since dictating the above I saw the annexed item in the *New York Herald Tribune* for today.)

HOFFMAN QUITS UNION JOB
ON PAROLE BOARD'S ORDER

Resigns as Manager of Local and Drops Out of Sight

Alexander Hoffman resigned yesterday his job as general manager of the Cleaners and Dyers Union, Local 239, in accordance with the order Thursday by the New York State Board of Parole that he was not to continue that post because the crime for which he received a four-to-eight-year prison sentence grew out of his employment.

Hoffman, forty-one years old, was convicted of attempted arson in November, 1940. He served only eight months of his prison term before his sentence was commuted on Dec. 19 by former Governor Charles Poletti. Hoffman resumed his task of organizing non-union dry-cleaning shops until the Parole Board registered its disapproval of his continuation of those activities.

Hoffman was not available yesterday. At the offices of the union at 403 Fourth Avenue Julius G. Cohen secretary of the local, said that Hoffman had appeared for only a few moments to hand in his resignation as general manager and then departed. Hoffman's press agent and Parole Commissioner Sanford Bates refused to disclose Hoffman's home address.

Mr. Cohen said that while Hoffman no longer retained his post in the union, he still had a union card and was entitled to all rights of a member. However, he said, Hoffman has divorced himself completely from all official activities of the union, an affiliate of the Congress of Industrial Organizations.

Commissioner Bates said he did not know whether Hoffman had another job, but that there were many available for Hoffman and other parolees at the board's employment office in the State Building, 80 Centre Street.

Saturday, January 9

Conference, which lasted until 6:15 P.M. This partly due to the habit of Stone, unlike Hughes' behavior, of carrying on a running debate with any justice who expresses views different from his. The result is not only the usual undesirable atmosphere created by contentious debate, but lack of that austerity of atmosphere which I thought so admirable in a scrupulous observance of each man's saying his say in turn without an interruption, as Hughes conducted the Conference, but also an inevitable dragging out of the discussion.

Dick Casey asked me to see him again and he turned up at nine o'clock and although he said he had to leave at about twenty minutes past ten, he did not leave until nearly half past eleven. He wanted to talk with me about Palestine and his relations with the Jewish Agency [1] people. He said "I feel a hostility on the part of the Jewish representatives whenever I see them, and I don't know why they should feel that way, so I come to you as the one man in the world who can make me understand their problems and possibly shed light on their attitude toward me personally." I told him I was greatly surprised, indeed dumbfounded to hear that any personal differences should have arisen between him and the Jewish leaders in Palestine, that this is the first I had heard of it, and I did not believe that however much they had made him feel their dissatisfaction with him, I am sure it had nothing what ever to do with him as a person, but rather that he now symbolizes the long experience they had had with the British Government in frustrating their hopes. I said that in order to understand the Palestine problem he would have to understand—what is very difficult for any outsider to understand—the position of Jews throughout the world (he interrupted at this point to say that that was exactly where he would like me to begin), or indeed for any member of a majority to understand the position and conditions of a more or less oppressed minority—the difficulty of an Englishman to understand what, as a matter of pure reason, is at times, or appears to be the behavior of the Irish or of the Indians.

I then tried to make Casey comprehend something of the position of the Jew in history, the resulting psychological state—at times aggressive, at times too deferential—and the resulting sensitiveness and preoccupation with grievances, or so it would appear to a person like himself who has no grievances because the Fates had been good to him. In order to make clear to him that the impact upon him of the Palestinian problems has behind it a long history, I read to him portions of my notes written in June, 1934, on my visit to Palestine. When he seemed so puzzled that the Jews should be constantly complaining to him about MacMichael (the High Commissioner in Palestine who, incidentally, is a nephew of Lord Curzon) and said how lacking in tact it was to speak to him, a member of the War Cabinet, critically of MacMichael, I

---

[1] At that time the Jewish Agency was the representative of the Jewish settlers in Palestine.

pointed out to him that, after all, MacMichael is for practical purposes the British Government for Jews in their daily lives, and while it is easy for him to say that the Jews should forget their differences until after the war, disregard of what he calls "differences" means life and death to the Jews, as they see their future.[2] I traced, as best I could, the relation of Palestine to the Jewish problem in the world, told him that perhaps the best way for him to understand the Zionist aspirations would be to read the speeches of that unsentimental, cool headed Scot, Lord Balfour, who was the author of the Balfour Declaration, and who thought that considering the contributions of the Jew in the history of mankind, a contribution directly related to the fact that the Jewish people lived in that strange and wonderful place called Palestine, made it not unimportant to the future of civilization that they be given the opportunity of seeing what more was in them for the benefit of mankind, but giving them the opportunities of a free life in that small territory, without dislodging the Arabs, considering the fact that such a vast domain for the Arab world was wrested from the Turks and given to the Arabs after the last war.

My sum total impression was that poor Dick Casey never in his life, gave a thought to the position of the Jew in the world in general, or to Zionism in particular, that he suddenly is confronted with problems for which he has no background, and which, being only a small aspect of his total responsibility, come to him as a nuisance and the Jews who bring these problems, as unreasonable nuisances.

He told me that Churchill is a staunch and uncompromising friend of Zionism, but when he tried to talk with him about some of the difficulties, Churchill just wouldn't listen. With considerable naivete, he said to me, "I tell you another great friend of the Zionist cause, General Smuts." The whole talk revealed that Casey not only knows nothing of the whole history of the Balfour Declaration and of Palestine since then, but he doesn't even know that there is such a history or that people like me know it.

The talk about Palestine occupied most of our time. He then went on to summarize the factors that explain the successful stopping of Rommel and their subsequent offensive—change of leadership, adequate preparation, appropriate matériel and morale.[3]

He also told me of the serious wounding of the youngest son of the Halifaxes, having heard from his wife from Cairo, that the lad's two legs had to be cut off, but that he probably will live, and that he sent a message to Mrs.

[2] Dissatisfaction with the British High Commissioner centered around two issues: the obstacles placed in the way of the admission of refugees from Europe and the slowness with which the British were recruiting and arming a Jewish Brigade to fight against the Axis.

[3] In early 1942 Rommel's Afrika Korps pushed the British back to El Alamein, the gateway to Alexandria and Cairo. Churchill replaced General Auchinleck with General Sir Harold Alexander and General Sir Bernard Montgomery. Under their leadership, the reinforced and now better equipped British Eighth Army swept Rommel back to Tripoli, where he prepared for a final stand in Tunisia.

Casey to send to Lord Halifax, "Tell father and mother not to fuss about me." Casey had to break the news to Lord Halifax who immediately summoned Lady Halifax to tell her, and Casey was full of admiration for the stoicism with which they behaved. Said Casey "My God, I don't mind saying I just couldn't take it as they have done."

Sunday, January 10

Went with the Athertons to Alexandria to lunch with the MacLeishes. Archie told of the new conflict between the OSS and the OWI in regard to control over so-called political broadcasting abroad. Evidently the Joint Chiefs of Staff have recommended that such authority be part of the military and therefore within the control of OSS. OWI say it is within the Executive Order of their authority, and the unresolved conflict is apparently still before the President.[1]

Monday, January 11

Sitting.

A message having come to Frank Murphy on the bench advising him that Wiley Rutledge's name had been sent in to the Senate to succeed Byrnes as Associate Justice, he told me, and then the following conversation ensued:

F. M.   I discovered Rutledge when, as Attorney General, I was looking for good men for Circuit Court places.

F. F.   Would it interest you to learn that some ten days before the President named me, he asked me to give him my views on Wiley Rutledge's qualifications for the Supreme Court, and I sent him a memorandum—after I had adequately informed myself—saying he was entirely qualified for this bench.

F. M.   That is surprising because the President never told me about it.

F. F.   Well, Presidents of the United States sometimes don't tell themselves things.

[1] In June 1942, Roosevelt had combined the Office of Facts and Figures, headed by MacLeish, the Office of Government Reports, and the Foreign Information Service of William J. Donovan's Office of the Co-ordinator of Information (later known as the Office of Strategic Services) into a new Office of War Information. He named Elmer Davis, a fearless and widely respected newspaperman and radio commentator, to head the O.W.I. It was given two different assignments—overseas it was a propaganda agency; at home it was supposed to present straight news. The armed services had already indicated they would not give up their control of the issuance of military information, either at home or abroad. They were less successful in their efforts to take over the control of political broadcasting abroad.

F. M. (laughingly) To show you the range of my influence there will be three men on this Court whom I recommended, one of whom will be President one of these days and another probably Chief Justice.

F. F. How many plugged nickels would you give for Bill Douglas' chance of becoming President?

F. M. Well, I think all the other contenders for the nomination will kill themselves off and that will leave only Bill.

F. F. I didn't ask you for his chances to become a candidate but his chances to become President.

F. M. Well, no Democrat will be elected in '44; but Bill will be named, I believe. I am only sorry that in order to gain what he believes to be the Catholic vote, the financial end of his campaign is being managed by Joe Kennedy and Johnnie Burns, and Brandon and Paul Shields.[1] But he will run in such a way as to make himself available the next time thereafter.

F. F. I am surprised, Frank, that it doesn't shock you to have this Court made a jumping-off place for politics.

F. M. Well, I don't like it.

F. F. Well, it's much more than a matter of not liking. When a priest enters a monastery, he must leave—or ought to leave—all sorts of worldly desires behind him. And this Court has no excuse for being unless it's a monastery. And this isn't idle, high-flown talk. We are all poor human creatures and it's difficult enough to be wholly intellectually and morally disinterested when one has no other motive except that of being a judge according to one's full conscience. And the returns are all in on judges of this Court who, while on the Court, have had conflicting political ambitions. We know all the instances and the experience is unedifying and disastrous.

F. M. Well I quite agree with you that it is not a good thing. I don't like it. But I am just telling you what I think will happen.

After the sitting, Moe Huberman, an old student of mine (1928 H. L. S.) who has for some time been in the Anti-Trust Division, came in by

---

[1] Joseph Kennedy, the first Chairman of the Securities and Exchange Commission, had brought William O. Douglas down from Yale Law School to work for the S.E.C. and later had suggested to Roosevelt that he appoint Douglas as head of the S.E.C. John J. Burn, the first Roman-Catholic on the Harvard Law School faculty, also was brought into the S.E.C. by Kennedy as Chief Counsel. When he left government service for private practice, he was on annual retainer from Kennedy. Paul Shields, head of a Wall Street brokerage house and father-in-law of Gary Cooper, was, wrote Douglas, "one of the few Wall Street men to support me in my effort to clean up the Stock Exchange. Brandon was head of the New England S.E.C."

arrangement and told me that he wanted me to hear at first hand of the circumstances which led him to leave the Department. In short, he said it has never been congenial to work with Thurman Arnold [2] who is a self-exploiting individual with essentially Fascistic leanings, and when finally the other day he asked him to give up the important work he was doing in connection with the war and to take on some anti-trust prosecution with which he was not in sympathy, he refused. When Arnold tried to turn the heat and tried to cajole him, his self-respect called a halt and he resigned. He said that what he most longed for was to get into uniform (he is classified as 3A having a wife and two children), but if that is not possible, he did not think he would go into any other civil agency of the government, and of the alternatives for practice, while he was assured of making a lot of money in Washington, he doesn't like that for various reasons of taste, and so it is a question of either New York or San Francisco. The latter place has the biggest pull for him, though it is naturally the most hazardous, and I strongly encouraged him to go there rather than to New York.

Before dinner Bob Sherwood and Archie MacLeish came in to ask my advice regarding the conflict of authority as between the OSS and the OWI, and more particularly the proper distribution of authority regarding responsibility for so-called political warfare as between the civil and military authorities. I suggested that no one was better fitted for the wise consideration of the problem than the civil head of the Army, to wit, Secretary Stimson. [3]

North Whitehead, now one of the advisors on American affairs of the British Foreign Office, here on a visit, dined with us, and the talk was mostly about Anglo-American relations along the lines of my conversation with Dick Casey the other day. Whitehead said that the center of difficulty was that Churchill was a great war leader preoccupied with the combative side of the war, and so that there is no spokesman in the British Government, what with negligible [?] feeling of the people of Great Britain, namely the indispensable [need] of building a world along the general lines of the Wallace-Milo Perkins, etc. talk. [4]

[2] Thurman Arnold, Assistant Attorney General in charge of the antitrust division, believed that the work of the division was "just as important during the war as it was prior to the war" because wartime procurement "created a great opportunity for conspiratorial agreements . . . with respect to prices, bidding, consolidations, and mergers." Henry Wallace in his diary for September 1, 1942 reported that at the W.P.B. meeting, "Don Nelson felt very deeply that Arnold was interfering with the war effort by some of the prosecutions which he is starting." In May 1943, Roosevelt appointed Arnold a federal circuit court judge.

[3] Robert E. Sherwood, playwright, member of the inner White House circle, was at that time director of the Overseas Branch of the O.W.I. In the conflict between the armed forces and the O.W.I., Stimson was on the side of the military.

[4] Wallace's speech, "The Price of Free World Victory," May 8, 1942, describing the war as a phase of the "people's revolution," and the peace that was desired as "a people's peace," had, in the absence of comparable definitions of war aims by Roosevelt and Churchill, an enormous reception.

Tuesday, January 12

Sitting.

Charlie and Jean Poletti were in for sherry. We again went over Charlie's problem regarding the Hoffman case and the upshot of the talk was that I suggested to him that he make a memorandum now, have it properly witnessed by Col. George Brownell, and give it to Jack McCloy for file in the War Department. What bothers Charlie is that he should be silent in regard to an action taken by him as Governor which he now knows was based partly on inaccurate representation made to him. My point to him was that neither [he] nor Gov. Dewey nor the N. Y. Parole Board can legally undo what he did, it is idle to make an avowal of the fact that he was misled because that would only add new fuel to the flames of controversy. It will be time enough to make a full statement when some duty, as, for instance, an appearance before a Congressional Committee, or some responsible accusation is made, if sometime in the future he should again run for office, make it appropriate and right to make public answer. Then he should read the statement which he will now prepare and file away.

Wednesday, January 13

Sitting.

Lunch—C. J. gave expression to some of the prevalent views about not being able to "win the peace" because Great Britain will want to return to the status quo and Russia has materialistic designs, and all that would provoke isolationism in this country. To which I replied by stating what I believe to be the true opinion of the British people, their desire, even more than that of our people for a postwar world à la Wallace, the necessity of resolving to aim for such a world with them instead of erecting old suspicions and prejudices and fears into barriers, that without such collaboration and insistence on agreement with the British, any kind of a decent world order is precluded.

Thursday, January 14

Sitting.

On argument today was a birth control case from Connecticut challenging the constitutionality of the Connecticut statute construed by the Connecticut Court of Errors and Appeals to be an absolute restriction against means of artificially controlling birth, even in the case of physicians seeking to give such

---

Milo Perkins helped Wallace with this speech and was speaking along similar lines. Frankfurter's secretary must have gotten this entry wrong. British popular feeling strongly favored a statement of war aims. Beveridge's "cradle-to-grave" plan for Social Security had been widely acclaimed. See Jan. 13th entry.

aid for reasons of health or jeopardy to life.[1] On behalf of the birth controllers the case was argued by Morris Ernst supported by Professor Borchard of Yale who supposedly is an expert on procedural problems presented by the case. The threshold question was whether the appeal was properly before us as it probably was not because of a failure adequately to lay, so far as the physicians were concerned, the restrictions upon their "liberty" by the construction which the Connecticut court gave to the Connecticut statute. The arguments by both Ernst and Borchard were lamentable—both revealed their incompetence so far as any understanding of the problem of federal jurisdiction is concerned. By contrast, the lawyer for Connecticut, William Beers of Connecticut, made an argument at once very engaging and highly competent.

Dined at Lefty Lewis' with Colonel Ned Buxton, Professor Langer, Sherman Kent and others of the OSS. General talk.[1]

Friday, January 15

Sitting.

Curtice Hitchcock [1] back from England—and it must be borne in mind that he is a very canny, unenthusiastic Scot reinforced by Vermont shrewdness and Cal Coolidge unenthusiasm—reports two outstanding impressions from his extensive tour of England and Scotland where he saw all sorts of people and talked with fifteen or so diverse groups. First, that he has not the slightest doubt

---

[1] *Tileston v. Ullman,* 318 U. S. 44 (1943).

The Court disposed of the case in a *per curiam* ruling ("by the Court" without indication of individual authorship). The opinion held that the plaintiff, a physician, was not the proper party to complain of the risk to the lives of his patients engendered by potential state enforcement against him of Connecticut's anti-birth control statute, as he could assert no injury to his constitutional rights, whatever the injury to his patients.

In 1961, in *Poe v. Ullman,* 367 U. S. 497, Frankfurter for the Court dismissed another attack on Connecticut's anti-birth control statute. This time, since the case was brought by a group of patients and doctors, the Court's argument was that it presented no justiciable issue, meaning that the Connecticut law was a dead letter one and not enforced. The Court's majority was a narrow five to four one, and among the sharpest dissenters was Justice Harlan, who, in his advocacy of judicial restraint, was usually quite close to Frankfurter.

The Connecticut opponents of the statute returned home, opened a clinic, got themselves arrested and criminally convicted, and when the case reached the Court in *Griswold v. Connecticut,* 381 U. S. 479 (1965), the issue was finally decided on its merits and the statute was ruled an unconstitutional violation of the right to privacy. Subsequently the Court went much further, upsetting a Massachusetts statute that banned the distribution of contraceptives and upholding the right of abortion as a constitutional right.

At the end of this development the question becomes unavoidable: did Frankfurter's philosophy of restraint mandate his position on this issue? Or was the doctrine of restraint a convenient device for evading an uncomfortable issue?

[1] "Lefty Lewis" was Wilmarth Sheldon Lewis of New Haven, authority on Walpole and formerly a Yale trustee.

[1] Curtice Hitchcock, president of the publishing house of Reynal & Hitchcock, had just returned from surveying the book situation in England.

that as a whole the mass of the English people are much more eager and ready for translating into action the Atlantic Charter and the Wallace ideas of a postwar settlement than our own people. Second, a surprising widely conscious new and deep interest in American manifested through the introduction of American history in the curricula of British schools and colleges, etc. etc., to a degree for which there is no comparable interest or understanding of things British on this side.

Dined at Dean Acheson's together with the Owen Dixons, the Australian Minister, the Governor Lehmans, and the Milo Perkinses. After dinner, when the men were alone, the talk was sticky and stodgy. I was confirmed in my view of Lehman—he is unimaginative, timid, conventional-minded, and, like most men who have held high office, preoccupied with his own past and his own future. When I asked him for some general observation on the differences between government in Albany and government in Washington, instead of commenting on the different ways of carrying on government, he launched forth into complacent remarks about his own job in Albany and his own job here and how much he likes both and how lovely everybody is to him, etc., etc. I was likewise confirmed in my impression of Milo Perkins—that he is a very interesting and intelligent fellow with enormous vitality and purposefulness, but what his purposes are I have never been able to ascertain because he never indulges in the free play of the spirit and plays his cards very close to his chest.

Saturday, January 16

Conference.

One of the matters we had up was an appeal from Ohio—*Dunn v. Ohio* [1]—which raised a very technical question whether a claim under the federal Constitution which was specifically proferred to the Ohio Supreme Court and had been before the Court of first instance in Ohio, the Court of Common Pleas, was saved and therefore gave us jurisdiction although it had not been formally placed on appeal from the Court of Common Pleas to the Court of Appeal of Cuyahoga County. The problem involved an interpretation of the formula used by the Ohio Supreme Court, to wit, "no debatable constitutional question is involved," and more specifically does that formula cover a federal constitutional question that was placed before the Ohio Supreme Court together with a state constitutional question when, as I have said, the federal constitutional question does not explicitly present it to the intermediate appellate court. The C. J. had originally recommended dismissal of the appeal on the ground that the federal constitutional question had not been saved in the court of appeal. I did not sufficiently attend to the matter and voted that way but when the C. J.'s draft of a per curiam opinion came around, it stirred doubts in me. And investigation confirmed the doubts and led me to conclude

[1] *Dunn v. Ohio*, 318 U. S. 739 (1943).
The Court dismissed the appeal in a *per curiam* opinion consistent with the views stated here by Frankfurter.

that according to Ohio practice, the "no debatable constitutional question" covered both federal as well as state constitutions. To that end I circulated a memorandum setting forth my grounds.

At the Conference, the C. J. elaborately replied to my memorandum and when I was asked to state my views, there followed what is in danger of becoming a habit with the C. J., of not allowing a Justice to state his views uninterruptedly when contrary to those of the C. J. but to argue almost every word that is uttered, thereby breaking up the discussion and making of it a needless contention, and, of course, causing a frightful waste of time. Several of the Brethren, especially Roberts and Black, have talked to me complainingly of this. When, last year, Lauson Stone the Chief's oldest son, asked me confidentially how his Dad was carrying on as C. J., I told him that I had only one qualification to make, and that is precisely the practice of which today's performance was such an egregious example, namely, his failure to observe what seems to me to be an indispensably wise order of procedure—for the C. J. to have his say, and then in order of seniority, for every other member of the Court to have his say without any interruption. Lauson said he recognized the phenomenon I was talking about and urged me strongly to speak to his Dad about it, saying that he would take it very well from me. Maybe he would—but I have not done so.

The Jim Byrneses were at dinner. Jim said two things that left one with concern: He thought that there was a real widespread absurd notion abroad in the land that the war is practically over, that the talks of Wallace and Willkie, in their preoccupation with the terms of peace, were stirring and stimulating such belief, and that he found the assumption that by summer it would be all over widely prevalent, particularly in the West and in the South. By way of illustration, he said he has it at first hand that Governor Bricker of Ohio is planning his whole campaign of winning the Republican nomination on the premise that the war will be over this year, and that he, as it were, would be "the honest Harding" ushering in a new period of normalcy. Secondly, he said he listened the other day to speeches by ten newly elected Senators, both Republicans and Democrats, and he never had such a sense of intellectual bankruptcy. He said there was not one thought or idea or bit of illumination in the whole outfit, and the only thing they talked about was that they were committed to abolishing "bureaucracy." Jim, who is not given to extravagant statements one way or the other, thought that the new Senate as a whole is about as poor, indeed he thought on a lower level, than any he had known about in his whole life.

Sunday, January 17

Lunch at Gene Meyer's.[1] Supper at the Francis Biddle's.[2]

---

[1] Eugene Meyer was publisher of the Washington *Post*.

[2] Francis Biddle was Attorney General.

Monday, January 18

Opinion day—beginning of recess.

Conference before and after Court.

One of the cases for Conference discussion was the review of the affirmance of the conviction of Nucky Johnson.[1] Several of the Brethren gave expression to views in voting to reverse because of alleged errors at the trial to which at the time no exceptions were taken. I let loose when it came to my turn by saying that while Taft was given somewhat to extravagant language, when he said "The administration of the American criminal law is a disgrace to civilization," he was overdrawing it a bit, in essentials that was a correct characterization. And there are two reasons for the low standards and inefficiencies of American criminal justice. Two contradictory influences—at one end are the brutalities of third degree methods and all that and the relatively violent and vulgar methods of prosecution compared, as I would say, with British standards, except that it would stir the fur of my Irish secretary to whom I am dictating this. At the other, is the tendency of American appellate courts, including the Supreme Court itself, to upset convictions on the most unreal grounds by forgetting that the printed record of what took place at the trial is not the basis for playing a meticulous formalistic game, called a quest for error, but an inadequate portrayal, as much as print can portray, of what took place during the course of the trial, in order to ascertain whether that which is complained of on appeal really touched the nerve centers of the living trial, and whether that which is complained of as an error in fact could have prejudiced the accused. This case is a striking illustration of a quest for error because a defendant who was sheriff of the county, with all that that implies, defended by a man who was United States Attorney, and therefore cognizant, not only of the appropriate procedures of the federal court, but also alert to the human factors that are so important in the criminal trial, now complains of alleged misconduct of the trial judge, to which at the time no objection was taken. And these so-called errors were raised by a new counsel, for new purposes, to wit, to persuade us of the enormities which were not realized contemporaneously. The eventual opinions in this case will show how this Court is dealing with this problem.

---

[1] *Johnson v. United States*, 318 U. S. 189.

Johnson, a Republican "boss" in New Jersey, was convicted of tax evasion. He appealed his conviction on the ground that it was error for the district judge to allow the prosecutor to comment to the jury on his refusal to answer certain questions. Johnson argued that his Fifth Amendment privileges against self-incrimination had been diluted by the judge's permitting the prosecutor to suggest to the jury that guilt might be inferred from refusal to answer.

The Court, in an opinion by Justice Douglas, held it was error for the district judge to have permitted the prosecutor to comment, but affirmed the conviction on the ground that Johnson had waived the objection. Frankfurter wrote a brief concurrence stating that he saw no error in permitting the prosecutor to comment on the failure to answer as, Johnson having taken the witness stand in his own defense, the district judge could have overruled his refusal to answer.

Dined with the Sam Rosenmans.[2] Talk was, of course, predominantly about things political—the President's final yielding to Ed Flynn's [3] insistence that he be "vindicated," that insistence having for some time taken the form of demanding appointment as Ambassador to China, which was compromised by sending Flynn to Australia. We talked a good deal about poor Missy Le Hand [4]—Sam Rosenman understanding, as very, very few people do the extraordinary beneficent role that Missy played in the Roosevelt Administration until her illness in 1941 because of the very remarkable judgment, disinterestedness, and pertinacity which she combined. Sam agreed with me that Missy's enforced withdrawal is a calamity of world dimensions in view of F. D. R.'s responsibility for world affairs. Sam said he always regarded her as one of the five most important people in the U. S. during the Roosevelt Administration, to which I replied that she seemed to me always to be the best most influential factor in the Administration, the President apart. One reason for this was, on which Sam and I agreed, that not the least important aspect of Missy's devotion to the President expressed itself in courageous truth-speaking to him. She was one of the very, very few people who was not a yes-man, who crossed the President in the sense that she told him not what she knew to be his view or what he wanted to hear, but what were, in fact, her true views and convictions. That she did all this with uncommon charm and persistence gives some indication of what her absence from the scene has withdrawn.

Tuesday, January 19

I. F. Stone of The Nation and PM, on urgent insistence, came to see me. He wanted to tell me the dubious and shifting talk he has had with Samuel Reber [1] of the State Department—who is concerned with French matters in

[2] Samuel I. Rosenman's association with Roosevelt dated back to the 1928 campaign for governor. He was the mainstay of the Roosevelt speech-writing team and during the war years served in addition as White House legal counsel, drafting many of the President's executive orders. He was part of the Roosevelt household and usually stayed at the White House when he was in Washington.

[3] Edward J. Flynn, political leader of the Bronx, had been Roosevelt's Secretary of State in New York and one of his top political strategists. He had stepped into the breach when James Farley broke with Roosevelt over the third term and managed the 1940 campaign. A cultivated man, he asked Roosevelt for an ambassadorship, but was obliged to ask Roosevelt to withdraw his name when it became clear the Senate would only confirm him with difficulty.

[4] Marguerite LeHand, an engaging, attractive woman, had become Roosevelt's personal secretary in 1920, and after his bout with polio in 1921 devoted herself to serving him. She, too, had become part of the Roosevelt household and worked devotedly until a stroke in 1941 disabled her. She lived out the final years until her death in 1944 as an invalid under constant medical care.

[1] Samuel Reber, a career diplomat, was Assistant Chief of the European Affairs Division. Widespread anxieties over United States readiness to work with Vichyites like Darlan were further fueled by reports that French civil authorities in North Africa were maintaining the anti-Jewish policies that the Vichy government had copied from Hitler's Nuremberg Laws.

that Department—regarding the lifting of some of the Vichy-Nuremberg decrees in North Africa. He said Reber told him there were all sorts of difficulties about lifting the anti-Jewish decrees without lifting the anti-Arab decrees. When Stone asked him what the anti-Arab decrees were, he talked vaguely and shiftingly. There is some talk that Reber is to be sent out to Africa to help work out the difficulties there. Stone said Reber was a typical State Department cookie-pusher—and the little I have seen myself of Reber, and what little more I know of him, justifies that description. He is one of these conventionally minded, unimaginative, formal "society" pursuing, little "professional" diplomats. He has about as much understanding of democratic processes as I have of thermo-dynamics.

In the course of his talk, Stone told me that according to Kenneth Crawford,[2] Berle said that the attribution to him of responsibility for the authorization of Otto of Hapsburg to raise an Austrian combat unit was my doing—that I had spread that rumor about him. This is utterly and completely without foundation, and a silly lie of Berle's to cover up his earlier lie that I was responsible for the Otto episode.

Attended a surprise dinner arranged by Ed Stettinius [3] to Captain Eddie Rickenbacker [4] who, for perhaps an hour, told with great particularity and unintended eloquence, the whole marvelous story of his Pacific Ocean adventure—the mishap to the plane that was to have carried him to China and the Far East generally to inspect our Air Forces, the subsequent unbelievable 21 days of himself and his companions on the two rafts—"I knew we didn't know where we were and I also knew that nobody could know either where we were or whether we were still alive, a helluva place from which to go and a helluva a place to which to come,"—and the miraculous rescue of all but a young Polish boy, Alec, whom they buried at sea.

Wednesday, January 20

Calvert Magruder,[1] the Senior Circuit Judge of the First Circuit, phoned me that he had been asked by the Department of State to serve as the chairman of a committee to investigate on behalf of Bolivia and this country, labor condi-

---

[2] Kenneth Crawford was head of the Washington Bureau of the newspaper *PM*.

[3] Edward R. Stettinius, Jr., former head of United States Steel, at that time was Lend Lease Administrator.

[4] Edward V. Rickenbacker, an American ace in the first World War, and head of Eastern Airlines, had been forced down while on a flight across the Pacific in 1942 and rescued after three weeks at sea on a life raft.

[1] Calvert Magruder had been selected by Professor Frankfurter as the first law clerk to Justice Brandeis, who later said to him, "Among all my law clerks Magruder was the best critic I had." Many of Frankfurter's own law clerks came to him after they had been with "The Judge," as they always called Magruder.

tions in the tin mines in Bolivia, upon which supply both the United States and Great Britain are dependent for tin. He said he had talked with the Chief Justice to ask whether to undertake such a mission would be within the ruling of the Judicial Conference against judges sitting in Labor Board cases, and the Chief Justice thought this was a very different problem and that it was for him, Magruder, to decide whether the condition of the docket in his Circuit permitted his leave of absence for whatever time this mission would take. I told him I agreed with the Chief, that there was no reason in propriety or anything pertaining to the function of the federal courts that should preclude his accepting this call, for the subject matter could never come before the courts. I told him that in view of his peculiar qualifications for this inquiry and the delicacy of the problems that were involved, I hoped he could arrange his judicial business so that he could go. I asked him whether he had considered that there may be a delicate diplomatic involvement, namely, that the State Department, through our Ambassador in Bolivia, had thrown the weight of this country against the labor demands in Bolivia. He said that he had not understood that was what the inquiry was about, and if that were involved he did not think he would undertake it. He asked me if I would talk to Dean Acheson about it—the official of the State Department who made the proposal to him over the phone. I did talk to Dean who rapidly rehearsed the circumstances of the affair and said that it arose out of a request of the Bolivian Government to have industrial economic questions investigated on behalf of both our governments and that he did not think the diplomatic row could possibly be inquired into. He said, however, that he would talk to Larry Duggan,[2] head of the Latin American work, and call me back. He did and said that Duggan said it was purely an economic investigation. I called Calvert back and told him the assurances Acheson had given and expressed the hope he would undertake the mission—involving the chairmanship of a committee of five—because of his ability in matters of this sort and the confidence that his report would arouse.

Thursday, January 21

The morning papers carried news, heretofore much talked about, that Robert Sherwood was going to North Africa to help straighten out the difficulties there, and more particularly as a counterpoise to Robert Murphy. I phoned him suggesting that before he goes he should have a full talk with Jean Monnet. The upshot was that Sherwood and I dined with Monnet at the latter's house. The whole North African-French situation was canvassed, not as a thing apart, but in its relation to the future France and the whole European problem, that is, more particularly the hopes and fears that are being inspired and should be inspired by what we do and do not do in regard to North Africa. Both Jean and I pressed on Sherwood the importance of a solemn commitment

---

[2] Laurence Duggan was State Department political adviser on Latin American affairs.

by the President, with which, of course, Churchill must associate himself so that there may not be an appearance of disagreement between the U. S. and Great Britain, that we deem ourselves the trustees of a future Free France, that no party outside of France could claim to be, and that we could not recognize the claim of anyone not called by the free will of France as a Provisional Government; that there is an ample provision in the French Constitution for the selection of a provisional government, when the central government is gone, as is the case, namely the *Conseil Generale* of the eighty-odd departments of France, the governing boards of the large administrative areas of metropolitan France, and three administrative areas in North Africa. Once such a general policy is solemnly announced to the French people and to the world, a direction will be given to all action, political debates will have to stop personalities will be reduced to their proper minor proportions, a French Army will be seen to be the instrument of a future Free France, and the present instrument, in subordination to the Commander-in-Chief, or a victorious France. Both Monnet and I are strongly of the opinion that Sherwood could be effective in Africa with General Eisenhower as a counterweight against Murphy only after the general policy was clearly announced to the world and given to him, as it were, as the authority for all the advice and urgings to be made by him in Africa. In other words, policy must be formulated here before one can have any confidence that execution will be wise in Africa.[1]

Friday, January 22

Had Dr. and Mrs. Weizmann for lunch. He has been in this country especially in connection with our rubber problem and has evidently contributed his great gifts as a chemist in connection with new synthetic processes. But he has been about the country much. He reports very great concern about the present temper of opinion which he thinks is extremely reactionary. As part of a reflex of that, but quite independently, he says he is shocked by the extent to which anti-Semitism is gaining ground in this country, quite unwittingly on the part of otherwise liberal-minded people. As he put it, "Hitler has won both here and in England to a less, but to an important extent, insofar as his campaign against the Jews is concerned." And that has been brought about by per-

---

[1] The political uproar over North Africa intensified when the press discovered that Marcel Peyrouton had gone from his refuge in Argentina to Algiers to become supreme political administrator in French North Africa. Peyrouton had been Vichyite Minister of Interior after the collapse of France, a post in which he was particularly harsh against dissenting countrymen and had promulgated Vichy's first anti-Jewish decrees. He had been brought to North Africa on Darlan's recommendation to Robert Murphy, who later said he had accepted him "without adequate information." On January 16 Roosevelt, who was at Casablanca meeting with Churchill, cabled Hull suggesting that Monnet come to North Africa to take charge of civilian administration. Hull, who had developed an obsessive hatred for the DeGaullists, vetoed the suggestion because he thought Monnet was too closely associated with DeGaulle.

meating the atmosphere, by a subtle process of infiltration due to constant reiteration of the Hitler line. The result is that both in this country and in England many people in government and other places of authority who have no sympathy at all with anti-Semitism, almost unconsciously yield to it as a matter of policy. This report from Weizmann is more than an ordinary man's estimate of opinion because Weizmann is one of those creatures who have a sixth or seventh sense in sniffing what is in the air.[1]

Saturday, January 23

Milton Katz asked to see me and when he came in the late afternoon, he stayed over an hour and a half. He went into considerable detail over the present situation in WPB, the immediate occasion for the difficulty being a new manifestation of the conflict between C. E. Wilson, President of the General Electric, who was brought down here to take charge of production as such, and Fred Eberstadt,[1] formerly of Dillon, Read & Co., an investment banker, who in conjunction with General Somervell, is constantly seeking to aggrandize authority (I knew something of Eberstadt from thirty years ago, through Emory Bucknor, after he left the law to join Dillon, Read, in connection with the Dodge-Chrysler row, a major litigation at the time. Eberstadt is a very able, utterly ruthless man, to whom the Prussian spirit can hardly be alien). The central difficulty is that Nelson is an utterly weak man incapable of exercising authority or making decisions if contending forces about him have to be composed. He is, as is well known almost deferential to Bernie Baruch's authority, who intermittently exercises it without the necessary responsibility and often the adequate knowledge for exercising judgment. Nelson is a weak man in more ways than one, and while he has real intelligence and capacity for under-

---

[1] Chaim Weizmann, a brilliant chemist as well as Zionist leader, came to the United States to urge the use of alcohol as a basis for synthesizing rubber, which had become necessary when Japan seized Indonesia and its rubber plantations. In the end the United States decided to manufacture synthetic rubber out of petroleum products. Weizmann also was arguing Palestine's capacities to absorb and sustain a much larger population than State Department experts would acknowledge was the case, and he was seeking to restrain the extremists among his fellow Zionists who were calling upon Great Britain to surrender the Palestine Mandate to the United States. He asserted that the future of the world depended upon friendly Anglo-American relations. "America doesn't want the mandate, and nobody wants to give it."

[1] The row between Eberstadt, who was backed by the armed services, and Wilson, who was backed by Nelson, caused Roosevelt on his return from Casablanca at the suggestion of Byrnes to ask Baruch to take over the chairmanship of the W.P.B. But within a few days it became clear to Byrnes that "for some reason the President did not want to appoint Baruch, and equally apparent that Baruch did not want to assume the responsibility of the office. . . ." Instead, Nelson counterattacked and, backed by Harry Hopkins, demanded and received Eberstadt's resignation, and also at Hopkins' suggestion agreed to turn over a large amount of the direction of the W.P.B. to Wilson. General Brehon B. Somervell was chief procurement officer for the army. He had been a top administrator of the Works Progress Administration under Hopkins and was one of the most powerful men in Washington.

standing, his experience as a subordinate in the Sears Roebuck organization, even though a highly placed subordinate, has evidently left in him habits of subordination, so that he is incapable of exercising with decision and despatch the authority which has been given him. According to Katz—and Monnet has indicated a similar view—the processes of production have really been brought into fine operation so that the gigantic program will certainly be carried out 80 percent, but could very easily through Wilson and the able production men whom he has brought down and could bring down, if they were not deterred by the confusion, reach 100 percent. The present row between Wilson and Eberstadt concerns the building of destroyer escorts and corvettes as part of the anti-U boat program. The submarine situation being what it is—submarines and the rubber deficiencies being the two most dangerous spots in the whole war situation—the controversy naturally has very significant aspects.

Billie Bullitt [2] came to dinner. General talk, a good deal of which played around the submarine hazard and the dilatory and unimaginative behavior of the Navy in coming to grips with this problem.

Sunday, January 24

Edgar Mowrer was most urgent in seeing me and when he came he told me the tale of his selection by Stettinius to go to North Africa on behalf of Lend-Lease, and the later—and present—resistance by Secretary Hull to his going including the latter's request to the Secretary of War that transportation not be provided for Mowrer. Evidently Elmer Davis has written a rather heated letter to Hull, giving some kind of an ultimatum though I do not quite understand why, if Edgar Mowrer is going for Stettinius, he (Stettinius) is not making the appropriate representations to the Secretary of State, rather than Davis on whose staff Mowrer happen to be. This incident opened up talk with Mowrer on State Department attitudes and activities, particularly those of Berle, who, according to Mowrer, has made [to] members of the OWI the most incredibly defeatist remarks, all leading to the proposition that we will have to do business with the Quislings everywhere. Edgar Mowrer is, of course, one of the most trained journalists of the day with a superb service of devotion to democratic ideals and anti-Fascist opposition. But it is very hard to believe that the things he reports as having been said by Berle were really expressed by Berle—even

---

[2] William C. Bullitt, Ambassador to the Soviet Union (1933–1936) and to France (1936–1941), had been one of Roosevelt's top advisers on foreign policy. He had one large shortcoming, a venomous jealousy of Sumner Welles, the Under Secretary of State, whom he was always seeking to replace. He had functioned as "Ambassador-at-large" since France's collapse, but without specific duties, and had now become special assistant to Secretary of the Navy Frank Knox. He told Henry Wallace on January 28, 1943 that he "would like to see Sumner Welles, Adolf Berle and Dean Acheson fired, and Cordell Hull given carte blanche." He also said that Peyrouton was as bad as he was being portrayed, but that "he will do a first class job in North Africa . . ." (*Wallace Diary*, edited by John Morton Blum, pp. 171–2).

though I well know that nothing can be so foolish or so incredible or so hostile to the avowed foreign policy of the President as to be incapable of being expressed privately by Berle. There is not one iota of doubt that Berle is almost pathologically anti-British and anti-Russian, and his anti-Semitism is thrown in, as it were, for good measure, though probably derived through certain personal hostilities and jealousies.

Marion and I had supper with the Stimsons alone. He wanted to relieve himself by talking for he has had a good many headaches recently—all of them attributable, as he says, to the fact that the conduct of the war reflects "disjointed administration," too many conflicting policies by agencies or administrators with conflicting authority as illustrated by the rubber situation, the manpower problem (a directive issued for McNutt's appointment without giving the Army the opportunity to express views on the proposed setup), and the conflict between Davis and Donovan regarding psychological warfare which, of course, is badly needed, but which cannot be effectively carried on when two agencies and two heads operate under two contradictory directives. I told Stimson that he had better make up his mind that orderly procedure is not and never has been the characteristic of this Administration—it has other virtues but not that. And so he had better reconcile himself to looseness of administration and the inevitable frictions and conflicts resulting therefrom which naturally go against the grain of an orderly, systematic brain like his. But I reminded him also that this is not his first experience with loose administration whereby much of his energy and thought is used trying to straighten out messes that should have never have occurred. The good thing about toothaches is that you don't remember past ones. So I reminded him how frequently during the time he was Secretary of War in Taft's administration he used to say, "I wish I didn't have to spend so much time stopping rat-holes." To which Stimson replied with great animation, "Did I say that then? I had forgotten. I have said it a great many times during the course of this year." To which I added, "Yes, you did say it a great deal, beginning with 1911 when you first came down here, and for the same reason that you are saying it now."

Monday, January 25

John Frank, law clerk to my Brother Black, asked to see me. When he came in he showed a good deal of uneasiness, saying he had something personal to say to me that probably would be very distressing and hemmed and hawed around so much that I yielded to the temptation to say that when he gets to be sixty he will learn, I hope, to be distressed without being discouraged. And so he finally said what was on his mind, which, in substance was the following: A junior officer of the Navy—I do not recall whether an Ensign or a Lieutenant—who was in Naval Intelligence, came to the Marshal [of the Court] to ask about Willard Hurst. Hurst came to the H. L. S. from Wisconsin where he had had a notable record, which he equalled at the Law School. He attracted my attention as one of the most scholarly minds I had encountered, particularly trained for historical research. He stayed with me a year as a Research Fellow and I then sent him to Brandeis as his law clerk. He then returned to Wisconsin; came to Washington several months ago with the BEW, and now is in the Intelligence of the Navy. He was being investigated before final detail was given him. The Marshal knew that John Frank was a friend of Hurst's, having been one of his pupils at Wisconsin. This Naval officer told Frank that what he called "the brass hats" are particularly anxious to guard against Communists getting into the Navy inasmuch as, in the view of those officers, our next war will be with Russia. He went on to say that the fact that Hurst was law clerk to Justice Brandeis naturally aroused suspicion that he was too leftist, when Frank suggested that I knew Hurst well and he might see me, the officer replied that it might be very undesirable from Hurst's point of view that his connection with me be known.

Throughout his recital Frank was very much disturbed. I tried to calm him by saying, "Of course the experience you had (it took place a few days ago) is disturbing in a way, but as I indicated to you at the outset, one must encounter such disturbances without being discouraged." I then probed Frank to ascertain whether the talk of the Naval officer reflected the views of a silly man. Frank said he was a graduate of the Yale Law School of two or three years ago, and had been a Naval Research officer. Apparently he reported the views of responsible senior Naval officers, at least when he spoke of the future war with Russia and the connection with Brandeis. Frank said he wanted to be very sure he was answering my question accurately since he thought it important, and that he could not speak with assurance as to the significance of all that the officer said. But he felt that the suggestion that a recommendation of mine might hurt rather than help Hurst was an inference that the Naval man drew from his assumption about the attitude of mind of the Naval Intelligence people.

Dined at Jean Monnet's with Col. Llewellyn, former Minister of Aircraft Production, now the Resident Minister of Supply in the United States, Sir Robert Sinclair, Chairman of the British Supply Board, Donald Nelson, C. E. Wilson, President of the General Electric, in charge of production for WPB, Sir Arthur Salter, Francis W. Gibbs, the Naval Architect, brought down here by Wilson, in charge of the ship building program for WPB, and Billie Bullitt who is now special assistant to the Secretary of the Navy. The talk, which lasted past midnight, dealt entirely with the necessary ways and means for meeting the submarine menace. The central difficulty is the conflict between the building program of the Maritime Commission and the program sponsored by the WPB on the basis of Gibbs' proposal to build in the quickest possible time the largest number of destroyer escorts and corvettes. That means, in view of the limitations upon the materials and facilities and manpower and skill in ship building a program of mass production—that is, building one type of destroyer escort rather than several types, and also cutting out the suggested improvements of the Liberty Ship with all the changes and the adjustments that that involves, and keeping on with the present type of Liberty Ship as ample and adequate for war purposes. The Maritime Commission evidently has an eye—as is true of some of the other agencies of Government—on post-war advantages in building ships helpful for post-war trade, and subordinating to that end the exigent demands of the war so that there should be a post-war trade, whereby we build merchantmen only to have them sunk with a continual threat to our supply lines and a resulting retardation of our striking power and a prolongation of the war.

Another difficulty that emerged with great clarity is the crying need in the Navy Department for an aggressive, imaginative younger Admiral whose sole responsibility will be the submarine problem, and who will therefore worry upon, hit upon, and aggressively urge offensive measures against the submarine menace. At present that concern is necessarily diluted because it is only one of many with which the higher command of the Navy is charged. In this connection Llewellyn told a very interesting story touching the U-boat menace in the last war. Things were getting bad in '16–'17 when Lloyd George summoned a meeting of the War Cabinet and all the naval authorities. Jellicoe was then First Sea Lord and when L. G. asked him what about a convoy system to meet the U-boat menace, Jellicoe said that he was opposed to it, that he wanted destroyers kept at home to guard the Grand Fleet. Someone had tipped off L. G. that there were some contrary views at the Admiralty, particularly those held by a junior officer named Henderson. "Is there a Commander Henderson present?" asked L. G. at this Cabinet meeting. The officer acknowledged his presence whereupon the P. M. asked him what his views were about the U-boat and the convoy system. Henderson said he was bound to disagree with the First Sea Lord, that he thought the convoy system was the answer to the U-boat menace; "Give me eight destroyers and let me try to bring a convoy safely from Gibraltar to the London docks. If that succeeds, then we can do the convoy system on a larger scale. If I fail, the answer would have been given in practice and not in theory that the convoy system is not the answer." Lloyd George thought that made sense, instructions were given accordingly, and as we know, the convoy system probably prevented England's starvation and certainly a serious menace to her life lines. As the naval officers left Downing Street to walk over to the Admiralty, a senior officer said to Henderson, "You certainly have cheek to express the views you did when Lord Jellicoe with all his experience and his great authority had announced his views in opposition to the convoy." Very shortly after when Henderson got to his room he had a summons that Lord Jellicoe desired to see him. Lewellyn was at that time at the Admiralty and he said that Henderson told him that when he was told to come to Lord Jellicoe's room his knees trembled on the way. When he got into the presence of Lord Jellicoe, the great man said: "Henderson, I sent for you first to shake you by the hand and congratulate you on living up to the best traditions of the Royal Navy. When an officer has convictions it is his duty to express them no matter how strongly his seniors may have contrary views. And I want you to know that no one more warmly wishes that you may be proved right about convoys than I do."

Tuesday, January 26

Kenneth Royall—with whom I have kept quite a close relation since his graduation in 1916, after which he became a leading lawyer in North Carolina, and who recently distinguished himself as counsel assigned by the President to defend the saboteurs in the proceedings before the Military Commission—came to see me to help him make up his mind regarding an offer for a change of position that has been made to him. He was brought up here by his classmate, Bob Patterson, the Under Secretary, to attend to some of the fiscal matters pertaining to procurement, for which he has not only considerable professional equipment but also the advantage of a personal relation with Lindsay Warren, the Comptroller General. The JAGD is hoping for a reorganization of that office whereby the various legal agencies that have grown up in the War Department, quite independently of the JAGD, would be brought under the centralized control of the Judge Advocate General. They want Royall to have charge of the litigation and other important activities of such a reorganized expansion of the JAGD, with the rank of a Brigadier General, if that should come to pass. He said in view of his relation with Lindsay Warren he thinks it is vital for the affairs of the War Dept. for him to continue his present responsibility—because that is a personal relation which could not be transferred to anybody else—no matter what other or added duties may be put upon him. With simple modesty Royall said that the one thing he wants to be sure of is to do what he can in his own limited way to help the conduct of the war. I told him that like so many difficulties in this world the solution may well be taken out of his hand—that such a reorganization as he speaks of, if the Secretary of War and the Chief of Staff were for it, and if they are for it, and he is asked to have one of the senior responsibilities for the new JAGD, he has no alternative but to accept.

Attended a lecture by Sam Morison, at Dumbarton Oaks, on the Morocco phase of the North African landing. Sam Morison at his best—lucid, expert, vivid, and witty. Afterward, we joined Bessie Morison and Marion at the Biddle's to talk over the 10 o'clock announcement of the Casablanca meeting between Churchill and Roosevelt—Biddle, Morison and I having heard it at Dumbarton Oaks, and the women at the Biddle's.[1]

---

[1] Roosevelt and Churchill conferred at Casablanca January 12–25. They agreed on plans to complete the conquest of North Africa as speedily as possible, gave the highest priority to the battle against the U-boat, and ordered the intensification of the strategic bombing of Germany while the force for the invasion of the Continent was being prepared. These military decisions were not, of course, described in the communiqué except in the most general of terms. There was a shotgun marriage between DeGaulle and Giraud, symbolized by the photographs of the two shaking hands

Wednesday, January 27

Ferdie Kuhn,[1] now in charge of the English branch here of the OWI—to lunch. Spoke of the avid interest of the British for knowledge of and understanding about our institutions and our people, and the poor service, largely owing to laziness, rendered by the correspondents of the London papers in Washington. Gave illustrations of the responsiveness of the British press for information furnished by the OWI office in London regarding American institutions, apparently the same but as a matter of fact very different from the comparable English institution, as for instance, the difference between a budget submitted in the House of Commons by the Chancellor of the Exchequer on behalf of the Government, and the budget message of the President to Congress. He also said that the knowledge about English people and institutions was woefully lacking among the American forces in Great Britain and very little has yet been done, apart from little handbooks, on the part of our soldiers to gain such knowledge and understanding.

This whole situation seems to me to present a marvelous opportunity for real "adult education" on a large scale as between ourselves and the British peoples in regard to one another, provided it is real education, that is, a conscientious and imaginative attempt at understanding and not a cheap or romantic desire to inculcate into one another a view of things for ulterior purposes.

The Monnets and the McCloys dined with us, because Jack McCloy is due to go to North Africa within a few days, as soon as the President and General Marshall have returned and given him appropriate instructions. There was, of course, much talk about the Casablanca meeting. All of us agreed that the results are very important from the point of view of military plans as well as enhancement of morale among the United Nations and dispiriting effects in the Axis countries, as well as the nourishment of hope in the Occupied countries. But all of us also felt that the hazards of such a trip for the President ought not to be incurred unless the military necessity really left no choice.

There was also talk about the French situation which plainly was not adjusted between Giraud and DeGaulle. And there is no reason to believe it will be adjusted so long as it is left on the plane of personality. DeGaulle will always find ground for objection for a full collaboration because, in my opinion, he and his advisors, or enough of them, have it in the back of their heads that the DeGaulle movement is not merely one of military resistance against Germany, and the recovery of France, but also one of political import,

---

in the presence of Roosevelt and Churchill, but as knowledgeable people quickly realized, that did not mean that the political problems had been resolved. Roosevelt and Churchill also proclaimed the Allied demand for "unconditional surrender," indicating thereby that there would be no compromise or negotiated peace with the Axis powers. This was meant to assure the Russians as well as Western opinion that the deal with Darlan did not mean a deal in the future with a Goering or a Matsuoka.

[1] Ferdinand Kuhn before the war had been chief of the London Bureau of the New York *Times*.

namely, to become the Provisional Government of France when she is liberated. And not until such hopes so far as the Allies are concerned are absolutely rejected, by a firm declaration between ourselves and the British that we shall recognize no Provisional Government established otherwise than by the liberated French people, will the present friction of personalities cease and collaboration become really effective.

Thursday, January 28

In recess. Worked on diverse cases.
Don Denman at dinner and spent the night.

Friday, January 29

In recess, working on various cases.

Max Lowenthal once more told me of the uncertainties regarding the fate of his position with BEW—he is concerned with the study of the various economic problems that arise in theaters of war in which the American Army is dislodging the Axis, and more particularly North Africa at the moment. I do not quite understand the reasons that make Milo Perkins, if not hostile, at least fearful of this activity. I suspect, however, he has an eye on the Hill and is fearful to give the appearance of not having "practical" people with him.

Jean Monnet telephoned to tell me of the death of General Dykes who was Secretary of the British Military Mission and apparently Field Marshal Dill's right hand man. He is, according to Jean, a really great loss—he was one of those men not outwardly in the public eye but a quiet powerful force in the actual conduct of the war.

All of which—Dykes' death due to a plane crash, and the news earlier in the day in Teheran which killed Childs, the former Minister of the British Embassy here—does not make me wish any the less that the President was safely in the White House ashore safely from Casablanca and Brazil and wherenot. I am not forgetting Robert Louis Stevenson's remark à propos of the people who continue to live under the shadow of eruptions of Vesuvius that, as a matter of fact, most people die in bed.

Alfred Cohn [1] for dinner and over night.

Saturday, January 30

Conference.

Attended Mary Acheson's wedding and later the reception at the Dean Acheson house. There I ran into Bob Jackson looking none too happy. He took

---

[1] Alfred Cohn, a heart specialist at the Rockefeller Institute, was one of Frankfurter's closest friends. The Frankfurters spent their summers with the Cohns at their capacious home in New Milford, Conn.

me off into a corner and said "Do you also feel as depressed as I do after these Saturday Conferences?" I replied that I certainly do not come away normally happy and certainly did not do so today because every time we have that which should be merely an intellectual difference gets into a championship by Black of justice and right and decency and everything and those who take the other view are impliedly always made out to be the oppressors of the people and the supporters of some exploiting interest. So it was today with regard to a case that involved merely a cool consideration of an order made by the ICC in regard to grain rates where grain comes to Chicago by way of barges over a short distance some sixty miles as compared with grain that reaches Chicago by rail from the Northwest and other much longer distances. The Commission issued an order which, in effect, deprived the short-run barge movement from rate advantages which it is unfair for it to continue to enjoy. Surely here was a question within a defined and confined area of judicial review over a determination of the ICC [1] in a peculiarly complicated field within its own special competence. And yet Black indulged in a harangue worthy of the cheapest soapbox orator to the effect that the Commission covered up in a maze of words the fact that it is "rail minded" and therefore in defiance of Congressional mandate deliberately and unjustly chokes off water borne traffic in competition with railroads, thereby gouging the farmer, the consuming public, etc., etc. The fact is that the record and the history of this whole grain rate problem and the legislation of Congress afford absolutely no basis for this Black harangue. The Conference voted five to three to affirm the order of the ICC—Douglas and Murphy contenting themselves with the usual "I agree with Justice Black." But it was all very painful and a perfect illustration so far as Black's harangue went, of Brandeis' remark to me, "Black hasn't the faintest notion of what tolerance means, and while he talks a lot about democracy, he is totally devoid of its underlying demand which is tolerance in his own behavior." Jackson went on to speak of the strange way in which Roberts is completely taken in by the systematic way in which Black, and more particularly Douglas, exploit Roberts' innocence. (In the earlier days here when Black talked more freely to me about the various Brethren, he said on more than one occasion: "Roberts is, I think, the most naive man I have ever known in my life—a fine character but as innocent as a child.") In connection with another case Roberts said that Douglas had some views contrary to those expressed in Roberts' opinion—it was the case of *Reconstruction Finance Co. v. Bankers Trust*, Nos. 387, 388 [2]—and that he thought we had better discuss these views, rather than to have the case go down and

---

[1] *Interstate Commerce Commission v. Inland Waterways Corp.*, 319 U. S. 671.

The Court, in an opinion by Justice Jackson, upheld the I.C.C. rate order as within the ambit of administrative competence. Justice Black, in a dissent, joined by Justices Douglas and Murphy, argued that whatever the technicalities of the matter, the effect of the I.C.C. order was to eliminate competition with the railroads from waterborne carriers, contravening the intent of Congress.

[2] *Reconstruction Finance Corp. v. Bankers Trust Co.*, 318 U. S. 163.

Opinion by Justice Roberts, concurrence by Justice Douglas, joined by Justice Black.

simply have Douglas file a dissent. Not having seen Douglas' dissent, I said so, expressing regret that somehow or other I must have missed the Douglas dissent, whereupon Roberts replied: "Douglas hasn't circulated his dissent, he merely showed it to me because he and I rather regularly talk things over whenever we disagree about an opinion, Justice Douglas is good enough to come and talk to me about it." This was news, at least to the extent that Roberts should state to the whole Conference that Douglas acts on this realization of Roberts' innocence which leaves Douglas to appear to talk to him in order to reach a disinterested common conclusion, if possible, but in any event, to make Roberts feel that he has no other interest except to reach a disinterested result. As Bob Jackson pointed out, that isn't what Douglas does when he, Jackson, or I have views different from Douglas.

Strangely enough, Roberts on more than one occasion has said that he cannot understand that so independent and forthright a mind as Douglas should always be me too-ing Black. Jimmie Byrnes who, like the rest of us, is greatly devoted to Roberts, but also amazed during the time he was on the Court, to discover Roberts' innocence. I once heard him mildly suggest to Roberts the fact that Douglas had political ambition—was running for the Presidency from here—and Roberts was as incredulous as a child. He reminds me in this respect of dear Julian Mack of whom I once said that experience passes through him without stopping. In their cultivation of Roberts, Black and Douglas go to perfectly fantastic lengths. Thus, Roberts told me with the greatest pride, that nothing more flattering had happened to him in all his life than to have Black and Douglas come to him, after Hughes' retirement, and say to him, "Roberts, if the President does not name a Democrat, we hope he will name you." Within the same week, Harold Ickes told me that "Bill Douglas lunched with me the other day and said a strange thing. He said I was just the man whom the President should make Chief Justice."

I enlightened neither to the Douglas technique. Except in cases where he knows it is useless or in cases where he knows or suspects that people are on to him, he is the most systematic exploiter of flattery I have ever encountered in my life. He tried it on me when he first came on the Court—every opinion of mine that he returned, he returned with the most extravagant praise, all of which ceased after I left him in no doubt that I did not come on to the Court to play politics on the Court but to vote in each case as my poor lights guided me.

Since the history of this Court was my business for a quarter of a century, I knew all there was to know, so far as print could convey it, on what had gone on behind the scenes and beginning with my friendship with Holmes in 1911, greatly reinforced during the course of the years, I learnt a good deal, of course, about the Court's doings since the time Holmes came on in 1902, and after Brandeis came here in 1916 and Cardozo in 1932, I learnt with cumulative intimacy from them about the inner workings of the institution and the behavior of the various personalities. As a result, I made one pact with myself when I came on the Court: that I would try to my utmost to continue to behave here as

I did as an independent scholar at Cambridge, that is, act on the best judgment I am able to summon with reference to a particular case regardless of where it would land me in relation to votes of other people on the Court and to eschew all combinations or machinations, active or tacit playing of politics on the Court. This of course does not mean that I would always express a dissent—many considerations enter into the expression or withholding of a dissent. Nor does it meant that the views that I reached independently might not be altered in disinterested discussion with one or more members of the Court or after Conference. That is the very essence of the Court, namely, that the views of individuals could be shared to the end that a collective conclusion may be achieved. That is why the Conferences should be the most important aspect of our labors, the free and full canvassing of all relevant considerations in the disposition of a case. But that is a wholly different thing from hunting in packs, presenting a solid phalanx, as part of a general parting within the Court as was true of what Learned Hand used to call "the four mastiffs"—VanDevanter, McReynolds, Sutherland and Butler, and as is true now of what everyone calls "the Axis"—Black, Douglas and Murphy. It is in this aspect of the matter that Jimmie Byrnes' remark reveals such an ominous situation—his remark that in the Senate Black controlled one vote, his own, out of 96 votes; on the Court he controls three votes out of nine in all important matters.

Sunday, January 31

Phil Graham,[1] now at the Officers Cadet School at Wayne Park, turned up on leave for a few hours. He was as delightful as ever and seemed very fit.

At Jim Landis'[2] for dinner together with the Speaker—Sam Rayburn. Sam feared that the next two years would be very bitter political years but thought that the division inside the Republican party on the question of isolationism may so split them up as to defeat their high hopes now of gaining power. He said the other day that there was a Republican caucus of the House and some of the leaders said the Republican increase in Congress was due to the people's support of isolationism which led a number of new members to resent bitterly any such interpretation of their election. The Speaker thinks that Willkie and Stassen[3] and other leaders who are in effect in agreement with the

[1] Philip Graham, Harvard Law School, 1939, was married to Katherine Meyer, the daughter of Eugene Meyer, the publisher of the Washington *Post*. He entered the Army as a private and rose to the rank of major. After the war he became publisher of the Washington *Post*. Graham was one of a select group of former Frankfurter students that also included Joe Rauh and Ed Prichard, whom Frankfurter enjoyed to the point of responding amiably to their taut, often spicy, demurrals from some of his *dicta*.

[2] James M. Landis at this time was head of the Office of Civilian Defense.

[3] Wendell Willkie, the Republican presidential candidate in 1940, and Harold Stassen, the youthful governor of Minnesota, were leaders of the liberal, internationalist wing of the Republican party.

present foreign policy of the country, are likely to make things warm for those, who if they had their way would name Taft of Ohio or Governor Bricker of Ohio or somebody as close to Harding as possible.

Tuesday, February 2

Court in session. Did work on cases.

Bill Douglas came in to discuss with me the Nucky Johnson case (No. 273, Oct. Term 1942). We went over the various grounds on which the conviction is sought to be reversed and Douglas agreed, as a result of further study of the record and the authorities, that none of them constituted prejudicial error excepting one and that he thought was a very close and fine point—the fact that Judge Maris sustained Johnson's claim of the privilege of self-incrimination in refusing to testify regarding receipt of gambling money in 1938—the year after that for which he was charged in the last count of the indictment—but allowing the jury to consider such refusal to testify as bearing on the credibility of Johnson's testimony. I told Douglas that in the first place I do not believe this action of Judge Maris did constitute an error—that having taken the witness stand, the accused could no longer appeal to his Constitutional privilege because he had none, that Judge Maris' assent to Nucky Johnson's refusal to testify was something that he did not have to do but was a favor granted to the accused, but that in the circumstances of the present case the fact that Nucky requested to be allowed to keep his mouth shut regarding 1938 was entitled to be taken into account by the jury as bearing on the truth or falsity of his explanation in admitting that he received gambling money for '35, '36, and '37. But, in any event, if error it was, it was not an error involving deprivation of a Constitutional right, it was an error pertaining to the ruling on evidence and a charge regarding evidence which, not having been excepted to, and for good reasons not excepted to, could certainly not now be availed of to upset the conviction. I spoke stiffly on the function of appellate review in criminal cases—that it was not a game or a discussion of abstract legal rulings, or rather an abstract consideration of possibly erroneous rulings, but had to do with correcting miscarriages of justice in the sense that an accused was convicted in disregard of orderly procedure with full opportunity in the trial court to correct any questionable rulings made in the course of the stress and strain of a criminal trial. I laid out the whole case in the light of the stenographic minutes which I had examined and concluded by saying that I cannot imagine a trial having been conducted with more scrupulous care and due regard for the rights of a defendant than the record shows has been the conduct of this case by Judge Maris. I pointed out that for fifty years, so far as I know, no criminal conviction has been reversed by this Court for such an error as we are now discussing when no exception had been made at the trail. Douglas feebly suggested that he thought there were such cases but he couldn't remember them. I told him I should be glad to have references to them. At the end, he said it all gets down to a very fine point. To which I replied that a conviction has no business to be upset on a point so fine—and not excepted to at the trial—that one who has as strong views as I have against any kind of unfairness in the conduct of criminal cases in the federal courts can't even see the point.

The talk was carried on in the best of temper and afterwards when we met later (the next day) in the Conference room before marching to the bench, Douglas said that the talk was very valuable because it showed that the case got down to a very fine point.

Wednesday, February 3

Court in session. Further work on Johnson case.

After Court I had two visitors, my friend Augustus L. Richards, and Robert Szold,[1] and later Milton Katz. The last told me the latest stage of the imbroglio in the WPB, poor Nelson's confusion, and what Milton calls his mental as well as physical sickness which led him to state to C. E. Wilson and others confidentially that he plans to ask to be relieved by the President and to recommend C. E. Wilson as his successor. There will ensue the usual tug of war for power, Eberstadt will try to urge that Baruch be appointed, under whose umbrella he thinks he can operate, etc., etc.

While one of these men was with me, Lee Watters (my secretary) passed me a note to say that Justice Roberts was in and was very anxious to see me before I left. I disengaged myself from my visitor and went in to see Roberts.

Roberts said he had a difficult question of policy to put to me and the following are substantially his own words:

"Douglas has been buzzing around me both yesterday and today with questions about the Nucky Johnson case. He told me that a study of the authorities convinced him that the attempted cross-examination of Johnson for the 1938 transaction was not improper in view of what had been elicited under direct examination, and he also thought that the withdrawal ordered by the judge of Johnson while counsel was discussing with Maris a question of law could not be made a ground for reversal since there was no objection to it and so the matter could be held to have been waived. That left only the question of the charge of Maris regarding the claim of privilege as affecting Johnson's credibility after he had allowed the claim. He thought that in view of the record from which it appears that they discussed this matter late in the afternoon, and the judge said "Well, let's think it over until tomorrow morning," and the next morning they started afresh, and there was no exception taken, that the objection had really been waived. Therefore, he (Douglas) felt that we ought to animadvert against sustaining a claim and yet allowing the jury to draw an adverse inference from it, but he was prepared to hold that there was a waiver and therefore no prejudicial error. I told him I was prepared to go along and then I

---

[1] Robert Szold, Harvard Law School, 1911, lawyer and Zionist leader. [See p. 21.]

am not sure whether Roberts said "I" or "he and I" went to see the Chief and the Chief said he was stymied by the failure to take an exception complained of, and in the circumstances, he was prepared to go along in sustaining a conviction. Douglas then asked me did I know how Black would feel about this, since Black had the strongest feeling against the impropriety of what Judge Maris did. I told him I did not know but I would talk to Black about it; so I saw Black and he said that if it were merely a case of ordinary lack of exception he would not think that that warranted a disregard of what he deemed gross unfairness but in view of the record in this case, in view of the fact that it was not just carelessness or oversight by counsel, he was prepared to go along with Douglas' conclusion.

But he raised a question of fairness to Douglas in having Douglas write this opinion in view of the fact that Douglas had written the Pendergast opinion.[2] Black thought it was rather unfair of the Chief to assign the Pendergast case to Douglas. (Pendergast is the Missouri boss who was convicted for income tax fraud and later sentenced for contempt of court in rigging up a fraudulent settlement of a case against the insurance company involving his bribery by something like three-quarters of a million. The Court reversed his sentence for contempt on the ground that the statute of limitations had run. Douglas wrote the opin. of the Court solely on the statute of limitations; I concurred with that conclusion but stated there was contempt; and Jackson dissented.) He thought here was a New Deal Justice writing an opinion to let out a Democratic boss, and so he was glad when the Chief assigned the Johnson case to Douglas the result of which was to let out a Republican boss because that would show Douglas' impartiality. But if we are to sustain Johnson's conviction, having reversed that of Pendergast, it wasn't fair to make Douglas write that opinion whereby it would appear that he let the Dem. boss out but kept a Rep. boss in prison. I [Roberts] then asked Black to go to the Chief and tell him that but Black had said that Chief Justices always exercise some care to take into account various considerations in making assignments which is so. Black said Oh, no, he wouldn't talk to the Chief and there we were at an impasse. And so I said to Black 'I'll talk to Frankfurter' and that's the question of policy I wanted to put to you."

I had to think fast in order to decide how to deal with this extraordinary recital. I had to decide quickly in my own mind whether to tell Roberts how

---

[2] *Pendergast v. United States*, 317 U. S. 412 (1943).

Thomas J. Pendergast, former Democratic "boss" of Kansas City, was jailed for criminal contempt of court for having deceived the court in the fraudulent settlement of a suit by several insurance companies against the State Superintendent of Insurance. The Supreme Court reversed the conviction on the ground that the statute of limitations had expired before the prosecution was begun. Justice Douglas, writing for the majority, left unresolved the question of whether Pendergast's conduct did constitute criminal contempt of court. Justice Jackson dissented, chiding his colleagues for not holding Pendergast in contempt. Frankfurter, in a concurring opinion, agreed with Jackson that contempt had been committed, but said he was forced to concede that the statute of limitations nullified the conviction.

shocked and outraged I was—the very notion of thinking about men after they were on this Court in terms of New Deal or Old Deal; the shocking irrelevance of whether any Justice would or would not be criticized for doing his duty, reaching the conclusion in a case that conscience required and writing on behalf of the Court the views of the Court whenever that task was assigned to him by the Chief Justice; the fantastic and repulsive implication that in writing the opinion in the Pendergast case it mattered that Douglas was a "New Dealer" and Pendergast a Democratic boss, and that in writing in the Johnson [case] that Douglas was a "New Dealer" and Johnson was a Republican boss, and that perhaps it was all right if we left all bosses of all parties off, that the only possible ground for any thought of unfairness in any criticism that might come to Douglas for being the organ of the Court could only derive because it might be unfair to political ambitions of Douglas. But I kept these and other thoughts to myself. To raise them would involve at least a tacit criticism of Roberts for not being shocked himself by the game that Douglas and Black were playing in this business, and it would also involve opening up the scheming of these two about which Roberts is as innocent as a newborn babe. So I have made no comment whatever on this phase of Roberts' communication but contented myself with saying that I was greatly relieved to infer that the conviction in the Johnson case would be sustained because I thought a reversal would be a grave miscarriage of justice and that I would be forced into the unpleasant duty of writing a dissent which would spell it out with great particularity, and I think really demonstrate that a reversal of the conviction instead of correcting a miscarriage of justice was creating one. I quickly summarized the record as I read it and told Rob. the legal investigation I had made. And then I said this:

"As for writing the opinion I have only this to say. That if the Chief desires me to write the opinion for the Court I shall be glad to do so. I am not asking for the assignment and have no desire for it, but I should not deem it an undue burden if it is given to me. And I shall be very glad to go with you to the Chief and tell him so. But I think it is better that you go alone, not only because you are the Senior Associate, and do not need to be reinforced by a Junior, but also because I am behind in my opinions and the Chief may not think I ought to be loaded up further, and he would feel freer to tell you that when I am not there. But I just want you to know that I shall be perfectly glad to do the job and if the only reason why the Chief would not want to assign it to me is because of my unfinished business, he needn't worry about it."

To which Roberts replied, "I understand you fully. You are both ready and able to take on the job. I'll talk to the Chief tomorrow. Of course I don't know how it will come out. Douglas said he is ready to write this opinion either way (another remark that shocked me, as though it made no difference whether the Court affirms or reverses a conviction), and even though he writes for affirmance, he may insist in not having the case taken away from him."

As I left Roberts' chambers, I bumped into Bob Jackson and repeated to him what had just transpired. He was, if anything, as deeply shocked as I was and said, "Roberts is just beyond me. He's a complete sap so far as under-standing men is concerned and those two fellows are just systematically playing on his innocence." Jackson expressed himself on the whole transaction in his characteristically felicitous way, full of indignation that anybody should be deemed a New Dealer after he is on the Court, or that the thought should enter a Justice's head if an opinion has to be written that he is dealing with a Democratic or a Republican boss. And he added, with ironic facetiousness, "I suppose the thing to do is to let out all bosses who commit crimes to show our impartiality." He was as distressed and saddened by this latest performance as I am.

Sam Rosenman and Bob Sherwood turned up at about ten and stayed late into the night talking over the North African situation, the President's inevita-bly limited opportunities and facilities for learning the facts of the political phases of the North African situation, the fact that he was stuffed full on his re-turn by Cordell Hull's hurt feelings and bitterness against the criticism of his (Hull's) policy (the President said to Sherwood, "The trouble with Cordell is, he can't take it."), the reliance on Robert Murphy, who is a nice fellow, but as Harry Hopkins says, very shallow, and the natural sidetracking of these political questions for the pressing military matters, although these questions while ap-pearing political, have the most important psychological bearing on military events.

Thursday, February 4

Court in session.

Yesterday's conversation with Roberts was much on my mind and I wrote the following longhand note to him:

Dear Roberts:

After sleeping on our conversation late yesterday afternoon, one reflec-tion will not down. And I'd conceal too much to suppress it. And it is this—I wince whenever I hear any responsible person talk of "New Deal" and "Old Deal" court or Justices. I'm incurably academic and cannot rid myself of the conviction that it is of the very essence of the function of this Court that when a man comes on it, he leaves all party feelings as well as affiliations behind. I certainly do not and have not since January 30, 1939 for one split second felt like or deemed myself, or deemed it right for any-one else to think of me, as a "New Deal" Justice.

Faithfully yours,
F. F.

After Court I told Stanley Reed the whole story. He was much surprised that Douglas should have been ready to change his view and vote for affirmance in the Nucky Johnson case, and when I asked him whether he wasn't shocked by the implications of the story, he said he wasn't. To which I replied, "You ought to be." He then said this, "I'll tell you why I am not. This illustrates the difference between you and me in our view of human nature. It is, as you know, my deepest conviction, you can't change people—you think you can. I'm sure you can't. Black always was a politician and he didn't and can't cease to be one by becoming a judge. And so things that you and I would never think about, such as the fact that Pendergast and Nucky Johnson are bosses— insofar as that has any relation to anything we have to do—he would instinctively take into account. He is one of these people who is sensitive to every current that might affect public feelings." To which I replied, "Well, all right, have it your way. Hugo Black is a politician—although a very bad one, I believe, because he takes short instead of long views, such as his complete panic in the last week of the 1940 campaign that the President would be surely defeated and his execrable advice that the only way he could possibly win is to make solemn promises from morning to night that, under no circumstances, would he ever consent to have this country go to war [1]—but what about Bill Douglas? You can have no such excuse for him. He's never been a politician, he was a professor." Reed replied, "But he is a politician now, though this episode about Nucky Johnson is a revelation to me. For I had assumed he had put all thoughts of the Presidential nomination in '44 out of his head, but plainly not." Reed also was surprised that Roberts shouldn't have seen that Black and Douglass, in view of their great intimacy, had of course arranged this whole business between them and were play-acting so far as Roberts was concerned.

Friday, February 5

Court sitting.

Roberts told me that after the receipt of my letter as set forth on February 4, he decided to "let nature take its course" and not to talk to the Chief about reassigning the opinion in the Nucky Johnson case.

Later in the day Douglas circulated his "memorandum" opinion for an affirmance of the Nucky Johnson conviction along the lines indicated by Roberts in his talk to me the other day. Having assumed that such would be the course of events I had prepared my small concurring opinion setting forth my conviction that Judge Maris had committed no error in regard to Nucky's cross-examination and therefore it was idle to talk about a "waiver" as the basis of affirmance rather than resting it on the fair conduct of the trial.

Jean Monnet told me of his talk with Harry Hopkins to whom he told of the cable from General Giraud asking him, Monnet, to come to North Africa.

---

[1] This is the first indication that Justice Black was among those, and there were many, who in the closing days of the 1940 presidential campaign, pressed Roosevelt to promise the country to stay out of war. "Your boys are not going to be sent into any foreign wars," Roosevelt pledged to America's fathers and mothers in Boston at the end of October.

Hopkins said that in the course of the President's discussion with Giraud at Casablanca, the President has suggested two or three Frenchmen who might be of help to Giraud on the side of civil administration and more particularly had suggested that Monnet might be of real value. H. H. therefore told Monnet that he should go but keep himself free of all entanglements with any of the French groups and go, in fact, as part of his present job in connection with the equipment of the French Army. Monnet told him of his conversation with Halifax—his duty to keep Halifax informed of all his doings inasmuch as he is an official of the British Supply Commission, and Harry said he would talk with Halifax and take care of matters. In the course of the conversation, H. H. told Monnet that the President liked Giraud very much, did not find him at all the kind of temperamental difficult person that he had been painted to be. On the other hand, the President found DeGaulle very difficult indeed. When the President suggested to DeGaulle that he actually take part in the fighting in North Africa, DeGaulle said he is no longer a military man, indeed he is no longer a free man, that he has become the instrument of a great political movement to which he owes all responsibility. He added, so Hopkins reported to Monnet, "Such a situation is not new in French history. There was Jeanne d'Arc."

Saturday, February 6

A few minutes before the Conference hour at twelve, as I came into the Conference room, Roberts took me into a corner looking plainly troubled. He said "Old man, I am terribly distressed by your concurring opinion in the Nucky Johnson case. I don't see why you have to pin a rose on Judge Maris." To which I replied, "Well, that's easy—I'll take out Judge Maris' name and simply refer to the trial judge." Roberts: "Oh, that isn't what I mean—it's deeper than that. In a case of such political implications as the Nucky Johnson case, I think it is very important for us to be unanimous and I wish you wouldn't insist on writing separately but join Douglas' opinion." F. F.: "I'm awfully sorry because I just don't understand what you are talking about. I don't understand this business about 'political implications' of the Nucky Johnson case. The problem is no different to me than it would be if it were the case of an unknown person named John Smith. Douglas' opinion says Judge Maris committed a grave error in his treatment of Johnson's cross-examination but the error can't be availed of here because no appropriate exception was taken, and so it was waived. I, on the contrary, think that Maris' conduct of the trial was conspicuously fair and there was no error." Roberts: "At least we ought to see what we can do and I don't think the case ought to come down Monday." F. F.: "That's entirely agreeable to me. I have no desire at all to hurry the disposition of the case but I think it is fair to say that this isn't a question of reading the record and not thinking out ideas. And I have studied the record with care and the record cannot be changed." Roberts: "Of course if you are adamant there is nothing more to do." F. F.: "I am sorry for I really don't mean to be unreasonable which doesn't mean that I am not in fact." Roberts: "Oh I know you don't intend to be unreasonable. But, as you know, I bare my breast to you and I am bound to say that you are unreasonable."

By this time the Conference got under way and in due course we got around to Douglas' Nucky Johnson memorandum. Roberts in substance stated to the Conference what he told me. When it came to my turn to speak I said it isn't pleasant to me to appear persnickety but I added "I suppose it's irrelevant to our job to be either persnickety or genial." I then went on to say that I am so innocent of some things that I didn't know such a person as Nucky Johnson existed until the petition of certiorari [1] came before us and that, so far as I am concerned, he doesn't now exist for me as a person. For all I am concerned, this is an anonymous case and I am trying to treat it as such regardless of anything except that which the record unambiguously, to me, reveals." Roberts then added, not at all in any petulant voice, "The case might as well then go down on Monday." To which Douglas at once said "I really hadn't planned to have it come down on Monday. I have to do some checkin' of the record." And so the case went over.

Sunday, February 7

Reinhold Niebuhr called to talk to me about the offer of Harvard through President Conant to become one of the University professors at Harvard—one of the five professorships at large, not confined to any particular department. Niebuhr gave the pros and cons—what it would mean to leave the Union Theological Seminary and his various activities in New York as against the opportunities Harvard affords for the promotion of his central intellectual and spiritual interests, to wit, the relation of the presuppositions of religion to social conduct. He was disturbed by a number of personal difficulties the Harvard move would entail, and more particularly the inevitable competitive aspects as between himself and Dean Sperry, the head of the Harvard Theological School, a dominantly Unitarian influence, and as chief preacher of the Harvard Chapel. He said Sperry himself is very fine about it and has no axe to grind but Mrs. Sperry—who, I interrupted, is characterized as one of the few really poisonous tongued people I have ever known—is doing a lot of mischievous talking, for, said Niebuhr, she really is poisonous. I told him that without minimizing personal difficulties of that sort if I were in his shoes I would forget all about them, trusting that time would take care of them, and decide the issue solely on whether Harvard or New York would give him the likelihood of the fullest opportunity for his special talents and interests. I tried to put Harvard in the proper perspective—what in my judgment he could rightly expect from the

---

[1] The Court's granting a writ of *certiorari* is a decision to take a case under review and call up the records of the lower courts in the case.

student body and the faculty. Of course I stated to him that it would be arrogant of me to have a judgment on the wisdom of going or not going—all that one friend can do for another is to help externalize the factors in such a problem to enable the person who has to decide to see the elements of the problem more clearly. On the whole Niebuhr seemed disinclined to go.

In the evening, we dined at the Monnets because he was anxious to discuss fully what seemed to him the possible far-reaching implications for him of his North African trip. He was plainly troubled as a Frenchman with all the anguish that must lacerate the souls of Frenchmen who were uncompromisingly anti-Nazi ever since the fall of France. And Jean seemed to feel that before he goes to France he must make up his mind whether to throw in his lot completely with Giraud because he had no doubt such would be the issue presented to him by Giraud. I was strongly of the view that precisely because he wants a liberated France with the position in a New Europe to which her historic position entitled her, and because such restoration of France was part and parcel of the whole Allied cause, it was his duty as a Frenchman, not to make any commitments that would make him inevitably a partisan of one of the contending forces in the pull of French politics. My own view was that he should go, as it were, on behalf and at the request of, the U. S. A. and Great Britain in connection with the equipment of the French Army and therefore the problem which he feared might arise when he actually conferred with Giraud would be taken care of before he got there. After a long talk that mode of proceeding seemed to satisfy Jean and it was resolved to work it out that way between Halifax and Hopkins.

Monday, February 8

Opinion day.

I learned from the C. J.'s law clerk (Bennett Boskey) that Black and Douglas first went to the Chief to ask him to have me withdraw my concurrence in the Nucky Johnson case and the Chief told him if I felt the way I did about the case he didn't see why I shouldn't say what I said in my opinion and that in any event he certainly didn't feel justified in asking me to suppress my views. After this failure with the C. J. they went to Roberts which led Roberts to talk to me as narrated in the conversation I had with him on Saturday.

Milton Katz urgently asked to see me and told me of the ruption inside of the WPB—the ruption of which Eberstadt is the center, who with characteristic ruthlessness and disregard of the ordinary canons of loyalty has for long been working, with and through the services whose agents are Bob Patterson [1] (a complete innocent) and Jim Forrestal (Eberstadt's former partner at Dillon, Read & Co.), to get rid of Nelson and push Baruch under whom, in view of

---

[1] Robert Patterson was Under Secretary of War and the War Department's representative on the War Production Board. James Forrestal, Under Secretary of the Navy, was also on the W.P.B.

the latter's age and inability to work ten hours a day as the job would require, Eberstadt would really run the show. Nelson, who evidently gets strength of purpose only at the last minute—or, as Jean Monnet says, sometimes after the last minute—has now resolved to block Eberstadt's maneuvers by putting Wilson at the head of production and getting rid of Eberstadt. Nelson is in fact ready to step out, but only if Wilson is named to replace him because in Nelson's conviction production problems have reached the stage where a technically equipped production man like Wilson and not a banker like Eberstadt, or generally equipped man like Baruch, can effectively direct things. On the other hand, apparently Jim Byrnes who for two years had thought that Baruch wisely should not take an official post but give the help of an "elder statesman" as the phrase goes about Baruch, now thinks, in view of all the press campaign and the feeling of confusion in the public mind that Baruch should for reasons of public impression be the right and wise appointment.

Tuesday, February 9

Sitting.

Wayne Coy [1] came to talk about the WPB situation. He is evidently strongly urging that Wilson be formally appointed to Nelson's place instead of letting Nelson, as it were, become the Chairman of the Board, and Wilson the executive head—a solution which the President proposed. Coy said he told the President that that is precisely the way not to do it because it will still further stimulate criticism that the President temporizes with problems instead of dealing with them decisively. While the President is considerably put out with Nelson he has also a strong feeling for him because of his devotion and his services and apparently is trying to keep him in some public post. Coy's solution is to send Nelson to Australia. Coy says Nelson is now standing firm—he will resign if Wilson is named but not otherwise.

Jean Monnet told me of a long talk he had with Hull, who at the President's request had sent for Monnet to talk over with him his mission to North Africa—at the President's request. Monnet said the talk was most satisfactory and that Hull was entirely agreeable to have him go along the lines of his desire, that is at the desire and the temporary release of the two governments.

Dined at Lydia Kirk's—the warm hearted and sturdy souled wife of Admiral Kirk who is Chief of Staff to Admiral Stark and the head of our Naval Mission in London. Among others was present Admiral Sir Percy Noble, the head of the British Naval Mission in this country, whose preoccupation is with the submarine problem he having been in charge of the Western approaches of Great Britain, that is, he has been successful in keeping submarines in check against the shipping entering British waters from the West.

---

[1] Wayne Coy, a management expert, was Assistant Director of the Bureau of the Budget.

Wednesday, February 10

Sitting.

Jean told me of his talk with H. H. and Halifax in trying to work out the details through London and here, so that he should go as he had planned to go—through notification by the two governments to Giraud before he gets there of the terms under which he is being sent.

Thursday, February 11

Sitting.

Ferdie Kuhn formerly of the N. Y. *Times* brought in MacDonald, the political correspondent of The (London) *Times*. MacDonald, a discerning and charming fellow, confirmed the impression one gets so widely as to the contemporary state of American opinion, to wit, that domestically it is veering towards conservatism, and internationally it is becoming more and more nationalistic. Wallace speeches, evidently, because they are pitched in terms and are conveyed with an atmosphere so easily susceptible of being translated into sentimental humanitarianism—the U. S. A. as Santa Claus—may well be more conducive against the very things which he is seeking to promote.

Friday, February 12

Court sitting.

Spent the night at Archie MacLeish's at Alexandria with the Achesons. Listened to the President's speech on his Casablanca trip. That opened up a long and animated discussion almost in the nature of debate with Archie and Dean who were depressed to the point of violent utterance regarding the North African policy. Both talked as though we had thrown away everything which we had professed to be fighting for. I tried to restore a sense of perspective in them, pointing out the practical difficulties which confront the President in conducting such complicated affairs, the kind of so-called compromises that the man at the top, be he Lincoln or Wilson or F. D. R., has to make, the President's own temperament which makes it absurd for Archie to have such fluctuating feelings about him, because the President is singularly unchanging in his methods, etc., etc. When Dean asked me "what would you have me do?" I talked Dutch to him and said it was his job to fight as hard as he can for the views that seemed to him right, within the Department, and that despair and exaggeration of acts which, however unpleasing, are not ultimate expressions of policy, are luxuries we cannot afford.

Saturday, February 13

Conference.

We had before us the appeal of the Government in the Petrillo case in which the District Court in the Northern District of Illinois dismissed the bill by the Government to enjoin Petrillo from continuing the rules of his union against recording and other practices that the union enforces on behalf of its musician membership.[1] There was some discussion whether the case was within the Hutcheson decision and the cases that followed. When it came to my turn, I said "I don't have to read the Hutcheson case at all because if this suit by the Government isn't prohibited by the Norris-LaGuardia Act prohibiting the use of injunctions in suits dealing with controversies about conditions of labor—then I don't know what is within the Norris-LaGuardia Act." Reed thought it would do the Court more credit to hear the case in view of the widespread publicity which the case has aroused. To which I replied that the only thing that does the Court credit is to do its job with complete indifference to all such extraneous considerations. Douglas felt strongly that we ought to hear the case and give the Government a chance to argue fully what it claims are distinctions between this case and the Hutcheson line of cases. Good sense finally prevailed and it was agreed by the majority to affirm the dismissal of the bill below because of the Norris-LaGuardia Act.

Sunday, February 14

We lunched at the David Findley's, Director of the National Gallery.

Monday, February 15

Opinion day. The Nucky Johnson opinions came down. Rutledge took his seat.

Tuesday, February 16

Dined at Jean Monnet's with McKittrick, President of the International Bank of Settlement at Basle. Mac, a very intelligent, sober-minded American, has been at Basle three years continuously with trips to Germany up to the time

---

[1] *United States v. American Federation of Musicians,* 318 U. S. 741 (1943).

The Court affirmed the dismissal of the government's suit in a one-sentence *per curiam* opinion that cited the Norris-LaGuardia Act's limitations on the issuance of injunctions in labor disputes.

, *United States v. Hutcheson,* 312 U. S. 219 (1941).

This decision, written by Frankfurter, affirmed orders of the district court quashing indictments of labor leaders for antitrust violations arising from their organization of boycotts of the products of certain companies with which their unions had a dispute.

that we entered the war, and since as well as before, advantageously placed to gauge the currents of German opinion and feeling. He also is intimate with Swiss folk who go to Germany and who have relations with Germans who come into Switzerland. He left Basle late in November before the great Russian successes, but even then Swiss people whose judgment he cared most about had reached the definite conviction not only that Germany cannot possibly win but that she couldn't last beyond this year. (This naturally interested me very much because I have been long of the conviction as I have often told Marion that the winter of 1942–43 would be the last winter of the war so far as Germany is concerned.) He said that those who were in a position to know assured him that Hitler himself has entered a stage of psychological instability—he is incapable of making decisions and adhering to them, he does not sleep well, and for the first time in his life, has taken to drink. Not that he gets drunk, but he feels the need of stimulants. McKittrick says Hitler may, after a few months, come back to his old form and dominate the situation. But it was very significant to McKittrick as it was to the rest of us that Hitler did not in person speak on the Tenth Anniversary of his regime. McKittrick says that no other person can hold the show together because of the terrific personal rivalries. He regards Himmler as the strongest of the Nazi leaders and of course Himmler has a large private army, the S. S. But apparently Goering also is recruiting his army—he actually advertised for volunteers to join the Goering Divisions. This, if true—and McKittrick said he had no doubt about it—is perhaps the most significant bit of news. For once a nation has groups of private armies the necessary cohesion for authority is cracked. It was because the Weimar Republic tolerated the private army that Hitler built up before he came to power that Weimar fell. Ditto Austria.

After McKittrick told us about the German situation we had a long discussion about the nature of the peace settlements. There were present Sir Arthur Salter, Bob Brand,[1] and Ben Cohen, besides myself. The difficulties and perplexities that the discussion developed led only to one agreement—that "It's going to be a hell of a mess." I wish the discussion could have been listened into by everybody because it had the great merit of trying to face difficulties candidly and fairly and not evade them or wrap them up with big, beautiful words, making the attainment of a peaceful and decent world as easy as rolling off a log.

Early in the day Katz told me that Nelson was going to centralize production authority in Wilson as vice-chairman and fire Eberstadt. He tried to see the President before doing so but was not able to do so. The evening papers carried news of Nelson's action.

[1] Robert Brand, a distinguished economist, had served as deputy chairman of the British Mission in Washington in the first World War and was financial adviser to the British at the Paris Peace Conference. He was a member of the British Food Mission in Washington in World War II, and Frankfurter described him "as one of the sweetest natures it was my good fortune ever to know." Sir Arthur Salter was the British representative in Washington for shipping problems.

Tuesday, February 16

Yesterday while I was in Conference, George Burton of the FBI phoned my secretary, Miss Lee Watters, to say that Mr. Hoover, the Director of the FBI, was very anxious to get some information to me and could he, Burton, see me for about five minutes. After the Conference was over, about six o'clock, I phoned Burton to ask whether he could tell me what was on his mind over the phone. He said he could not, so I arranged to see him this morning. I saw him at ten o'clock and then he told me that Mr. Hoover was very anxious to get to me the following:

One of the informants of the FBI had advised them that a man named George Rukert, known to the informant, had tried to enlist the informant in a plot hatched by Rukert and others to assassinate me. The informant promptly advised the FBI and they are covering the situation and are quite confident they will be able to ascertain whether this is a crackpot enterprise or whether it has some substance to it. There was to be a meeting of Rukert and his associates last night and the FBI were covering it and expect to have some information today. For the moment Mr. Hoover desired me to know of the matter at this stage but had no wish that I should in any wise change my mode of life or behavior or be protected by guards.

I told Burton that this made it appropriate for me to show him a card postmarked Los Angeles giving me warning of proposed violence against me. I told him that I had kept the card because my law clerk who had seen the card was under the impression that similar threatening cards in the same handwriting had come to Justice Murphy, and he thought I might want to see him about it. Of course I had received such postcards and letters from time to time and I always tear them up. Burton asked me hereafter not to tear up such communications but to turn them over to the Department as they have people who classify these communications and draw at times important clues from them.

I concluded the interview with Burton by asking him to thank Mr. Hoover for advising me and to say to Mr. Hoover that I shall go about my business without any change whatever and keep myself entirely at the service of Mr. Hoover so far as this matter is concerned. I told Burton that I do not take any stock in these threats and plans of assassination but that, of course, I have to keep in mind also that if there is anything serious in them the maids who work in our house and the staff here are involved and therefore I await Mr. Hoover's suggestions and wishes. For the rest, I shall forget it.

Wednesday, February 17

Now that Eberstadt was out the forces behind him were moving hard to supplant Nelson and have the President appoint Baruch. They have evidently won the support of Jimmie Byrnes who, I am sure, is wholly disinterested in his motives, has no other desire except to promote the necessary war production, but, on the other hand, is acting largely on the information fed him by Jim Forrestal and does not know what has been going on at WPB in regard to the relevant issues. Jean Monnet and Milton Katz phoned me to see me this evening, told me of the whole situation, talked things out, and were profoundly convinced that to put Baruch as nominal head of WPB would be a calamity for the production program as well as a source of mischief for the President, because Baruch would bring in all the sources that had been indulging in these mischievous leaks against the President for some time, to wit, Arthur Krock and David Lawrence, and Malcolm (I believe is his front name) Stone, the chief editorial writer for Roy Howard. They also felt confident that the President himself, so far as his own desires go, still does not want to put such great official authority into Baruch's hands as he has consistently refused to do so for two years. It all depends on Nelson. If he will stand firm and tell the President what he has told Katz and others that he will gladly retire for Wilson, but will not resign for Baruch because that appointment to him would be a calamity (not because of Baruch as a person but because the situation needs somebody like Wilson and not somebody like Baruch), Monnet and Katz were confident that the President would not fire Nelson but would somehow or other work out the situation.

Thursday, February 18

Heard Madame Chiang Kai-shek in the Senate.[1] The exquisiteness of her entire presence—the delicacy of her figure as she stood there sheathed in black, beautifully emphasizing the rich black sheen of her hair and the delicate charm of her face—and speaking, as she did, in a pleasing voice and with faultless English diction—was a striking commentary on the silly sense of superiority of Western people and the still sillier arrogance that somehow or other man is a creature superior to woman.

Saturday, February 20

Sam (Judge) Rosenman phoned me and talked about the WPB situation. I told him in substance that I was not competent to say who should be put in Nelson's place or whether Nelson should be replaced. What I was sure of is that the man at the head of WPB must be one who is actually capable of running the organization ten hours a day for six days, and that Baruch certainly is physically and psychologically not capable of doing that. The war production

[1] Madame Chiang Kai-shek had arrived in the United States at the end of November for medical treatment—and also as a political emissary from her husband who felt that China and the Pacific Theater were being neglected in Allied councils. Madame Chiang, beginning with her address to Congress, swept the country up in a wave of enthusiasm for China. America's military leaders feared she might even unhinge the basic Allied strategy of "Europe first."

process cannot be run by intermittent flashes—occasional wise advice of a general nature—which is the function that Baruch has been exercising and could only exercise if he were formally made head of WPB; that I speak as one who was on Baruch's War Industries Board during the last war when Baruch like the rest of us was twenty-five years younger. Moreover, since Baruch has close associations with sniping newspaper men like Krock and David Lawrence and Roy Howard, as well as partisan critics like Clare Booth,[1] the fact that he could only give intermittent energy to such a job would inevitably give opportunity for these irrelevant outsiders to become part of the whole enterprise on the public side of it. In a single word, my view was that while Baruch's appointment would result in what is called "a good press" for a short honeymoon period, honeymoons are notoriously brief and the problems and production are technical, humdrum problems not to be solved by glamour and a good press. Sam said "You are speaking words of wisdom and you ought to tell all that to the President. You should come up and see him." To which I replied "No, I should not. Of course whenever the President wants to talk to me about anything about which I am free to talk, I shall tell him frankly what I think. But it is not my business to volunteer views although of course you are free to tell him the substance of our conversation."

The Monnets (Jean is shortly leaving for North Africa), the Herbert Feises, and Bob Brand, among others dined with us. When the men were alone, we got on to India and I told Bob Brand that that which might seem weakness to a stiff-necked, unimaginative man of rigid character like Lord Linlithgow, the Viceroy of India, were he to release Gandhi because of the latter's hunger strike, probably would appear to the millions of Indians who view such things from a totally different angle, as an act of humanity and generosity. And magnaminity, I believe, never is bad statesmanship. The difficulty, of course, is that the Western peoples and Indians view things quite differently—and when we say the Indians are unreasonable and irrational, we simply mean that we cannot understand them. What I am afraid of is that should Gandhi die during confinement—which I am sure is his aim—he will be made a Christ of by the humble people of India. For myself, I regard him far from being a Christ. To me he is a man of very considerable worldly cunning and guile. The question is not one's intrinsic judgment of Gandhi but how his life and death would be viewed by those most concerned—the millions of Indians.

Sunday, February 21

Luncheon at the White House with the President and Mrs. Roosevelt and eight other miscellaneous friends of theirs. During lunch Mrs. Roosevelt raised the Gandhi hunger strike problem, expressing her own great fears of the conse-

[1] Clare Booth Luce, dramatist, wife of Henry Luce, the publisher, Congresswoman from Connecticut, was sharp-tongued—as in her characterization of Henry Wallace's speeches as "globaloney."

quences of not letting Gandhi out, and when she asked the President to do something about it, he indicated with some show of impatience that he had been at work on the problem, that she was not raising questions that were new to him and while he indicated that she expressed to the British the feeling that Gandhi should be let out, the British had difficulties he could not overcome.

The President told in some detail of his sessions with Giraud and DeGaulle—so that at first hand I heard the story of DeGaulle's replying to the President when asked to take the field in France that he was no longer a military man but had become the leader of a great national movement, like Jeanne d'Arc—"I am the Jeanne d'Arc of today" DeGaulle told the President. The President said he received that with a serious face and did not smile, but when on the following day, he said to DeGaulle "After all, our first job is to win this war. France can be liberated only if we win this war. So let's work out a practical program between you and General Giraud." General DeGaulle replied, "That is easy. The last war furnishes the answer: General Giraud is the Foch of today and I am the Georges Clemenceau." The President said, "I then had to laugh and said 'Now, see here, General DeGaulle, I knew Georges Clemenceau and I don't think I ever knew anybody who was less spiritual than Clemenceau. You can't be both Jeanne d'Arc and Clemenceau." To which DeGaulle replied, "It is not at all difficult. That's just what I am." The President commented on his two interviews with DeGaulle by saying "I think he is a little touched here"—tapping his right temple.

Had supper with the Stimsons. The Secretary is very much concerned with what he calls the ballyhoo of the press over that charming emissary of China, Madame Chiang Kai-shek, together with the bribe on behalf of other theaters of war to lead the President, with his goodness of heart and optimistic spirit, to "syphon" war supplies away from the African and European theaters, and thereby to handicap that effort. The President, said Stimson, is clear about policy but allows himself to be persuaded by visitors like Madame Chiang Kai-shek to make commitments to China and elsewhere, the inevitable effects of which are to reduce our striking power in Africa and Europe.

Sunday, February 21

On our arrival at the White House, the usher told us that the President wanted to see us in his study. He greeted Marion and me with his customary warmth and gaiety of spirit and quickly launched into fun-making by telling Marion with mock solemnity that he was sorry to see I could no longer button my last vest button, etc., etc. He then asked with genuine eagerness about the Murray children and Oliver,[1] what news we had of them, etc., etc. On turning

[1] Oliver Gates was one of the three children of Mr. and Mrs. Sylvester Gates, member of the London bar who had studied with Frankfurter and helped him in analyzing the record in the Sacco-Vanzetti case. At the height of the London *blitz* the three Gates children, Ann, Venetia, and Oliver, had lived with the Frankfurters and all of Washington, including the President,

to his Casablanca trip, I heard him for the first time, so far as I recall, express displeasure about an experience of his, namely, the air trip. Evidently he dislikes traveling in the air as it gives him a strange feeling of not wanting to do anything—although he does not suffer from air sickness—or read anything, leaving him with a feeling which to me sounded very much like the state in which one is greatly fatigued. He concluded this aspect of his talk with "And as for fleecy clouds—I never want to see another fleecy cloud in my life." But with this phase of the trip out of the way, he told with his usual zest of the extraordinary and wonderful strangeness by which he could dine with the Sultan of Morocco and have a visit with the President of Liberia and breakfast or lunch with the President of Brazil, all within a day or so.

Monday, February 22

Sir Girja Bajpai, the Indian Agent General, came to have tea with me. He has been in the habit of doing this ever since he came to this country and brought to me a letter from Sir Maurice Gwyer, the Chief Justice of India. He was, of course, full of the Gandhi business and said it is a clash between the two authorities, the Viceroy, Lord Linlithgow, and Gandhi. He is confident if Halifax had been in India events would never have taken this turn—that Halifax certainly would have terminated Gandhi's confinement at once danger to his life brought in a new factor in the situation. Bajpai does not anticipate violence or tumult on a large scale should Gandhi die, but he feels there might be stoppage to the war industries which might greatly hamper the war effort. He is sure, however, that the long range results will be very bad indeed. Gandhi dead will be more powerful than Gandhi alive: he will embitter the situation between the Indians and the British, and above all, he will stimulate the forces of violence and help to usher a period of terrorism and assassination in. Gandhi has been against violence, to be sure against the Japanese, where it has been bad, but also against the British. Nehru has never been anti-violence but has accepted such a policy only as a matter of expediency. Having had a father and mother die through frustration and now his political and moral preceptor (should Gandhi die) because the British did not release him, Nehru's expediency is not likely to be on the side against violence. Moreover, if Gandhi were to die naturally the Congress Party would break out into feuds because of the rivalry among the remaining leaders, but if Gandhi dies of the hunger strike, Nehru will become the undisputed leader.

---

delighted in the Justice's tales of their doings and sayings. Finally, the President said he wanted to see these remarkable children, so, accompanied by their nanny, they called at the White House. Later Frankfurter called the President to thank him and tell him what a marvelous impression he had made upon the children—all, except Oliver, he added, who seemed to be a little reserved in his reaction. That troubled Roosevelt, Frankfurter later said. "Send him over alone," Roosevelt urged, "and give me twenty minutes with him alone." It really troubled Roosevelt, Frankfurter commented, "that someone had held out against his charm."

Before leaving, Bajpai, in a rather poignant way, said he had a personal problem that he would like to put to me. While of course he has no responsibility for the conduct of the Indian Government because he is not a member of that Government, he nevertheless disapproves the action taken by the Viceroy—who is the Indian Government—and naturally would like to identify himself with the emotions of his people by giving up his post and returning to his country. On the other hand, all his life he has tried to discipline himself against making emotional decisions and therefore he has to consider lest, yielding to an overpowering emotion he do something that does not help his people any and may exacerbate feeling still more between the moderate Indians and the liberal-minded British. Thus the debate is balanced in his own mind between quitting should Gandhi die and doing what he can do by staying. And so he asked me what I thought about it, saying that naturally it would not do for him to discuss such a question with the people in the State Department or with Halifax because they could not advise him. He turned to me as a friend. I told him that I could say with all humility that I feel the poignancy of his situation and I have ever since Gandhi's hunger strike began. His people and he, in particular, have been much in my mind. I told him I assumed his inquiry was a rhetorical question—a way of thinking out loud and seeing how his thoughts sounded when they were externalized. And I said I would like to think about what he had told me before I ventured an opinion. Bajpai said he would be grateful for an expression of my views because this is the greatest crisis in his whole public life—that he wanted to put to one side the natural feeling of resentment and disappointment that twenty-seven years of effort towards ways of moderation between the British and his people should seem to have come to naught. On the other hand, he wishes to act to satisfy only one audience and that was his own conscience. He left on that note and I took him to his car and bade him au revoir.

Jean Monnet called up to say he was leaving tomorrow morning for North Africa. Everything worked out as he had wished and even better. He is carrying a strong letter from the President to General Eisenhower. He remarked laughingly, "I am not a modest man but I would never have written such a letter for myself as the President has given me." He goes on behalf of the Joint Munitions Board and to that effect has a formal letter of instructions from Harry Hopkins, the Chairman of the Board.

Tuesday, February 23

Worked on opinions.

Wednesday, February 24

Worked on opinions.

Thursday, February 25

Jay Allen came for lunch. He returned from Casablanca, where he was the representative of the OWI, last Saturday. In his characteristically ironic and mordant style, he summarized the North African situation recalling—as I well knew—that he had supported our Vichy policy as a necessary tortuous course in dealing with a situation as ambiguous as that created by the debacle of France and the German occupation. And so, he said, he had no quarrel with the arrangement made with Darlan, and even an appointment like Peyrouton, though wholly unnecessary, could be defended. He said he was a believer in the principle of "but he is now our crook"—referring to the old story of a political lieutenant complaining to the "boss" over the appointment of someone, and the boss saying "What's the matter with him?" and the follower replying, "Don't you remember only last year you said that so-and-so was a crook?" To which the boss answered, "Yes, but he's now our crook." Allen says if you are going to use people like Nogues,[1] you have got to use him on your side, infiltrate his administration with our friends and not allow him to operate with our enemies, etc., etc. Allen says that most of our Army people are not only ignorant about all these things but on the whole, by inclination, rather more comfortable with the Vichyssoise crowd, the Nazified Frenchmen, than those who for their convictions of liberalism either had to leave France or were put in prison, etc. Our diplomatic arrangements were in the hands of and guided by Robert Murphy who Allen knows well and with whom evidently he has had some unvarnished talks. Jay gave me a number of episodes touching Murphy and the sum total impression left on my mind is that Murphy is a soft-spoken smoothie with easy charming manners, but lack of deep understanding of the forces at play. All that Allen said confirmed the impression that Murphy left on Harry Hopkins when the latter spoke of Murphy as a very shallow man. One trouble with Murphy, says Allen, is that although he is up from the ranks, he is like so many people, who have not had the advantages of the so-called well born, but wish they had them, more "Grotty" than the men who actually went to Groton in the State Department—which has its own amusing implications in that Berle, the worst influence in the State Department, did not go to Groton, and Sumner Welles and Dean Acheson, who are constantly opposing his reactionary views, are Groton products.

Jay said he had a good short talk with Sumner Welles and at Welles' request is putting his analysis of and views on the North African situation in a memorandum for Welles.

Sir Owen Dixon, the Australian Minister, came for tea to tell me that he had cabled to his Prime Minister, suggesting the desirability of a short trip to

---

[1] Auguste Nogues was the five-starred French Resident-General in Morocco. He had ordered his troops to resist the Allied landings, until persuaded by Darlan to stop fighting.

Australia for the purpose of talk on a number of vital problems. Quite unexpectedly, the reply came from Evatt (who is Minister of External Affairs) that they thought that it was a good idea for Dixon to come for awhile but adding that Evatt would come here to represent Australia during Dixon's absence. Dixon said he never contemplated such a sequel to his proposal. He then discussed the potentialities for irritations and conflicts that Evatt might bring due to his temperamental self-assertions, intensified by the feeling that the emphasis on the European theater of war subordinates the threat of Japan and therefore minimizes Australia's dangers. Dixon said the latter feeling is encouraged by MacArthur's restiveness who, while the New Guinea fight was on, was engaged but is now a little inactive again, and in any event had been somewhat disturbed as to his own future command in view of the decisions taken at Casablanca and the possibility of Wavell's future responsibility. Dixon himself feels that there is no occasion for any new or special concern regarding the Australian situation, and he added with charming whimsy, "Of course it would be unpatriotic to suggest that Australia's exposure is partly inescapable because she is such a large island in the Pacific waters."

Friday, February 26

The Chief asked to see me and apparently all he wanted was to relieve his mind about the difficulties that the present situation on the Court presents, and especially the difficulties of making assignments of cases when he is so limited in his choice by reason of the fact that three members—he laughingly said "the Axis" which is now a common sobriquet of Black, Douglas and Murphy—are practically a solid block on any question that divides the Court, and a solid block at that through their strange subservience to Black. I myself had an illustration of that today in connection with two cases I had on behalf of the Court, involving the admissibility of confessions obtained while defendants were under detention for a considerable time without the help of friends or counsel and in violation of law against being promptly brought before a magistrate.[1] The opinions held the admissions improper but rested that conclusion on the policy

[1] *McNabb v. United States*, 318 U. S. 332; *Anderson v. United States*, 318 U. S. 350.

Both McNabb and Anderson appealed federal convictions based on confessions that had been extracted after prolonged questioning while they were kept isolated from family, friends, and legal counsel. Both contended that the use of their confessions at trial denied them due process of law, and cited in support a series of cases overturning state convictions on similar grounds which had been decided by the Supreme Court between 1940 and 1943.

In both cases, Frankfurter, writing for the Court, skirted the constitutional issues and reversed the convictions on the strength of the failure of the arresting officers to comply with statutory requirements that persons arrested be brought promptly before a judicial officer. Although Black, Douglas, and Murphy concurred, they wanted to go further and void the conviction on grounds of unconstitutional self-incrimination. Reed dissented because even the narrow grounds on which the Court was acting he feared broadened "the possibilities of defendants escaping punishment by these more rigorous technical requirements in the administration of justice."

behind the statute requiring the arresting officer to bring the persons promptly before a magistrate because of the abuses that such detentions breed, leaving undecided whether, as a matter of fact, the confessions were in legal conception involuntary and "coerced" and therefore in breach of constitutional rights. Black & Co. wanted to go that far which would carry very serious consequences in upsetting convictions which the state courts had sustained—the two cases in question being prosecutions in federal courts under federal law—and therefore entailing grave questions in the administration of criminal justice throughout the forty-eight states. Black talked to me about this with almost naive recognition of the fact that he is the leader of the "Axis" in that he said "I had a talk with Bill (Douglas) and Frank (Murphy) to consider what we would do about your confession cases. We may be able to go along with you since you have strengthened your opinion and are leaving open, as I see it, the Constitutional ground on which we would like to go." Later on Frank Murphy said, after teasing me about reference to English practice, "There is much in your confession opinion that is very attractive to me and that I think will be very wholesome, and I don't know yet what I shall do. Hugo and Bill and I were talking about it, and I don't know yet what we'll do." Later in the day Black told me he had talked with Douglas and that he was ready to join me, and asked whether I had yet heard from Murphy. It all would be very funny if the joke weren't on the Court.

Friday, February 26

Gil Winant phoned to say he was very anxious to see me before he went back to his London post. Unfortunately we were going out to dinner so I proposed he turn up at 7 o'clock and we could have at least an hour's talk since we were dining around the corner. He has been rather ill and has had what could not have been a minor operation, and seemed more wistful than he does even normally. Marion thought he was a lonely man. He wanted to talk about the state of opinion of this country and Anglo-American relations. He seemed very much distressed by the general and intensified attitude of hostility toward the President, manifested by the new Congress, etc., etc. And he had forebodings of that opinion upon the nature of the peace settlement. I told him I was not worried about the soundness of the body of American opinion as a potentially reasonable state of mind. But that I was worried that so little continuous and effective education of that opinion was being pursued; that practically everybody feels as he does about a common purpose on the main outline for the Allies and the world in general, but they are depending on the President in very large measure to do it, and that it is just humanly impossible for the President to discharge his responsibilities for the actual conduct of the war and also serve as the nation's schoolmaster. While, to be sure, there is no other person who can really affect the mind of the whole nation—barring the qualified exceptions of a few people like Wallace and Stimson—what is needed is that men of influence in their different regions, or men who can influence relatively small bodies of people, should make it their business to deal with that side of the war problem as their almost professional job. That led us to talk about the English situation and the similar dissatisfaction with Churchill's failure to concern himself, except in a very negligible way, with creating the right opinion for the right kind of a peace because he is wholly concentrating on winning the war— which, God knows, is job enough for any statesman. Gil told me that Harold Laski is quite hopeless about Cripps and the leaders of his own (the Labor) Party,[2] and that's why he is going after Churchill and appears to place himself in an attitude of sniping against Churchill although he and Churchill are on a friendly footing, and Churchill is very understanding and generous about it. That led to a considerable talk about Harold in the course of which I gave him very specific messages for Harold, first to explain why I am not writing him— the reason being that I cannot talk about real things since to my knowledge the letters are censored and it would do neither Harold or the things he cares about nor the President in the present state of reckless and irresponsible hostility to the President, any good if I said the things that are on my mind. Secondly, I thought Harold's strategy in attacking Churchill all wrong, not furthering his aims and making mischief he does not intend. I should suppose a wise course would be to recognize that Churchill has only one aim and that is to win the war, that his energy and interest and aptitude are naturally absorbed by that indispensable condition, i.e. winning the war to win the peace, that he respect Churchill's intention to lay down responsibility when the war is won, and that therefore he go after his own Party leaders and address himself to them in insisting on the necessary moral and intellectual preparation for making the military victory fruitful. But the thing that I said I wanted him most to convey to Harold is a sense of my abiding and enveloping affection for him and that while my thoughts do not get on paper, for the reasons given, I constantly hold converse with him in my mind.

Saturday, February 27

Conference.

Sunday, February 28

Lunch at the Adolph Miller's. Present were the Peterses, the former Swiss Minister, and Frank Noyes, the owner of the Washington *Star* and former President of the A. P.

---

[2] The Beveridge Report, which recommended the establishment after the war of a "cradle-to-grave" system of social security, had precipitated a broad discussion of postwar objectives. Labor Party backbenchers favored a stronger endorsement by Parliament of the Report's principles than the Government was willing to accept. In the Division on the Report on February 18, almost all Labor Members of Parliament except for the leadership voted against the Government. Sir Stafford Cripps was Leader of the House. Laski politically felt "very much alone" at this time and often said to his wife Frida "Felix was fighting Churchill's war and he the people's war." (Kingsley Martin, *Harold Laski*, p. 129.)

Monday, March 1

Court sitting.

Dinner at Halifaxes with Lord Hailey (the distinguished Colonial administrator) and Admiral Maitland, R. N. (who has just come over to join Sir Percy Noble in connection with a more aggressive strategy by the Allies against the U-boat menace). Maitland is a quiet spoken, tart, witty, shrewd sailor man who went through the Dakar mess [1]—in fact, it was his ship that carried DeGaulle. He gave a fascinating account of the ill conceived and still worse executed enterprise of the Free French Dakar tragedy. He also gave the most illuminating explanation I have had yet of the nature of the U-boat menace—the program of construction on the part of the Germans, the enormous furtherance of the effectiveness of that program through acquisition of the French ports, the objectives in bombing those ports in order to destroy the facilities for servicing the U-boats by destroying the installations, though the concrete pens built by the Germans are almost impossible to demolish, the furthering of aerial means of detection, etc., etc. The great problem is to get long range aircraft or air bases for short range craft. If the Azores could be used for air fields there would be nothing to it. There was a quiet bitterness in Maitland's tone when he spoke of the fact that the oldest of Britain's allies, Portugal, would not make these bases available.

Tuesday, March 2

Court sitting.

Rabbi Berlin of the Mizrachi (the organization of Orthodox Jews), a member of the Jewish Agency in Palestine, called. He summarized the familiar situation in Palestine, the hostility of the present High Commissioner toward the Balfour Declaration and Jewish development in Palestine, the need for an outlet in view of the European situation, the dependence of effective and decent consideration of European Jewish problems after the war on adequate public opinion supporting Churchill and this Government, etc., etc. He told me how much they looked to me for active support and asked me whether I could, in view of my position be the formal spokesman for Palestine when the time comes. I told him that my judicial office precluded that, but that he and everyone else knew not only where my sympathies were but where my convictions were regarding the relation of carrying out the policy of Balfour and Wilson and the two governments that are primarily committed to the Balfour Declaration after this holocaust is over.

---

[1] In September 1940, a combined Anglo-Free French force, whose objective was to establish General DeGaulle in Dakar, failed to overcome the garrison there. Vichyite morale had proven to be much better than the Gaullists had said, and the operation turned into a fiasco.

David Ginsburg,[1] the counsel of the Office of Price Administration, called in a rather agitated mood. He feels, I think not unnaturally, that the OPA is the keystone to the maintenance of a proper war economy—to prevent all the evils of inflation—and OPA is apparently sailing in heavy waters. Leon Henderson had to resign because of the enemies he had amassed in Congress and the forces that brought about that undesirable end are still operating. Henderson's successor, Senator Prentiss Brown, is a very high-minded, patriotic, intelligent person. But his whole antecedents make him unable to realize with sufficient quickness that a man in that post has to be absolutely ruthless against demands for special exemptions from general rationing and price fixing rules. While he has been very good in saying no as demands are made upon him by former colleagues in Congress, both Senators and others, the drive is accumulating by the mere fact that he entertains these appeals. Once the dam is loosed it will, of course, be difficult to hold the water in along the whole line of war economy and the desirable need of economic stabilization. Fierce hostility to the President is moving a good many partisans and narrow minded stupid people like Dick Wigglesworth of Massachusetts (whom I knew well as a former student and who has not a brain in his head). Then there are the meretricious, largely undercover, anti-Semitic, anti-"bureaucrat," anti-"radical" people through whom it is being fanned and stimulated in all sorts of ways, and Dave thinks that it is best for the OPA that he should get out, though Prentiss Brown, with whom his relations are intimate, will have none of it.

I asked Dave what his military status is and he said he assumed he would in due course be called. I expressed vigorously the view to him that if Prentiss Brown is the man I think he is then he ought to stand up and fight and do it publicly and drive out all these men and the dark influences that thrive because the issues are not publicly exposed. And that, as far as he was concerned, he should let the requirements of the war take their course, namely, to stay at his post if Prentiss Brown wants him to until he is drafted and then refuse to have a claim of deferment made on his behalf but let the draft take its course.

---

[1] David Ginsburg, one of the Frankfurter "hot dogs" in prewar Washington, was an outstanding lawyer, with a talent for conciliation and devising solutions. Shortly after this entry Ginsburg resigned as General Counsel of the Office of Price Administration and entered the armed services as a buck private. Roosevelt took the unusual step of publicly praising him. "Here is a young man who was working day and night on our war effort," he wrote O.P.A. Administrator Prentiss Brown, "long before some who now attack him realized the danger to which our country was exposed. I know, as you know, how diligently, ably and painstakingly David has worked for over two years to help develop the necessary legislative and administrative price controls essential to maintain economic stability and prevent ruinous inflation. Even before Pearl Harbor Mr. Henderson [former Price Administrator] told me that David was eager to get into the Army, but that he could not spare him. . . ."

Wednesday, March 3

Court sitting.

Arthur Lourie [1] came to talk to me about his future. He came to the Harvard Law School for some post-graduate work from South Africa and after some time at the bar he became attached to Weizmann and the Zionist office in London. He said he has a feeling of frustration for the ZOA in America and wonders whether he ought not go to the bar or some Government work. The latter would require giving up his British citizenship which he does not like to do. I urged on him the importance of men of his training and powers of detachment in the difficulties that lie ahead and told him he ought not to leave until he gets an authoritative position which would give him a better opportunity for exercising his talents than that which he now has.

Thursday, March 4

Attended religious services at the White House on the tenth anniversary of the President's inauguration.

Court sitting.

John Foster Dulles [1] called to tell me of the work he has been doing as chairman of the Committee on the Peace of the Federated Churches of Christ. His opposite number in England is the Archbishop of Canterbury. Dulles said that they have finally agreed to six simply and briefly worded objectives for the peace—I thought them admirably stated. He is proceeding quietly to enlist support throughout the country before starting meetings for popular support. I told him I was wholeheartedly sympathetic towards his effort—that if we are to get a decent peace we must secure that which President Wilson did not after the last war—namely, mass opinion behind decent peace aims. It was my view that at one extreme is a relatively small body of isolationists and imperialists—people who do not realize the transforming changes that have been wrought in the world—and on the other hand are so cocky and so self-conscious about the United States that they think we alone can rule the roost. At the other extreme

---

[1] Arthur Lourie remained an aide of Weizmann's and with the establishment of Israel had a distinguished career in its diplomatic service.

[1] John Foster Dulles was a Wall Street lawyer with Sullivan and Cromwell who had fought the New Deal representing the utility interests. In politics he was an ally of New York Governor Thomas E. Dewey. His fundamental interest, however, was foreign affairs, his grandfather, John W. Foster, having served as Harrison's Secretary of State and his uncle, Robert Lansing, as Wilson's. He was active in the affairs of the Federal Council of Churches, serving as Chairman of the Council's Commission on a Just and Durable Peace. The statement that Dulles showed Frankfurter became known as "The Six Pillars of Peace." In addition to urging the creation of a successor organization to the League of Nations, it asserted that international affairs must be conducted in conformity with moral law.

are people like ourselves who have long thought about the problem—also only a few in number—and who appreciate that the U. S. is not merely of the world but in it and that our own peace and security will absolutely depend upon the peace and security of the world. In between is the great body of opinion that is disturbed and aware that something is going on in the world, but which is capable of having its fears and fatigues exploited unless efforts like his win them to an understanding that our security is absolutely dependent upon world security.

We dined at Sylvia Monnet's with Joe Alsop [2] who has just returned from China and India. His own conviction about our Chinese relations is that we romanticize the wrong things about China but fail to give them the kind of material help that they really need. He spent three days in Delhi seeing our Minister, Bill Phillips,[3] there and said that, to the surprise of many people, he is taking quite an independent line on India and thinks that the Viceroy's policy is shortsighted and wrong, but also thinks that it would be disastrous for the United States to intervene in the Indian situation since we would not have the power and would not assume the responsibility of straightening out an almost impossible difficulty.

Friday, March 5

Court sitting.

Shertok [1] of the Jewish Agency in Palestine called and in the course of an hour reviewed the situation in Palestine, in London, and here so far as the outlook for Palestine in the peace is concerned. He said that there were conversations under way at least by some of the British representatives in the Middle East, as, for instance, the British Resident in Trans-Jordan, looking toward a solution of the Palestine problem outside the limits of the so-called White Paper which envisages a federation of Syria, Lebanon, and Trans-Jordan in which the Jews would not be limited to a minority status in Palestine. So far as London is concerned their general attitude toward a decent peace is one of readiness to work out an arrangement if this country will take its due share in international responsibility with a fear, however, that the U. S. A. might lapse into isolationism as it did last time.

Saw Dr. N. Siravaj who had phoned on his own initiative. He is one of the Depressed Classes and represented the Untouchables at the recent Pacific

---

[2] Joseph Alsop, a grandnephew of Theodore Roosevelt and nephew of Eleanor Roosevelt, was a widely syndicated columnist.

[3] William Phillips, career diplomat and close family friend of the Roosevelts, was in India as the President's personal representative. His report to the President in April 1943 was highly critical of British policy in India, a policy under which twenty thousand Congress leaders remained in jail without trial.

[1] Moshe Shertok later Hebraicized his name to Moshe Sharett. He served as Foreign Minister and Prime Minister of Israel.

Relations Conference. It was interesting to hear the case of the Untouchables at first hand—their dissatisfaction with Gandhi and even hostility to the Congress because of the disregard of their economic and political interest and the unfavorable position which even the Cripps proposals placed them in because of deference to Congress opinion put to one side their claims. Dr. Siravaj went so far as to claim that although there are 60 million of them the census figures actually show only 40 million—that is, the latest census figures—which would imply a decreasing fertility rate as well as a large death rate in the last few years, neither of which is true. Dr. S. is of the opinion that at the core of the Indian problem is an agreed settlement between the two communities—the Hindus and the Mohammedans (the Congress denies the Untouchables even their religious status as Hindus).

Henry Hart [2] called in a state of considerable agitation to say that Dave Ginsburg had resigned as counsel for the OPA because of a number of actions taken by Prentiss Brown and more particularly by some of the people he has brought in like Senator Herring, which if persisted in as part of a policy would shipwreck the whole program of price maintenance and economic stabilization. Henry says the difficulty with Brown is that he does not realize that in making concessions here and there, as for instance, yielding to an insistence by Senator George for an extra allotment of sugar to the Coca Cola people in Georgia— breeds demands for such further individual concessions and makes it impossible to hold the lines. Ginsburg is arranging with Brown—with whom his relations are very friendly—to have Henry become Acting General Counsel and he discussed with me ways and means by which to bring about the education of Brown as quickly as possible to the nature of the problem with which he has to deal and the firmness with which he must adhere to a realization that the task he has in hand cannot be accomplished by dealing with individual instances as individual instances and not as part of a total scheme in which a concession here and there carries with it impulses of disorganization and disintegration.

Hamilton Fish Armstrong [3] was at dinner and spoke of his concern regarding the state of American opinion and the nature of the problems now presented for a decent peace much along the lines of the discussion between John Foster Dulles the other day. He said Secretary Hull is largely concerned with vindicating his own past policy and that he is really not in constructive control of things, that he is away with intermittent colds but that the one thing that he, Armstrong, is sure of, is that Hull will never resign. Welles seems to have the right outlook and appropriate direction regarding the future most of the time

[2] Henry Hart, one of Frankfurter's students, had been sent by him as a law clerk to Brandeis. He became a professor at the Law School and took over Frankfurter's seminar in legislation and sent him his law clerks." [O]ne of my pet products here . . ." Frankfurter had fondly written of him in 1937 in a letter to Roosevelt.

[3] Hamilton Fish Armstrong was editor of *Foreign Affairs* and a specialist in Danubian affairs. In 1938 just before the *Anschluss*, Frankfurter had urged Roosevelt to appoint him ambassador to Austria.

but every once in a while he, Armstrong, wonders whether the Advisory Committee of which Armstrong is a member is really fulfilling the functions of an Advisory Committee—namely, that its views are conscientiously being considered—even if not accepted—or merely acting as a façade behind which decisions are taken "irregardless."

Later Herbert Bayard Swope and his wife came in and Swope told of the informal committee consisting of Baruch, Byrnes, Admiral Leahy, Hopkins, and Sam Rosenman, which is functioning as a sort of *ad hoc* War Cabinet on specific matters, and more immediately manpower and food. Swope says he does not know who is opposing—perhaps the President himself—a formal acknowledgment of the existence of this committee with formalized powers. I told him that I knew nothing about it but it would not be unlike the President to let the thing remain in an informal state and see how it unfolds.

Saturday, March 6

Conference.

After Conference, Brother Reed said to me he felt very unhappy by the indications of the state of mind of the new member of the Court as revealed by his attitude at the first Conference. Reed said he seemed to vote wrong on all the important issues, and wrong because "He is another one of these fellows who wants to do what he calls justice in the particular case without heeding the consequences in other situations not immediately before the Court, or in the general administration of justice." When I told Reed that it is a good sign for him to realize all is not for the best in the best of possible worlds but that he ought not to be disappointed in Rutledge, that that was to be expected from him, that he is one of these men who fails to remember what Holmes said it was the first duty of a civilized man not to forget, namely, that he is not God. Rutledge evidently is one of these evangelical lads who confuses his personal desire to do good in the world with the limits within which a wise and humble judge must move. I said "He will be very conscientious and very earnest and formula-ridden and perhaps too easily taken in by big, noble sounding words."

We dined at Ellen McCloy's with the Stimsons. I had a very intimate talk with Stimson alone in which he told me of his deep anxiety over the uncooperative attitude of the Navy in fighting the submarine menace. Important inventions of a high order have been made for the detection of the submarine and the transmission of information for the location of the U-boats whereby bombers are enabled to reach the marauders in an incredibly quick time and increasing enormously the toll of the U-boats and correspondingly decreasing the threat to our supplies. Stimson said it would greatly shorten the war if only what he called "the damned Admirals" would not be habit-ridden in operating Navy facilities as though it were an independent service. I asked him what the real reason for this stonewall attitude on the part of the Navy was and he said the real trouble is that they never had an Elihu Root as a Secretary who reorganized the Navy and created a kind of a Staff and Line arrangement which Root introduced for the Army. "Instead they have a lot of fuddy-duddy Admirals who live in the past and cannot adjust themselves to the needs of this swiftly changing, scientifically developing, present day war." Stimson said he is at work at the whole problem with a view to storming the President and see if the President cannot cut through all the Navy barriers.

Sunday, March 7

Captain Hussy, who is the right-hand man for Lord Mountbatten of the British Commandos, and being a great friend of the Gateses phoned to give us news of them. Marion asked him to lunch. He was here about a year ago trying to work out ways and means for appropriate shipping for what eventually became the North African landing. He was good enough to say that the dinner I gave him in order to meet Bob Lovett [1] and Dean Acheson and Jean Monnet and Bob Patterson and others made it possible for him eventually to persuade our people to the arrangements which made such a landing [possible]. He is now here on some very important plans which require the close cooperation of our Army and Navy because amphibious operations are involved. He said in England the Commandos are practically a unified arm of Army, Navy and Air, whereas here the greatest block to effective action is a separateness almost bordering on hostility between the Army and Navy, and it's a most difficult thing to get joint action from them. His talk was almost an echo in another field of the war effort to what Stimson said the night before. Hussy said that in all future operations utmost collaboration will be indispensable because even in Africa the losses we had were due to inexperience in collaboration, and there we hardly encountered opposition because of the Darlan business, etc., but in the plans that are afoot we will have the stiffest kind of opposition and therefore unity of effort becomes indispensable. He says it is almost funny but the fact is that by tactful labor—and infinite tact is indispensable, he said—the British can almost do more with our Navy in getting collaboration than can our own Army. Which reminds me that Stimson said the night before when I said that we have had no Secretary of the Navy for decades to break through the Admirals—he replied, "I'd break through, all right, if I got a chance." As I have no doubt he would and as I have no doubt he is right in saying "Frank Knox is completely in the hands of the Admirals and they do what they please with him."

Monday, March 8

Court sitting. Opinon day.
Continuation of Conference all morning.
Worked on cases late into the night.

---

[1] Robert A. Lovett, a Navy flier in World War I, an investment banker, was Assistant Secretary of War for Air.

Tuesday, March 9

Continuation of Conference beginning at 9:30 until we went on the bench. After sitting the C. J., Black and I spent until past six as a committee of the Conference to formulate questions for the attention of counsel on reargument of the Texas oil cases (Nos. 495–496 and 528, *Burford v. Sun Oil Co. et al*).[1] It seemed to me that the Chief's attention was flagging toward the end of our meeting and his mind certainly was not quick and alert, naturally enough. We had been at it from 9:30 without interruption which is sheer madness— nearly nine continuous hours—on intellectual problems of real difficulty calling for the utmost concentration, but more than that, involving the tension inevitable in group discussion as compared with the calm of solitary work in one's own study. The long hours of our Conferences seem to me a very bad way of doing business that we have to do, and I am greatly disturbed about the future if the Chief does not make it a flat rule to terminate Conferences after four hours and also, incidentally, if the Court does not realize the bearing of keeping down our docket, of not taking cases simply because three men (which usually brings a fourth) feel that an injustice has been done in the lower court, although the litigation necessarily has already been before two courts and does not involve any far-reaching general principle or a novel point in federal law calling for settlement by this Court, on the quality of our work.

At Herbert Swope's request I saw Mr. George Kennedy who is writing a full-dress article on Stimson and his conduct of the War Department. In sum I told him that Stimson happened to combine what are, so far as I know, unique qualifications for the creation of the Army necessary for the kind of war in which we find ourselves, namely, his knowledge of the War Department by reason of his past service as Secretary of War, his distinguished experience in the last war, the moral authority that these two factors give him in the eyes of the generals, his knowledge of the relation of military to political questions, and particularly understanding of Far Eastern problems both by reason of his service as Secretary of State and as Governor General of the Philippines, his very high standards for competence and his good judgment of men as illustrated in his civilian heads, Patterson, Lovett, and McCloy, but above all his infectiously disinterested character and courage which enabled him to bring the

---

[1] *Burford v. Sun Oil Co.*, 319 U. S. 315 (1943). Rehearing denied, 320 U. S. 214.

An oil company sued the Texas Railroad Commissioner in Federal District Court, challenging his grant of an exception from the regulations that required minimum spacing between oil wells. The District Court refused to take jurisdiction over the case, finding that it was not in the public interest to protect the rights asserted. The Court in an opinion by Justice Black approved the action of the District Court.

Frankfurter, in a dissent joined by Chief Justice Stone and Justices Roberts and Reed, maintained that as long as the Constitution provided for jurisdiction over controversies between citizens of different states, and the judicial code specifically lodged such jurisdiction in the district courts, the latter were without discretion to refuse to take jurisdiction over an otherwise proper suit between citizens of different states on public policy grounds.

full force of his mind and experience to bear as Secretary of War in this gigantic struggle.

Wednesday, March 10

Court sitting.

Thursday, March 11

Court sitting.

Shertok called and put to me three questions: [1] (1) What kind of legal sanctions would I say were necessary for arrangements that may be made at the peace; (2) the Ben-Gurion-Weizmann row; (3) the general situation in this country regarding peace arrangements, particularly in relation to Palestine. I answered: that I knew nothing about the second question but it is a silly and tragic waste of limited forces; as to the first question, I thought it idle to work out details of sanctions for the arrangements to be arrived at through the peace as it all depends on two things, namely, the strength with which public opinion will be behind the governments both here and abroad in England for realizing that not only must some secure provision be made for European Jewry but also that Palestine is the one sure solid aspect for such determination; public opinion must be educated to the realization that such an adjustment can be made with full fairness to the Arabs through a confederation or whatnot which gives ample room to the Arabs in Syria and Trans-Jordan and Saudi Arabia, leaving Palestine in a very special situation.

We dined at Sir Owen Dixon's, the Australian Minister. He told me that he had instructions from home that he is to await Evatt's coming and not go to Australia until he arrives. It is difficult from this end to make competent appraisal of Japanese purposes in the Pacific, that so far as we know she may be taking defensive measures against the invasion of Java or offensive measures against Australia.

Friday, March 12

Court sitting. We heard the reargument of the Schneiderman case,[1] being a review of the decision of two lower courts which decreed the revocation

---

[1] Why Shertok raised these questions about the future of Palestine at this time is not clear. British policy in the Mandate still was guided by the British White Paper of 1939. There were three points in that policy—that Palestine was to become an Arab state in five years, that there would be limited immigration during those five years, and none thereafter without Arab consent. If adhered to after the war, Dr. Weizmann and his colleagues considered it a nullification of the Balfour Declaration's pledge of a Jewish homeland. Just before Weizmann came to the United States to work on synthetic rubber, he was called in by Churchill, who told him his plan was to make Ibn Saud of Arabia "boss of the Middle East, providing he settles with you." (C. Weizmann, *Trial and Error* [New York, 1949], pp. 425–427.)

[1] *Schneiderman v. United States*, 320 U. S. 118 (1943).
Wendell Willkie had represented Schneiderman in argument before the Supreme Court on

of a naturalization certificate granted to one Schneiderman on the theory that it was illegally granted because he was not attached to the Constitution of the United States. The two lower courts held that the proof showed his allegiance was to an alien system, to wit, the Communist regime in Russia. Much of the argument centered on the questions whether knowledge of a body of literature showing the nature of the Communist Party and various subsidiary Communist organizations, was actually brought home to Schneiderman so that the lower court may have been warranted in finding that those principles were his principles sponsored, avowed, and disseminated by him. To that end the Chief Justice asked Mr. Fahy, the Solicitor General, a series of questions and answers according to which Schneiderman appeared to have expressed his personal acceptance of what are deemed to be "principles" opposed to those principles of the Constitution. Brother Black then asked "Is there anything more than his agreement to general political talk?" To which Fahy said, "There is nothing more than Schneiderman's agreement with this general political talk." I followed that question up by asking Fahy, "Is it suggested that the Communist Party has no principles?" At which Black turned to me with blazing eyes and ferocity in his voice and said, "The Hearst press will love that question." I replied, "I don't give a damn whether the Hearst press or any other press likes or dislikes any question that seems to me relevant to the argument. I am a judge and not a politician." "Of course," replied Black "you, unlike the rest of us, live in the stratosphere." I made no further comment but resisted the impulse to say that in any event I do not change my views and votes on cases before this Court because of newspaper criticism. The reference is to what Douglas told me in the fall after we had decided the Flag Salute case. Douglas said, "Hugo would now not go with you in the Flag Salute case." I said "Why, has he reread the Constitution during the summer?" Douglas replied, "No, but he has read the papers."

In the afternoon Jackson, in the course of a talk about the problems before the Court, again reverted to his own very great unhappiness on the Court. He said, "I have a rather long expectancy of life and I don't know whether I want to spend it in this atmosphere. It is an awful thing at this time of the Court's and country's history, with the very difficult and important questions coming before this Court, to have one man, Black, practically control three others, for I am afraid Rutledge will join the Axis. But on the other hand, I say to myself it would be rather cowardly to leave the field to them. But I can tell you that it is very sad business for me and it isn't any fun to be writing opinions to show up some of their performances." I did the best I could to soothe him, adding, "Well, in any event, you don't have to decide this afternoon what you are going to do with your life."

November 9, 1942. The case was discussed in conference on December 5 and 12 and Frankfurter made summaries of the discussions. Since the case is a significant one, and occasioned in conference a highly personal statement by Frankfurter, analogous to the one he made in his dissent about this time in the *Barnette* flag-salute case (see Introductory Essay, pp. 71, 72), his notes are included in their entirety.

Saturday, March 13

Conference.

NO. 2—SCHNEIDERMAN V. UNITED STATES

Summary of discussion at Conference on Saturday,
December 5, 1942.

C. J.   (After giving the facts in some detail said it boiled down to this:)
Are there in the documents with the knowledge and dissemination of
which Schneiderman charged, things which, if you advocate them, are so
contrary to the principles of the Constitution that a person so doing lacks
attachment to those principles? The most important document, Exhibit
26, is not in the record, but even without it the whole program sponsored
by Schneiderman is the antithesis of the Constitution—and there is nothing in it that accords with the Constitution. It is difficult to escape saying:

1. Schneiderman was charged with knowledge of documents.
2. He participated in spreading and inoculating people with these
   ideas, including,
3. Overturning our government by force.
4. Later recession or denial of party programs does not detract
   from their central qualities.
5. The District Court could have disbelieved Schneiderman's
   professions of attachment, etc. I am as strong a man for freedom as anyone but surely Congress may say that no one
   should become a citizen who is not attached to the principles
   of the Constitution, and a person is not attached to the principles of the Constitution who is attracted to another system
   which excludes every notion of our Constitution.

ROBERTS: I agree with you, Chief Justice, and I have very little to add. It
is very unfortunate that law officials put up this case at this time. But that
is for them and not for us.

I had this view right along—the view that men who become naturalized
must be attached to the principles of our Constitution. That is our historic
policy commanded by Congress and it should be our cool view to adhere
to that policy of the government. As to Exhibit 26, I have no difficulty in
finding that it was in fact admitted in evidence and not merely marked for
identification. The petitioner moved to exclude that document with others. The trial judge refused this motion and that is tantamount for me to
an admission. That the document was in fact in the case was treated so
throughout.

BLACK: I think the other way and should reverse. (That is all Black said.)

REED: I also am inclined the other way and will state my reasons for that view briefly. (Reed then went on to express views based on the record but I really could not follow them.)

FRANKFURTER: I spoke rather at length, prefacing my remarks by agreeing with Roberts at the unfortunate necessity that compels us to consider the case. (I referred to my views which some doubtless deemed vehement last spring, on the question of postponing the case.) I thought then, and I think now, that when it is a question of administration of the Court's business, consideration of the effects of our action outside the technical record of the case are relevant. Last spring it seemed very important to me that the case should not be heard at the time because of the posture of things in the world. For myself, I cannot understand why the government did not confess error in this particular case and let it go at that. But that is their concern and not ours. The case is now here for adjudication. And when we are confronted with the duty of deciding, I am sure all of us agree that we have but one duty and that is to go down into our consciences as judges and bring up what we find and without any heed to any consideration that is not relevant to the legal questions presented by the record. In other words, my job and my exclusive duty is to reach a conclusion on the materials that are relevant to the issue raised by the decree setting aside a certificate of naturalization—that is, the relevant legal materials in the light of the record. And so this case has nothing to do with the second front or the fifth front or Russia or our relations with Russia or with what will or won't be the possible consequences of deciding one way or another.

I am saying what I am going to say because perhaps this case arouses in me feelings that could not be entertained by anyone else around this table. It is well known that a convert is more zealous than one born to the faith. None of you has had the experience that I have had with reference to American citizenship. I was at college when my father became naturalized and I can assure you that for months preceding it was a matter of moment in our family life, and when the great day came it partook for me of great solemnity. Later on, as an Assistant United States Attorney in the Southern District of New York—with all that New York implies in the making of new citizens I represented the Government in naturalization proceedings in the federal court. As one who has no ties with any formal religion, perhaps the feelings that underlie religious forms for me run into intensification of my feelings about American citizenship. I have known, as you hardly could have known, literally hundreds of men and women of the finest spirit who had to shed old loyalties and take on the loyalty of American citizenship. Perhaps I can best convey what is in my mind if I read to you from a letter written me by as distinguished an historian as is now alive when he went through this experience of becoming an American citizen.

> There is in this country a wider area of generosity than in any other country,—at least in Europe. It is this feeling that one is at home here that conquers you little by little. And one fine day you feel that you are no longer an exile but a citizen in your own country. When I took my oath I felt that really I was performing a grand function. I was throwing away not my intellectual and moral but my juristic past. I threw it away without any regret. The Ethiopian War, the rape of Albania, the Spanish crime, and this last idiotic crime, had really broken my connection with sovereigns, potentates, and all those ugly things which are enumerated in the formula of the oath. It is a wonderful formula. Your pledges are only juridicial and political. You are asked to sever your connections with the government of your former country, not with the people and the civilization of your former country. And you are asked to give allegiance to the Constitution of your adopted country, that is, to an ideal life.

> Thus, I took my oath with a joyous heart, and I am sure I will keep it with the whole of my heart as long as I am alive. [The historian was Professor Salvemini of Harvard.]

In other words, American citizenship implies entering upon a fellowship which binds people together by devotion to certain feelings and ideas and ideals summarized as a requirement that they be attached to the principles of the Constitution.

That phrase, as we know, began practically with the beginning of this nation. It is an historic phrase and it certainly is not empty of all meaning—just rhetorical flourish—and it certainly does not mean that you are attached to the principles of the Constitution if you want to overthrow the scheme of society of which the Constitution is a framework simply because one of the principles of the Constitution is the right to amend it. In other words, one can hardly be attached to the principles of the Constitution merely because one is ready to undo the Constitution and the Constitution affords means for doing so. If the "principles of the Constitution" is so vague as to be meaningless then we had better erase from our books opinions reaching far back which talk about the principles of the Constitution as the means whereby liberty and justice is secured and vindicated—opinions like Van Devanter's on *Hebert* v. *Louisisana* (272, 312) [1] in which he speaks of the fundamental principles of liberty and justice which

---

[1] *Hebert v. Louisiana*, 272 U. S. 312 (1926).

Hebert appealed his Louisiana conviction for bootlegging, and the length of the sentence imposed by the state court. The Supreme Court upheld the conviction and the sentence, and in *dictum* (language superfluous to the result reached) stated that the Fourteenth Amendment, which did not affect Hebert's conviction, required that state action "be consistent with the fundamental principles of liberty and justice which lie at the base of all our civil and political institutions . . ." at 316.

lie at the base of our civil and political institutions (272 at 316) and the whole series of the more recent opinions like *Chambers, Edwards* v. *California,*[2] and the rest. The simple truth of the matter is that apart from the issues of this case, however large the phrase "principles of the Constitution" may be, all of us around this table are in substantial agreement about the essentials of our scheme of government and society which the Constitution brought into being and which characterize our political and social life as a nation.

And so the real question is whether we can say that the two lower courts were not, on this record, justified in finding that Schneiderman was not attached to the principles of the Constitution. And to answer that question I ask myself another: Suppose precisely the same record had come up not from a decree revoking citizenship but denying an application for it. For under the *Tutun* [3] case (270,568) the denial of a petition by an alien for admission to citizenship could be brought here. To me it is simply inconceivable that if on this same record a district judge had originally witheld citizenship from Schneiderman because he was convinced that Schneiderman's loyalty was enlisted by another fellowship than that which binds us together and therefore was not attached to the Constitution as the binding force of our political fellowship that we would have reversed. I say this in no disparagement of Schneiderman's moral qualities. I have known the Schneidermans and a good many of them well since my college days, and I have admired, and still do admire, their devotion to their ideals. They are the salt of the earth so far as character and selflessness goes. But they are devoted to a wholly different scheme of things from that to which this country, through its Constitution is committed. Of course the district judge had a right to reject all of Schneiderman's perfect disavowals. That which to Mr. Willkie seemed so important—to prove that Schneiderman was attached to the Constitution because of his smooth and complete and perfect testimony on the witness stand—looks to me rather in the other di-

[2] *Chambers v. Florida,* 309 U. S. 227 (1940).

A forceful opinion by Justice Black for a unanimous Court that held it a denial of due process for a state to use at trial a confession obtained after the defendant had been held incommunicado for five days of continuous questioning.

Edwards v. California, 314 U. S. 160 (1941).

Edwards appealed his conviction under a California statute that made it a misdemeanor to bring an indigent into the state. The Court, in an opinion delivered by Justice Byrnes, held the statute to be an unconstitutional incursion by the state into the regulation of interstate commerce which under the Constitution is reserved to the federal government. Justices Black, Douglas, Murphy, and Jackson all believed that the statute ran afoul of the Fourteenth Amendment's prohibition of abridgment by the states of the "privileges and immunities of citizens of the United States."

[3] *Tutun v. United States,* 270 U. S. 568 (1926).

A decision that held justiciable an appeal from a district court's denial of a certificate of naturalization.

rection, for as a judge I do not have to be innocent of that which as a man I know, namely, that deception and lies in the interest of their holy cause are well recognized instruments in the tactics of Communist officials.

Of course I am not suggesting that mere membership in the Communist Party indicates lack of attachment to the principles of the Constitution. Many a person is a member of the Communist Party merely as an expression of his deep feeling of injustice about the iniquities and hardships of our present society. I am not talking about an ordinary member. We have before us this record concerning a passionate lad who, since his sixteenth year, had dedicated himself as an active organizer and important official of the orthodox creed of the Communist party. It is still true that no man can serve two masters when two masters represent not only different, but in this case, mutually exclusive ideas. At least that is what the District Court found and that is what the Circuit Court of Appeals affirmed. Had they found against the Government, I should not have been warranted in setting my judgment against that of the District Court and the Circuit Court of Appeals. Since they found for the Government, equally so I cannot say that the District Court judge was disentitled to find what he did and that the Circuit Court of Appeals was disentitled to affirm what the District Court found.

I have only one more thing to say. I cannot deal with this case any differently than I would deal with a case involving a Bundist. I have recently had occasion to show Brother Murphy a book some of us got out before this war started, based entirely on German documents, to prove that Germany adheres to the old notion that once a German always a German, and therefore is ready and indeed encouraged, American citizens of German origin to serve for Hitler's Reich. Now suppose such a case came here, as it well may come, on a record not dissimilar from this, how can I have a different attitude toward a decree revoking the citizenship of an American of German origin simply because Naziism is loathsome to me whereas Communism, although in its methods and practices it is hostile to everything I care about, is in its ultimate ideals directed towards human welfare and human dignity?

DOUGLAS:　I am also inclined to vote to reverse. (He said no more.)

MURPHY:　I am also inclined the other way, though not as strongly as I was, and I should reverse. (He said no more except to add after a pause) I should like to see what is written.

C.J.:　How can anything be written when we are equally divided?

ROBERTS:　But Chief, we are not equally divided. Jackson is out of it (he left soon after the discussion got under way), and so we are four to three for reversal.

C.J.: Well, let's vote.

DOUGLAS: (At this point Douglas vigorously said:) I don't think we should vote. Inasmuch as there is no full majority, I don't think we ought to go on with this case. We ought not to decide a case of this importance on such a line-up.

C.J.: Well, what do you suggest?

DOUGLAS: Well, I think we ought at least to wait until we have another Justice.

(At this point there was more or less a hubbub in the discussion but Murphy joined Douglas in saying he too thought we ought not now to decide the case. For one thing, he said we ought to have a reargument or otherwise it would not give us a chance to clear up the problem of Exhibit 26.)

ROBERTS: It is as cleared up as it ever can be cleared up. The Government has filed a reply brief in which they tell you everything that the record permits them to tell. We have all the light there is.

(The C. J. again suggested that we in any event take a vote whether the case goes down or not. Black said he was ready to vote, but he too thought it was better that the case should go over. Reed said he would rather like to have the case go over. Frankfurter said nothing throughout this discussion about taking a vote or not. The Chief said he thought Justice Reed was entitled to have the case go over if he felt he wanted it to go over until next week.)

NO. 2. SCHNEIDERMAN V. UNITED STATES

Summary of discussion at Conference of Saturday,
December 12 [1942]

The Chief called up the *Schneiderman* case, expressing the view that we ought to try to make some disposition of it and at least have our votes recorded.

DOUGLAS: (Douglas said that before the vote is taken he would like to state why he is for reversal so that there is no misunderstanding around the table.) If the case here had only the circumstances the Chief Justice mentioned last Saturday I would feel differently, namely, that it was proved that Schneiderman himself was committed to an immediate program of action by force and violence against the Constitution. But I don't feel that the record made that clear, and what is prominent in my thinking, as at present advised, is that the Court did not sufficiently define the appropriate criteria. On the record what is clear is

(1)   that Schneiderman himself was not guilty of any disobedience of law;

(2)   that he did not collect funds to incite against the overthrow of the Government, and

(3)   that the Communist Party is engaged, as the later documents show, in becoming an American Party, and

(4)   that, while a great deal of the stuff in the record goes against my grain—it is not fair to attribute the views to Schneiderman. And so, as at present advised, I would set up the proper criteria to be applied and then remand the case to the District Court for application of these criteria.

The Court then voted:
  For reversal
    Black
    Reed
    Douglas
    Murphy
  For affirmation
    Chief Justice
    Roberts
    Frankfurter

The Chief Justice then stated that at the last Conference the suggestion was expressed by the majority that the result be not announced and that the case be held for the present. The Chief Justice said that it was for the majority to determine and he invited their views.

BLACK: (Black was strong against handing down the opinion.) If necessary, I would hold it for the duration because of the misuse that would be made by our enemies—particularly as I assume the Chief Justice will write—

C. J.:   I shall certainly write.

BLACK: I had assumed so and I think particularly with the prestige of the Chief Justice writing a dissent in a case like this, it would prejudice us without enemies.

REED: I would hold the case, if necessary, until after the war because of the risks of the war situation.

DOUGLAS: I would hold, not because I think the decision would affect the conduct of the war but because, as I am advised, the Government has a number of cases pending in the district courts for revocation of naturalization certificates and we ought to hold it until we have a full bench so that there may be an authoritative ruling to guide the Government in the district courts in cases now pending.

C. J.: (The C. J. interrupted—) I think Congress is entitled to be informed so that, if necessary, it could pass legislation and a new judge might make it a four to four Court, giving no guidance to anybody.

(But several of the majority thought a divided Court would be just right.)

MURPHY: Ordinarily I think we ought to face things and decide promptly but when three of the majority of four are for postponement I will go for putting it over.

C. J.: It will be put over. [See p. 259.]

Sunday, March 14

Luncheon at Mr. Alfred Noyes' with the Adolph Millers and Madame Peter.[1] Fascinating discussion concerning Wilson and F. D. R. and more particularly—since the Millers had known the President intimately during the whole of the Wilson Administration and everybody there had known him for some time—about his qualities, especially the effect of his sickness on him. There was a general feeling that long illness drove him in upon himself, made him more reticent and more self-reliant. His conviviality was only on the outside as he tended to give himself intimately to but an irreducible few.

Monday, March 15

Conference before we went on the bench for delivery of opinions and afterward until 6:30. We were thus in Conference for about eight hours, a perfectly indefensible way of deliberating on the kind of stiff issues with which we are concerned.

Tuesday, March 16

Bill Sheldon's funeral at Arlington.

Wednesday, March 17

Work on "When Irish Eyes are Smiling" opinion.
I had Mrs. Roosevelt (who came to see the bust of Brandeis) to luncheon

[1] Frankfurter in dictating this entry may have confused Alfred Noyes, the British poet and novelist, with Frank Noyes, publisher of the Washington *Star* and former president of the Associated Press. Two weeks earlier he had been at Frank Noyes' with the Adolph Millers and Madame Peter. The latter's husband, a member of the International Red Cross, was in the United States to charter a fleet of "mercy ships" to sail under Red Cross and Portuguese flags and carry medical supplies and other comforts to prisoners of war and civilian internees in Axis lands. The Adolph Millers were among the closest friends of the Franklin Roosevelts during the Wilson years. Adolph Miller had been one of Wilson's first appointees to the newly created Federal Reserve Board.

with the members of the Court. Justices Douglas and Murphy were the only ones not present.

We dined at the Halifaxes with Eden. There were present in addition three members of Eden's mission to this country, to wit, [William] Strang, the Permanent Undersecretary of the Foreign Office; [Harry] Crookshank, a representative of the Minister of Information (a first rate man); and [Oliver] Harvey, Eden's secretary. Also, besides ourselves, there were present Frances Perkins and the Walter Lippmanns. When the men were alone, Halifax put to us what he called Eden's "problem"—that he was to appear at an off-the-record lunch and meeting of the two committees on Foreign Relations of Congress and he wanted Walter's and my views as to what Eden should say and how he should say it. Walter Lippmann spoke up first and said in effect (what he had written in an article recently) that the Committees on Foreign Relations consisted of a lot of awful people with very few exceptions and he advised Eden "to tell them a story in narrative form"—that they like to feel they are told something they did not know. He repeated several times "to tell them a story that will make them feel they are in on things although the story would not be anything of new or important nature." When he was asked what kind of a story (everybody looked a bit puzzled), he said he did not know just what kind but he thought they would like one. Then there was some talk about what kind of a story—the story of the near collapse of England in 1940—to which Halifax said "They know all that"—or the story of the Greek debacle or the Egypt threat—all were thrown around the room. During all this time I contained my utter disgust over Walter's silly and contemptuous assumption that the two Committees consisted of a bunch of little children who had to be told some diverting "story" and that the appearance of Eden before the two Committees presented a problem in evasion, something to be got over by some verbal trick. I finally spoke up and said to Halifax, "Let me be the Devil's Advocate. After Mr. Eden will have said a word of appreciation for appearing before the members of the two powerful committees, it does not seem to me he can say 'Now I will tell you a story about Egypt or whatnot.' I do not quite see how he will ease into story telling. What is the impression that he really wants to leave with the members and who are they? I then went through the members, one by one, of the Senate Committee, summarizing the composition by saying that with the exception of two or three truly hostile people like Clark and Nye and Shipstead,[1] so far as the Senate Committee is concerned, they are mostly men of good will who are, however, largely ignorant through remoteness from the problems of international living and the relation of the United States to international organization. It is really the question of teaching calculus to people who are not firmly rooted in the multiplication table. So as I see it, the real

---

[1] Senators Bennett Champ Clark, Democrat of Missouri, Gerald P. Nye, Republican of North Dakota, and Henrik Shipstead, Farmer-Laborite of Minnesota, were leaders of the isolationist bloc in the Senate.

question is what kind of an impression will they carry away from the whole experience. And that depends on the feeling that will be aroused in them regarding the major concern in their minds—what is the so-called British Empire after, what are the purposes of British policy in the world. Now everybody who goes to England comes back, no matter how prejudiced—at least so far as I have noticed—with a feeling not about the British Government but about the British people. What needs to be done for most Americans is to supplant the picture they have in their minds about Great Britain—which is a caricature of the body of English men and women—with actualities. And so, as I see it, the real task for Mr. Eden is to stir the imagination of these Senators and to give them, at least to a measurable degree, the experience they would have if they actually went through Great Britain and at first hand got a sense of the mass of British men and women and realized they are pretty much the same kind of people as American men and women, and on the whole want the same kind of a decent world. At this point, Eden interrupted to say "What you say is illustrated by Willkie's experience. I saw a good deal of him when he first came to London. We had a pleasant time but he was full of doubts and worries and criticisms. Then he went off by himself to see the English men and women, and it is that experience that stirred in him the feelings that he afterward expressed about the people in England." Halifax also agreed that that was the important note to strike. I went on to say that one must make them feel that you have no cards up your sleeve, that there are no secret treaties, etc. Notes on all this were taken by Harvey and once or twice Eden himself made notes. The discussion then went on to some of the questions which might be put with the intention of embarrassing Eden by people like Clark and Nye et al.[2]

I exercised as much restraint as I could and I do not think the Britishers had the slightest intimation of the disgust I felt over Walter Lippmann's feeling of contempt and cynicism, and how tawdry it all seemed compared with the high flown, noble talk he gets off in his column.

On leaving, Halifax told me very confidentially that he had seen the dispatch from Harold Macmillan, who is the British Minister of State for North Africa, to the P. M., setting forth the course of negotiations in North Africa, which led up to Giraud's speech and the elimination of the Vichy influences and the abrogation of the Vichy decrees and the restoration of the laws and practices of the French Republic in North Africa. Macmillan had stated in

---

[2] Eden's meeting with the Senators went off uneventfully. He laid particular stress on his ideas about a postwar world organization, making it clear that, contrary to an impression created by Churchill, it should be a world, not just a European, council, with China as one of its mainstays, and emphasizing again that the British were in the war against Japan to the very end. Eden may have learned more from his appearance than he gave, for at the end of his visit, according to Hopkins' notes, "Eden said he had learned of the importance of Congress and particularly the Senate in any postwar discussions and he had not fully understood the working arrangement between the President and Congress. He found it pretty difficult to envision the wide separation of the powers of the executive and legislative branches" (Sherwood, p. 719).

his dispatch that the whole course of events had been largely due to Monnet's wise and effective efforts.[3]

Thursday, March 18

At work on opinions all day.

Friday, March 19

T. V., (Dr. T. V. Soong, the Foreign Secretary of China and brother of Madame Chiang Kai-Chek), came to lunch. This was the first time I had seen him since his return from China whither he had gone last November. He greeted me with affectionate warmth. He summarized the Chinese situation and in telling me things he talked to me as to no other person because, after all, he is Foreign Secretary of his country and it is his business within the fair limits of truth to give the encouraging and not the discouraging side of the picture to this country, and more particularly not to talk about the difficulties that he sees ahead in China after the war is over. As is well known, there has been some strain between the Generalissimo and T. V. T. V.'s stay in China this time wiped out all difficulties and he says in all his relations with his brother-in-law he has never felt such assured friendship as this time. He was able to straighten out many matters in the internal affairs of China and Chinese relations with ourselves, and more particularly in the relations between General Stillwell and the Generalissimo where there has been friction.[1]

He summarized the economic situation which, while bad, he was confident would not lead to a breakdown unless, of course, a great military defeat occurred such as the taking over of the large rice regions by the Japanese. The fact of the matter is that low as the food standards in the Army are, they are being met. The Generalissimo's hold on the country is unquestioned although there is some grumbling that he tries to do everything himself. T. V. thinks that is the greatest danger once the war is over—the absorption and centralization of authority in the Generalissimo and the inability of any one man taking all the decisions that he has to take or even remotely making them all

---

[3] On March 7 General Giraud, in his capacity as French Civil and Military Commander in Chief, had formally severed all ties with Vichy and declared that "a decree signed in Vichy has no effect in French Africa." In effect this repealed all Vichy laws, including the Nuremberg law restrictions on Jews that the French had copied from the Nazis. Giraud also abolished the department dealing with Jewish affairs, which as late as March 2 had officially published two additional anti-Jewish decrees.

[1] General Joseph W. Stilwell, "Vinegar Joe," had been sent out to command the China-Burma theater in February 1942. By the end of the year he had become increasingly bitter because of the neglect of the Chinese theater by the Allied chiefs, and although in agreement with Generalissimo Chiang Kai-shek on this matter, he also was feuding with the Generalissimo because he thought more could be done with the limited resources assigned to the China-Burma area.

wisely. While there is, of course, great concentration of authority both in Downing Street and in the White House, the difference is that in both those countries there is an established machinery of government, and the decisions that are taken by the P. M. and the President are on the whole carried out. But the whole tradition in China is to regard government as an instrument for *not* doing things and therefore there is not that machinery or those habits whereby the decisions of the Generalissimo, such as they are, can be or will be able to be, adequately carried out. T. V. thinks that after the war the present grumbling will reach a real volume and the modern needs of China will require a considerable change in the disposition of power now lodged in the Generalissimo. The difficulty is, of course, that Chiang Kai-shek is so overwhelmingly the ablest figure in Chinese life that the people about him are dwarfed and responsibility is not developed which is partly cause and partly effect of his ability and authority, but more particularly his habit of doing work by himself instead of training other men to share in his responsibility.*

T. V. visited India for the first time in his life and said the experience made a radical change in his view of India. The state of that society offended him deeply as a "modern." To see sacred cows running the range in the streets of Bombay, to come close to the whole caste system and the untouchables and all the rest, made him realize that India is still in such medieval state that there probably is—brutal as it sounds—no other way to solve its problems except for England to get out even though civil war will inevitably result so that these awful institutions will be shaken to their foundations. England either cannot or will not deal properly with the Indian problem nor has Gandhi and his movement touched the basic difficulties of India.

Saturday, March 20

Worked all day in Library of Congress, and more particularly in vault, going over Jefferson's original papers—236 folio volumes which had been carefully arranged by him, meticulously indexed both chronologically and alphabetically, and now beautifully mounted.[1]

---

* (T. V. said that as he sat at Cabinet meetings he was struck with seeing the same old faces that he had seen five or six years ago. He noticed a great deal of incompetence among the Generals and civilians. The Generals were mostly older men as in the case of Russia. But what struck him was the people—when he came in contact with the mass of the people he felt his strength renewed as did Antaeus when he touched Mother Earth.)

[1] Frankfurter had been invited to deliver the Jefferson bicentennial address at the Library of Congress on April 13. He took the address most seriously, not only going through Jefferson's papers in the Library's vault but spending a weekend at Charlottesville. In his speech he focused on the way that "misuse and manipulation" of some modern devices, including "chain newspapers, cheap magazines, popular polls, the movies and the radio," had complicated the problem of making democracy work. For democracy, in his view, was "the reign of reason" and the media had "enormously enlarged opportunities for arousing passions, confusing judgment and regimenting opin-

We had the McCloys and Sylvia Monnet to dinner. McCloy just back from North Africa where he had—one inferred from his modest talk—what one would have guessed about it—a major share not only in working out the political problems but also, and primarily, a number of major military changes to secure completer cooperation among Americans and British (who, at General Headquarters are a beautifully united force, Jack said, because a few men at the top, Eisenhower, Cunningham,[2] and Air Marshal Tedder, and the French who thus far have been rather insulated from the central direction of GHQ). Jack was greatly impressed by Gen. Giraud—who evidently is really a General of high caliber but has been out of the world of the imponderables—questions of public opinion in the U. S. regarding the Vichy decrees and failure to restore the rule of the French Republic—during his years of confinement in a German prison and since. But evidently Jean Monnet and Jack made great headway in getting Giraud to understand these things once he was made to realize through Jack, as spokesman for the President, that the French Army will be looked to as the most natural thrust once the invasion of the Continent is begun.

Sunday, March 21

We lunched at the Robertses. There was present Congresswoman Rogers of Massachusetts who is a member of the Foreign Relations Committee. She said that Eden made a really excellent impression upon the members of the Foreign Relations Committees of both Houses.

Worked the rest of the day except during the time that I was interrupted by a visit from Ben Cohen who was much concerned about the drive against maintaining stabilization of prices through what he regards as a very self-regarding behavior of Congressmen from the agricultural districts, and the failure to resist them in compromising with them, and the effect of such indulgence of the farm interests upon other interests, more particularly labor.

Monday, March 22

Worked all day and evening writing opinion.

Thursday, March 25

Dean Acheson phoned me to say that David, his son, is going off to sea soon and he would like to see me before he went. I asked both of them to lunch with me in my Chambers. When Dean came he said first, "Let me give

---

ion." Frankfurter's speech was completely overshadowed by President Roosevelt's address the same day at the Jefferson Memorial on the edge of the Tidal Basin.

[2] Admiral Sir Andrew B. Cunningham was the naval commander of the North Africa expedition.

you some documents. They are cables that have just come to you from Jean Monnet." I asked Dean whether I should read them right away and return them and he said no, he would leave them and I could return them later. I took copies of the following cables for my own files:

Secretary of State   Algiers
Washington   Dated March 21, 1943
URGENT   Rec'd 11:18 p.m.
452, March 21, 4 p.m.

FROM MURPHY
Your 494 March 18, midnight

After careful reading of the text of the statement written by Edouard de Rothschild [1] which he intends to give to the press we here arrive at the conviction that he either has not read Giraud's public declaration of March 14 and the declaration and ordinances subsequently published or he or the group for which he is spokesman for propaganda purposes have deliberately chosen to place a patently false interpretation on them.

The following comment has been prepared in consultation with an un-biased legal specialist. I believe it represents the facts and controverts the statements made by Rothschild which smack of the hysterical.

One. General Giraud by an ordinance of the fourteenth of the current month abolished the laws relating to the Jews which were of Nazi inspira-tion. The right to practice the liberal professions including the holding of public office, the right to own property and freely to manage their prop-erty, assets and all business enterprises, and the right to attend institutions of learning of all degrees are now entirely guaranteed to the Jews. In the civil registry records the Jew is no longer indicated as of a race apart. General Giraud wished to efface an odious past by ordering the reinstate-ment of all public officials, agents and employees excluded because they were Jews. With the same objective he ordered that property sequestered under provisional administration would be restored to the Jews and that

---

[1] Although General Giraud had followed up his action of March 7 with even more specific ac-tion on March 14, abolishing Nazi-inspired laws in all districts, he had also abrogated the Cre-mieux Decree of 1870 and thereby deprived Jews born in North Africa of French citizenship. This placed them on the same level as the Arab population of North Africa. Giraud said that the 1870 Decree had given Jews a privileged position. It was the abrogation of this Decree that had caused Baron Edouard de Rothschild of Algeria, speaking for Algeria's Jews, to protest Giraud's actions. He acknowledged that the General's statement "raises great hopes and contains many encouraging and gratifying elements" but these were nullified by the abrogation of the Cremieux Decree. The Jews of Algeria had automatically become French citizens since 1870 and it was difficult not to see racial discrimination in Giraud's repudiation of all of Vichy's decrees except its abrogation of the Law of 1870. On the side of Giraud and his advisers, including Robert Murphy, it was argued that to confer automatic citizenship on Algerian Jews but not Arabs would infuriate the latter.

the sales of real property and other assets would be null and void. It follows that Rothschild's affirmation that the decisions of General Giraud are obscure and insufficient is false.

Two. Jews both in France or descendants of parents born in France remain French citizens. The affirmation made by Rothschild that they lose their citizenship is false.

Three. The Cremieux decree only concerns native Algerian Jews. It is abrogated but in the near future a procedure will be established for the acquisition of citizenship by native Algerian Jews who desire to become citizens. It should not be forgotten that elections, following the precedent of 1914–1918, are deferred until the end of the war, that is to say until the liberation of metropolitan France. Therefore native Algerian Jews who desire it will have ample time to become citizens and participate in those elections. Rothschild's affirmation that Jews will be unlawfully deprived of voting power is also absolutely false.

WILEY

Secretary of State   Algiers
Washington   Dated March 22, 1943
URGENT   Rec'd 5:33 p.m.
453, March 22, 5 p.m.

FOR THE SECRETARY FROM MURPHY

The following is for Justice Frankfurter from Jean Monnet to be transmitted to Frankfurter at the Department's discretion. This would be for delivery to Frankfurter only if the Department considers it advisable also to show Frankfurter the statement written by Edouard de Rothschild published in N.Y. Times of March 19th. "I am shocked at the incomprehension shown by certain interpretations in the United States of the measures taken by Giraud wiping out all discrimination against Jews and also by the harmful interpretation of the abrogation of the Cremieux decree. The telegraphic reply sent by Algiers to the Department's telegram No. 494, March 18, midnight represents an accurate statement made after consultation with an unbiased and best qualified legal specialist. I hope that you can help in straightening out any possible misunderstanding. If any points remain doubtful to you please cable me through Murphy."

WILEY

Sunday, March 28 to Friday, April 2—
Charlottesville visit

Visited the General Watson's at Charlottesville—working on Jefferson Day address.

Friday, April 2

Justice Roberts told me of the President's invitation to preside over the International Conference for Refugees in Bermuda sometime in June. I told him how glad I was and that he has accepted.[1] I said I hoped he would not feel any urge about accelerating the date of the Conference. International conferences (I said) do not inevitably succeed even when there is ample preparation for their work, but they certainly never succeed if there is not ample preparation. And from what I know about the whole international situation and what is being thought and done about it both in England and the United States, far too little has been done to make the issue of the Conference a very promising one. Roberts said he supposed there is very little we can do except make the right kind of a gesture, but the gesture is important. I said of course I knew nothing about the problem—which was not a modest disclaimer but the fact. I told him some of the people who really are knowing in the matter, to wit, Fred Keppel, who is Chairman of the Committee of Appeals for Visas of Refugees, and George Warren, Director of the International Immigration Service.

Saturday, April 3

Conference. Discussion of curfew bell cases.[1] My remarks on basis of Chief's statement of how case got here, etc.

In a dissenting opinion by the Chief in one of the Jehovah free speech cases, *Martin* v. *Struthers*,[2] Stone characterizes the ordinance that was sustained by the Court in that case as an "exercise of totalitarian power." I said to Roberts that I thought Stone in the eagerness to make a point was really betraying his own sense of regard for the influence of this Court in that he used a vituperative adjective which excites temporary popular passion, that really the Chief Justice of this Court ought not to condemn an opinion which he happens not to agree with as "totalitarian," when in simple truth, the majority of

---

[1] The International Conference in Bermuda was essentially an Anglo-American affair. Justice Roberts withdrew his acceptance because Chief Justice Stone thought it unwise for members of the Court to take on extra-judicial governmental assignments. The purpose of the conference was to consider "more effective governmental action on behalf of refugees." It adjourned without effective action because few countries were willing to take in the refugees. The Jewish settlements in Palestine were prepared to receive them, but the British, fearful of stirring up the Arabs, adhered to the 1939 White Paper policy of keeping Palestine's doors as tightly closed as possible.

[1] *Hirabayashi v. United States*, 320 U. S. 81 (1943).
This challenged the constitutionality of a wartime curfew order on the West Coast that applied to Japanese Americans.

[2] *Martin v. City of Struthers*, 319 U. S. 141 (1943).
Justice Black for the Court held that a city ordinance making a license necessary for door-to-door circulation of pamphlets, as the Jehovah's Witnesses were doing, violated freedom of speech and press.

the Court care as much about free speech as he does. Roberts replied, "Now see what I have been up against ever since I have been on the Court. Stone just cannot help lashing out when he finds himself in a dissent."

Thursday, April 15

Court sitting. (Francis Kirkham, Reuben Oppenheimer, Charles Merzes at house.)

Dinner at Stimson's. (F. D. R., H. L. S. and La Guardia)

Friday, April 16

Court sitting.

Visit with President Quezon.

Dinner at Bullitt's. Ickes, Francis Biddles, Achesons, MacLeishes. Reason for present feeling about Willkie, F. D. R., etc.)

Saturday, April 17

Conference.

Sunday, April 18

Miss Goldmark at the house.[1]

Delightful afternoon visit with Hughes.[2] His vigor and the charm of his mind, show no sign of his 82nd year. There was talk about Jefferson, and Hughes gave special emphasis to one characteristic of Jefferson's—his imperturbability throughout his life despite the acrimonious political controversies in which he was engaged.

Monday, April 19

Opinion day. Conference continued forenoon and afternoon, interrupted by going into Court for opinions.

At Conference long discussion of the Texas Oil cases [3]—Black at his

---

[1] Josephine Goldmark, sister-in-law of Brandeis, was a woman of remarkably disciplined intelligence. She did the research, first for Brandeis and later for Frankfurter, in the minimum wage and maximum hours for women cases.

[2] Frankfurter, always interested in the history of the Court, treasured his talks with the former Chief Justice. He was a frequent caller.

[3] See footnote, p. 207.

worst, violent, vehement, indifferent to the use he was making of cases, utterly disregardful of what they stood for, and quite reckless when challenged once or twice regarding the untenability of what he was saying. I spoke at some length, I hope quietly, just laying out the long history of the nature of judicial power and stating why these cases would present an appropriate exercise of judicial power, and that we could not, with any regard for the teachings of the past and proper regard for federal legislation conferring jurisdiction on the federal courts, deny the right of the federal courts to adjudicate a controversy where a clear right under Texas law was presented simply because we felt—as indeed I felt—that it is much more appropriate to conduct such litigation in the state court instead of in the federal courts.

Dined at the Lefty Lewises to have the benefit of their experience regarding the housing problem with which we have been confronted, namely, the decision of our landlady to put the house on the market and thus subject us to the terms of the lease in case she gets a buyer.

(While on the bench, in reference to what I had said two weeks ago in Conference in regard to the action of the Conference in allowing the Dewitt curfew order case to come here by way of certification in order to prevent the block of Judge Denman's opinion—a decision of the Circuit Court of Appeals on the merits and the publication of the opinion by Judge Denman the contents of which were deemed undesirable to be published, Frank Murphy handed me the attached note.)

Felix—

Speaking of capacity for indignation—I consider it a rare and choice quality in any man.

Two weeks ago—on our Saturday afternoon conference—you were at your peak in your righteous wrath about choking off a judge you have nothing in common with and who was espousing beliefs we probably all disclaim. It seemed to me that while our brethren were not party to it that there was put in motion just what you said—a scheme to gag a judge.

Tuesday, April 20

Continuation of Conference. At the end of it Brother Roberts came into my room and said that on Saturday he went home after the long Conference tired and dispirited, and yesterday he went home after another long Conference tired and dispirited again. "Just because," he said, "of what we did on Saturday and yesterday, and the way we tear up law with complete indifference to the precedents or the consequences. Black with his vehemence and vitality and lack of savoir faire and ruthlessness and unflagging industry will before long absolutely control the Court. He now has two votes as a matter of course—Murphy's and Douglas' (I cannot understand the latter with his training and his academic experience), and all he needs is another one, either Jackson's or Rutledge's and when there is another vacancy on the Court, with the present trend of things, he will practically have the majority in his pocket. I am very blue at the prospect." Roberts then reverted to the "Texas" cases—cases involving the jurisdiction of the federal courts over the Texas Oil proration cases— and said the way Black just rode roughshod over everything and everybody—"I simply cannot understand why Jackson should go that way, for you never laid out a problem more conclusively or more beautifully than you analyzed the question of jurisdiction in that case." To which I replied that a difficult problem confronted me and probably if I had been wise I would not have said anything, because in order to say anything I had to spell it out in detail and at least in the manner in which I did it appeared to be very professorial—not that I mind being a professor because that is what I am and I was appointed to this Court as a professor, so to speak. Roberts: "It was your duty to do what you did and I would have been very unhappy if you did not do so." "Well," I replied, "as a matter of self-respect I just could not be silent when such hog-wash was emitted by Black with fanatical disregard of the truth of the cases and statutes which he threw together haphazardly without relevance and without meaning except generally to create an atmosphere of confusion and intensity of conviction."

Roberts went on to say, "Of course, one difficulty is that the present Chief is not strong at the helm—you were on the Court long enough to see with what mastery Hughes presided over our Conferences."

Wednesday, April 21

Governor Neeley of West Virginia called to say that he is taking the affirmative in a debate shortly in which the question is whether a fourth term would be proper for the President in case the war is still on, and as a means of assuring an effective peace. He has written his speech but he wondered whether he could turn to me as a student of American history and politics to ask me to jot down any ideas I may have on that subject. But he went on to say "If to do so will in the slightest embarrass you, you don't have to give any reasons for saying no." To which I replied: "I am going to say no and without much circumlocution tell you why I say no." The Governor interrupted to say "You don't have to give me any reason. Your 'no' is reason enough for me." I then said, "I want to give you the reason and it is that I have an austere and even sacerdotal view of the position of a judge on this Court, and that means I have nothing to say on matters that come within a thousand miles of what may fairly be called politics." Governor Neeley said, "I quite appreciate your attitude and I had to screw up courage for three days before putting this to you, as I myself was doubtful of the propriety of doing it." I replied, "Questions are not improper but some answers are." He then asked me whether I knew Max Lerner and I said I did and I gave him his address.

Monday, April 26

Bob Sherwood called—just back from Africa—to say that it is a perfect Godsend to have Jean Monnet in Africa. He says he cannot imagine what course the political developments would have taken if Monnet had not been there to straighten out things as gradually he is straightening them out. Bob, who before he went to Africa thought it was all hunky-dory and easy to straighten out the DeGaulle–Giraud difficulties, evidently has come back a somewhat wiser and sadder man.

Tuesday, April 27

Roberts said to me today, with a really anxious tone of voice, "What is a man with my views and feelings to do with an opinion like this of Douglas' in the *Bailey* case? [1] (*Bailey* v. *Vermont Railroad* is a piddling employer's liability case—one of those commonplace actions by an injured or dead railroad employee against the railroad under the Federal Employers Liability Act. For various reasons the brotherhoods are on the whole opposed to the introduction of the Workmen's Compensation Plan to injuries on railroads and insist on the archaic plan of compensation for loss of life or limb on the basis of negligence, instead of regarding such losses as inevitable in the conduct of the railroad enterprise and thereby to be compensated for on an insurance basis.) Why does Douglas in writing an opinion in a single case like that, instead of just saying it was a close case and therefore was a case for the jury, go off and make a stump speech on a soapbox which really makes the Court a laughing stock when it does not degrade it?" Roberts went on in this way with a great deal of feeling. I said to him that I have my own painful thoughts about this sort of thinking and the more painful because I know the answer to his questions, namely, that is the opinion of a judge who has political ambitions, and is not thinking about

---

[1] *Bailey v. Vermont Railroad*, 319 U. S. 350 (1942).

Under the Federal Employers' Liability Act a workman was entitled to compensation for an industrial accident only if he proved negligence on the part of the employer. On most of these cases Frankfurter found himself at odds with the Black-Douglas group over whether the Court should review the evidence in cases where lower courts had found no liability. "Considering the volume and complexity of the cases which obviously call for decision by this Court," Frankfurter wrote in 1949 in *Wilkerson v. McCarthy*, 336 U. S. 53, "and considering the time and thought that the proper disposition of such cases demands, I do not think we should take cases merely to review facts already canvassed by two and sometimes three courts even though those facts may have been erroneously appraised. . . . For this Court to take a case which turns merely on such an appraisal of evidence, however much hardship in the fallible application of an archaic system . . . may touch our private sympathy, is to deny due regard to the considerations which led the Court to ask Congress and Congress to give power to control the Court's docket. Such power carries with it the responsibility of granting review only in cases that demand adjudication on the basis of importance to the operation of our federal system; importance of the outcome merely to the parties is not enough."

the Court or his Court job. To which Roberts replied: "I know you and others tell me that but it is hard for me to believe it." I answered, "You will admit, will you not, Roberts, that I have said very little to you on this subject and only rarely have referred to it." Roberts: "Yes, that is true but people in whose judgment I have confidence tell me that constantly and still it is hard for me to believe." I remarked that every man must make his own judgments and I do not want to disturb his faith but the fact of the matter is that not long after Douglas came on the Court it was as plain as a pikestaff to me that he was not consecrated to the work of this Court but his thoughts and ambitions were outside it. And for me such ambition in a man corrupts his whole nature— especially if he is a judge, as the history of this Court amply proves. Roberts said he was very much distressed, and said it had come to the point where lawyers don't care any more about precedents or what this Court has decided or what may be relevant legal arguments—that they try to aim at what they think social and political prejudices of a majority are. I said that when an opinion like that of the Bailey case comes around, I cannot but recall my mother's remark to us as children—that we should hold ourselves dear. I should think that that was particularly applicable to the Supreme Court of the United States and that an opinion of this sort writes us down as cheap. It presents a great difficulty to me because one hates to swallow all the tripe of such an opinion simply because one agrees with the result, and I equally dislike concurring in the result and thereby seeming to have a personal difference with Douglas.

Wednesday, April 28

Geoffrey Faber called. He is the head of Faber & Faber, the well known London publishers. He is here now as a return visitor on behalf of the British publishers—whom Curtice Hitchcock recently visited from here. Like all Britishers he is interested in the currents of opinion and hopes of collaboration between the British and ourselves after the war. I gave him my views—being in substance those set forth in my letter to Stafford Cripps last July.

Thursday, April 29

A buffet supper at the Danish Minister's. Talked with Hambro,[1] the former Norwegian Foreign Minister, and Arthur Salter about the Russo-Polish difficulty and the general question was canvassed whether this was an eruption

---

[1] Carl Hambro was President-in-exile of Norway's Parliament. As the Russian armies approached the prewar frontiers of Poland, relations between Moscow and the Polish government-in-exile in London, headed by General Sikorski, deteriorated. In April the Germans announced they had discovered in the Katyn forest a mass grave of Polish officers and accused the Russians of having executed them. Sikorski asked the International Red Cross to investigate. The Soviet Government thereupon broke relations with the Polish Government in London and moved toward recognition of a group of Polish Communists in the U.S.S.R. as the Polish Government.

of the long process of friction between Poland and Russia or whether it had dangerous implications for division among the United Nations, and more particularly between Western Powers and Russia. Hambro spoke with a good deal of power about the feeling of the small nations against the tendency of Moscow, London, and Washington to run the show and inevitably to get into what he called "imperial tendency."

Friday, April 30

Lunch with Prich.[1] Late afternoon, Main Johnson, Ottawa newspaper man, came to office. Archduke Otto and his brother at the house later.

Sunday, May 2

Saw Secretary Stimson who had just returned after perhaps a fortnight's absence from Washington inspecting encampments, particularly those presenting various phases of artillery problems, throughout the country. He said that Knox is very much disturbed over signs that political considerations, i.e., the next Presidential election, are influencing the disposition of questions. For the first time Stimson reported Knox as saying he has doubts about the wisdom of having entered the Administration. For himself, Stimson said, "I won't say that I have seen evidence of political motives asserting themselves, but I feel the presence of such considerations in the atmosphere and I am very sensitive to atmosphere." "I am not suggesting," he went on to say, "that in anything the President has said or done have I seen the slightest sign of political considerations, but it is the people about him, the little sycophants that always play about the throne, who, I believe, are full of political preoccupation. Somehow or other I am feeling that my presence in the Administration is less welcome than it has heretofore been." I told him that I was glad he saw not a trace of any political attitude on the President's part. I then went on to ask him whether he thought Harry Hopkins was moved by such consideration. He answered emphatically that he was sure Harry was not thinking about such things—that quite the contrary, before he left on his Western trip Harry was helping him

---

[1] Edward F. Prichard of Kentucky was one of Frankfurter's favorite students at Harvard during his last years there. A man of immense bulk, of engaging wit and bonhomie, he delighted Frankfurter with his endearing brashness. Herbert B. Ehrmann gave an example in *Felix Frankfurter: A Tribute* (p. 98). In a seminar session just after Roosevelt had nominated Frankfurter to the Court, the Professor had suggested a new approach to some problem in administrative law and asked "Prich" what he thought of it. "That," exploded Prichard, "is the most tenuous legal proposition I have ever heard." To which Frankfurter replied mildly, "I hope, Mr. Prichard, that your capacity for surprise has not been exhausted." "No, it has not," Prichard came back, "and I'll tell you why. You can never tell what one of these new judges may decide." Along with MacLeish he had edited *Law and Politics* (1939). In 1943 he was working with Judge Fred M. Vinson of the Federal Court of Appeals who, within a few weeks of this entry, was appointed Stabilization Director under Byrnes and who took Prichard with him.

vigorously—trying to get action on the anti-submarine campaign, and that Harry promptly got in touch with him after his return. "Well," I said "I am sure Jimmie Byrnes isn't thinking about politics." And Stimson was equally sure. "It is these minor figures who are buzzing about the President with their eyes and minds on '44. What I am concerned about is, in the first place, the interests of the country, what it would mean to us as a nation to have the conduct of the war embroiled in political controversy, and equally I care about the President, for his own sake and his own place in history. Any deflection from exclusive attention to war to politics would mean a great deal to his place in history." We then went on to talk about other things, but as I was about to leave, he took me to the door and said with great gravity, "I count on you, Felix, to let me know when my presence here is an embarrassment to the President, when he would on the whole prefer to have somebody else in my place. I count on you to tell me the very minute that he feels that way. For I do not want to stay a day longer than he wants me to stay." I told him that he would recall how there were busybodies around Taft and T. R., respectively, who helped foment and promote differences between T. R. and Taft and thereby creating and widening breaches instead of making it their business to maintain the friendship. And so I hoped that just as the President would keep in their places people who buzz about him, so he, Stimson, should not listen to talebearers and people generally who, instead of being preoccupied about the war find time to stir up things, that after all what matters is the President's attitude, what he says and does and feels and so long as he, Stimson, has no ground for believing that the President does not want him to stay, he ought not to be thinking about the subject at all.

Monday, May 3

Opinion day.

George Rublee dined with us and we talked about our old friends, Phil Littell, B. Hand, Ned Burling and the other Cornishites, and then at last about the prospects of the war.

Tuesday, May 4

On several occasions heretofore Frank Murphy told me that my opinion in the Broadcasting case seemed to him "singularly fair, calm, and difficult to answer." Today he repeated these remarks saying the following:

"Why do you reserve your best opinion for a case in which I have to dissent.[1] I have reread your opinion and it is very fine and very fair. Hugo [Black]

---

[1] *Federal Communications Commission v. National Broadcasting Co.*, 319 U. S. 239 (1943).

The Court upheld the power of the Federal Communications Commission to regulate the major networks in the public interest. Frankfurter wrote for the Court majority of five. Murphy and Rob-

and Bill [Douglas] are very disturbed because I am dissenting and they have tried to dissuade me from doing so. I want to tell you why I am doing it. Both as Mayor of Detroit and Governor of Michigan I have seen many excesses of administrative agencies and if we allow these excesses to go unchecked and have the administrative agencies take over the courts, we will have practically totalitarianism. And so I want to check these excesses. Now that has nothing to do with this particular case and I would not be dissenting if it did not concern this general field in which I am so much interested."

At this point I interrupted to say:

"Well, Frank, why didn't you agree with me when I wrote opinions for the Court, checking excesses in the Phelps-Dodge and the Chenery cases? [2] I think I am at least as strong as you are where the specific cases establish excesses."

Without commenting on this interruption Murphy went on:

"And that is why I am writing in this case. Now Hugo and Bill think I have some other motive and so, since I want to be wholly just, I have been examining myself to see whether by chance I am influenced by any consideration. It may be that unconsciously I am influenced by the fact that I do not like the idea of having Tommy Corcoran put Fly in as Chairman of the F. C. C."

At this point I again interrupted to say:

"Did he? I don't know anything about that. Anyhow, and so what?"

---

erts dissented. Black did not participate and Rutledge had not heard the arguments. Frankfurter argued that the Communications Act of 1934 gave the Commission its regulatory authority. If such an exercise of authority was unwise, the fault lay with Congress, not the Commission. The majority also denied that free speech was infringed by withdrawal of a station's license as a penalty for violating an F. C. C. regulation. "It is not for us to say the 'public interest' will be furthered or retarded by the chain broadcasting regulations," Frankfurter wrote. "The responsibility belongs to the Congress for the grant of valid legislative authority and to the Commission for its exercise."

Murphy's dissent contended that, "By means of these regulations and the enforcement program the Commission would not only extend its authority over business activities which represent interests and investments of a very substantial character, which have not been put under its jurisdiction by the Act, but would greatly enlarge the control over an institution that has now become a rival of the press and pulpit as a purveyor of news and entertainment and a medium for public discussion." The Commission assumed this function "as a mere incident of its duty to pass on individual applications" for station licenses and that was "an assumption of authority to which I am not willing to lend my assent." The F. C. C. should ask Congress for new legislation, he advised.

[2] *Phelps-Dodge Co. v. N. L. R. B.*, 313 U.S. 177 (1941).

The Court held that under the Wagner Act a company can be required to hire applicants who were never previously employed by the company, but who were refused jobs because of their union activities and affiliations. The company was also required to give "back pay" from the time they applied until they were hired.

SEC v. Chenery Corp., 318 U. S. 80 (1943).

Frankfurter for the Court, Black, Reed, and Murphy dissenting, Douglas not participating, ruled that Commission orders were reversible where they could not be sustained on grounds found by the Commission itself.

F. M.: "Well, I know all about it because it was at Tom's request that I gave the former Chairman (McNinch) a ten thousand dollar job so as to create the vacancy into which Fly was placed. And I don't like Tom's performances."

To which I replied: "That hasn't a blessed thing to do with the validity or invalidity of the particular regulations that are now before us and are challenged as being in excess of the powers which the Congress conferred upon the F. C. C."

Murphy went on to say that he had talked with the Chief about this case and that the Chief agreed that "Your opinion is perhaps the finest thing you have done since you have been on the Court and that it is a very fine job indeed."

"My opinion is all contained in the first six lines of what I have written which states my general point of view. And the rest of the ten pages are just saying the same thing in many different ways in a legal form."

Jackson reported the Chief as saying that he was very sorry about the majority opinions in the Jehovah Witnesses cases last Monday, that as opinions they were inexcusable, they did not properly formulate or discuss the issues, that he was in an impossible situation in that having said all that he had to say in his dissent in the *Opelika* case last Term, he could not now rehash what he had then said, he could not make those who were writing the majority opinions in which he agreed with the results, write opinions to suit his views, and so he was in a practical box of having to agree to opinions that he was ashamed of.[3]

Herbert V. Evatt and Mrs. Evatt dined with us. He is in a much more equable and composed mood than he was a year ago. Then he was really frightened by the prospect of a Japanese invasion of Australia and the lack of adequate understanding, as he believed, both in London and in Washington, of the Pacific situation. He now says that there is a much more balanced view of the relation of the Pacific theater to the war in its entirety. Last time he was critical of almost everybody, especially Churchill, and our people, barring only the President—except that he thought the President was misinformed by his military advisers, etc. But this time he found fault with nobody and expressed

---

[3] *Jones v. Opelika*, 361 U. S. 584 (1942); *Murdock v. Pennsylvania*, 319 U. S. 195 (1943).

In *Opelika* the Court had narrowly sustained an Alabama municipal ordinance licensing street vendors. The majority contended that the licensing provision did not infringe upon liberty of expression or religion, even though such ordinances were applied to witnesses peddling religious tracts. Stone, Murphy, Black, and Douglas had dissented, and Black and Douglas in an unusual statement had repented of their views in support of the flag-salute decision written by Frankfurter in 1940, the *Gobitis* ruling. Opelika was reversed on rehearing 319 U.S. 103 (1943). In Murdock, the decision handed down on May 3, 1943, Douglas, writing for the majority, with Reed, Frankfurter, Roberts, and Jackson in dissent, ruled that such license fees were a tax on the free exercise of religion and therefore invalid.

general appreciation of our efforts and of what he calls our growing understanding.

Wednesday, May 5

We dined at Eugene Meyer's. The Wayne Coys and Ben Cohen and Prich were present. There was a good deal of talk about Lewis and a rather pessimistic line of talk by Coy, Prich and Ben in attributing the awkward situation into which John Lewis has got the country and the Administration to what they call the "liquidation" of the New Deal and the failure to anticipate by appropriate measures the grievances Lewis is exploiting.[1] I rather talked Dutch to them and indicated that defeatism and pessimism are luxuries we cannot afford, that they seem to forget that reforms are not to be won over night, and that the goals of a decent society constitute a process which must be constantly fought for, and that they must not get weary of welldoing. I also insisted that with what may well be close to two million men scattered the world over in the armed services, millions upon millions of Americans are now immediately related to the larger issues of the war and that they ought to be won to those larger issues rather than have their energies diverted and confused by all the political talk that emanates from Washington.

(Note on May 4th—Evatt said he thought the Court is making a fool of itself in the Jehovah Witnesses cases. It looks to him as though the Chief is taking a position in regard to freedom of speech and is now making a fetish of it and applying it to cases where it simply has no relevance.)

Friday, May 7

Milton Katz asked to see me and came to ask my judgment on a pressing invitation he has had from O. S. S. to plan their intellectual work under Whitney Shepardson.[1] This would necessitate his leaving WPB and he canvassed

---

[1] John L. Lewis, head of the United Mine Workers, had broken with Roosevelt in 1940. Now in defiance of a general "hold-the-line" order on wages and prices, he had ordered the bituminous workers to strike when the operators did not agree to the contract terms he demanded. Roosevelt asked the miners to go back to work in the interests of the war effort and directed Ickes to take the mines over if necessary. The miners did return to work, but the basic issues remained unsettled and there were more strikes, official and unofficial. Public opinion and much of labor was hostile to strikes in an industry so essential to war production, especially when millions of men and women were in the armed services, and Congress, over Roosevelt's veto, enacted the Smith-Connally anti-strike bill, but Lewis did obtain a favorable contract for his miners.

[1] Whitney Shepardson was chief of secret intelligence in the Office of Strategic Services. Milton Katz did join the O. S. S.

with me the present situation of WPB and the possible consequences of his pulling out. He thought things were on an even keel now but of course difficulties may arise within a year and I expressed to him my general doubts about a person having his relation with all the plans being replaceable, although I recognized the attractions of the O. S. S. because of its more proximate relation to the actual conduct of the war. Since, in any event, he would not leave for a month I told him I would think about it.

George Creel [2] came to talk with me about a full-dress article he is writing on Stimson and the War Department and he wanted to verify not only the circumstances in Stimson's past but also his own judgment of the unique qualifications of Stimson for his present post. Creel wrote that Stimson is the only man in the whole war administration who brought to the task precisely the experience one would wish a person to have if one had ideal qualifications to choose from. He was to me particularly interesting in emphasizing the skill with which Stimson manages men and drives his team—unlike the situation in the Navy or in the other big war agencies, with all their constant squabbling. And I think Creel showed perception in emphasizing what he called the native dignity, and what I would call the moral authority of Stimson.

Saturday, May 8

Dined at Dr. Rajchman's (the adviser to Dr. T. V. Soong) together with T. A., the younger of the three Soong brothers. Rajchman told me that T. V. is greatly disturbed at the turn of events and that the Generalissimo has been sending rather fierce cables in view of the conversations at this end with General Stilwell who has, as I have long known, a very limited view of the Asiatic theater. Evidently Madame Chiang Kai-shek has been messing up things by discussing things with the President about which she is completely ignorant. Apparently Wavell is in entire accord with Chiang Kai-shek and will press adherence to the decisions taken at Casablanca and the conversations that will soon take place. [1]

Judge Wyzanski [2] came to see me much disturbed about black market of-

---

[2] George Creel, who was in charge of government propaganda and information activities in World War I, was a frequent contributor to *Collier's* and other publications. His article, "Secretary of War," appeared in *Collier's*, August 7, 1943.

[1] At Casablanca Roosevelt and Churchill had approved plans for ANAKIM, a land offensive to reopen the Burma Road and an amphibious operation to recapture the port of Rangoon, but the struggle was still raging in Allied military councils to get the infantry divisions, planes, and landing craft needed to launch the operations. Churchill was due to arrive in Washington, where this and other matters would be under discussion. General Sir Archibald Wavell was the ranking British Commander in the ABDA (American, British, Dutch, Australian) area.

[2] Judge Charles E. Wyzanski, Jr., a Frankfurter "hot dog," had come to Washington in the mid-Thirties as Solicitor in the Department of Labor. He had then moved to the Department of Justice, where he served until appointed a federal judge.

fenders in Boston. He wanted my general attitude in meting out sentences. The specified incident which came up was a sentence by him of a pretty bad offender whom he had given six months in jail. Thereafter the Attorney General called him by long distance to ask him whether he would not reconsider the sentence and make it lighter in view of representations that had been made to him, Biddle. Wyzanski then called both the U. S. Attorney and the counsel for the prisoner before him, said he does not believe in having any communications about sentences without seeing both sides, told them of the communication that he had had from the Attorney General, and then said he would not change the sentence. I told Charlie that he was absolutely right, that the Attorney General was absolutely wrong, and that it was a characteristic performance of irresponsibility on the part of Francis Biddle—that he was not a bad man or a wrong-doing man but a heedless fellow because he did not take things with sufficient seriousness. The fundamental fact about Francis Biddle is that he is an amateur in his view of life. Charlie said: "Well, you remember what you told me five or six years ago when I consulted you on behalf of Secretary Perkins and asked you what you thought of Francis Biddle as Chairman of the Labor Relations Board." I said I did not remember just what I said and Charlie said: "Well, you said he was much too la-de-da." I replied: "Did I say that? It is still my view. And la-de-da is not good enough in wartime."

Wednesday, May 12

After several efforts on my part to get hold of Dave Niles,[1] he finally turned up. He has recently been the victim of about as outrageously unjustified an attack—a campaign of vituperation—as has been launched against anyone in the New Deal. A Congressman from Michigan, Bradley by name, let loose a harangue on the floor of the House charging Niles with being the great spider-weaving center trying to introduce Communism and Fascism—all in one—and all the other isms. In doing this work he is part of a conspiracy consisting of me and Harold Laski and Jim Landis! They lugged in Jim Landis because he wrote the report in the *Bridges* case, holding Bridges was not a Communist. The real animus I had supposed was anti-Semitism and anti-Rooseveltism with Dave as a good target because through him they could hit at Harry Hopkins. But Dave told me a story that makes the matter much more difficult. After Bradley's speech was published, Senator Wheeler phoned to Dave. Niles and Wheeler have been friends for nearly twenty years and Dave has been very, very intimate with the Wheeler family until the difference between the President and Wheeler made Dave withdraw from the Wheeler intimacy. Wheeler called up

[1] David K. Niles was one of Roosevelt's "anonymous assistants." During Harry Hopkins's brief campaign for the presidential nomination in 1938–1939 before he became ill, Niles was his chief political adviser and strategist. In 1940 he was the director of the Norris-LaGuardia Committee for Roosevelt and Wallace and after his appointment by Roosevelt had become a favorite whipping boy of the isolationists.

to express sympathy and invited Dave for lunch which lasted three hours. He told Dave that the stimulus of this recent attack against him is none other than Joe Kennedy who thereby is not only venting his gorge against the New Deal, but more particularly his personal resentment against Harry Hopkins and me, whom he, in his foolish and ignorant way, blames for his exclusion from participation in the conduct of the war. I don't suppose it ever enters the head of a Joe Kennedy that one who was so hostile to the whole war effort as he was all over the lot, and so outspoken in his foul-mouthed hostility to the President himself, barred his own way to a responsible share in the conduct of the war.

Dave seems to be really hurt partly because his family has been crucified by this performance in that his aging mother who is an invalid with heart disease has had to hear all this awful stuff about Dave over the radio and by anonymous letters that have been sent to her about Dave. He said the President had been very nice about it—assuming, and rightly enough, that such attacks are what he calls "occupational risks," but Dave does seem to be hurt and Harry Hopkins has not manifested the kind of friendship he should in the face of this assault upon Dave when in good truth it largely derives from, or rather stems from, Dave's devotion and service to Hopkins in the past.

Dined at the Percival Chubbs, Joe Alsop's brother-in-law; dinner in honor of General Chennault.[2] There were present also President Conant, Lew Douglas, Jim Forrestal, and Alfred Cohn. Chennault made a very deep impression on me. He evidently belongs to the breed of rare fighters—the Jackson, Montgomery, et al. breed. He is all concentrate, imaginative, resourceful, grim, though when his face breaks into a laugh it has the charm and simplicity of a child. The substance of his talk was that the nature of Chinese geography—the fact that all communications that amount to anything are by water—and the habits of the Japanese who are wonderful fighters to the death within the rules that they know but helpless and disconcerted by the unexpected, makes it possible for 600 planes (fighters and bombers) to accomplish in a very short time what it would take years and years for ground forces to attempt. And he thinks time is of the essence because after all the Chinese have been at it for five or six years, war weariness is bound to set in, and the Japanese are very

---

[2] Major-General Claire Chennault, organizer of the American Volunteer Group (the Flying Tigers) which had been absorbed into the Army Air Force, now commanded the Fourteenth Air Force, based in China. Supported by Chiang Kai-shek, he was pressing for the matériel and men that would enable him to launch a major offensive. But General Stilwell, the top American commander in the China-Burma theater, felt Allied resources should go into the development of a ground force capable of carrying out the reconquest of Burma. He feared that the only result of an air offensive that was not backed up by adequate ground forces would be to provoke the Japanese into wiping out the Fourteenth Air Force's airfields in China. Both Chennault and Stilwell had been summoned to Washington by Roosevelt to argue their case during Churchill's presence there. Chennault, aided by Joe Alsop (and Madame Chiang Kai-shek), was the more effective lobbyist and Roosevelt came down on his side, primarily, as he told General Marshall, as a political matter. He feared the collapse of Chiang Kai-shek's regime and wanted to do what he could to shore up the Generalissimo's authority.

skillfully trying to exploit the peace desire of the Chinese and also the easily stirred prejudice that the white man is trying to conquer China. After Chennault's analysis of the Japanese, Ambassador Grew told a striking story. He said he once asked a well known Japanese how it is that the Japanese Army—one of the best in the world—fighting against an unmilitary people such as the Chinese, should not have succeeded in vanquishing them. The Japanese replied with marvelous lack of humor, "The answer is that the Chinese do not know how to fight—they don't fight the way people should fight."

Thursday, May 13

Dined at the Bob Brand's with John Maud who is here on behalf of the Food Ministry. We had detailed talk about the prospects of the Food Conference.[1] John read us a draft of the position that Great Britain is planning to take, expressing her readiness for a very positive and vigorous program of collaboration not only in dealing with the food needs for the short run, as it were, after hostilities come to an end, but also for the larger vistas that the Food Conference should open up, namely, tackling malnutrition and satisfying the food needs of depressed countries and depressed populations in all countries, and also for the success of the economic program to realize such food aims.

Friday, May 14

Learned Hand was in for lunch. We talked about everything under the sun. He was at his best, perceptive, full of disinterestedness, curiosity, witty, and speculative.[1]

[1] At the invitation of President Roosevelt, a United Nations Conference on Food and Agriculture convened in Hot Springs, Va., on May 18. Roosevelt defined its purpose, saying that nations "must take all necessary steps to meet the essential nutritional needs of the world population. . . . Society must meet in full its obligation to make available to all its members at least the minimum adequate nutrition." (*Public Papers and Addresses*, 1943, p. 212). It was the first United Nations Conference and resulted in the creation of a permanent U. N. organization, later known as the Food and Agricultural Organization.

[1] In the autumn of 1942 Frankfurter had pressed Roosevelt to appoint Judge Learned Hand to the seat vacated by Byrnes. Frankfurter called Hand "the only man worthy to rank with Holmes, Brandeis and Cardozo." Frankfurter thought Roosevelt would have appointed Hand, had it not been for his age, for to have appointed Hand, who was 71, would have revived memories of his court-packing plan which had been centered on the age of the justices. That may have been Roosevelt's chief reason for not appointing Hand, but Roosevelt had surprised Douglas at a poker game in early January, saying "Learned Hand is *not* going to be appointed." When Douglas protested that Hand was a fine judge, Roosevelt explained, "This time Felix overplayed his hand." Twenty people that day had asked him to appoint Hand, "Twenty, and every one a messenger from Felix Frankfurter." Roosevelt paused. "And by golly I won't do it." Francis Biddle, who was Attorney General at the time, told Hand, "If Felix hadn't pushed, pushed, pushed, you'd have had a better chance—if he hadn't been so importunate." (Freedman, pp. 671–676; William O. Douglas, *Go East Young Man*, pp. 331–332; Learned Hand, COHP, p. 105.)

At Herbert's Feis's to a dinner to Richard Law, the Under-Secretary of Foreign Affairs. There were present also the Michael Rights (the new head of the British Chancery) and Congresswoman Luce. Later on the McCloys came in. As we walked home—the McCloys, Marion and I expressed common astonishment at the dullness and humorlessness of Mrs. Luce. She is undoubtedly what Dick Law calls "decorative," i.e. has all the style that money can buy and a slim figure can carry off, but no real charm, no beauty except big and attractive eyes (doll's eyes that close and open), no give and take of spirit or mind. She behaves like a school teacher who has learned her lesson. She makes little speeches and has unmitigated self-assurance and altogether seems to me an extraordinary triumph of a build-up. Marion said I behaved very badly in that I treated her at no point seriously, in fact, indifferently. But Marion was also aware that Mrs. Luce did not know that I was pulling her leg all the time. The point was that I wanted to avoid any serious discussion with her. I wholly distrust her motives.

Saturday, May 15

Dined at Paul Appleby's—the Undersecretary of Agriculture. Present were the Vice President, three leading members of the British Food Delegation, John Maud, and Lionel Robbins, the economist. The head of the Australian delegation, Dr. Coombs, was also there (a very able and hardheaded fellow, it appeared to me). Mordecai Ezekiel of the Department of Agriculture was another guest and the various issues that will arise at the Food Conference were canvassed. The consensus of opinion is that an opportunity of really doing something is very good indeed. It was realized that there were two phases to the Conference—searching technical inquiries with a view to specific constructions by the various committees of the Conference, and public education so that the desired ends which it hopes are to be reached will have behind them enough public support for necessary action both here and in Great Britain more particularly.

Re: *Lepke* cases: At Conference Nos. 606, 610, 619—*Buchalter* v. *New York*, were considered.[1] The Chief went through item by item and found that none

[1] In February the Court had denied a review of the trial of Louis (Lepke) Buchalter, once labeled "Public Enemy No. 1," and two associates, Emanuel Weiss and Louis Capone, for the murder of Joseph Rosen. Lawyers for the three had contended that they did not receive a fair trial; that the jurors were prejudiced; that the publicity about "Murder, Inc." had built up an atmosphere in which a fair trial was impossible; and that the District Attorney, William O'Dwyer, had further prejudiced the case by holding the trial during his campaign for Mayor of New York. In March the Court had reversed itself and agreed to review the case. It gave no reasons, and the only additional argument for review that had been presented by the defendants' lawyers was the narrowness of the margin, four to three, by which New York's Court of Appeals had upheld the conviction. In an opinion handed down June 1, Justice Roberts, for a unanimous court, held that the defendants had had a fair trial [321 U. S. 780 (1943)].

of the claims proving [denial of] due process was made out and therefore thought the case should be affirmed. Roberts agreed and said he still had a hunch that the men were crucified but said the argument was very disappointing and the case was not made out so he was ready now to dismiss it. Black said he was not prepared to affirm because he did not know there was anything to affirm—and in a subtle way indicated that the mere presence of error in a criminal trial did not give rise to a federal claim. In a covered way, he indicated his view that there can be no violation of due process unless there was a denial of one of the specific provisions of the Bill of Rights, such as the privilege against self-incrimination, etc., etc. Generally his attitude was that this was a frivolous case and that the *certiorari* should be dismissed as having been improvidently granted. Douglas sang the same song and said that though he finally voted to bring it up, he now sees there is nothing whatever in it and he thinks we ought to dismiss it. When it came to me, in view of the attitude of Black and Douglas, the latter of whom left the table and sat in one of the big soft chairs where McReynolds used to sit when he was bored, I spoke at length on the importance of the case and the reasons why to me a disregard of our responsibility not to have taken this case in view of the preliminary showing made on the petition for rehearing and more particularly the opinions of the Chief Judge of New York and of the three dissenting judges, would be wrong. I said I hear a great deal of talk about granting freedom of utterance to opinions that we loathe. I thought it was no less important to vindicate people we despise. People like Lepke who for me are human vermin, should receive from us the same consideration as others—if not it simply means that we do not care for law as such and we are in the same position as those in Russia and Germany where it is enough that people are wicked in the eyes of the authorities, and it does not matter that appropriate procedure is followed to establish wickedness. I said I simply cannot with all deference understand a point of view which regards the absence of a few Negroes more or less on a Southern jury a momentous constitutional question, but can seriously suggest that the solemn condemnation of this trial as lacking in fundamental fairness is so frivolous as not to have even warranted an argument at the bar of this Court. (Three of the judges—one of them Loughran, a Catholic, who would not easily find such unfairness frivolous—agree with my view.) I can understand it only on the assumption that we wipe out the requirement of due process as a basis of constitutional protection, independent of the specific enumerations of the Bill of Rights, and thereby wipe out the glorious history of seven centuries of Anglo-American public law. It cannot be that a physically extorted confession would upset a conviction but a subtler way of framing a conviction by having the prosecution collaborate with the chief witness for the state in the giving of dishonest answers in a vital issue in a case, does not offend our fundamental sense of decency which is the essence of due process. This could only be on the assumption that we cannot trust five members of the highest court of the land to exercise a judgment of whether or not a thing does offend fundamental decency because forsooth they would vest too much discretionary power in a majority of the Court who, one would suppose, are disciplined by the responsibility of their office and the great tradition of the history of this Court. Are we really prepared I said, to say we are morally impotent to apply due process as historically it has been applied and instead twist and contort in all sorts of funny ways other provisions of the Constitution to accomplish the same result, or at least results that sometimes are desired to be accomplished? I made it very clear that I would not acquiesce in a dismissal of the case because that would imply that the issue tendered by the petitioner for rehearing, even if established on the record, would not constitute a violation of due process. Nor would I think that the case that was made out was so frivolous as to warrant dismissal. It is simply a case for affirmance on the ground that the petitioners did not establish their case.

After Conference F. M. came to my room and said he wanted me to know that if nothing else was accomplished by taking the Lepke cases (he was disqualified from participating), the remarks that the case called forth from me at the Conference would have made it worth while. He said "It was good for every member of the Court to hear every word that you said." He added that if he had sat in the case he would have been troubled about something that I did not mention, namely, that both the District Attorney and the judge were running for reelection while the case was on, which, to his mind, had a great deal to do with their conduct.

Sunday, May 16

Lunched at the Burling's [1] cabin in Virginia. A rather large party for the Hands, including the Robertses, the Jacksons, and John Lord O'Brians, etc. My talk was mostly with Frances Hand, and I gathered from her that Learned is very much perturbed at the course of the decisions of this Court. (Learned interested me at luncheon the other day in saying that he finds greater uncertainty and lack of clear discussion in the opinions of Stone in recent years, more particularly since he has become Chief, and he attributes it to the fact that so long as he was with Holmes and Brandeis, and later Cardozo, he had the guidance of those great men. I said nothing to B about that. In the first place, I had not thought of the matter in that light, and as I listened to him I realized that the matter is much more complicated that he is aware of.

Monday, May 17

Dined at the T. V. Soong's with the Prime Minister of Canada.

---

[1] Edward Burling, senior partner in Covington, Burling, Washington's most prestigious law firm. "Its ten miles up the river, on the Virginia side," said Learned Hand. "Lovely."

Tuesday, May 18

General Chennault, his aide Colonel Morgan, and Joe Alsop were to lunch with me; only the aide as General Chennault was called away on urgent business immediately after arriving.

Wednesday, May 19

At noon Court went to Congress to hear Churchill's speech. I lunched afterwards at the Australian Legation with Herbert Evatt.

Thursday, May 20

Dr. Chaim Weizmann lunched with me.

T. V. Soong called greatly disturbed at the course of events at the Pacific Council meeting, and doubts cast by Churchill on conclusions supposedly reached at Casablanca and thereafter, implemented by Council at Calcutta which T. V. attended regarding Burma offensive.

T. V. showed me minutes of the Calcutta Conference in order to have my opinion whether he was right in asserting a commitment was made at Calcutta regarding the Burma offensive. I could not read the minutes otherwise than in the manner T. V. interpreted them. T. V. apparently talked out bluntly in reply to Churchill and after the meeting Churchill and Harry Hopkins told him that the matter is not definitely settled and not to cable the Generalissimo. He thought he would have to report. I advised him before he did report to send a draft of the report to the President, and ask him whether that was a fair account of what transpired. He said he would think it over and show me the memorandum he would submit to the President.

Friday, May 21: T. V. said after sleeping over it that instead of sending the President a memorandum he would try to see him, and he had secured an appointment for noon on that day. He then went over the ground and said he would report to me what transpired. T. V. turned up later in the afternoon and showed me a minute which he made of his conversation with the President for transmission to Chungking. He was very much pleased with the interview; found the President very sympathetic. He said that the day before he tried to act as mediator by saying the strategy remained but the tactics may have to be changed and that he could so advise the Generalissimo. The Chief of Staff was at work on the terms and he was hopeful of the report he would bring in by Monday.[1]

[1] Justice Murphy took a rather cynical view of Felix Frankfurter's off-the-bench activities and interests. "Justice Murphy was full of gossip about the quality of the men around the President," Henry Wallace noted in his Diary, May 31, 1943. "He especially has it in for Felix Frankfurter and Harry Hopkins. He says Felix gets great joy out of being the power behind the throne, out of

Friday, May 21

Dinner at the British Embassy to meet the Prime Minister. The host was, of course, Lord Halifax. The guests—the P. M., Lord Leathers, Minister of Shipping; Lord Cherwell, Malcolm MacDonald, Governor General of Canada and son of Ramsay MacDonald; Ronald, the P. M.'s secretary; Richard Wood (Lord Halifax's son, his youngest, recently back from Africa with two legs lost in action); the Americans—the Chief Justice, Byrnes, Undersecretary of War, Bob Patterson, Assistant Secretary of War, John J. McCloy, Ed Stettinius, Lew Douglas, William L. Batt, Eugene Meyer, and myself.

Saturday, May 22

Conference.

Sunday, May 23

Worked all day. (Johnson case.)

Monday, May 24

Continued Conference—discussion of the *Stephan* case [1]—the traitor in Michigan who aided an escaped Nazi flyer. Strong urging by Murphy to take it. Roberts and Rutledge also voted to take it. On the merits I did not think there was any question that called for taking it but urged the importance of granting *certiorari* under the rule that sometimes the conviction of three members of the Court that a matter is important calls for granting *certiorari*. I myself did not want to vote that way because I did not want to encourage the tendency of having a fourth always join three others, particularly when, in so many cases of minor consideration, there are now almost always three for taking them if a "little fellow"—as in a negligence case or a farmer case—namely, Black, Murphy, and Douglas. I did not want to create a precedent of always having a fourth go along because that made it a rule of three instead of four.

---

writing speeches for the Secretary of War and suggesting to the President that he should set up a War Labor Relations Board. He says he contacts the representatives for foreign countries and then talks in a large way about the situation being very grave in China, says Felix is completely sycophantic as far as the English are concerned. . . . According to Murphy, Felix and Hopkins are behind the strong build-up for Jimmie Byrnes. . . ."

[1] *Stephan v. United States*, certiorari denied, 318 U. S. 781 (1943), rehearing denied, 319 U. S. 783 (1943), application for direct review denied, 319 U. S. (1943).

Stephan was sentenced to death for treason. Justices Murphy and Jackson disqualified themselves from consideration of the original petition for certiorari. Justice Murphy dissented from the denial of the petition for rehearing.

Such a rule would defeat the capacity of a court to do its real job. Black felt that while he was strongly against taking it, if the three asked him to join them he would. Roberts said as the oldest, "I emphatically do not want you to join me on any such basis." Roberts afterwards told me that Black had come to him and told him if he wanted him to vote with him he would. Roberts did not want to enter into any such arrangement.

Tuesday, May 25

The Edwin Watsons to dinner. Talk about the President and Churchill, their present relations.

Wednesday, May 26

Dinner at the White House in honor of President Barclay of Liberia next to whom I sat. I asked him for his prophecy regarding the effects of the war upon Africa in view of its embroilment in the actual struggle. He said it all depended on President Roosevelt's views about world organization, and more particularly if the freedom of the people would become effectuated after the war. I was sitting on the other side of President Barclay, a seat removed from F. D. R., and toward the end of the dinner (during most of which F. D. R. let me carry Barclay), he turned to his guest and we had a threesome, continuing the conversation I had had with Barclay concerning the effect of the war on Africa. The President made an interesting observation about Churchill and his outlook on world affairs. He said Churchill is of course preoccupied with the concerns of England, and is somewhat limited by England's experience, etc. When I suggested that Churchill is an old man or at least feels like one and wants to get through with the war, F. D. R. said "That's the way he talked in all my meetings with him until Casablanca and this one, and now he no longer says what he used to say, that all he wants is a big victory and he'll quit." I continued to press my point that Churchill may fear he feels he is an old man, and the President said "I suppose I ought not to say this, and you keep it to yourself, but I have a feeling when I am with Winston that I am twenty years older than he is." The impression was not that the President felt that he was an old man himself, and that Churchill had great buoyancy, but rather that there was a boyish immaturity about Churchill, that the President had a greater seasoning. I myself am rather skeptical of this. It makes me wonder whether the President is not a little misled by Churchill's vitality into minimizing Churchill's depth of discernment, as possibly Churchill in turn does not fully appreciate the sophistication of the President. Not that each does not appreciate the other for they give every impression of joy and happiness in the companionship of the other.

Thursday, May 27

Sumner Welles came to lunch with me. Talk about problems of Palestine in relation to world settlement—the duty from the point of view of peace and decency of having this country and Great Britain talk with forthrightness to the Arabs and more particularly to Ibn Saud about the rightful claims of Arab countries—through the independence won for them by the Allies—to develop empty Arab countries and to allow ample scope for Jewish development in the little notch of Palestine. Welles was in entire agreement and talked like a statesman. He was also very emphatic in saying that to him a peace was unthinkable that does not take proper safeguards against racial or religious discrimination.

Dr. Weizmann came to tea and surveyed the Palestine situation and more particularly the reasons for Great Britain's foolish, timid, and self-defeating policy in Palestine.

Friday, May 28

Jack McCloy came to talk about recent efforts to cause difficulties by suggesting neglect of the European theater of war and transferring everything to the Pacific. He said Billy Bullitt had written a very foolish memorandum [1] to the President full of his anti-British feelings, giving expression to this pro-Pacific policy, and he had asked him to show a copy to Stimson. Stimson endorsed it by saying that it could only come from a mind essentially disloyal to this country. Apparently this is a concerted effort to divide energies. The elements in the problem are anti-British, anti-Russian, anti-Roosevelt, feelings exploiting the easy comprehension of Americans of the Japanese dangers and the natural desire to deal with Japan.

Later T. V. Soong came to see me. He had been authorized to send a message to the Generalissimo that the decision taken by the Joint Staffs would carry out in substance the conclusions reached in Calcutta for the campaign against Japan. T. V. spoke of this recent silly business of trying to make it an exclusively anti-Japanese war. He said the one happy feature in his tiff with Churchill was that he was able to say he had had no truck whatever with the Chandler-Bullitt idea of minimizing Europe and concentrating on the Pacific. He says the trouble with Bullitt is that he not merely has an anti-British and

[1] The Bullitt memorandum to the President, May 12, 1943, one of several that he sent to Roosevelt in 1943, is presented in full in *For the President*, edited by Orville H. Bullitt (New York, 1973), pp. 591–595. Bullitt feared that after the defeat of Germany, Britain and Russia would leave the United States to fight Japan alone. He also feared that Russia, with the destruction of Germany, would seek to dominate Central and Southeastern Europe. He proposed, therefore, that the United States demand hard and fast commitments from Britain and Russia that they would go to war with Japan with all of their forces as soon as Germany was defeated, and that they agreed to the establishment of a united, democratic Europe. If they rejected such a commitment, the United States should alter its world strategy and concentrate upon the defeat of Japan.

anti-Russian feeling—in the case of the latter ever since his love turned to hate—but that while he is a man of ideas, he has no judgment.

John Lord O'Brian and Milton Katz called to express their concern about the new dispensation in the conduct of the civilian aspects of the war by the establishment of the Office of War Mobilization with Jim Byrnes as its head.[2] They said the new scheme can be either very good or very bad—very bad if Byrnes' organization will actually undertake to run production and thereby to dislocate the phenomenal progress and results achieved in war production. On the other hand, if the new scheme is merely an effective way of avoiding rows like those between Jeffers[3] and Bob Patterson, etc—in short, a program and policy determining control, then it will be precisely what is needed. I told them that while I had no more information than they did, I had no doubt that it could not be a dislocating agency, but must be a concentration of the noncombative aspects of war administration. The evolution of this organization, the powers that have been given to it, its membership, above all, the intellectual and temperamental habits of Jim Byrnes, preclude, at least in purpose and general endeavor, the taking of the production process and such dislocations as O'Brian and Katz indicated had occurred from time to time in the past. Katz said of course intention is one thing and knowledge is another. To which I quite agreed, and therefore said the important thing is for Wilson to assume that the new organization is one promotive instead of destructive of the War Production Board and therefore he should choose his earliest opportunity of educating Byrnes, to the extent that he has to be educated, into the problems that O'Brian and Katz explained to me and their relation to the new setup.

Sunday, May 30

Had a long talk with Stimson apropos of the new Office of War Mobilization. He said he assumed that this is the long delayed and much needed effective systematization and centralization of the non-combative aspect of the war, and he added laughingly, "I assume the President is not going to fire me tomorrow." He spoke warmly of his confidence in Byrnes. I told him something about Vinson,[1] of whom he did not know, expressing my confidence in Vinson's disinterestedness, competence, and knowledge of governmental affairs. It was plain enough from his talk that with his characteristic habit of concentration on essentials he will take all he has into this new job, just as he has been

[2] On May 27, by executive order, Roosevelt established an Office of War Mobilization and named Byrnes Director of War Mobilization and placed the W.P.B. under him.

[3] William Jeffers, President of the Union Pacific Railroad, was rubber "czar" charged with implementation of the report of the Baruch Committee on ways to end the rubber shortage. When he set about building synthetic rubber plants, the Army and Navy resisted, contending that such plants would divert men and materials from more urgent military needs.

[1] Judge Fred M. Vinson was named by Byrnes as Director of Economic Stabilization.

lately preoccupied in recent months with getting aggressiveness into the plan to combat the U-boat menace. His heart is, of course, on the combative side of the war, and he hates to be withdrawn from that to any extent whatever. He was very happy about the outcome of the Churchill-Roosevelt Conference in which Churchill had to make a number of concessions to the President's views—which were Stimson's views—regarding future strategic operations. But to swallow the pill Churchill made a request which the President granted rather to Stimson's disgust, namely, to allow Churchill to take General Marshall with him because of the great confidence that both sides of the ocean had in General Marshall. No doubt Churchill wanted to have Marshall make the most effective presentation on the other side of the conclusions reached here.

At last the long efforts of everyone, and more particularly in recent months, of Jean Monnet, to bring General Giraud and DeGaulle together led to the meeting of the two and the constitution of the new French Council. Giraud asked Jean to sit on that Council as one of his representatives. Naturally enough, he could not refuse. The road ahead seems to me most precarious, largely because of DeGaulle's personality, his conception of himself—he once said to the President he is the modern Jeanne d'Arc—as well as the great spiritual sickness amongst the French because of the fall of France. It will require all of Jean Monnet's infinite patience and complete disinterestedness and extraordinary resourcefulness, to evolve the necessary atmosphere of good will necessary to revive the forces in France that will enable her to take her place again as a great nation.

Monday, May 31

The *Schneiderman* opinion [1] was circulated today after months of incubation. I know not in what incubators, except that it largely reflects cunning and

---

[1] *Schneiderman v. United States*, 320 U. S. 118 (1943).

Schneiderman was a Communist Party Organizer whose naturalization twelve years earlier was challenged by the government, which successfully contended in the district court that Schneiderman's commitment to the Communist Party at the time of his naturalization was inconsistent with the "attachment" to the Constitution required by the Naturalization Act. The Court, in a massive opinion by Justice Murphy, reversed. Skirting the question of whether the government had the power to raise such a tardy challenge to a grant of citizenship on the grounds not of fraud, but of error in the finding of "attachment" to the Constitution, Justice Murphy wrote that the government had not adequately proven that Schneiderman was not attached to the Constitution. The principles of political liberty implicit in the Constitution, the Justice wrote, required that the statute be construed to set high standards of proof for denaturalization.

Justice Douglas concurred in the majority opinion but added that in the absence of fraud he did not believe that a grant of citizenship could be revoked for lack of attachment to the Constitution. Should the Congress act specifically to preclude communists from citizenship, then denaturalization would be proper whenever the government could show that a naturalized citizen had been a communist at the time he was naturalized.

Chief Justice Stone, in a dissent, joined by Justice Frankfurter and Roberts, argued that no special standard of proof was set by the statute. The government, wrote the Chief Justice, had proven that Schneiderman was not attached to the Constitution when naturalized, and that his naturalization was therefore illegal and invalid. [See pp. 208 ff.]

disregard of legal principles to which Hugo Black gave expression from time to time in connection with this case. It is one of those extraordinarily shortsighted opinions which, to accomplish an immediate end, is quite oblivious of its implications for the future. Roberts, after he read it, was deeply disheartened. He said "It is one more of these efforts to bring the Court into disrepute." The Chief will write the dissent and while he is a very rapid worker it is most unfortunate that the major effort that is called for in exposing the mischievous fog and cynical confusion of the opinion should be done under pressure at the end of the Term. It is the kind of writing that requires much reflection and the sureness and delicacy of phrasing that only adequate time can produce.

Tuesday, June 1

F. M.—quite on his own—discussed the *Schneiderman* case with me. (See bound volume of opinions for this Term for detailed description of what was said.)

NOTES ON THE SCHNEIDERMAN CASE

Tuesday, June 1—quite on his own initiative Brother Murphy spoke to me with great perturbation about his opinion in the *Schneiderman* case. He said that while he believes everybody should be allowed to have his opinions about things, on the other hand Congress is entitled to make conditions of citizenship and to make one condition attachment to our Constitution. And so, as a matter of law, he said his opinion "skates on the thinnest possible ice—awfully thin." What really bothered him, he said, was his dislike of having a person's citizenship cancelled ten years after it was conferred. I mildly suggested that that was none of our business—if the lower court could justify finding that at the time the oath was taken there was not the fullhearted commitment of loyalty to this country but attachment not to a transformation of this country to something else but attachment to the commands of an outside authority in regard to political matters, then it is our business to enforce what Congress has commended and not overrule the legislative power.

Later, at lunch, when there was some talk about the *Schneiderman* opinion, Roberts, to my great surprise, said to Black that a reading of it made him, Roberts, feel that the author of a goodly portion of the opinion was Black. The latter blushed and hesitated for a minute and then said he wished he had written it as he would be proud to be the author. He was plainly evasive in what was a wholly unexpected aggressive remark on Roberts' part. That night the Robertses dined with us and he seemed pretty sad—afterwards Marion said rather bitter—about the affairs on the Court. He said while everybody takes it for granted that Douglas is moved by political considerations and political ambition, it is awfully hard for him to believe that when Douglas from time to time assures him to the contrary, a man can be so "outright hypocritical" as that would imply, if in fact Douglas was gunning for high political office. I left

Roberts to his doubts and worries and made no comment. (Incidentally, during the course of the day, Jackson, who has no illusions on the subject of Douglas, told me something that is very funny indeed, namely, that the line that is going round about Douglas is that he is the great successor and follower of Brandeis—as Jackson said, "He has about as much in common with him as black has with white, but since his death Douglas sees a great deal of Mrs. Brandeis so as to absorb Brandeis' philosophy through her." Admirable woman that Alice Brandeis is, to regard her as the spring at which one refreshes oneself on Brandeis' philosophy, is egregiously funny.

Wednesday and Thursday, June 2 and 3

Work on *Flag Salute* case.

Ham Armstrong dropped in after dinner just to say hello and stayed long enough to tell of the very unhappy friction within the State Department and particularly because of the feelings of suspicion on Hull's part toward Welles. Every time a newspaper article appears, and more particularly by that scavenger, Drew Pearson, indicating that Hull is only nominal Secretary, Hull attributes such articles to direct inspiration by Welles. Armstrong said he told the Secretary that at a time when the greatest country in the world is engaged in the greatest war in the history of the world, it is too awful to have the head of the premier Department of the Government suspect disloyalty on the part of his subordinates. He, Armstrong, does not believe that Welles is anything but loyal but if Hull thinks otherwise he ought to do something about it. To which Hull replied he is a great believer in giving people rope enough to hang themselves. In other words, the situation is as bad as possible, with resulting indiscipline in the Department. Hull is notoriously one of the most sensitive and suspicious people who ever held public office.[1]

Friday, June 4

Work on cases.

Graham Spry to lunch. He is intimate of Sir Stafford Cripps and was with him in India, etc. He is now here on loan to the Foreign Office to tour the country in order to report on American opinion and more particularly on opinion about Britain's colonial relations. He said that Cripps has, of course, greatly shrunk in public importance since last year, but he agreed that his public importance was factitious in that it was falsely inflated through Russia's entry into the war and the public identification of Cripps with Russia. Cripps now has a technical job—that of Minister for Aircraft Production—in which his technical competence (he was an outstanding patent lawyer) is brought into

---

[1] In September 1943, Roosevelt felt obliged to choose between Welles, whom he preferred as his top diplomatic adviser, and Hull, whose support he needed on the Hill, and Welles resigned.

play and also his practical faculties. Also he was relieved from the uncongenial task of being the government's advocate in the House as the leader of the House. Spry, who is a Canadian, said what strikes him most about the present English situation is the substantial unity of feeling and oneness of the public— of the great bulk of the population and of the Party. There is an extreme Right and an extreme Left—actually uninfluential. In between is a great body of Center-Left opinion.

Saturday, June 5

Conference. Long discussion regarding the Japanese case.[1] It was provoked by a concurring opinion distributed by Douglas, two-thirds of which was, in the language of Frank Murphy, "The most shocking thing that has ever been written by a member of this Court." As he said, "a regular soap-box speech." F. M. said to me that Douglas thought the Chief's opinion, in talking about the war power of the Government, was partly addressed to the American Legion. "Well, if the Chief's was addressed to the American Legion, Bill's was addressed to the mob." It was full of cheap oratory about America winning the war and all that sort of stuff. But toward the end he left the door wide open to have any American citizen independently prove his loyalty—before a court— because while he expressly left that case open he also wrote that he did not mean to decide that the issue was "justiciable." Black expressed the view that in time of war somebody has to exercise authority and he did not think that the courts could review anything that the military does. But on the other hand, he would not allow a thousand habeas corpuses to be brought, and if he were the commanding General, he would not let the evacuated Japanese come back even if the Court directed that to be done. Jackson indicated that Douglas' opinion was a "hoax" in that it promised something that could not be fulfilled. Roberts and I strongly supported the great importance of having the Court bend its every effort towards securing common agreement in formulating a result as to which apparently we are all agreed—with the possible exception of Brother

---

[1] *Hirabayashi v. United States*, 320 U. S. 81 (1943).

A unanimous Court sustained the wartime curfew regulation controlling the movement of American-born Japanese in the West. Chief Justice Stone for the Court stated that the regulations were military necessities within the power of the Army Commander in the region. "We cannot close our eyes to the fact, demonstrated by experience, that in time of war residents having ethnic affiliations with an invading enemy may be a greater source of danger than those of a different ancestry."

The Court did not in this opinion rule on the validity of the evacuation regulations under which Japanese-Americans as well as Japanese aliens had been herded in detention camps, a policy that was later called "our worst wartime mistake." But at the end of 1944 in *Korematsu v. United States*, 323 U. S. 214, a Court majority upheld the Civilian Exclusion Order that barred Japanese-Americans from certain West Coast areas. Justice Black for the Court said the order was "constitutional at the time it was made." Frankfurter wrote a concurring opinion, and Roberts, Murphy, and Jackson dissented.

Murphy who still has his worries about drawing the line on the score of what he calls "ancestry." (I good humoredly chided him about his Indian opinions—their being based on the fact of ancestry, namely, on the fact that Indians are Indians.) The matter went over after the Chief expressed the eager hope that all who have ideas so far as expression or omission is concerned should let him know them and he would do his best to meet the variant suggestions.

Black strongly objected to any reference to the exclusion of the Japanese as a law and policy of this country or to the prohibition against intermarriage, from which might have resulted feelings that in case of Japanese invasion there may be temptation given to Japanese on the Coast, even though nominally citizens, that may well have justified the evacuation order by the military. Black said, "Even if that is true, I do not think it should be said because I am against saying anything that may give the propagandists of our enemies a lift."

Sunday, June 6

Work at home.

Monday, June 7

Saw President Benes of Czechoslovakia at the Legation for about an hour. We talked on general European situation, and what he called the moral problems that will follow victory—and about Russia, and the Jewish problem.

Dined at the Brazilian Embassy. Talked with Ambassador Martins on the Argentinian turnover [1] and he raised the question of the position of Austria to future peace—as mediator between East and West, the relations of the Balkans, etc.

Tuesday, June 6

The Chief phoned to tell me about developments regarding the Japanese opinion. Black and Douglas had promised on Saturday to talk with him with a view to meet their difficulties. They had failed to do so and he had received today a letter by Douglas making conditions leaving out all views pertaining to the Japanese and temporary connection of this order and openings for judicial relief by habeas corpus—conditions wholly impossible for him to meet or for the rest of us to agree to. In his letter Douglas said he does not know what Black's views are, and the Chief has heard nothing from Black. On the other hand, the Chief has had a long talk with Jackson who is very eager to join the Chief's opinion and the Chief is confident he can meet a number of suggestions that Jackson made.

[1] An Army coup had ousted the neutralist (in wartime parlance "isolationist") government of President Castilio.

Wednesday, June 9

Had luncheon at William Clayton's (Commerce Department)—for Dick Law and John Maud of the British Food Mission. Lord Halifax, Jesse Jones, Billy Bullitt, Nelson Rockefeller, were some of the others present. Billy brought me back to the Court and I told him when I have time I would like to talk with him at length about a matter that greatly disturbed me. He wanted to know what it was and I told him of the anti-Semitic talk attributed to him. He, of course, said it was sheer nonsense. I said if I did not think so I wouldn't be talking to him at all, but while I didn't want to talk about it now because there was not time I will talk later, because though I assume he does not entertain anti-Semitism himself, his tongue, sometimes in anger or hastily, may give expression to things that may encourage anti-Semitism in others.

Thursday, June 10

Worked until 2 A.M. on *Flag Salute* case.

Friday, June 11

Work on *Flag Salute* case.

Roy Harrod of Christ's Church, Oxford, came to dinner and we talked about our English friends, Maurice Bowra,[1] et al, and gradually drifted into talk about post-war problems. Herbert Feis later phoned and joined us. We also talked about the Giraud-DeGaulle difficulties, DeGaulle's insistence on his way, more particularly on having those whom he regards as Vichyites put out of power in Africa, failing to see he may hold up for months the military program.

Saturday, June 13

At Conference Roberts told me that he regarded my first two sentences in the Flag Salute case "more and more a mistake and he hoped that I would let him know why I put them in." [1] I told him that it is not pleasant for me even

---

[1] Roy F. Harrod, one of the young tutors at Oxford when Frankfurter was a visiting professor. An economist, he later wrote a life of John Maynard Keynes. Maurice Bowra, an outstanding Greek scholar, was a don at Oxford. Isaiah Berlin was one of his protegés. Frankfurter described Bowra as "witty, powerful, generous and uncompromising. He's abundant, an abundant source of life." [*Felix Frankfurter Reminisces*, p. 258]

[1] See Introductory Essay, pp. 71, 72. *West Virginia Board of Education v. Barnette*, 319 U. S. 624 (1943).

In *Gobitis* in 1940 the Court in an opinion by Justice Frankfurter with Chief Justice Stone alone dissenting, upheld a Pennsylvania law which required school children to salute the flag. The First

indirectly to make a personal reference for he well knows that any kind of public manifestations are temperamentally disturbing to me, but one has to forego one's personal dislikes at times. From the time of the *Gobitis* case I was literally flooded with letters by people who said that I, as a Jew, ought particularly to protect minorities, etc., etc. And when the Flag Salute issue again became prominent through Judge Parker's opinion on the question we are now deciding, I began to have a new trickle of letters telling me my duty, more particularly because I was a Jew and an immigrant. I therefore thought for once and for all I ought to put on record that in relation to our work on this Court, all considerations of race, religion, or antecedence of citizenship, are wholly irrelevant. Roberts said he had not realized that at all and that makes a difference and satisfies him. I have good reason for believing that Roberts spoke to me about it at the instigation of Black. What moved Black I do not know except his general philosophy about not mentioning such things—he is a great fellow for keeping things under cover. To me, on the contrary, to keep all reference to anti-Semitism or anti-Catholicism hidden is the best kind of cover under which evil can operate.

Monday, June 14

Before we went on the bench, F. M. said he would like to say to me "as a friend" and "for your benefit" that it would be a mistake for me to keep in the opening sentences of my Flag Salute opinion. I asked him why. He told me he thought them "too personal" and that they would be "catapulting a personal issue into the arena." I said I could understand that a reference to the fact that I am a Jew would be deemed to be personal if I drew on that fact as a reason for enforcing some minority rights and invoking the protection of the Constitution to declare legislation unconstitutional. But I do not see what is "personal" about referring to the fact that although a Jew, and therefore naturally eager for the protection of minorities, on the Court it is not my business to yield to such considerations, etc. In any event, the sentences will stay in because they are not the products of a moment's or an hour's or a day's or a week's thought—I had thought about the matter for months and I deem it necessary to say and put into print in the U.S. Reports what I conceive to be basic to the function of this Court and the duty of the Justices of this Court.

Amendment, the Court ruled, did not deprive the states of the power to adopt such a policy. In *Barnette* the Court found unconstitutional a similar requirement adopted by West Virginia after the *Gobitis* ruling. Justice Jackson writing for the Court noted that it was the purpose of the Bill of Rights to "withdraw certain subjects from the vicissitudes of political controversy, to place them beyond the reach of majorities and to establish them as legal principles to be applied by the courts" (319 U. S. at 638). Thus it followed that the First Amendment did foreclose the states from requiring school children to make expressions symbolizing beliefs which they did not hold. Justice Frankfurter alone dissented. The regulation, he averred, was offensive to his personal beliefs, but his function as a judge excluded such considerations. He could not read the Constitution, he wrote, to give the Supreme Court the power to forbid West Virginia to select the means by which to instill patriotism in its children.

At lunch, after the opinions were delivered, the Chief Justice said he had meant to speak to me about one part of the opinion, namely, that part in which I referred to the five prior decisions of the Court sustaining the compulsory Flag Salute. He had meant to tell me that while what I said about the prior decisions made him "writhe," he felt perhaps he should justly writhe because, after all, although he had had his doubts at the time he did not speak up and so far as the record goes, he shared in those prior decisions. But Cardozo did speak up at the time one of these decisions was under discussion and expressed his doubts as to the Constitutionality of the legislation, but the others felt so strongly about it that he suppressed his doubts. Whereupon Black said that he also had had his doubts and had actually voted against the Flag Salute but then finally had suppressed his doubts and that if I wanted to, of course I could take the record as it stood. I said that of course I can only go on the face of the record and that this goes to the very core of my position, namely, that to declare legislation unconstitutional is an act of such delicacy that it should not be indulged in unless there is no reasonable escape, that the fact that Justices join in sustaining legislation and do not hold an act unconstitutional is the vital fact whatever doubts they may have entertained. What matters is what they did and not what their private doubts were. But I want to go beyond that and recall that two of these cases arose very soon after I came on the Court, early in '39, and that when they were discussed, Chief Justice Hughes called attention to the prior decisions but said that in view of the fact that there was a new member on the Court, to wit, I, he asked me whether I had anything to say. And I remember vividly replying that it seemed to me clear that the prior decisions were correct, that this legislation, however foolish and unwise, was not unconstitutional and that I would not see any point in having further argument— writing the matter out, because I did not see, with all respect to the present membership of the Court, that the reasons given by Cardozo in *Hamilton v. Regents*, 293, U. S., could be improved upon. Not only that, but after the *Gobitis* case came up I circulated the opinion and sent a copy of it to Brandeis (I did of all my opinions, because though retired, he was officially still a member of the Court), and he said: "After I read it I assumed you would get the whole Court with you."

The Chief's talk at lunch was a variation of that which he had previously told Bennet Boskey,[1] who on Saturday told Philip Elman, my law clerk, that the Chief would tell the Conference my reference to the past decisions would have to be changed because the fact was that he, Stone, and Cardozo had taken a contrary view on two of the earlier cases but had been so vigorously opposed by the rest of the Court that they swallowed their doubts. Stone said nothing whatever about this at the Conference on Saturday and said nothing to me about it until the conversation above narrated.

After lunch, Roberts told me that while human memory is treacherous he is as sure as he can be that no such protest by Cardozo took place at any time at

[1] Bennet Boskey was Chief Justice Stone's law clerk.

Conference. When one of these cases came up the Chief asked whether anybody thought there was need for writing an opinion, and he, Roberts, spoke up and said that he thought that the case should not be dignified by calling for argument in the writing of an opinion. He also remembered vividly Brandeis' sole remark, "I would affirm without opinion."

Tuesday, June 16

I. Berlin at lunch with me.

F. M.'s talk with me about Douglas' concurring opinion is the *Schneiderman* case. (See bound book for full notes on this talk—with *Schneiderman* case papers.)

Ed Murrow [2] came in to see me after dinner. We talked about English and American opinion regarding the war. He is greatly disturbed about the awful reactionary feeling he found on this side and more disturbed with the preoccupation with the Presidency in '44 instead of concentration on the war. He finally said he came to ask my views on a personal problem in the utmost confidence. Brendan Bracken, the Minister of Information, has told him that the BBC is to undergo a reorganization—it is to be vested in the hands of two directors: one for the business and financial management and the other for its program side—everything relating to the content of what goes over the BBC. Bracken said after full consideration the P. M. has authorized him (Bracken) to ask Murrow to take the program directorship of the BBC. Murrow said this offer had its "amusing" aspects. I said "How amusing?" He said, "Well, can you imagine an American broadcasting company asking an Englishman to take charge of it?" He told Bracken that he would have to come to this side and consult three or four people. Bracken asked who they were, and when Murrow named me as one, Bracken gave him leave to do so. We then discussed the pros and cons. Murrow's chief concern being that when peace comes there may be real conflict of views between this country and Great Britain, and that would place him as an American in charge of the BBC in an awkward position. He said he would not care about people now saying that he had gone over to the British but he would be bothered by a real conflict of interest in the days following the war. I said to him that any kind of a decent world order for me presupposes the resolute determination of this country and Great Britain to overcome whatever differences there may be between them; that, if we cannot have collaboration it is just idle and silly talk to think we can have collaborative relations for the peace of the world with Russia and China. That being so, I welcome every effort in the direction of collaboration and that the British should ask an American like Murrow to take charge of the BBC is a very ex-

---

[2] Edward R. Murrow, London correspondent of the Columbia Broadcasting System, whose "This Is London" broadcasts during the blitz brought home to Americans the realities of the war in Europe.

traordinary thing and shows how far they have gone in their determination for collaboration; that of course there are great difficulties in such an enterprise for him but in these days the only way to deal with big problems is to be greatly daring. He should make it perfectly clear that the conditions under which he would take hold were these; he should only take the position for the duration of the war so that both should be free under the very different circumstances of the peace to reexamine their respective positions; but that for the duration of the war it seems to me an experiment well worth trying and I hoped he would do it.

Talk with Murphy:

Tuesday, June 15—Frank Murphy came to see me greatly wounded by the Bill Douglas concurring opinion in the *Schneiderman* case and the circumstances attending it. This is what he told me:

Douglas had made some suggestions as to the effect that the grant of citizenship is a judgment which ought not to be subsequently cancelled except for reasons of fraud and that the Government did not establish fraud in this case. Murphy thought he had made Douglas' point and that Douglas was wholly satisfied with his opinion. On Saturday, at Conference Douglas was insistent almost to have the opinion come down on Monday because he wanted to leave for the West on that day. And it was finally agreed to have it go over because Murphy wanted to have more time to deal with some of the arguments made by the Chief Justice in the dissent. On Monday afternoon, after Douglas had left town, Murphy, like the rest of us, received copies of Douglas' concurring opinion in which he not only went on the ground of the finality of the original grant of citizenship but enforced his argument by saying that of course if Congress wanted to provide that citizenship should be denied to anyone who is a member of the Communist Party they would do so. Murphy said that the printed copy of the opinion was the first notice he had that Douglas contemplated filing such an opinion and that he left town without having made any attempt to see him or talk to him. Murphy was deeply wounded—he said he was "shocked by such behavior," and it was hard for him to get over the perpetration of such "skullduggery" in what was supposed to be a temple of justice. He said it was just like Douglas' behavior in the *Bethlehem* [1] case in which he first learned that Douglas was proposing to hand down a dissenting opinion five minutes before we were to have gone on the bench, and that he had to ask the Chief Justice to postpone the decision in that case because of the unfair

---

[1] *United States v. Bethlehem Steel Corporation*, 315 U. S. 289 (1942).

A government suit that arose out of contracts made with Bethlehem Steel to build ships during the first World War on which the company had earned very large profits. The Court, in an opinion by Justice Black, upheld the company's position. Chief Justice Stone and Justices Roberts and Jackson recused (disqualified) themselves. Justices Douglas and Frankfurter dissented, the latter arguing that in time of stress the government under the war power can regulate prices and control contracts. Justice Murphy wrote a separate opinion, concurring in the ruling of the Court but castigating the company for its conduct. (See entry, November 21, 1947.)

position in which this shift on Douglas' part would place him. Murphy was well aware of the fact that at the heart of Douglas' concurrence in the *Schneiderman* case was his desire to let himself out by agreeing with Murphy's result in not taking away Schneiderman's citizenship, but on the other hand, taking care of the anti-Communist sentiment by saying that of course Congress could proscribe the Communist Party. I have never seen Murphy in quite such a state. He was deeply outraged at Douglas' behavior which he took very personally—and naturally enough—and he said he was hurt because he thought he agreed with Douglas in so many essentials.

Wednesday, June 16—I went to Frank Murphy and told him that I was very much concerned about the whole Schneiderman situation and more particularly in view of the position in which Douglas' opinion placed him. I told him I was going to talk to him with absolute candor. In substance I said this:

"I just know you cannot be happy about the result in the Schneiderman situation. I know it cannot really satisfy your conscience. The fact of the business is that both your opinion and the Chief's are full of unrealities. The short of the matter is that the Soviet Government, after the last war, expected a Bolshevist Revolution throughout the world. Its expectations miscarried because they were based on the very false assumption that class solidarity is stronger than national solidarity—in other words, that the masses in France and Belgium and Germany are united by stronger ties with the masses in Russia than the people in any one of those countries are with one another. Events proved that nationality is a more powerful force than alleged economic interest. And so, after a little while, the Soviet Government fashioned the Comintern—The Third International—as the instrument of the political export business of the Soviet and the Communist Party. In each country there was a branch office of this international export business of the Soviet Government. And those who were running the branch business in the various countries were, in fact, political instruments of the Soviet regime. Of course, many, many people who became Communists in the United States were perfectly devoted and loyal Americans, but found in Communism a practical expression of their hopes for a better society. But the active managers of the Communist Party were the knowing and eager instruments of their foreign masters, the Comintern, and the Comintern was, as I have said, the instrument of the Soviet Government. Now Schneiderman was not just a member of the Communist Party. He was in charge of the local branch of this foreign political business in Los Angeles, and as such, when he became a citizen, his whole life had been committed to his foreign principal, i.e. Russia, and therefore the two lower courts were wholly justified in finding that he was not attached to the principles of the Constitution."

At this point Murphy interrupted and said "That is the real point of the case. You said that to me after the argument in the *Schneiderman* case and I have realized ever since that that is the real point."

"Now, as a matter of fact," he went on, "my instincts are satisfied with the result in the *Schneiderman* case but not my understanding of the law. And I suppose on this Court we sit as lawyers. And so I think the Chief has the better of the law in this case but the faith of my whole life is wrapped up in support of Liberty."

To which I said that when he says his instinct is satisfied with the result, all he means is that he does not like to have Schneiderman have his citizenship taken away. But on this Court we are not sitting as Santa Clauses, or as the makers of policy. When he says that as a matter of law the Chief has the best of it, that is where his duty ends—with what the governing legal principles are. Therefore I hoped that he would act on what he so clearly says our legal duty is—which would divide the Court 4 to 4. Nobody would be writing opinions, and this general problem, namely, the basis on which a grant of citizenship can be revoked because of want of attachment to the principles of Government, could be discussed and adjudicated in a much calmer atmosphere when the Bundists come before us next Term. "For, while it may not be true of us," I went on to say, "you know very well, Frank, that it is true of some of the members of the Court that the dominating consideration in this case is thought of Russia and Russia's share in this war. And because of that legal principles are going to be twisted all out of shape. And when we get the case of the Bundists next year there will be some fine somersaulting."

He said he would be thinking about that a good deal but he was afraid he could not now change his position because he could not act the way Douglas had acted. I tried to tell him how absolutely different the two cases were—that he changed his mind the last minute in the *Terminal* case a week ago because my dissenting opinion had convinced him that he could not go along with the opinion Bob Jackson had written for what was then the majority of the Court, and that not only did I see nothing improper but everything that was most proper and honorable for a man to be acting on what his legal conscience tells him should be the result in a case.

He took all this talk in the friendliest spirit and said he would think about it but he was afraid it was too late.

Thursday, June 17

Marion and I dined with Stimson alone. Mrs. Stimson has gone to Long Island for the summer. He seemed particularly fit and buoyant. He told us of the culmination of his long effort to get adopted an offensive attitude toward the U-boats. The enormous advances in scientific discoveries and detection devices whereby planes can spot the U-boat when it comes above the surface though it may be fifty or more miles away, and the speed of the planes, have been utilized by Army bombers with demonstrable success. This procedure has enormously cut down the toll of the U-boats both on the Atlantic (the great reduction in tanker losses, etc.) as well as the British in their Coastal Command in the waters off England. But since U-boats are a Navy concern, the Navy with obstinate institutional resistance has been unwilling to yield to Stimson's proposal that the Army planes engage in this U-boat offensive but under Navy control—under Army command until the Navy itself can fit out its own planes for this service. Admiral King has been absolutely stubborn about it, but as Stimson said, "While the Army has finally lost in its proposal we have won in our defeat, because the Navy out of sheer defense has been converted to the idea and promises in a very reasonable time itself to have the necessary air command for this U-boat offensive, and King is going to be in command himself. The President is fully aware of the institutional jealousy in the Navy but he seems to be loath to crack down on the Navy—he hopes to have results achieved by persuasion. Stimson feels that the fight against the U-boat is for practical purposes won in the sense that the right methods have been adopted and the means for using them are being made effective.

I had talk about Africa with Stimson and he said "You think well of Jean Monnet, don't you?" I said I did—as well as I did of almost anyone in Washington, that he is absolutely first rate in all the things we care about—in devotion to his country, France, with complete indifference to any French factions. Stimson said that was his view, that he has a very high regard of Monnet, but that there is a good deal of talk going around that Monnet has now sold out to DeGaulle. He went on to say that poor old Cordell Hull, who is all jittery about the French situation and almost irrational about Monnet, said he had sold out to DeGaulle. I said that was all rubbish of the worst sort, that De Gaulle, as everyone knows, is the most powerful single symbol in the effort of French liberation and that Monnet is not selling out to him, because he is single-minded about France and therefore is trying to prevent a French civil war. He has to discuss with DeGaulle and compromise just as the President has to go to Congress with Army matters and compromise for the public good. Stimson said that was entirely his view and that it is very difficult to talk with Hull he is so touchy and "irrational on this subject."

Friday, June 18

Dined at Fotitch's—the very able Yugoslavian Ambassador. There were present among others, Hamilton Fish Armstrong, Herbert Feis, Harold Butler, and Sir Wilmot Lewis, the Washington correspondent of the London *Times.* The latter was full of the action taken in the afternoon by the House cutting off all appropriations for the OWI for domestic work because of peeve against Elmer Davis for his speech before the Newspaper Guild in Boston the other day. In that speech he was critical of the lack of perspective in the reporting of Washington news in the press and also of some of the criticisms in the Congress in regard to conflicts and confusions in the war administration. When someone said "Well, Davis was pretty accurate in what he said," Lewis, who has been in the service of the London *Times* for more than thirty years and knows this country thoroughly, said, with sharp irony, "Pretty accurate? Entirely and completely and scrupulously accurate and that is just the trouble. That is why he is now fetching it." I said I thought it a striking illustration of the untouchability of the press, that thus far Elmer Davis every time he spoke, spoke in praise of the press, but the slightest deviation from adoration of the press is a sin against the Holy Ghost and off goes his head. "And that is what is called freedom of the press." To which Lewis replied "Don't talk to me about the freedom of the press. That is a phrase that is to be used only to the youngest cub reporter." Lewis said also that "Here is Elmer Davis with all his long record of independence and honesty and yet because he dares, and gently enough, to tell the press of its shortcomings in reporting the war effort, he becomes overnight a political hireling and a Presidential hireling and a Presidential mouthpiece, etc., etc."

I left with Ham Armstrong, who told me he saw Sumner Welles that day and put in his hands the minutes of a recent small private dinner of the Council on Foreign Relations at which Dr. Weizmann stated the Zionist case. Armstrong said he told Welles he wanted Weizmann's analysis and answers to questions in the files of the Department because there is a small clique in the Department that is systematically working against decent Palestine policy and is generally anti-Semitic. Of course Berle and the Middle Eastern Division—with Wallace Murray at its head—have been anti-Zionist all along and are at it all the time. But they have been powerfully reinforced under cover by Myron Taylor and Isaiah Bowman and Pasvolsky,[1] who operate through Secretary Hull. Evidently Hull is pursuing one policy and Welles another.

---

[1] Myron Taylor, former President of United States Steel, was Chairman of the Intergovernmental Conference on Refugees and the President's representative at the Vatican. Dr. Isaiah Bowman, geographer and President of Johns Hopkins, was active in State Department policy planning and in his approach to Palestine was persuaded that the country's absorptive capacities precluded large scale immigration. Leo Pasvolsky was a special assistant to Hull and Chief of the Division of Special Research.

((1945–1946))

THE HIGH COURT
UNDER TRUMAN

There is no Diary for 1944 and only one entry for 1945. That deals with the savage clash between Justice Jackson and Justice Black, a confrontation that had far-reaching consequences in the spring of 1946 when the new President, Mr. Truman, considered a successor to Chief Justice Stone. In his selection of Vinson, Truman did not consult any member of the Roosevelt Court, including Frankfurter. In part that was because he wanted to avoid the factions in the Court. But it also reflected for Frankfurter the change in relationship that set in with Roosevelt's death in April 1945.

He was no longer the intimate counselor of the President. "When a great tree falls," he wrote in the Harvard Alumni Bulletin *(April 28, 1945), "we are surprised how meagre the landscape seems without it. So when a great man dies . . . when he is gone, life seems thinner. . . ." The words were not his own but they caught what millions, including Frankfurter felt, and the sense of emptiness was especially poignant and painful for those like Frankfurter who had been close to Roosevelt.*

His relations with Truman were satisfactory but impersonal. It was now through his daily walks with Dean Acheson, who quickly became one of Truman's most valued advisers, that we hear what is happening at the top levels of the new administration. The Diaries conclude with a substantial number of entries for 1946, 1947, 1948.

The chief change in the Court was occasioned by the sudden death of Chief Justice Stone on April 22, 1946. Speculation about a successor immediately centered on Justice Jackson since it was known that Roosevelt had considered appointing him Chief Justice in 1941. Jackson had been absent from the Court since 1945 in Nuremberg as the chief American prosecutor at the war crimes trials. As Truman pondered his selection, reports circulated that Black, and Douglas as well, had sent word to the President that they would resign if Jackson were named Chief Justice. Regarding Murphy's attitude, see November 19, 1946 entry.

Then on May 16 a column in the Washington Star traced Black's feud with Jackson to events arising out of Jewell Ridge Coal Corp. v. Local No. 6167, 325 U. S. 161 (1945). The United Mine Workers local in that case successfully argued that miners were entitled to "portal-to-portal" pay. The decision was a narrow five to four one, with Stone, Roberts, Jackson, and Frankfurter dissenting, and Black voting with the majority. This was on May 7, 1945, and the coal company promptly sought a rehearing, arguing that Justice Black should not have participated since the UMW local was represented by Crampton Harris, who twenty years earlier had been a law partner of Black. Customarily motions for a rehearing are denied without opinion, but in this case the Chief Justice, knowing how strongly Jackson and Frankfurter felt, proposed a two-sentence opinion denying rehearing on the ground that "this Court is without authority and does not undertake to pass upon the propriety of the participation by its members in the decision of cases brought here for review." Jackson was willing to accept that statement, but Black declared "any opinion which discussed the subject at all would mean a declaration of war."

This was "bullying," Jackson said, and decided himself to write an opinion "to keep self-respect in the face of his threats." Jackson's opinion, concurred in by Frankfurter, concluded that "there is no authority known to me under which a majority of the Court has power under any circumstances to exclude one of its duly commissioned Justices from sitting or voting on any case." This will give the reader the background needed to understand the first Diary entry in this section, the memorandum dated June 9, 1945.

An awareness of this feud, President Truman indicated, was one reason why he went outside of the Court for his nominee as Chief Justice, and on June 7, 1946, he named Fred M. Vinson, who was then serving as his Secretary of the Treasury. He regarded Vinson as the person "capable of unifying the . . . Court and thereby improving its public image."[1]

Jackson's disappointment erupted in the form of an astonishing letter that he sent to the Senate and House Judiciary Committees and that he released in Nuremberg. He approved of Vinson as "an upright, fearless and well-qualified man," and went on to explain that the new Chief Justice did not face "a mere personal vendetta among Justices which can be soothed by a tactful presiding officer. This is utterly false. The controversy goes to the reputation of the Court for nonpartisan and unbiased decision." He then reviewed the Jewell Ridge case and the request for a rehearing. "I did not say that it was wrong of Mr. Justice Black to sit, but I did say that it was for him to decide and that responsibility for his decision should not be by inference put on the Court." He reviewed the "declaration of war"—"bullying" exchange and then ended on a note that embarrassed even his most ardent partisans. Black's sitting on Jewell Ridge was not

---

[1] Quoted by Henry J. Abraham, Justices and Presidents (New York, 1974), p. 227.

a question of "honor" but of "sound judicial policy." If the practice was ever repeated "while I am on the bench, I will make my Jewell Ridge opinion look like a letter of recommendation by comparison." [2]

Arthur Schlesinger, the historian, placed this letter in its kindliest context when he dismissed it as "the act of a weary and sorely beset man, committed to a harassing task in a remote land, tormented by the certainty that the chief justiceship had now passed forever out of his reach." [3]

On June 10, 1946, the day of Vinson's appointment, Frankfurter sent Murphy a note summarizing what he thought had happened to the Court under Chief Justice Stone:

> *Today ends another epoch in the history of the Court—the quinquennium of the 1941–1945 Terms. Of course there have been many shortcomings in the past and some striking instances of what Chief Justice Hughes so aptly called "self-inflicted wounds." But if I were translated into a classroom and had to tell my students what I thought about the period just closed, I would have to say the following—assuming, of course that I lived up to Holmes' injunction "never lie to the young!":*
>
> 1. *Never before in the history of the Court were so many of its members influenced in decisions by considerations extraneous to the legal issues that supposedly controlled decisions.*
> 2. *Never before have members of the Court so often acted contrary to their convictions on the governing legal issues in decisions.*
> 3. *Never before has so large a proportion of opinions fallen short of requisite professional standards.*
>
> *It would relieve me of much unhappiness if I did not feel compelled to have these convictions. But they are based on a study of the history of the Court which began from the day I left the Law School just forty years ago and on first-hand detailed knowledge of what has been going on inside the Court during the last thirty-five years.*
>
> *Of all earthly institutions this Court comes nearest to having, for me, sacred aspects. Having been endowed by nature with zestful vitality, I still look forward hopefully to the era which will open on the first Monday of October next.* [4]

---

[2] U. S. News and World Report, June 21, 28, 1946.

[3] *Arthur M. Schlesinger, Jr., "The Supreme Court: 1947" Fortune, January, 1947.*

[4] Frankfurter Papers, Library of Congress.

June 9, 1945

Memorandum dictated by Justice Frankfurter.

At the close of today's conference Justice Murphy addressing the Chief, said that he did not find the portal-to-portal rehearing matter (No. 721, of October term, 1944) on the conference list. Accordingly the Chief said, "Let's take it up at the end of our list." When that point was reached, Murphy said that Justice Frankfurter's views had come in so late in the forenoon that he thought it was perhaps wise to let the matter go over another week, that he wanted some more time to think about it. (Murphy's reference was to a letter sent by F. F. to Black setting forth the reasons why F. was joining Jackson in his memo on the rehearing reaction. A copy of that letter is hereto attached.) The Chief responded that he was entirely agreeable to having the matter go over; he saw no reason why it should not if such was the desire of Justice Murphy. Justice Black intervened to say that he was ready to have the matter go down. No other member of the Court made comment, and it was understood that the matter was to go over and that the case was not to go down on the Monday.

Immediately after this disposition Black passed a note to Murphy.

Shortly after I returned to my room Jackson phoned me to say that this matter was going down Monday after all. In order to ascertain what had happened I tried to get hold of Murphy, who had left the building and gone to his hotel. Upon reaching him there by phone I inquired what he had in mind about my views. He said in effect the following: "Why, I merely used your letter as an excuse for bringing up the matter. I thought your letter was well set up; it was very frank; I examined every word of it carefully and there is nothing in it that ought to give you any concern. I thought it was a very good letter, but I used it merely as an excuse to gain time. Time is our great friend and that's why I suggested what I did. Saturday a week ago was the saddest day I have spent on the Court. I wish Hugo had not said anything but had left some of the rest of us to defend him as I would any Brother. But instead he said what he said and appeared to try to silence Bob and to intimidate him. You know how far anyone would get with me if they threatened me, and I could well understand how Bob felt, why it was necessary for him to make the statement in return. After that it was natural for the matter to get into the situation in which it now is. That's why I tried to play for time. But Hugo at once sent me a note in which he told me that he was annoyed that I had brought the matter up and that it would cause more publicity to delay the matter and he wanted the thing to go down. So I suppose it will go down. But I told the Chief after the conference that I was just hoping that time would heal things and straighten out the matter, but that Black wrote me a note that he did not want any delay and wanted the case to go down."

I said, "Well, will the case go down on Monday?" In a kind of sighing, pathetically weak voice Murphy replied, "I suppose so."

April 4, 1946

Miss Watters (my secretary) told me that the Chief Justice wanted to speak to me and I told her to phone in and say I was coming in to see him since I have found it easier for the dispatch of business to talk with him face to face rather than over the phone—I think I have noticed a diminution of the acuteness of his hearing. After his opening remark that he has nothing but troubles, the following colloquy took place:

C. J.   "Douglas is very restive under the assignment I made to him of the railroad reorganization case (*Denver & Rio Grande Reorganization*, Nos. 278, 282 of this Term.) [1] His ostensible reason is that he has already written a reorganization opinion. But I think the real reason is that there is a good deal of agitation in Congress, and perhaps elsewhere in regard to these railroad reorganizations, and he does not want to be subjected to criticism and get involved in this matter."

F. F.   "I should think that the fact that he wrote a prior railroad reorganization opinion would be a reason for his writing this one also and not a reason against it. It seems to me rather funny that because a man is a specialist in the field he does not want to write an opinion in that field."

C. J.   "On the other hand, I do not think I would want the men on the Court to be exclusive specialists in a particular field so that they only write the opinions dealing with that subject all the time."

F. F.   "Well, that is not this situation because Douglas has had only one railroad reorganization case and Reed has had one so it can hardly be said that to write another reorganization case makes him the exclusive specialist in that subject."

C. J.   "Anyway, he is very restive about writing this opinion and wants to get out of it, and since you are in dissent in the case you cannot write it, Reed would get too involved in it and that means that I would have to take it over, but I haven't any case that I can give to Douglas, instead of this railroad reorganization. And since you seem to be pretty loaded up, I was

[1] *Reconstruction Finance Corporation v. Denver & Rio Grande Western Railroad Co.*, 328 U. S. 463 (1946).

Justice Reed did write the opinion for the Court in this case. It affirmed the district court's approval of a reorganization plan that was objected to by one class of creditors. The Bankruptcy Act provided that the district court might override such objections if it found them unreasonable. Justice Frankfurter dissented, arguing that the overridden objections were entirely reasonable in light of the fact that the war profits earned by the Denver & Rio Grande could have been used to make payments to the complaining class of creditors, but instead were used to make capital improvements, thereby leaving the claims of the complaining class almost wholly unsatisfied. See also entry for February 4, 1947.

wondering whether there wasn't a case that you could transfer to him. I was thinking about Tex-Mex, unless you are particularly anxious to write that." [2]

F. F. "That is the one case, Chief, in which I haven't opinions actually in process and which I shall be glad to put at your disposal to do with as you will. I do want to say, however, that I think it is very bad for the Court for men to get out of writing opinions which have been assigned because, for considerations having nothing to do with the working of the Court but relating entirely to their thoughts elsewhere, they prefer not to incur criticism from sources they do not want to offend. I think that is very bad indeed and ought not to be encouraged. It is indispensable for the work of this Court for the Chief to make the assignments—to make the best disposition he can of the particular qualities and experience and capacities of the various members of the Court—and then for each Justice to take the assignments without demur, and to attend to the job heedless of all extraneous considerations. The *Tex-Mex* case is at your disposal, but I do want to indicate that what you regard as the real reasons for Douglas wanting to get out of the writing of the opinion in the *Denver & Rio Grande* case are considerations that should not be allowed to operate on the Court.

Apropos of the Chief's remark that Douglas is restive about "writing the *Denver and Rio Grande* case," I add the following. Last Tuesday afternoon, April 2nd, Douglas and I were to meet in the Chief Justice's room preliminary to a session with the advisors of Chairman Keogh of the House Committee to revise the jurisdiction of this Court. Shortly before the three o'clock hour the assignment slip had been circulated and I found that the case of *Angel v. Bullington*, [3] which I had assumed was to be discussed further at Conference had been assigned. When I came to the Chief's room I found Douglas already there. I then told the Chief that I noted that *Angel v. Bullington* had been assigned and I had been under the impression that it was still under discussion by the Conference and was to be discussed further. The Chief then said, "Well, I will get hold of Black and maybe we can have that case go over and that would help, because Douglas would like to be relieved from writing the *Denver & Rio Grande* case. I could then take that case and give Black one of my cases and that would take care of Douglas' situation." The Chief then got hold of Black

---

[2] "Tex-Mex case." *Thompson v. Texas Mexican Railway Co.*, 328 U. S. 134 (1946). Justice Douglas wrote the opinion in this case. It related to a contract dispute between the railroad and the trustee in bankruptcy of another railroad.

[3] *Angel v. Bullington*, 330 U. S. 183 (1947).

In an opinion by Justice Frankfurter the Court held that the issue of the state court's jurisdiction over Bullington's suit against Angel had been decided by the North Carolina Supreme Court and could not be relitigated through the federal courts. Justices Reed and Rutledge dissented.

on the phone and repeated to him our conversation. Black then said he would consult the others and see whether the vote that had been taken once was to stand or was left in doubt. After a little while he reported that those who had voted in the majority wanted him to go ahead and write the opinion and so the matter was left. Douglas said nothing throughout this discussion when the Chief told first me and then Black that Douglas wanted to be relieved of the *Denver, Rio Grande* case.

Shortly after the Chief told me that Douglas was restive about writing the railroad reorganization case and asked me whether I could assign *Tex-Mex* to Douglas, I went into Reed's room to discuss one of the cases. But before doing so I asked him whether he had seen the reassignment. He said he had not seen it but that Douglas had told him about it when they came back from the swearing-in of Vardaman [4]—Reed having been there to administer the oath and Douglas as a spectator. Reed had been home for the last two days and so had not taken note of the assignments of the opinions this week. He asked Douglas what his assignment had been and Douglas replied—Reed paused and said "let me get his exact words"—in these words: "The Chief assigned me the railroad reorganization case and when I saw him I said I had supposed he was going to take that himself. And then the Chief assigned it to himself and gave me the *Tex-Mex* case."

I then told Reed exactly what the Chief Justice had told me about the circumstances of the reassignment.

I annex the reassignment slip, a copy of a letter of mine to the Chief and a copy of the Chief's "memorandum for the Court."

April 4, 1946

Dear Chief:

I hope it has been your experience with me that I am not self-concerned with regard to the work of the Court. But there are considerations having nothing to do with self-concern that lead me to ask you to circulate a memorandum to the Brethren something to the effect that, "in connection with the reassignments made this day it is appropriate to say that Mr. Justice Frankfurther did not ask to be relieved of Nos. 42 and 384."

Incidentally, it is not without humor that Nos. 42 and 384 also involve railroad reorganization.

Faithfully yours,

(signed) F. F.

The Chief Justice

---

[4] Commodore James K. Vardaman, a Missouri political associate of Truman, had been appointed his naval aide in May 1945, and in January 1946 was named by Truman to the Board of Governors of the Federal Reserve System and sworn in that day.

October 15, 1946

On the walk down Dean [Acheson] gave me an illustration of the difficulties of running the State Department. He said he read in the newspaper that Jimmy Byrnes was to make a radio address on Friday night, October 18th, on his return. The President told Dean that he had seen this in the newspapers and he asked Dean whether he knew anything about it, because he, the President, plans to address the opening session of the U. N. on Wednesday of next week. Dean said that all he knew was what he saw in the paper and he was about to ask the President what he knew about the proposed speech by Byrnes. They both agreed that it was unwise for Byrnes to talk first, rather than to have the President speak and then say he is asking Byrnes to report to the Nation, etc. There were natural difficulties for Dean to suggest to the Secretary not to speak and he thought that the President might talk to Byrnes directly. The President said he would phone to Byrnes in Paris. When Dean got back to the Department, he was shown an exchange of cables between Benton (the Assistant Secretary in charge of publicity, etc.) and Byrnes. Benton had cabled to Byrnes without consultation or even advising Acheson that he had done so, that the radio people were eager for Byrnes to speak and were trying to keep time open. In response to this, Byrnes fixed Friday night. Dean says this kind of thing happens all the time, although he had given orders that no communication be had by anyone with Byrnes without advising him (Dean), so that he may know what is going on.[1]

Sat in Court. Arguments continued in Nos. 4 and. 5, the dissolution

---

[1] Byrnes did speak on October 18 and Truman on October 24. This was not the first time that President Truman was nettled by the failure of Secretary of State Byrnes to defer to him. In January 1946, on Byrnes's return from Moscow where the Council of Foreign Ministers had been meeting, Truman sharply rebuked him for his failure to keep the President adequately informed, and ended his letter, which he asserts he read to Byrnes, with the famous statement, "I'm tired of babying the Soviets." At the Paris session of the Council of Foreign Ministers, which ended in October, Byrnes's policy of firmness toward the Soviets, which he thought was in line with Truman's views, was undercut by a speech by Henry A. Wallace on September 12, in which the then Secretary of Commerce called for a spheres of influence approach to world affairs. "We have no more business in the *political* affairs of eastern Europe than Russia has in the *political* affairs of Latin America, western Europe and the United States. . . ." Wallace also asserted that the "danger of war is much less from communism than it is from imperialism, whether it be of the United States or England." Although this was correctly understood to be an attack on the policies of Byrnes, the press was advised that the speech had Truman's approval. Byrnes from Paris informed the President that if he could not keep Wallace from speaking out on foreign affairs, then he, Byrnes, should be permitted to resign. Since Wallace was unwilling to remain silent, Truman requested his resignation. That was on September 20. There was, therefore, great interest in Byrnes's report to the nation. An interesting Court sidelight to the Wallace speech is recorded in his Diary (p. 615). He went to see Justice Black, Wallace noted. "Black said he thought we were headed straight for war with Russia. He said that the only trouble with my speech was that it didn't go far enough. . . . He said he had given a speech on the same subject last summer and that he had gotten a lot of the data from Ben Cohen. In fact, Ben had written quite a lot of the speech. . . ."

decrees against American Power and Light and Electric Power and Light; heard No. 37, *Ballard v. U. S.* involving the prosecution of the leaders of "I Am," one of these strange California religious sects, for using the mails to defraud and raising interesting questions as to the reaches of claims of religious freedom; heard Nos. 6–10, *United Brotherhood of Carpenters and Joiners v. U. S.*, a reargument, prosecution of one of these price-fixing arrangements between union and employers.

At five o'clock the Court paid its annual visit to the President. He was in formal attire and apologized for what he called this "rig," saying that he had been informed that the Court would attend "in tails." As an indication of the depreciation of appropriate formality on formal occasions, one of the brethren said, "This is not the old Court," as though dignity in addition to being intrinsic may not also have outward manifestations. Most of the members of the Court did not even wear dark suits. The President was friendly and warm, as he has been on all the few occasions at which I have seen him, and I again was impressed with a kind of natural charm about him. There was tea and coffee, bourbon and scotch—and all sorts of accompaniments. The talk was empty pleasantries, except that a reference to Jimmy Byrnes led the President to show how he smarts under criticism. This morning Mr. Lippmann had a column entitled "Mr. Byrnes Failure" giving his general outlook on the wrong theory on which the Peace Conference was conducted, that the wrong issues were projected. And the President indicated with a great deal of asperity how criticism gets under his skin. I am constantly impressed by the extent to which second-rate people around here are preoccupied with newspaper comments. The duty of a real statesman is to charge the atmosphere with his purposes and outlook. Columnists are important because mediocre and second-rate people treat them as important, and too often, even if they do not let their policies be shaped by them, allow their energies to be wasted by them. There was of course a good deal of clicking of cameras as we went into the White House and a rather disgusting scene as we left. It has been the custom in the past for the Court to be photographed on leaving the White House. But this time Vinson brought Truman out too and there was shown a general deference to the Hollywood aspect of Washington.

Stanley Reed took me home and we sat in the car in front of my house talking for a good half hour. Reed surprised me by his free talk about Vinson. I say surprised me, because Reed is usually on the bandwagon of authority, he is usually for the new King and is uncritical of those on top. Of course, he knows Vinson of old and when Vinson's appointment was made he was very frank in his expressions of Vinson's inadequacies for the job. When I asked him what Vinson was like, he replied, "He is just like me, except that he is less well-educated and has not had as many opportunities." I then said, "Well, why didn't the President appoint you?" To which he replied, "That's what I asked myself," adding, "Of course, I would have appointed neither Fred nor myself. I know a good deal about the history of the Chief Justices of this Court and the great ones have been men like Marshall, Taney and Hughes, men of recognized pre-eminence before they [Diary breaks off abruptly here.]

October 17, 1946

Drove to airport with Dean Acheson to meet Jimmy Byrnes' plane coming from the Paris Conference—the usual mob of movie and still photographers and of reporters and the usual fusillade of questions pertinent and impertinent to which not only Byrnes but Mrs. Byrnes were subjected. I don't know how many Roman holidays there were in Rome in order to satisfy the crowd, but with our vulgar press, with the pace set by those who have neither self-discipline nor taste, every occasion is sought to be turned into a Roman holiday and it requires not only great forbearance but also great skill, the skill of subtlety and agility, for a high official like the Secretary of State not to make costly blunders and possibly affect international relations with what he says and how he says it, or what he doesn't say and how.

Byrnes, with his usual charm, had all the outward appearance of ease and cordiality. When I had a word with him, however, he seemed to me very taut, with the tension of a man not tired by an uncomfortable air trip but with a tautness which reflects inner fatigue. I ventured to speak to him on the importance of getting a few days sleep at home in South Carolina before he plunged into difficulties here. I could see plainly enough that he was not going to do that, although he did say that I talked just like Maude, and when I told her what I had said I could see that she had been strongly urging refreshment for him and that he was resisting it on the notion that he cannot afford to take a rest between now and the meeting of the U. N. I was tempted to quote—but did not—what Brandeis said to me at my last talk with him, that on the whole he thought the greatest mistakes that men make derive from two weaknesses: (1) the inability to say no; and (2) the unwillingness to take a vacation when they should and therefore going on in the making of important decisions when their judgment was fatigued and not well poised.

Sat in Court—heard Nos. 12–19, *Cleveland v. U. S.*, reargument, the so-called celestial marriage cases, being convictions under the Mann Act of practitioners of one of the dissident Mormon group; No. 20, *United Fed. Workers of America (C.I.O.) v. Mitchell*, involving the constitutionality of the Hatch Act forbidding political activity to federal employees; and No. 54, involving prosecution under the Hatch Act for political activity of a State employee paid from a federal grant.

Called on Chief Justice Hughes and was with him for about an hour and a half. His summer had evidently so refreshed him that he seemed to me not one wit less vigorous in body or mind than when I came down here in 1939. He says, however, that he fatigues much more easily, that there are not as many hours a day when he is vigorous. After some preliminary pleasantries we launched into talk, as is usually the case when I see him, about foreign affairs and we spent most of the time talking about Russia. It began when I asked him what books he had been reading during the summer and he said he had been reading fewer than he had expected because he had been trying to keep up with the "rushing world." He summarized with his characteristic detailed accuracy, giving dates and quoting with precision when relevant, the course of events pertaining to our problems vis-à-vis Russia since the close of the War. He is as far as he can be from being a red baiter, quite the contrary, he fully appreciates the almost pathological effects upon Russia of the number of Western aggressions against her during the course of the nineteenth and twentieth centuries, and heeds also the stresses and strains within Russia and the logical compulsions of her "ideology." What struck me this time very forcibly, as it has in the past, is that Hughes, now that he has no position to defend nor any responsibility for action, is mainly preoccupied with trying to understand things, and to be very tentative and doubtful about any answers, fully aware of the complexity of these world forces and the action of forces in the pursuit of predominantly national interests.

Murphy whispered to me on the bench, " 'They' are trying to make me sit on the Hatch Act cases [1] and I can't do it, because as Attorney General I advised the President that the Act was constitutional and urged him to sign it. I can't now sit in a case and take the other view—what will people say?"

To which I replied, "They will say what they are entitled to say if you do that. But who is 'they?' Has the Chief (I asked blandly) asked you to sit?"

F. M. —"Certainly not, you know who I mean by 'they.' "—and the indication was plain that it was Black and Douglas. He went on to repeat that they asked him and that he can't do it.

And I answered, "Frank, I had supposed that whether a man is disqualified in sitting in a case is a matter for his own conscience to determine and this was established by now, and no one ought even to make a suggestion to another unless his view is invited. If they ask you why don't you tell them to go to hell, and not try to bludgeon you."

He went on to repeat two or three times like a nervous child that "he couldn't do it." And finally, bored with the performance, I said "Why, of course you shouldn't yield." And he then said that he was writing or had written a note telling the Chief that he will not sit in these cases.

---

[1] In 1939 Congress had passed the Hatch (Political Activities) Act, barring federal officeholders below the policy level from active participation in politics. The Act was passed in response to allegations of improper activities in the 1938 elections by W.P.A. workers and was meant as a rebuke to Roosevelt and the New Deal. The case referred to by Murphy was brought by government employees as a test of the Act's constitutionality. It was first argued in December 3, 1945 and reargued on October 17, 1946 and decision was handed down February 10, 1947, *United Public Workers v. Mitchell*, 330 U. S. 258. The Court rejected the claim of unconstitutionality by a vote of four to three. Reed, speaking for Vinson, Frankfurter, and Burton, held that the statute was not an unconstitutional invasion of rights. Black, Douglas, and Rutledge dissented, Jackson and Murphy did not participate.

October 18, 1946

Dean told me this morning that Byrnes had given him his proposed speech reporting on the Paris Conference for consideration and that it raises a number of difficulties in his mind. Thus Byrnes only once, and that not in any explicit laudatory sense, refers to President Truman, but refers to Roosevelt about six or seven times and to himself any number of times. I told Dean I thought that was particularly bad inasmuch as the papers are making much of the silly notion of the failure of the President to meet Byrnes at the airport, as if it had some significance. Dean had not read that the papers explained it by saying that Byrnes and Vandenberg looked around when they arrived as though they were disappointed at not finding somebody, whereupon Dean is supposed to have whispered something to Vandenberg who passed it on to Byrnes that "Harry has a cold and could not come." Dean says that the thing was made out of absolute whole cloth as I well know as he and I were standing together for ten or fifteen minutes, or more, while the photographers were clicking their cameras before he approached Byrnes. I said to Dean that the President gets himself into these difficulties because of his careless way of good fellowship, as in this case he went down once or twice to greet Byrnes on coming in from abroad, or to say farewell when he was going off, without realizing that great significance would be attached to his not doing it—as is happening this time. Dean agreed that nothing would be easier than for Byrnes to give basis for people in the White House to "needle" the President, and in a psychopathic way make Truman feel that Byrnes is trying to appear to be the maker of foreign policy, independent of the President and thus beget friction between them. That would not only be bad insofar as the personal relations between the President and the Secretary of State are concerned, but of course would be very detrimental in point of view of policy and would add another important element of friction and confusion in an atmosphere that is already too murky.

October 18, 1946

Sat in Court. Heard argument in No. 84, the Oklahoma Hatch Act case was concluded; No. 40, *U.S. v. Carmack*, the silly controversy about the condemnation by the United States of a site devoted to local government purposes held by a township in trust; No. 21, reargument, *Champlin Refining Co. v. U.S.*, in which the issue is whether the refining company is a pipeline under the Interstate Commerce Act. Argument begun.

Dined at the Sherman Kents [1] with Sherman's sister, the widow of Stanleigh Arnold, a dear friend of mine who was counsel for the Forest Service in

---

[1] Sherman Kent, a historian, was a high official in the Central Intelligence Agency. In 1949 he published *Strategic Intelligence*.

Gifford Pinchot days, and later helped me in the Mooney investigation, and the James Cooleys, he a Harvard Law School man, 1930, and she an extremely intelligent woman. We listened to Secretary Byrnes' report on the Paris Peace Conference. I was eager to know the consensus of opinion of such an intelligent group. Sherman had to leave before the speech was concluded, and the general impression was that the temper was good, that it allayed rather than encouraged the war talk with which the atmosphere has been recently charged, but that Byrnes was not particularly enlightening as to what the real differences between Russia and us are, or what the explanations are of the stubborn resistance of Russia to the general rules of fair dealing which he laid down as our policy. Cooley thought that he could not be more illuminating, because Byrnes is in the midst of trading and therefore he would not take a position. To which I replied that as there are certain unalterable issues of principle that ought to be concretely stated, because as to these, on the very fact that they are unalterable principles, there is no room for negotiation and therefore clear enunciation of precisely on what positions we take a stand, not only to let the Russians know, but adequately to educate the mind of the American people should be made.

October 19, 1946

First Conference in which argued cases were taken up. The way Vinson dealt with them gives further evidence that he is likely to deal with complicated matters on a surface basis. He is confident and easy-going and sure and shallow. Of course it is a heavy burden that he is taking on and one must give him ample time to show his qualities, but he seems to me to have the confident air of a man who does not see the complexities of problems and blithely hits the obvious points. He does it all in good temper and with dispatch. He evidently has been told that Stone used to fumble over things and allow talk to be too loose and confused and so he is probably driving for results. But Hughes showed that mere executive competence—keeping things moving in an orderly way—does not preclude thoroughness of consideration by the Chief Justice. After all, our task is dispatch consistent with adequate consideration.

Reed took me home and said he was rather disappointed by Vinson's performance, since he did not do as well as he had expected him (Vinson) to do.

We had the Owen Robertses and the Chief Justice Groners [1] (with whom the Robertses are staying) in for cocktails. There was good-natured chafing about the Court, and of course I said nothing except that things are going pleasantly, and talk turned to Hughes and Stone. Roberts, Groner and I agreed on Hughes' extraordinary qualities, his intellectual powers and his tolerance of contrary views and the free atmosphere that prevailed at Conferences when Hughes presided the atmosphere was free, but whatever inhibition was felt was

---

[1] D. Lawrence Groner, Chief Judge of the U. S. Court of Appeals for the District of Columbia. He had administered the oath of office to Vinson when he was sworn in as Chief Justice.

due not to Hughes' restriction of discussion, but derived from the influence of his intrinsic authority. One just did not drool or needlessly talk if Hughes was around. Roberts and I said nothing about Stone's ineffectiveness, because of Roberts' warning to me that Groner is a great admirer of Stone, but our very silence about Stone's quality as a Chief Justice furnished an obvious contrast to our enthusiasm about Hughes.

Herrman Blumgarts and Jonas Friedenwalds [2] came to dinner—a good deal of somber talk initiated by Herrman (who is as lively and as charming as ever) regarding the world situation. Poor Herrman wanted some comforting or cheering comment upon the situation of the world. Jonas made one remark that reflected a good deal of thought on his part. He was of the opinion that we have about five years within which to work out peaceful accommodations with Russia, because he thought the prospects of doing so after they have acquired the atomic bomb on their own will be rather slim, and he gave them about five years to do so. Of course that estimate is a guess on anybody's part, but Jonas is not only one of the most thoughtful men I know, he also has a good deal of scientific understanding of these matters and wise judgment.

October 20, 1946

Arthur Schlesinger wrote me the other day to say that he was at work on an article on the Supreme Court for *Fortune* [1] and asked to see me. I fixed the forenoon of today, and he duly showed up. I asked him what he had done by way of reading and seeing people to equip himself for the job. He then told me what he had read, and he had read all the things that are worth reading. As to people—he had already seen every other member of the Court except the Chief Justice whom he is to see shortly. (From some remarks he made, I gathered that a good many talked freely to him, though not for quotation, and he said that Black was the only one who, though cordial, was tight and insisted on talking about the *Age of Jackson*, saying that he made it a practice since coming on the Court never to talk to anyone about the Court. I did not tell Arthur Schlesinger that that of course is not true, that in the case of partisans of his, he talked with considerable freedom to get his self-righteous interpretation of his actions into circulation.) He had a long session with Judge Learned Hand, a whole afternoon with Paul Freund, had also seen T. R. Powell, Henry Hart,

---

[2] Hermann Blumgart, an outstanding internist connected with the Beth Israel Hospital in Boston, was an old friend of Frankfurter, as was Jonas M. Friedenwald of Johns Hopkins Hospital in Baltimore. He was one of the country's foremost ophthalmologists whom Frankfurter had gotten to know well when he was on the medical faculty at Harvard.

[1] Arthur M. Schlesinger, Jr., a winner of the Pulitzer Prize for history for his *Age of Jackson*, completed his article in time for the January 1947 issue of *Fortune*. Its title read "The Supreme Court: 1947," and the subtitle said, "Nine Young Men, appointed by Democratic Presidents, will be on the bench in a Republican era; the Justices are not divided on political issues but on the understanding of their function."

Fred Rodell of Yale, Tom Corcoran, and Eliot Janeway, the latter a *Time-Life* man. I asked him why he wanted to see him and he said that he wanted to see people who were close to those on the Court and he knew that Eliot Janeway was a great buddy of Douglas'. He saw Corcoran for the same reason, knowing that Corcoran is engaged in promoting Douglas for the Presidency. I told him that the Court was the one subject concerning which I had knowledge about which I was not free to talk with him. He said he was aware of that, that he did not expect me to talk about personalities, and wondered if I could not say anything about the governing ideas for the Court aside from the restrictions which naturally enough I imposed upon myself. I said that it seemed to me that the important thing for a man like himself to do was to educate the American people as to the nature of the function of the Court and the nature of the duties of the judges; more particularly that the framers of the Constitution had decided not to make the Court another branch of the legislature; that the liberals all threw their hats up in the air when Brandeis cautioned the Court against becoming a super-legislature, and the point of that was not that the so-called old Court legislated in undesirable ways, but that it legislated at all, and that it is not merely a confusion of function but dishonesty to want the Court to legislate so long as it legislates in the kind of way that people like or to approve the Court's doing so when it does so. I then pointed out the silliness of the reports of Pritchett [2] out in Chicago in giving what Krock and Company call the box score of the Court, being an analysis of decisions solely on the basis of results, whether one votes for or against the Government, for or against labor, for or against this, that or the other thing. At the core of such an attitude was, of course, the assumption of belief that there is no such thing as law and that law and opinions are just ways of clothing themselves in legal jargon. Schlesinger said that there is a school of thought, particularly centered in Yale, which believes that and believes it is a question of whether your side or the other side is going to use the Supreme Court for its purposes. I told him that such an attitude was of course just as wicked as it was dishonest.

Max Radin [3] came to lunch, full of his bubbling talk about everything under the sun. He was interesting about the increase in California's population. The war industries brought a large increment of Negroes in particular, for various reasons, and they have remained there and are creating considerable social problems for California.

Was at dinner given by Whitney Shepardson [4] in honor of Barrington-

---

[2] C. Herman Pritchett, a professor of political science at the University of Chicago, was at work at the time on *The Roosevelt Court* (New York, 1948) which was filled with the tables on voting alignments to which Frankfurter objected.

[3] Max Radin was professor of law at Stanford University. He was an authority on Roman law and Jewish history and the author of *Law as Logic and Experience*.

[4] Whitney Shepardson was Director of the Carnegie Corporation's British Dominions and Colonies Fund, and had C.I.A. connections.

Ward, editor of *The Times*, London. Present—Sir Wilmot Lewis, Washington correspondent of *The Times*, Herbert Elliston of the *Washington Post*, Colonel Eddy of the intelligence service of the State Department, [William P. M.] Burden, Assistant-Secretary of Commerce and Bob Jackson. The talk was about the Nuernberg judgment [5] and a good deal of discussion as to the feeling of opinion in both countries regarding the "tough" policy of Bevin and Byrnes. Barrington-Ward was of the opinion that what he called the dialectic exercises at the earlier London Conference regarding rows between Bevin, Molotov, and Vishinsky on the whole led the extreme conservatives to make a hero of Bevin for the wrong reason, but in the aftermath left a feeling of concern whether every opportunity to work out reasonable accommodations between the Soviet and the Western powers had been availed of. In a rather long *tête-à-tête* with Barrington-Ward we agreed that somehow or other the feeling of disquietude in both countries to which Wallace has given voice is rather considerable and that while it it difficult to be concrete, it was important somehow or other for the purpose of enlightening and enlisting public support, as well as giving due notice to the Russians, to be much more specific than either Byrnes or Bevin has been as to just what it is about which we will be firm "with force if necessary." There was some interesting talk about *The Times* and I was rather surprised to learn that the editorial team of *The Times*—the people who do the leader writing—is about a dozen. Barrington-Ward said that while the pen of a particular person may, of course, write the particular leader, it is the product of a good deal of consultation and collaboration by people who intellectually live together, and not only as to specific articles, but from day to day interchange information and views. Elliston was curious about the authorship of the leader on the Nuernberg judgment, which he and I agreed was the most impressive thing written by any periodical, and Elliston wondered whether it had been written by some specialist from without. Barrington-Ward said that it was not; that it was written by a staff member, but one who knew months in advance that he would be called upon to write on the Nuernberg trial and, therefore, had occupied his mind by following the proceedings, etc., etc.

Both Elliston and Eddy reflected concern over the Argentine situation, disclosing a row between Messersmith and Braden, the Assistant-Secretary in charge of Latin American affairs.[6] According to Eddy, Vandenberg and others

[5] The Nuremberg International Tribunal on October 1 found Goering and eighteen other Nazi leaders guilty on some or all counts of an indictment that charged conspiracy to wage aggressive war, crimes against the peace, crimes against humanity, crimes violating the laws of war.

[6] Spruille Braden, Assistant Secretary of State for Inter-American Affairs, had been Ambassador to Argentina, where Colonel Juan Peron had declared him *persona non grata* after his criticism of the suppression of a free press. He favored a policy of isolating Argentina in the hemisphere. He was succeeded in Buenos Aires by George Messersmith, whose speeches in Mexico, where he had been stationed, about the coming war with Russia, had offended the Mexican government. Messersmith and the military favored a policy of reconciliation with Argentina. Byrnes supported Braden.

want Braden's scalp, and he and Elliston were strong supporters of Braden and thought that if the matter came to a head, Byrnes' action would be a test of his power and his wisdom.

October 21, 1946

I told Dean this morning of what Eddy and Elliston had said regarding the Braden-Messersmith affair, and he confirmed that the matter may come to a head and that it is loaded with dynamite. Evidently, while Byrnes was in Paris, Messersmith, as is his custom, was flooding Washington with long letters— sending them to newspapers and to Senators and others—complaining against Braden, making all sorts of charges against him and strongly backing the policy of Peron. Apparently, Vandenberg and Connally and others think that Braden is a bull in a china shop. Dean said he had a long session with Byrnes on Saturday about this and was not at all made happy by the outlook. Byrnes wants to clean up the mess in Argentina so that they can have the Rio Conference with Argentina out of the way. Dean explained the complications of the situation. Peron is apparently behaving outrageously, taking over the universities, imprisoning the justices of the supreme court, except for his own followers, and according to Sforza,[1] who was down there recently and reported on the situation to Dean, the present conditions in Argentina are similar to those that he was familiar with in Italy immediately before Mussolini took over. Furthermore, Dean pointed out to Brynes that if we support Peron the way Messersmith proposes it will appear to fall into the pattern of having us support reactionary regimes wherever the position arises—Darlan, the monarchy in Italy, King George in Greece, etc. etc. He said to Byrnes that one or two can be explained but that if we have six of them, there is too much to explain. He advised Byrnes to insist on certain compliances by Peron as a prerequisite of proceeding with the Rio Conference. Dean said that the matter is complicated, because the Senators have rather invited Latin-American diplomats to take up matters with them directly and Vandenberg and Company finally told the Latin-American diplomats that the State Department was conducting our Latin-American policy and that they must deal directly with the Department. Dean said that the "sixty-four dollar question" in regard to Argentina is whether this Government will help arm Argentina and he thought the answer was perfectly clear that it should not. I told him that Elliston thought that the visit of the Argentine Minister of War, Von der Becke,[2] was arranged by some of the War

---

[1] Count Sforza, an exile from Mussolini's Italy, had been favored by the United States to head the successor regime to Mussolini, but had been vetoed by the British. He returned to Italy after Mussolini's fall and was a member of the Constituent Assembly.

[2] General von der Becke, former Chief of Staff of the Argentine Army, came to Washington in June 1946, but, wrote Dean Acheson, "I received him coolly under the watchful eye of Spruille Braden . . ." [*Present at the Creation* (New York, 1969), p. 189]. General Robert L. Walsh was connected with military intelligence. The War Department was intent on a policy of furnishing arms and military missions to Latin America.

Department people, what Elliston calls some of the "underlings" of Eisenhower, though not by Eisenhower himself. Dean thought this might be true; General Walsh was particularly active in connection with the Van der Becke visit.

Sat and heard conclusion of argument in No. 21, *Champlin Refining Co. vs. U.S.*; and reargument of No. 22, *Levison v. Spector Motor*, involving the application of the Fair Labor Standards Act to the motor industry.

October 22, 1946

Sat in Court and heard the conclusion of No. 22, *Levinson v. Spector Motor Service* begun yesterday; heard No. 41 *Pyramid Motor Freight Corp. v. Ispass*, involving the application of Fair Labor Standards Act to motor industry: heard Nos. 42–45, *Vanston Bondholders Protective Committee v. Green*, concerning validity of contract for payment of interest on coupons.

Dr. Nahum Goldman of the Zionist Executive called. He has been in Europe engaged in formal discussion with the British. He had five or six talks with Bevin whom he found friendly enough, but belligerent at the suggestion that he, Bevin, was trying to liquidate Zionism. He hotly denies this and says that he is a friend of Zionism. Goldman cannot fathom what the real position of the Attlee Government is in regard to Palestine and what policy, if any, it has. He says that while Attlee has shown a conciliatory attitude on occasion, the matter has always to be referred to Attlee and he thinks his attitude is really hostile. One difficulty in the situation is that Bevin and Attlee think that Truman's intervention is just a campaign gesture that will pass with the election. If the British are once convinced that Truman really means business and that Anglo-American cooperation generally is involved, Goldman is hopeful that the hard cake of the Attlee-Bevin intransigence will soften. The action of the Attlee government in regard to Palestine is entirely the doing of Attlee and Bevin—the Cabinet really is not confused on the basis of policy but confounded from time to time with the demand of emergency military action. Both Bevan and Dalton are very unhappy about the mess into which the Labour Government has got and are eager for strong support from this side in their opposition to the Attlee Palestine policy. Goldman told me that he had a long talk with Dean Acheson, who says that this Government is completely behind the partition scheme and is anxious in every way actively to promote it. Acheson asked Goldman for suggestions to that end. The latter told him that it is important to talk plainly to Bevin when he gets here for the United Nations meeting and that it is also important that this Government talk directly to the Arab states and not leave all negotiations to the British. Acheson assented and told Goldman that as a matter of fact the State Department had sent a circular letter to our representatives in all the Arab States directing them to tell the Arab Governments to which they were accredited that the President's pronouncement represented the true American policy and that they better not have any doubts about it. It was interesting that at his press conference today Secretary

Byrnes stated, when asked about Palestine, that the President himself is directing that policy.[1]

October 23, 1946

Sat in Court; heard No. 23, *Gibson v. U. S.* (reargument), review in criminal prosecution under Selective Service Act of propriety of classification by
draft board; No. 86 *Dodez v. U. S.* same; beginning of No. 24, *Halliburton Oil
Well Co. v. Walker* (reargument), use of functional language to describe combination patent.

We dined at Mrs. Dwight Davis,[1] one of the most charming of hostesses,
where talk is always good, for the atmosphere is so free of all stuffiness and the
boredom of empty formality. Francis Biddle who has just returned from Nuernberg talked in his usual pleasant, but semi-frivolous way about Nuernberg. He
was very critical of Lord Justice Jeffrey Lawrence, and said that if he had
presided more firmly he could have brought the trial to an end within four
months instead of nine months. (I do not take Francis' criticism at face value.
Moreover, I am of the opinion that there was a wisdom deeper than Francis
could see in giving the defendants all the rope they wanted to take, so that there
could not be any possible claim in history that Goering & Company were shut
off from making what they deemed a proper defense.) He said that the ablest
man in the prosecution was Sir Maxwell Fyfe, who began the prosecution as
Churchill's Attorney General, but continued in active command after the

[1] Despite British Labor's traditional support of the Zionist cause, the Labor Government, headed
by Prime Minister Clement Attlee and Foreign Minister Ernest Bevin, adhered tenaciously to the
British White Paper policy of restricting immigration to Palestine to 1,500 a month, this in the face
of a resistless tide of Jewish refugees, survivors of the holocaust, flowing toward Palestine. Impatient
with United States advice to open Palestine's doors while America's were kept closed, Attlee
proposed, and Truman accepted, an Anglo-American Committee of Inquiry. In April 1946 this
Committee recommended the issuance of 100,000 entry certificates, the number of Jews then in
the refugee camps in Germany and Austria. Truman embraced this proposal, but since its implementation would be the responsibility of Britain, Bevin accused Truman of pressing to have Jews
admitted into Palestine because Americans did not want any more Jews in New York City. A second Anglo-American Committee ended inconclusively; meanwhile the British Government had
embarked upon a policy of deporting "illegal" immigrants. On October 4, 1946, the Jewish Day of
Atonement, Truman again advocated entry of 100,000 and said also that some plan based on partition "would command the support of public opinion in the United States." Simultaneously, the
British were making a last-ditch attempt to persuade Arab and Jewish leaders to work out some accommodation. A few weeks after this entry Bevin indicated to Jewish leaders in New York, where
he was attending the General Assembly of the United Nations, that if he could not get agreement
between Jews and Arabs on a permanent solution of the Palestine problem, Britain would give up
its mandate to the United Nations. In April 1947 Britain formally requested that the Palestine
problem be placed on the agenda of the General Assembly. Aneurin Bevan and Hugh Dalton were
leaders of the left wing of the British Labor party.

[1] Mrs. Dwight Davis, the former Pauline M. Sabin, had been active in the Republican Party in
the '20s and '30s. Her husband, a lawyer and banker, was former Governor-General of the Philippines.

Attlee Government came in with Sir Hartley Shawcross, the Labour Attorney General, as the official leader.

Katherine Biddle asked me what I thought about the directorship of UNESCO which had been offered to Francis. I told her that this is a job with great possibilities, but that it will have to be fashioned by the director primarily, and no one ought to take the job who has not a zealot's passion for it. She told me that since literary and other artistic people have heard about the offer to Francis, they have been strongly urging acceptance on the Biddles, because they think it is the only thing that matters in the world—promotion that is, of the cultural purposes which UNESCO represents. I told her that of course that is so—literary people and artists usually have little understanding of and therefore deprecate political forces and expect everything from UNESCO. But just because their expectations are so high, it makes it important that something be accomplished by UNESCO. Katherine Biddle smiled and said, "You are evidently politely suggesting that Francis is not fit for the job." To which I said, "Not at all, but I am implying that he ought not to take it except in a deep missionary spirit." On the way home Dean told me that Francis asked him what he thought about the UNESCO job, and didn't he think it a soft job. And Dean replied that it was the very opposite of a soft job, that it has to be made out of whole cloth. Francis went on to say that he reminded the President of the latter's remark to him, Francis, when he saw him a year ago, that if he ever had any specific post in mind to let the President know about it and he would see what could be done. And so he, Francis, told the President that if there was a vacancy at the Paris Embassy he would like it. Dean said that in the first place there is no vacancy in the Paris Embassy, that Caffery [2] is doing a good job in Paris, but, in any event, the Paris Embassy is more like a soft job because, after all, an Ambassador really does not shape policy, but is to a considerable extent a high-class messenger boy.

October 24, 1946

Walking down with Dean this morning I asked him why it was that, when the Russians some time ago proposed before the Security Council an inquiry into the number of Allied troops in former enemy countries, doubtless with an eye particularly to British troops in Greece, etc., we did not join them and ask for an inquiry into the extent of the soldiering in all the occupied lands. Dean said that that was precisely what the State Department proposed. The situation was this, he told me: the Russians proposed an inquiry into the number of troops in non-enemy countries, like Greece, etc., and the State Department urged on Byrnes that we sponsor such a resolution by extending the inquiry to a census of the troops in all countries, except as to troops within their own coun-

---

[2] Jefferson Caffrey, a career diplomat, had been Ambassador to Brazil and was now Ambassador to France.

tries. Byrnes took it up with Bevin, who opposed it strongly, because he said that that would mean a disclosure of the number of British troops in Palestine, Indonesia, Egypt, etc. And his opposition was not that it would show the British troops so large, but that it would show how small, how incompetent Great Britain really was militarily. The State Department countered that suggestion by saying that they did not think the American proposal would be accepted by the Russians, because they would then have to make disclosures which they did not want to make and the rejection would then be theirs, and Great Britain would take a very small risk in acceding to it. Russian experts in the State Department also objected to the suggestion, saying that Great Britain would be telling the truth and Russia might not. Dean's wise answer to that was that if Russia palpably lied about the size of troops in countries where she has them, we would broadcast the fact and discredit her estimates. Dean thought, as I did, that that was a great mistake on Bevin's part and showed a lack of wisdom. Dean said the matter is coming up again before the Assembly of the United Nations.

Sat in Court, heard completion of No. 24, *Halliburton Oil Well Co. v. Walker*; and beginning of No. 11, *Alma Motor Co. v. Timken-Detroit Axle Co.*, Federal Royalty Adjustment Act, suit by patent licensee for declaratory judgment as to patent validity, infringement, and liability for royalties.

October 25, 1946

Sat in Court and heard No. 26, *U. S. v. Alcea Bank of Tillamooks* (Reargument) compensation by U. S. for extinguishing original Indian title; and No. 50, *U. S. v. H. P. Foley Co.*, action for breach of contract for failure by U. S. to make performance possible within time originally set.

Harold Rosenwald called and told me that he and Rogge and two others are going into practise and he told me that at the suggestion of a federal district judge (whose name he did not give me) one of the Garssons, whose names have been involved in so-called war contract scandals with Representative May, has asked Rogge to be his counsel in case any prosecutions are brought against the Garssons.[1] I told Rosenwald that there are two schools of thought on the

---

[1] The Garssons, Henry M. and Murray, were charged with war profiteering and the Senate War Investigations Committee had also turned up evidence that Representative Andrew J. May, Chairman of the House Military Affairs Committee, was their patron and protector, in return for favors received. O. John Rogge was a special assistant to the Attorney General and chief prosecutor in the wartime sedition cases. He had gone to Germany after the war to collect evidence to use in the postponed sedition trials, but when the Justice Department refused to release his report on what he had found because, Rogge alleged, it would embarrass prominent Americans, he began to divulge its contents in speeches and leaks to the press. On that very day Attorney General Tom Clark dismissed him for violation of long-standing departmental rules on the confidentiality of reports such as his. In 1947 he set up a law firm, Rogge, Fabricant, Gordon & Goldmann, that specialized in corporate law and tax work. Harold Rosenwald, a former student of Frankfurter's, returned to Boston to practice.

question of representing people in criminal cases: John W. Davis thinks that anybody has a right to be defended in a proper way, and that if anybody is accused and wants to retain him, Davis, he will represent the accused within the limits allowed by the law, and Davis has gone very far in holding the view that it is impossible for lawyers to sit in judgment and then refuse to defend people whom you may regard as reprehensible. On the other hand, Emory Buckner believed he could pick and choose those he defended and, if a man appeared to him reprehensible, it wasn't up to him, Buckner, to defend him. I told Rosenwald I agreed with Buckner's view—that I did not think it was a lawyer's duty to defend a man, though of course every man has a right to defense and, if necessary, court must assign counsel. So, the whole problem lies in the realm of taste and preference and so he must decide these matters for himself. Of course, I know nothing about the charges against the Garssons, but whatever they are charged with, I do not think that is reprehensible for a lawyer to defend them so long as it is done with complete regard to the ethical requirements of the question.

Rosenwald told me that after the mistrial of the Sedition cases in the District Rogge recommended a dismissal of the indictments, because he thought it was impossible to secure prosecutions, but that Tom Clark did not feel free to act on that recommendation, because he was afraid of the attacks that would be made on him by Walter Winchell.[2]

October 27, 1946 Saturday

Conference—Vinson conducts the Conference with ease and good humor, disposing of each case rather briefly by choosing, as it were, to float merely on the surface of the problems raised by the cases. Black, who, since Court opened, has appeared to be all sweetness, let loose for the first time in expressing his views on the Hatch Act, the law by which Congress has drastically forbidden political activity by Government employees, or even by State or city officials who are carrying on activities financed by the federal government. His thesis was that the right to vote carries with it the right to convince other people how to vote and therefore any attempt to limit the right of employees does violence to our whole democratic society. It led me to say to myself, "Oh, Democracy, what flapdoodle is delivered in thy name." Not the less so because it was all said in Black's irascible and snarling tone of voice. When it came to my turn, I thought it appropriate to call attention to the fact that we have had good demonstrations in other countries of maintaining the

---

[2] On November 22, Chief Judge Bolitha J. Laws of the United States District Court dismissed the Government's case against the surviving defendants in the mass sedition case. In July 1942 a Special Federal Grand Jury had indicted twenty-eight persons for conspiracy "to interfere with, impair and influence the loyalty, morale and discipline" of the armed forces and "to cause insubordination, mutiny and refusal of duty." The first trial began in 1943, dragged on for eight months, and ended in a mistrial when the presiding judge died.

forms of democracy—the one party system whereby those who wield the political machinery of government can perpetuate themselves permanently in office and prevent the true play of democratic forces.

November 1, 1946

At lunch the Chief Justice referred to an item in the gossip column of Leonard Lyons to the effect that he, the Chief, has Kelley [Paul L. Kelley, Administrative Assistant to Vinson] as a barrier, and that Kelley was blocking approach to the Chief to such an extent that even the Justices could not see him with the result that two Justices passed notes to one another saying, "Clear it with Kelley." The Chief said Kelley was much disturbed and that of course he was not presuming to play such interference and that if any members of the Court want to see him, the Chief, there will'not be the slightest difficulty. The Chief went on to say that Kelley had been with him since 1934 and would not behave toward the other Justices in such a manner, if for no other reason than because of Kelley's devotion to him the Chief. To break the dead silence around the table I said that if Kelley had been in Washington for ten years, I assumed that he is no longer bothered by what the scribblers in the newspapers say. Vinson said that he was greatly bothered, etc., etc. I gathered that the Chief was also disturbed lest it imply some criticism of him for having Kelley. After thinking about it, I phoned to the Chief to say that so far as my office was concerned—both my own experience and that of my secretary, whose standards and judgment in all matters of behavior I rate very high indeed—we had nothing whatever to complain of, and quite the contrary, there was the quickest readiness to have me come in to see him, the Chief, on the few occasions I wanted to do so.

Professor and Mrs. Niels Bohr [1] called. Mrs. Bohr, whom we had not

---

[1] Dr. Niels Bohr of Denmark, Nobel Laureate in Physics and Director of the Institute of Theoretical Physics in Copenhagen, had been smuggled out of Denmark in 1943 by British Intelligence and had assisted British and American scientists in the development of the atomic bomb. He was equally concerned, however, with the fateful consequences that would flow from a failure to achieve in time international agreement—in the first instance among Britain, the United States, and the Soviet Union—on the use and control of the new force. In the summer of 1944 Bohr through Frankfurter had submitted a memorandum to Roosevelt warning that whatever advantages the United States and Britain had in atomic development were temporary and pleading for what he called timely "concessions regarding exchange of information and openness" in return for agreement on effective control measures. However, Roosevelt and Churchill at Quebec in September 1944 decided to keep the project secret from Stalin, and Dr. Bohr was labeled a security risk. International control did have high priority with the United States and Britain in the postwar period. The Acheson-Lilienthal report in April 1946 recommended that the headstart that the United States had in atomic development be used to secure agreement on the creation of an international authority which would have a monopoly of the atomic bomb. Truman turned these proposals over to Bernard M. Baruch to translate into "a workable plan." The Baruch group's changes and additions included a provision for automatic, veto-free sanctions against violators of a control treaty, an addition that in the view of Acheson and others made it highly unlikely that Russia would negotiate

seen before, is a most charming, warm-hearted woman, who must have been very lovely in her younger days. He and I went over familiar ground in regard to the bomb situation, reviewing his great concern about the poison of suspicion that is raising havoc among the scientists the world over. But he struck a new note in indicating that some of the political situations are affecting scientists, as in the case of Professor Blackett of England who, in order to promote friendly relations with Russia, is minimizing the importance of the bomb. On the other hand, some American scientists are getting panicky and catching the fear that is now so much on the increase in this country about Russian designs. Bohr thinks that the Baruch line is doomed to failure. Bohr supported the judgment of Eberstadt, Baruch's most vigorous assistant. As Bohr put it trenchantly, "You can't solve this problem by flattery (referring to Baruch's constant assertions of the purity and generosity of our own motives). You can only do it by a readiness for and real show of compelling sacrifice all around."

November 2, 1946

Lunched with Adolph Miller, who reminisced mostly about Herbert Hoover. He and Hoover became intimate friends during the first World War and afterwards were nextdoor neighbors. Hoover consulted Miller on public matters during the Wilson administration, after he became Secretary of Commerce and while he was President. I knew from F. D. R. that there was a small group, consisting of Franklin Lane, F. D. R. and Adolph Miller, who looked to Hoover as Wilson's successor and hoped that he would be the Democratic candidate, and they were terribly disappointed when Hoover announced himself a Republican in the futile hope of gaining the Republican. nomination. After Harding was nominated, Hoover asked Miller's advice on an offer that had been made to him by the Guggenheims. Their smelting operations had gotten into a tangle and they offered Hoover a million dollars a year to take charge of all their affairs. Hoover said he didn't care about the money, he had no desire to leave his two sons riches, and he had an income of forty thousand dollars a year. But Leland Stanford, his college, to which he has always been deeply attached, was in need of funds and the opportunity of making it for his college attracted him. Miller advised him strongly against acceptance, telling him that he, Hoover, had opportunities for public service that he ought not to abandon. In due course, he became Secretary of Commerce during the Harding and Coolidge administrations. Miller, who was on the Federal Reserve Board, began in 1925 to tell Hoover of his fears concerning the speculative development in the country which was then becoming rampant. Hoover agreed with

seriously on the matter. In the light of what is known now it is highly dubious that any Western proposal to share knowledge would have induced Russia to turn over control of atomic weapons to an international authority. The Soviet atomic objective in the immediate postwar years was to neutralize Western stockpiles by "ban-the-bomb" propaganda while pushing frantically to obtain the bomb itself.

Miller and from time to time talked about doing something, but never did. Following the Black Friday of Hoover's Presidency Hoover from time to time called on Miller for his views and for his suggestions and repeatedly agreed with the drastic proposals made by Miller against the jaunty and timid optimism of the financial interests of Wall Street, particularly under the leadership of Ben Strong, the President of the Federal Reserve Board. But, again and again, Hoover would agree with the analysis of the situation, but fail to act according to his better judgment. Miller summarized his view of Hoover by saying that he was politically the most cowardly man he ever knew.

Mr. Stimson never spelt it out that way, but it tallies with the experiences that Stimson had with Hoover on things like signing the Smoot-Hawley Tariff Act, the Moratorium, etc. Hoover would say again and again, "That is the thing to do, but the people wouldn't stand for it." He was wholly incompetent in smelling public opinion and wholly unwilling, apparently to educate public opinion to his own understanding. He lacked insight into the imponderables. I am reminded of what Chief Justice Taft told me early in Hoover's administration. He, Taft, was proposing the Wickersham Committee on law enforcement. While that was primarily concerned with prohibition, Hoover was generally eager to overhaul what he deemed the obsolete "legal machinery." Taft in telling me about it said, "When Hoover speaks of 'legal machinery,' " and then came the famous Taft chuckle, "he thinks it really is machinery."

Did the *certs* for next week.

November 3, 1946

Worked on the *Donnelly* case (Nos. 38 & 39) and wrote some long-hand letters.

November 4, 1946

Lunched with the Chief and some of the other Justices, and being the day before election the talk naturally was about the election. The suggestion was made that we guess the outcome of the election and the Chief went down the table and called first on Black as the senior member. Black played perfect innocence and said he did not know how the election would go, because he is so out of things that he doesn't even know what Senators are running in what States. It was all so fantastic that I said with quiet irony, "It is a great pity that you were not in the Senate, because then you would have known about politics." He smiled a knowing smile and said, "Well, if I had stayed in the Senate, I would have kept up with things." Afterwards, Reed said to me, "Wasn't Black funny?" And I said, "I wonder if he thinks we are all saps in assuming that he is so completely immersed in the law and the work of a judge that he does not even know that an election is going on. There is nothing more naive than a man who thinks he is so sophisticated that other people are saps and are taken in by his pretenses." To which Reed replied that he was not thinking of the rest of us—he, Black, had in mind one person and that was Fred. To which I said, "Do you think Fred is such a sap that he believes poor Hugo thinks of nothing but law and learning?" I went on to say that a friend of mine, on being told how placid everything is around the Court and how agreeable our Conferences are, etc. replied, "It is like a new girl at school when every boy is courtin' her." To which Reed replied, "I have seen a great deal of courtin' here since October 1st." And Reed went on to say, "But Black *was* funny." I said, "Yes, Black has given several manifestations of this complete withdrawal from the world. And poor Bill Douglas says he does not even read the papers any more." I then said with ill-concealed irony, "The Court is really suffering from an excess of unearthiness."

Dave Ginsburg had called to ask if he could see me and he came in at the tail end of the afternoon. He looked concerned and said he is troubled by what he is experiencing in the practice of law. Ginsburg was one of the ablest of the younger people in the war administration, one of the most influential brains in devising the Price Control scheme and "holding the line" as long as it was held. After he went into uniform he was utilized on key work, first in London as to supply matters, and later in the military administration in Germany. He told me, quite confidentially of course, that he and Galbraith, who was the economist in the O. P. A., were called in by Jimmy Byrnes to draft the program which Byrnes will give as the policy of this country at the meeting of the Council of Foreign Ministers. Ginsburg agreed that the Potsdam Agreement was a calamity and said the real difficulty was due to the fact that poor Truman did not realize the power that he is capable of exercising just because he is President, that he does not know what levers to pull—indeed he does not seem to know that there are levers to pull. I put to him my dissatisfaction with the Potsdam Agreement, as well as with the present situation, which is that Germany is treated not as part of Europe but as an organic whole. Dave agreed, but said that now it is important to insist on the Potsdam terms because if it were all ripped open the outcome of the negotiation would be even worse. Russia's policy is to withdraw capital goods from Germany and Austria, to obtain reparations through current production, and to have the use of current production which is the product of imported Allied supplies and to obtain 51 per cent control of Austrian and German enterprises that were allowed to continue.

As to the practise of the law, he was deeply concerned by the pressure under which lawyers find themselves and by the things that one is asked to do that he does not deem consonant with the standards of a learned and honorable profession. Evidently he has been having great success and turning away much business, but carrying himself with the thought of shifting over to some one country like Austria or Germany so that he could be of use as a lawyer in the international field. He is impressed now, as he was while he was in government, with the behavior of some of the agencies of trying to win at all hazards—this apropos of some observation of mine that government lawyers ought not try to win, but to win justly—and he thinks that the great bane of private practitioners is that in trying to advise their clients of what is right and wise, they identify themselves too much with their clients' desires. Dave has high standards of character as well as real insight and understanding of our social economic problems.

November 5, 1946

Election Day. The Chief asked to see me and told me how much he liked my draft opinion in No. 3 *Freeman v. Hewitt*.[1] He said that it handled "smoothly," in the good sense of "smoothly," the difficult questions with which it was dealing, namely the powers of States to tax where interstate commerce was involved. He then spoke to me about the opinion Reed had circulated in the *United Brotherhood* case, Nos. 6 to 10.[2] He was all exercised about that and thought it was an outrageous opinion, because in effect it took labor unions out of the Sherman Law. He then said, "I know Stanley well and I think I understand how he comes to take such a position. Stanley was counsel for the B. & O. Railroad and other such big concerns, and he had the reputation of being a conservative and when he was appointed to the Court there was a prophecy that he would be a conservative. I watched his work from the time he went on the Court and I think he is pretty conservative about most things, but I think he is going whole hog in these labor cases just to refute folk who thought he was going to be conservative." Vinson then read successive portions of Reed's opinion and hammered them. And when I asked him, the Chief, what he thought ought to be done about the opinion, he said, "By gad, something has to be written and I wondered whether you wouldn't want to write the dissent." I agreed to draft the dissent for consideration by the Chief and Burton, the other dissenter. He then suggested that there was no hurry about having the

[1] *Freeman v. Hewitt*, 329 U. S. 249 (1946).

Justice Frankfurter for the Court wrote that in the area of invalidating a state tax, the Court need not wait for Congressional action, but should apply "the principle that the Commerce Clause was not merely an authorization to Congress to enact laws for the protection and encouragement of commerce among the states, but by its own force created an area of trade free from interference by the states. In short, the Commerce Clause even without implementing legislation by Congress is a limitation upon the power of the states."

[2] *United Brotherhood of Carpenters v. United States*, 330 U. S. 395 (1947).

This was a criminal prosecution of various employers and unions for conspiring to monopolize interstate commerce in millwork and patterned lumber in the San Francisco Bay area. At issue was whether Section 6 of the Norris-LaGuardia anti-injunction act exempted unions from the conspiracy provisions of the Sherman antitrust law. Justice Reed for the majority ruled that Section 6 did restrict the responsibility and liability of the unions. Justice Frankfurter dissented vigorously. In an opinion concurred in by Chief Justice Vinson and Justice Burton, Frankfurter said that the majority had wholly misconstrued the Congressional intent behind Section 6, that Congress had intended only to keep unions from being held responsible for "the conduct of individuals in whom was lodged no authority to wield the power of the union." The majority had now imposed conditions for union liability which would be "practically unrealizable."

case go down next week, indicating that it is just as well not to have such a split in a labor case right at the beginning of the Term, and inferentially, at the beginning of his Chief Justiceship. After I left his room, he came after me to tell me why he had assigned to me the *Donnelly Garment Co.* case, 38 to 39,[3] another labor case. He said it was a complicated case and since Stanley had some doubts about it, I probably was more likely to persuade him in what I wrote than anybody else.

Phil Kurland and Lou Henkin dined with us. The two boys are helping me in connection with the Cardozo lecture before the Association of the Bar next January. I have entitled the lecture "Some Reflections on Statutory Construction." As law material for that lecture I shall use the light that is shed by the decisions of Holmes, Brandeis and Cardozo on statutory construction. The two lads are helping me to analyze the opinions of these three Justices, and this was the first of a series of meetings in which they will report to me their gleanings from these opinions and the light that they shed on the general problem of statutory construction.

November 6, 1946

Professor Bohr came to luncheon. I had always suspected depths of sagacity about human affairs in him, but today he revealed it more than ever before in his shrewd comments on people and in particular on Vannevar Bush.[1] I had always regarded Bush as a man of great guile—I said to Marion that I thought he was a very cunning horse trader. Bohr confirmed this entirely by indicating that he really did not know what Bush thought about the major political problems raised by the atom bomb. He said that Bush was a very able man, that he thought he was reliable. Then Bohr said, "I must tell you a nice little story." He then told of a late Danish statesman who was a charming and able man but suspected by many people of being too smart—not reliable. On his death his leading opponent said, "I do not agree that so and so is not reliable. I have always found him very scrupulous. I could always rely on his word, but it was always necessary to listen sharply to what he did not say." Bohr in new terms conveyed to me his old apprehension that the situation among scientists is greatly deteriorating and he felt that the moral feeling in countries was deteriorating, because of the growing feeling that the bomb should never have been

---

[3] *National Labor Relations Board v. Donnelly Garment Co.*, 330 U. S. 219 (1947).

Ever since the 1930s the Donnelly Garment Co. of Kansas City, which had potent political connections, had sought to prevent the International Ladies Garment Workers Union from organizing its workers. In this case, the Court in a unanimous decision written by Justice Frankfurter upheld an N.L.R.B. order that the company union be disestablished. The decision reversed a lower court ruling that N.L.R.B. procedures had violated the due process rights of the company.

[1] Vannevar Bush, president of the Carnegie Institute, had served during the war as chairman of the National Defense Research Committee and Director of the Office of Scientific Research and Development. He had emerged from the war as the government's chief science adviser.

used at Hiroshima and Nagasaki. For instance, he, Bohr, had seen Hoover the other day, and Hoover said it was a crime to have dropped that bomb. Of course that is not what Bohr thinks. Bohr fully realizes that the decision was taken after the most careful consideration and as an exercise of judgment by men who had the responsibility of making it. Stimson was perhaps the chief adviser of President Truman in making that decision and he said no decision was ever more justified. There is a great deal of ignorant twaddle about the needlessness of discharging the bomb, because the Japs were almost defeated. Nothing was farther from the truth, we were all poised for a land invasion of Japan, which was to be undertaken on the assumption that it might involve casualties running into a million, and the termination of the war resulted in not only the saving of the lives of hundreds of thousands of American lads, but the lives of many more Japanese than were the victims of the bomb. Bohr said that to attain peace in the world would be an heroic result and heroic results cannot be achieved without some heroic contributions, and that is why some new direction must be taken by America to avoid an atomic armament race. He, Bohr, told me that he had had a talk with Dean Acheson yesterday and that he found Acheson unusually enlightened and understanding and appreciative of the necessity for something very different than the hopeless Baruch talk.

I took Inverchapel (the British Ambassador) to see Hughes. We were with him about an hour and a half and the vitality and trenchancy of Hughes' mind is best conveyed by what Inverchapel said when Hughes' door was behind us. He said, "What an extraordinary old man. How alive and mellow! Do you suppose we will be even remotely anything like that when we are eighty-four?" It was the day after the election and so there was some preliminary talk about the situation created by our Democratic President and the Republican Congress.[1] Hughes talked of the difference between such a vast Congressional vote against the administration and a turn in the tide through by-elections, or otherwise, against the Government in England. He spoke of the almost impossible task of the Presidency. "On the one hand, we elevate the President to exalted heights, and, on the other hand, we treat him cruelly and make all sorts of demands so that he is expected to christen every baby that is born." He spoke of the absurdities and horrors of press conferences. When Inverchapel said that, after all, the Prime Minister has to meet six hundred members of the House of Commons, Hughes pointed out the differences—advance notice has to be given of questions for the Prime Minister and they have to be given in writing, the Prime Minister has the aid of technical advisers, etc., etc. Hughes said that no man ought to be a public servant who is not ready to serve, but also no man ought to be a public servant who is not ready at any moment to step out. I added that no man ought to be President who hasn't the "zest for life," and Hughes quickly added, "for that kind of life." I accepted the qualification and suggested that since the Civil War Teddy had had such zest and Franklin. And

[1] In the 1946 elections the Republicans gained control of both the Senate and the House of Representatives for the first time since 1930.

Hughes said: "And there you stop." "Teddy enjoyed every minute of it in the White House and I think Franklin did too." Hughes added that Wilson did not have a good time in the White House, because he had what he, Hughes, liked to call a "psychic kick"—a constant inner kick against doing what you have to do in the Presidency.

From this subject we went on to Russia, and Hughes told Inverchapel that he was eager to know, "if you are free to say" whether or not he found that Stalin has a free hand and what are his relations with the Polit Bureau. Inverchapel said that the Polit Bureau is divided into the Westerners and the Easterners—terms that Stalin himself used with Inverchapel. The Westerners, of course, believe in accommodation with the West and the Easterners disbelieve in such a policy and think that no good can come of it. Stalin is the leader of the Westerners and Molotov of the Easterners. While, of course, Stalin has to take account of the Polit Bureau, he, Inverchapel, on a number of instances has seen him overrule the Polit Bureau, and it has happened in his, Inverchapel's, presence. Two things worry Stalin and affect the control of the Western School. Stalin is worried, so far as the United States is concerned, about an economic slump, with its vast consequences to the world, and, so far as Great Britain is concerned, he is worried lest the Labour Party will not get another term of office after its five years are up. What he is anxious about in reference to both the United States and Great Britain is stability in those countries; he wants to be able to count on their policies. Inverchapel said that the difference between Molotov and Stalin can best be described by saying that Molotov is like a streetcar—once it is put on its tracks it can only go on its tracks—whereas Stalin is more like a motorbus, winding in and out of the different streets. "You can reach Stalin's mind," Inverchapel said, "if you can make him laugh. He has a lively sense of humor, and if you can strike that, you can make him see things." When Hughes expressed his wonder whether the people would not eventually tire of the low standards of living, Inverchapel said he did not think so. "They are accustomed to very low standards, lower than those under which they now live." He said that during his three or four years stay in Russia he was always on the look out for dissatisfaction, but that he is sure that there is no hope in thinking that the Russian people will rise against their rulers. Moreover, no outside influences are allowed to reach them and what tiny trickles do get through are far outweighed by the controls that are exercised. According to Inverchapel we must be very, very patient as well as firm and above all, we must be right. We cannot afford to be in the wrong on any issue that arises with Russia.

The Chief Justice took us to the door with a sprightliness that belied his years, and just as we got to the door the maid brought him the evening paper and I saw the headline, "GOP captures Senate." When I said to the Chief, "I see the Republicans have the Senate too," he said with gaiety and vigor, "That's fine—but what will they do with it is the question." And thus, of course, he put the crux of the situation presented by the election.

Inverchapel insisted on my going back to the Embassy with him to have a drink and he struck me as being harried by his job. He said that he gets no time to read. He asked us whether we were free to dine with him at a dinner he was giving to the Andersons (Sir John and Lady Anderson).[2] This led me to ask him if he were booked up all the time with guests and he said "Yes, the Embassy is a regular hotel. But, if you don't ask prominent Britishers to stay, they are offended." He then went on to say that he had the "psychic kick" that Hughes talked about, that he is in rebellion against the things he is doing. This attitude of Inverchapel's rather surprised me, considering the fact that dipolomacy has been his life job, that he has excelled at it, and that more particularly, he naturally looked forward to this Embassy as the culmination of his career. It may have been an off day, but I have no doubt that he has to do thousands of jobs that go against the grain.

We attended a dinner at Joe Alsop's in honor of the John Andersons. The other guests were Alice Longworth, Pauline Davis, the Averell Harrimans,[3] the George Kennans [4] (he was counselor in our Moscow Embassy and is one of the sharks on Russia, but is now very gloomy and defeatist on Russian-American relations) and Frank Kent.[5] When the men were alone, talk turned to the outcome of the election and there was a good deal of gloom from Joe Alsop and others as to the control of Congress by the "other gang." John Anderson expressed the rather customary view of even experienced Englishmen regarding the inherent difficulties of the American scheme of Government. I listened for a long time and finally made a rather vigorous speech against the talk that the interim Congressional election creating a clash between the President and Congress makes a stalemate, a vacuum, etc. etc., and all the usual talk precipitated by Senator Fulbright's foolish suggestion that the President appoint a Republican as Secretary of State and resign. I said to Anderson that a government needs some coherence or else there is chaos and eventually tyranny, that in England the coherence comes from history and that with us it comes from the Constitution and a defined disposition of government powers, that all this talk about the impotence of our government, because the President is a Democrat and Congress is Republican, wholly leaves out of account the intrinsic powers of the Presidency. Of course power does not exercise itself and therefore

[2] Sir John Anderson had been Chancellor of the Exchequer in Churchill's wartime Cabinet and in charge of Britain's atomic program.

[3] Averell Harriman had been Ambassador to Russia at the time of Roosevelt's death and after that Ambassador to Great Britain. He was about to be appointed Secretary of Commerce, the position vacated by Henry Wallace.

[4] George Kennan, chargé d'affaires in Moscow. His dispatch in early 1946 elucidating Soviet policy had had a profound effect on U. S. government thinking about relations with Moscow. He predicted that Soviet policy would use every possible means to infiltrate, divide, and weaken the West; he asserted that it was hopeless to try to reach a *modus vivendi* with the Stalinist regime, and proposed a defensive policy on the part of the noncommunist world that was translated into the word "containment."

[5] Frank Kent was a conservative columnist with the *Baltimore Sun*.

a President may not avail himself of the power of a Presidency, but so far as the intrinsic situation is concerned, the election only formalizes what has been existing since Truman succeeded F. D. R.—the President did not control the Congress and the Congress had essentially the same bi-partisan combination that it will now have. There are two aspects that it is important for the foreigners to appreciate about our situation: (1) the vast control that the President has, unimpeded by Congressional authority, over the conduct of our foreign relations, and (2) that the Presidency is a pulpit, a sounding board for focusing issues. In my view, President Truman is now freer than he was to exercise his authority, because now he does not have to make any concessions to the Republican leadership, where he was naturally handicapped in the way of camaraderie and good fellowship that was against him. Averell Harriman said he had not thought of it in that light, but it struck him as a sound analysis that the President is now freer than he was and has hardly lost any power that he had before the election.

November 7, 1946

Dean Acheson turned up in the morning to read me something he has drafted as a possible statement for the President to comment on the election. He told me that he went down to meet the President yesterday and that, as he expected, there was not a soul there to meet him.[1] This shed some light on the absence of imagination on the part of other members of Cabinet. Dean said the President asked him to come to the White House for talk. Some of the White House entourage were making incredibly absurd suggestions, one being that he should call the Senate in session for submitting a lot of nominations for U. S. Attorney, Marshal, etc. I could hardly believe my ears. It was so inconceivable that anybody but a lunatic would make such a suggestion. It would of course be the worst possible thing for the President to do. He would be assuming a role not only of partisanship, but partisanship for the sake of patronage. Dean said that Ross [2] and Vardaman quickly stepped on that proposal. When I told Dean that I thought the President was freer than he had been, he said that that was what the President thought and said that really nothing had happened and there had not been a change in the control he had of Congress. The President asked Dean to draft something and Dean wanted me to look at it. It was an admirable statement, the essence of which was that the people had spoken as far as Congress was concerned and all ought to recognize that while of course no one should surrender his convictions, it is very important in the interest of the

---

[1] It had been a Cabinet custom in Roosevelt's time for administration officials to troop down to Union Station to meet President Roosevelt on his return after an election. This time Acheson discovered he was "a reception committee of one."

[2] Charles Ross was President Truman's press secretary. He had formerly been chief of the Washington Bureau of the St. Louis *Post-Dispatch*.

country to examine what action or non-action those convictions require. I had only one suggestion to make, that it should be stated that if everyone will keep the country as a whole in mind, there won't be any deadlock or stalemate or vacuum. I told Dean that I hoped that the President would take that statement and make it his own and that I would watch with interest to see whether he does so.

Marion and I drove to Jenkintown and to the Roberts' with whom we spent the night. As always, they were warmly hospitable. Of course they had a feeling of satisfaction over the Republican victory and more particularly over the defeat of people like Guffey.[3] When Elsie Roberts, in a girlish way, said how wonderful it was, Roberts, with a stern face, said it was not wonderful at all, the responsibility which this brings to the Republicans is almost overwhelming, and he went on to say that some of the good men who had been elected to the Senate did realize their responsibility for formulating a program within the limits of their agreements and to take the public into their confidence. Roberts was troubled by all this talk about cutting the taxes, which of course would be a very mischievous thing to do. He recognized with great regret the lead that the New York vote gave to Dewey [4]—Roberts himself felt that all-in-all Vandenberg [5] would bring to the Presidency the most experienced and most sober judgment.

November 9, 1946

Conference went off smoothly and with relatively little discussion in the way in which the new Chief conducts conferences, that is, difficult problems are dealt with in their shallow aspects.

November 10, 1946

Mark Howe [1] came down from Harvard to take back with him all my letters from Holmes. I told him they were at his disposal for his most convenient use. Inasmuch as there is a good deal of repetition in Holmes' letters to various

---

[3] Senator Joseph F. Guffey of Pennsylvania, a veteran Democrat in the Senate, was one of those who had gone down in the Republican sweep.

[4] Thomas E. Dewey, the Republican Governor of New York, had been the Republican presidential candidate in 1944. His landslide reelection in 1946 automatically made him frontrunner for the 1948 presidential nomination.

[5] Senator Arthur H. Vandenberg, Republican of Michigan, had created a sensation in January 1945 by repudiating his former isolationism and wishing success to the United Nations. Roosevelt promptly appointed him to the United States delegation to the San Francisco Conference that established the United Nations. From that time on Vandenberg had become the symbol of bipartisanship in foreign affairs. As a result of the Republican capture of the Senate he became Chairman of the Senate Foreign Relations Committee and president *pro tempore* of the Senate.

[1] Mark DeWolfe Howe. See Introduction, pp. 54, 55.

people, he will sift those of mine which he wants to use and have them photo-stated, as they are all destined eventually for the Law School collection.

Went to a tea at the Reed's given for Maxwell Anderson, the author of *Joan of Lorraine.* It was one of these typically silly and meretricious Washing-ton parties. Winifred Reed characteristically had cabinet members and other people whom she could not possibly have known, but whom she asked because that is the kind of a person she is, and they came because people come if asked by a Justice of the Supreme Court.

Joe Rauh phoned and talked about the President's order of decontrol and its effect upon housing. He said Wyatt [2] (the housing expediter) and Paul Porter (OPA) were the only ones who stood against taking controls off. He said that Paul Porter vigorously contested the claim that the law is so bad that it is unworkable. In any event, the President's statement was making it appear praiseworthy to do what was highly questionable. He said that Wyatt is in a head-on collision with George Allen of the R.F.C., and other agencies of the Government and the week will show whether the whole housing program will have to be given up; at best only part of it can survive. Joe told me that Tom Corcoran had told him that the Solicitor Generalship—the outgoing Solicitor General having been elected Senator from Rhode Island—had been put at the disposal of Ed Pauley. Joe naturally thought that was a very peculiar thing to do considering Pauley's [3] relations to the oil interests, etc. I did not tell him that McGrath told me about two weeks ago very confidentially that the new Solici-tor General had been decided upon—Mathes, now a District Judge in Califor-nia. I knew nothing about him, but inquiry at the Harvard Law School, of which he is a graduate, class of 1924, showed that he was not a very good student there. I also wrote to Sayre MacNeil, who in his round-about way indi-cated that Mathes is not a man who stand on his own two feed. [4] [*]

[2] Joseph L. Rauh, Jr., former law clerk to Frankfurter, was assistant to Wilson Wyatt, who was on leave from his position as mayor of Louisville and serving as Housing Expediter. There was enormous pressure for housing and the industry was impatient to get rid of all controls, especially controls administered by men who were not reachable.

[3] J. Howard McGrath, the outgoing Solicitor General, had been elected Senator from Rhode Island. Edwin Pauley, a California oilman, had been nominated by Truman in January 1946 as Under Secretary of the Navy. Secretary Ickes, testifying before the Senate Naval Affairs Committee on the nomination, said that Pauley had asked him to use his influence with Roosevelt to stop a Justice Department suit to have the tidelands oil deposits declared to be in the federal domain. In return Pauley said there would be hundreds of thousands of dollars in campaign contributions. Ickes, after blasting the Pauley nomination, resigned from Truman's cabinet. Truman continued to back Pauley, but the latter asked him to withdraw his name when it became clear he would not be confirmed.

[4] Judge William C. Mathes, Harvard Law School, 1924, remained on the Circuit Court bench. Philip B. Perlman was appointed Solicitor General. Sayre MacNeil, Harvard Law School, 1911, was Dean of Law at Loyola University of Law in Los Angeles.

[*] Entry for November 12, 1946, omitted. It discusses a private individual's emotional illness.

November 13, 1946

Sat in Court and heard No. 53 *United States v. Sheridan*, concluded; No. 25, *Unemployment Compensation Comm'n. of Alaska v. Aragan*, concerning eligibility for compensation under Alaska Act of union members stranded in U. S. by failure of contract negotiations; *Hickman v. Taylor*, No. 47, Contempt conviction for failure to answer interrogatory claimed privileged under Rule 33, Rules of Civil Procedure.

At the request of Luther Evans, the Librarian of Congress,. [Frederick H.] Wagman of his staff came to consult me on whether they should have a ceremony to signalize the forthcoming deposit of a copy of the Magna Carta in the Library of Congress. I told Wagman that, in view of the fact that there was a very considerable ceremony when the Lincoln Chapter copy of the Magna Carta was deposited in the Library for safekeeping during the war by Lord Lothian and another public ceremony upon its return into the hands of the British Ambassador, a public ceremony would seem anti-climactic.[1] The only thing that I thought might be appropriate would be to invite some scholar like Roscoe Pound to discourse on matters of public interest in regard to the new copy of the great Charter and to have a few guests who are interested in such matters.

Ralph Page came for a hurried lunch between Court sessions. He writes a non-partisan, reflective kind of a column in the Philadelphia *Bulletin*, owned by Edward McLean, the head of the Associated Press. The *Bulletin* has an enormous circulation, making its appeal as a so-called family paper. Doodle (Ralph Page) has been away from Washington and asked me what has happened in the course of the few months to the so-called liberals and progressives. Apparently, what Doodle called the "good folk" think that they must be "all for Russia," because foolish people or reactionaries are all against Russia and he wanted to get some bearings for himself as well as understanding of the antics of people like Wallace, Ickes, etc. He referred to Ickes' fierce attack on David Lilienthal in today's Washington *Evening Star*. I disposed of the latter quickly, by telling Doodle of Ickes' animus against Lilienthal which derived from Lilienthal's successful resistance to the greedy effort of Ickes, as Secretary of the Interior, to bring TVA under the control of his Department. He made a similar effort to have the Forest Service turned over to him and Gifford Pinchot's successful resistance led to Ickes vendetta against Pinchot and his foolish attempts at glorifying Ballinger. I tried to tell Doodle that one must see these things in perspective and the confusion and conflict among different brands of progressive movements is almost inherent in progressive movements and their great

---

[1] Of the four originals of the charter of 1215, the Lincoln Cathedral Charter was considered the most perfect. Of the two copies in the British Museum, the Lacock Abbey copy was the only fully legible one, and it was coming on loan to the Library of Congress by authorization of the House of Lords.

danger. I referred him to Asquith's summary of the difference between a conservative party, which has its great ally in inertia and the cohesive force of conservatism, and the motley groupings of a liberal movement. I promised to send him a copy of Asquith's letter to Margot which seems to me to illumine so admirably our own problems. It is found in Spender and Asquith's "Life of Lord Oxford and Asquith," Vol. I, p. 103:

> It is of course a much easier thing to lead their party (the Tory) than ours, as you and I will find if we ever have a share in the work. The function of the Tories in these days is neither to originate nor to resist *a outrance*, but to forestall inevitable changes by judicious compromises in the interest of threatened classes and institutions. They have, just as much as the old Tories had and even more wealth, property and the vis inertiae on their side, and as their game is a difficult one and full of intellectual interest, they admit a vast deal more than they used to do of the higher intelligence of the country. But they need neither intuition, initiative, constructive power (except of a low kind), nor (what is rarest of all) the ability to organize and concentrate the scattered discontent and diffuse enthusiasm of a half-educated society.

F. D. R.'s great achievement was precisely his capacity to weld together discordant elements which normally fight among themselves, instead of agreeing on the things on which they can agree and pushing them to fruition.

Ed Weeks of the *Atlantic Monthly* came to tea. He said that the *Atlantic* circulation had increased from what it was in Ellery Sedgwick's best days, some hundred thousand, to about a hundred and thirty-seven thousand, but he seemed troubled about competition due to new entries in the magazine field. Evidently Henry Luce has long had plans underway for a new monthly. Talked about changes in the *Atlantic* format, etc., to make it more popular. Both Marion and I urged him strongly to let well enough alone and to assume that there is a public that cares for the kind of sedateness which the *Atlantic* has. That seemed to be his feeling, but he evidently is being pushed by business associates. During the course of the discussion Walter Lippmann came to pick up Weeks, who was his house guest. Lippmann talked to Weeks generally about adhering to one's convictions and changing one's views in case one is convinced that one's views are wrong, but, in all events, asserting one's convictions. As he left he said that the two most important things these days that people seem least able to do are to resign and to recant. He left with that noble utterance and after he had gone, Marion said, "How characteristic of Walter, he always has the highest moral standards for others."

Marion and I saw Olivier's "Henry V"—an English technicolor movie. I have not seen a movie for years, but I cannot believe it possible that there has been a finer bit of photographic art on the screen than the Battle of Agincourt. Marion recalled Alfred Cohn's remark that Olivier's acting made you feel that "he was a king every minute he was on the scene." Olivier was indeed always regal.

J. A. Spender and Cyril   [Diary breaks off.]

Thursday, November 14, 1946.

Pach, the well known New York photographer, was down to take photographs of the members of the Court and he asked me whether I could help him to get an appointment to take the President's photograph in order to add the President to a new addition of their book of the photographs of the Presidents whom they had taken from the time of Grant. On the urgings of Marshal Waggaman, [Thomas E. Waggaman, Marshal of the Court] I called up Charlie Ross, the President's press secretary to put Pach's case for him. He told me of the difficulties of giving an appointment to one photographer rather than the whole group of photographers, because then every other photographer thinks he should have an individual appointment. He finally suggested that Pach write him and he would try to do what he could "to get Pach out of my hair, though thereby to get a lot of people into my hair." What interested me was the extreme sensitiveness that Ross disclosed about criticism of him. When I suggested that I assumed he was quite oblivious to the criticism that is inevitable in view of the light that beats upon the throne, he said with an unconvincing effort at sturdiness, "Yes, I am fast growing a thick skin," reflecting thereby the thinnest of skins. Poor Charlie Ross is a man of sterling character and greatly respected by his profession and by all who know him. But evidently he is devoid of that shrewd and shallow streak of camaraderie which should enable him to get on well with the members of his own craft. As a result, he has been the target of rather cruel criticism. The strange coincidence whereby Charlie Ross' high school classmate at Independence, Missouri, became President of the United States, made him press secretary—a job for which his sensitive character would not at all call him.

Sat in Court and heard No. 27, *Bruce's Juices, Inc. v. American Can Co.*, concerning violation of Robinson-Patman Act as defense to a suit on contract; No. 28, *MacGregor v. Westinghouse Electric & Mfg. Co.*, price-fixing clause in patent license, effect on estoppel of licenses to challenge validity of patent; Nos. 70 & 71, *Katzinger Co. v. Chicago Metallic Mfg. Co.*, begun, concerning same as No. 28.

Archie MacLeish came in to talk with me about the Directorship of UNESCO. Archie himself has been the choice of the members of UNESCO and has resisted their importunities, although again and again the temptation has been almost too much for him. Ada's strong influence has been against it. She does not want him to repeat the unhappy experience he had in the harness of public life at the State Department. MacLeish is leaving for Paris where a Director is to be chosen. This country is putting forth Francis Biddle, whom the English will not swallow. Their candidate is Julian Huxley, who has been in charge of the provisional organization. Archie asked me how I felt. I said I would not vote for Biddle, and told him that the best way to state my reason is that I know that Biddle would give up UNESCO the day after he became its head, if the President offered him the Ambassadorship to France which is really what he wants. Nobody ought to take the leadership of UNESCO, unless he has a burning zeal for the potentialities of UNESCO in promoting peace among the peoples of the world. Francis is fundamentally not a serious character. He is bright and his impulses are alright, etc., but he cares too much for Francis Biddle and for life as a show. Archie said he agreed entirely, but he is in a bad fix, because he is under instructions to do everything he possibly can to have the other countries agree on Biddle up to the point of avoiding friction between Great Britain and the U. S. A. on the subject. He said he phoned to Biddle who was at Sea Island, Georgia, to apprise him of the British opposition, and Biddle said he thought the British opposition was not against him, Biddle, but against having an American at the head of the organization, which, of course, is not true, because Julian Huxley will promptly retire in favor of Archie and the British would be delighted to have him. Archie said that Francis told him he had a "channel" to both Prime Minister Attlee and Bevin. Archie said the "channel" was Sir Hartley Shawcross, who is the Attorney General in Attlee's Cabinet and who was the Chief British Prosecutor in Nuernberg where Biddle came to know him. Archie also had a phone talk with Sir John Maude, the Permanent Undersecretary of the Ministry of Education, who knows Francis Biddle well and says England is strongly opposed to him.

On the bench today Frank Murphy whispered to me, "I have carefully read your opinion in *Freeman v. Hewitt* (the opinion denying States the power to tax the gross receipts from interstate commerce). It is a very fine opinion and correct." To which I replied, "Then you are going to join it." To which F. M. answered, "Oh, no." And then I said, "What a perfect summary of your attitude [this] is of much of your performance on the Court: you see the right but for some reason or other having nothing to do with the merits of a case, you go in the other direction." Whereupon, Murphy sort of buried his face in his hands and then said, "I have thought a good deal this past summer of the things you have said to me, and of how true they are." To which I answered, "Yes, but you will persist in sinning against the light."

After we got off the bench, the Chief motioned to me to see him and when I came into his room he said "What is happening around here? I haven't heard anything for several days." I did not know what he had in mind particularly, and so I began to talk about the situation regarding the *Ballard* case— whether we can smoke out the majority who want to reverse on the jury business to face the merits.[1] He then said, "I am ready to move in whenever I have

---

[1] *United States v. Ballard*, 332 U. S. 78 (1944).

Ballard, head of the "I Am" cult, claimed to be a divine messenger with supernatural healing powers. He and his family used the mails to solicit money and members, and the government

to, but I want to take my time about it and not do it too soon. If I have any special ability, it is that of getting on with folk and I want to do it here without making people feel that I am unduly moving in and that is why I rather thought it would be unwise for me to move in on the *Ballard* case." By "moving in" it became clear he meant taking the initiative on questions before the Court and asserting such intrinsic authority as the position of Chief Justice gives. The situation in the *Ballard* case was this: that was a prosecution of leaders of a professed religious sect known as "I Am," who extorted a great deal of money from the gullible in California by claims of miraculous performances. They were indicted and convicted for using the mails for a scheme to defraud.

November 15, 1946

Sat in Court and heard No. 70, 71, *Katzinger Co. v. Chicago Metallic Mfg. Co.*, concluded; No. 36, *Carter v. People* of the State of Illinois, concerning failure to appoint counsel for defendant in capital case until after plea of guilty.

Sunday, November 17, 1946

Caught up with some back correspondence with Katy Watters.

Ernest Gruening, the Governor of Alaska, came to lunch and before we sat down Herbert Feis dropped in and the two of them spoke soberly, but not hysterically, about the possibility of the confusion resulting from the election, not because the Republicans will be taking over Congress, but because of the lack of leadership on the part of the President. Gruening felt strongly, and I thought wisely, that it was fortunate and not unfortunate that, if the Republicans were to have the Houses, that full responsibility for the legislative branch will be theirs.

---

charged them with using the mails to defraud. They claimed religious persecution, but the trial judge refused to submit questions to the jury relating to the truth or falsity of "I Am" doctrines, in order not to lend substance to their claims. He confined the issue to whether the defendants in good faith believed their claims and on that basis the jury found them guilty. The Supreme Court in 1944 upheld the trial judge, but five justices, concerned with the claims of religious persecution, sent the case back to the lower court for argument on the constitutional issues. Stone, Frankfurter, and Roberts, who had voted to uphold the district judge, had been opposed to sending the case back.

When the case reached the Supreme Court a second time in 1946, instead of being argued on grounds of religious liberty, the case was dismissed because of the exclusion of women from the grand jury which had indicted them and the petit jury which had convicted them. Frankfurter and Burton, with Vinson concurring, attacked this decision, because, argued Frankfurter, the defendants had not raised the issue of exclusion of women in their first appeal; moreover, the absence of women on juries did not violate due process. Frankfurter was particularly exercised because the Court, speaking through the majority, had given no hint of its position on the validity of the prosecution under the First Amendment.

Monday, November 18, 1946

Dean Acheson told me this morning on our walk down that he was very much disturbed about the general current of affairs and for two reasons. In the first place he is much disturbed lest all the talk that the election will not affect our foreign relations because Vandenberg will be at the head of the foreign relations committee and is responsible for the bi-partisan development of our foreign policy may turn out to be more talk than fact. He said that he had a talk with Vandenberg on Saturday about the renewal of the trade agreements and Vandenberg indicated that he might not have a free hand in the matter and that as to domestic affairs he must be very careful about Taft. Dean Acheson pointed out to him that many questions of foreign policy have their domestic aspects and that, if, as to all of them, he will have to defer to Taft because domestic affairs are in Taft's bailiwick, there won't be much of a bi-partisan foreign policy. I should suppose that this would be particularly so if Taft gets any kind of encouragement to assume that he has a veto power over the stand which Vandenberg is to take as Chairman of the Committee on Foreign Relations. Dean was also disturbed by his conversation with the British regarding the financing of a unified Anglo-American zone. The British professed to be absolutely up against it and asked us, substantially, to bear the whole cost of the obligation. Dean made it plain that neither Congress nor American opinion would stand for that and the British seemed rather hopeless about it.

Tuesday, November 19, 1946

Apropos of nothing in particular, Murphy asked me while we were on the bench, "I wonder if Bob Jackson knew what went on here last spring?" I replied that I thought Bob was pretty busy in Nuernberg. Then he said he wondered if even I knew what had gone on. He then proceeded to say that he could understand why Black would be hostile to Jackson and try to block his becoming Chief Justice, but he could not understand why Bill Douglas should feel that way. He said that Douglas had come to see him one day and said, "You know Father White well (Father White is Dean of Catholic University Law School). Why don't you get him to reach the White House in opposition to Jackson?" Murphy refused to do so and Douglas said that he guessed there were other ways of getting it done. Murphy indicated that the endeavor was to bring both Catholic and labor opposition to bear against the appointment of Jackson.

Wednesday, November 20, 1946

While sitting in Court Frank Murphy again turned to me out of a clear sky and said: "You make me Ambassador and I will resign from the Court and then you can get a good judge to take my place." Then he went on to tell me what good qualifications he had for the Indian post, that he knew the East, etc., etc. Since only yesterday Murphy spoke to me of Bill Douglas' reference to Father White, I called his attention to the fact that Father White was in Court listening to the arguments in *Everson v. Board of Education,*[1] dealing with transportation in other than public schools. Murphy said, "You know what this case is about—why don't they tell what it is about? All this legislation is legislation to hurt Catholic schools." To which I responded with a bland face, "Well, why don't you enlighten everybody, since you are peculiarly qualified to state that that is the issue, if that is the issue." I then asked him whether he had invited Father White to attend this argument and Murphy nobly responded that because of the Catholic interests involved he would not even speak to White. This was before luncheon. After luncheon Murphy said to me "Where do you suppose Father White was lunching?" And he called my attention to the fact that immediately after lunch Bill Douglas was not on the bench and neither was Father White in Court, and that both returned to their respective seats sometime after.

Thursday, November 21, 1946

Dr. Katju, Minister of Law and Justice of the United Provinces in India, with a population of some five million people, called. I had seen a letter by him recently (in the *Times* of London) and so broached the subject of it—capital punishment. He said he had strong views against capital punishment, both because there was no evidence to indicate it was a deterrent and, human fallibility being what it is, it was too dangerous a remedy in view of the number of miscarriages of justice.

Friday, November 22, 1946

Worked at home all morning on draft of opinion in Nos. 42–45, *Vanston.*
On the bench Murphy said that he had read my opinion in the *Carter* case [1] (holding that there is no basis in finding on the record before us that the

---

[1] *Everson v. Board of Education of Ewing Township,* 330 U. S. 1 (1947).

By a five to four decision the Court ruled that New Jersey public school funds raised by taxation could be used to reimburse the parents of parochial school students for their transportation to and from school. Black wrote for the majority, which included Douglas, Reed, Vinson, and Murphy. Rutledge, writing for Frankfurter, Jackson, and Burton, asserted that the First Amendment prohibited "every form" of public aid or support for religion. And Jackson, in a separate statement that was joined by Frankfurter, charged the majority with setting back the clock because the prohibition against establishment of religion cannot be circumvented by a "subsidy, bonus or reimbursement."

[1] *Carter v. Illinois,* 329 U. S. 156 (1946).

This was one of many right-to-counsel cases on which the Roosevelt Court divided. Although in 1932 Frankfurter had called the Court's reversal of the conviction of the Scottsboro boys because of the denial of the right of counsel "a notable chapter in the history of liberty," in 1942 he had supported the Roberts majority opinion in *Betts v. Brady,* 316 U. S. 455. In that opinion Roberts had

right to counsel was improperly denied) and that while I was right in my opinion that the law does not justify us in reversing the case, because on the record there was no basis for finding denial, he Murphy wanted to go beyond the law and go on grounds of humanity.

The Chief Justice again revealed to me his undue sensibility about criticism of the Court and the undesirability of continuing the practice of oral opinions, because of the inevitable tendency, when there are divisions, of assuming an advocate's tone in delivering the opinions, thereby giving a basis for newspaper talk of hostilities among the members of the Court. I did not encourage this line in him, it being a practice since the beginning of time. I suggested that after all, the newspapers only print what is in the written opinion and not what is orally expounded.

Prichard turned up later and said amusedly that the Chief Justice said to him (the Chief is a very close friend of Prichard's), "Everything is going smoothly—I don't think there is a man on the Court who doesn't like me." Prich told this with knowing amusement. Vinson is a very ingenuous creature and of course Prich is the opposite. Prich said, "Poor Fred Vinson is certainly foolin' himself by his idea as to what is smoothness. The nice man is going to have an awakening sooner than he thinks." Which reminds me that Dean told me the other day that he saw the Chief at dinner and Vinson asked him if he had noted that Black and Jackson had agreed in the first batch of cases and how well things were going in the Court, and Dean said to himself, "Old boy, you don't know nothin'." When Dean said that I told him that I never can understand how people can go through life with a vast experience, such as is true of both Vinson and Roberts, and still remain as ingenuous as those people are. It reminds me of dearly beloved Julian Mack, one of the best brains I ever knew who was simple-minded about human motives and human ways, to whom I was led to say once, "Julian, experience goes through you without stopping."

Murphy's name having come up in a talk between the Chief and me, I

---

argued that the Sixth Amendment was not extended to the states through the Fourteenth Amendment and that the right to counsel of indigents in less than capital cases was not a general constitutional right. The Court subsequently see-sawed back and forth on the issue. In the 1944 term Black, Douglas, Murphy, and Rutledge had prevailed in favor of the defendants; in 1946 in several cases including *Carter*, with Frankfurter writing for the majority, the Court ruled against the defendants on the right-to-counsel issue. The matter was finally settled in 1963 in *Gideon v. Wainwright*, 373 U. S. 335, where Black for the Court overturned *Betts v. Brady* and held that the equal protection of the laws clause under the Fourteenth Amendment required that counsel be appointed for indigent defendants in all criminal proceedings. The *Carter* case was a little unusual in that Murphy did not have the support of Black, Rutledge, and Douglas and had been cautioned by his clerks that he should not take notice of facts outside of the record that had been reviewed below nor should he imply that there never could be a waiver of counsel in a capital case. "Legal technicalities doubtless afford justification for our pretense of ignoring the plain facts before us," he wrote in his dissent, "facts upon which a man's very life or liberty conceivably depend. . . . But the result certainly does not enhance the high traditions of the judicial process. In my view, when undisputed facts appear in the record before us in a case involving a man's life or liberty, they should not be ignored if justice demands their use."

told him by way of amusement of Murphy's successive remarks to me on the bench that if he were made Ambassador to India, there would be room for appointing "a good judge" in his place. Today Vinson said, "I didn't say anything the other day but I took note of your remark about Murphy and something may come of it. I wouldn't hesitate in the slightest to tell the President about it, but I do not want to go out of my way in doing so in view of the Lewis controversy and the Court.[2] And so I shall wait my chance."

Saturday, November 23, 1946

The usual Saturday morning before Conference—last minute circulation of opinions or changes in outstanding opinions and the need for accomodating one's own opinions to them or qualifying one's prior agreements or dissents. Brandeis once told me that he thought it ought to be a rule of the Court not to hand down any opinion unless it had lain over a whole week after agreement had been reached. I wish we had adopted such a rule. The deliberative process requires it.

Conference engendered rather more friction, particularly in connection with the first opinion which the Chief circulated, No. 26, *U.S. v. Tillamooks.*[1] Stanley Reed has written a rather stiff dissent and the Chief showed extreme sensitiveness about it, as indeed he did to me yesterday when he said he did not quite understand "why Stanley should write a dissent in such strong terms." In driving home after the Conference Stanley Reed described the atmosphere of the Conference as "sultry." And when I said the Chief seemed to be rather sensitive he said, "Yes, he is very sensitive. You must remember he comes from

---

[2] The country was again resounding to John L. Lewis's thunder. In May 1946 the government had taken over the bituminous coal mines in order to keep them in operation, but a week before this entry, Lewis had informed the government that unless it agreed to reopen certain terms of the contract, he would strike the mines, whether they were government operated or not. The President responded to this with an order to Attorney General Clark to "fight John L. Lewis on all fronts," and on November 18 the district court had issued a restraining order against the threatened strike. Nevertheless, on November 21 every coal mine was shut down. The government returned to the court and on December 4 Judge T. Alan Goldsborough fined the union three and a half million dollars and Lewis personally ten thousand dollars. On December 7 Lewis ordered the strikers back to work.

[1] *United States v. Alcea Band of Tillamooks,* 329 U. S. 40 (1946).

The Tillamooks, an Indian tribe residing in Oregon, sued the United States under a newly enacted statute, claiming a right to indemnification for Indian lands taken in the last half of the 19th century. The Court, in an opinion by Chief Justice Vinson, joined by Justices Frankfurter, Douglas, and Murphy, held that under the statute the Indians were entitled to recover for the taking of their "interest" in the land. Justice Black concurred separately.

Justice Reed, joined by Justices Rutledge and Burton, dissented, arguing that irrespective of any right to sue under the new statute, the Indians had no legal rights to their "aboriginal" lands which the government was required to extinguish by payments. The morality of this rule was not a justiciable question, Reed asserted. "It is not for the courts of the conqueror to question the propriety or validity of such an assertion of power."

the mountain region in Kentucky. It makes a lot of difference whether you come from a community where you assume everyone is ready to help everyone else, or from the mountains where you are brought up to be suspicious and distrustful. And as I said some time ago, Fred Vinson has all those qualities."

Sunday, November 24, 1946

Sir Hartley Shawcross, the Attorney General of England, came to luncheon. He is one of those Englishmen with a very good mind, strong capacities and considerable charm. He acquitted himself admirably at Nuernberg where he made the opening and closing speeches—leaving the prosecution to his predecessor, Sir Maxwell Fyfe. Shawcross was brought by John Balfour, the British Minister, and his wife, and we had good and gay talk about sundry American manifestations which were new to them, and also a good deal of talk about the press, because of the recent action of the House of Commons in voting for a Royal Commission to investigate the state of the press. Shawcross said that one of the great differences in the content of the press between this country and England was the vogue of columnists and he could hardly assimilate the kind of leakages which Drew Pearson so widely exploits. He was very troubled about the Royal Commission on the press, because he didn't think anything could be done legislatively and it could serve only the purpose of education through appropriate publicity. And he thought that would require a chairman of philosophic understanding and power and he did not know of any British judge now sitting who has those qualities and chairmanship traditionally goes to a judge. I asked Shawcross who did make the selection and he said, ultimately Attlee did, but largely on the recommendation of the Lord Chancellor and the Lord Chancellor usually recommends for a chairman the judge whom they can most easily spare from judicial work.

Did this week's *certs* and cleared up most of my birthday correspondence.

Noticing that Ickes was speaking on the radio about the Lewis coal strike situation, I was curious to hear what he had to say, anticipating that he would, as is so often the case with him in these matters, be guided by personal venom. One would suppose that even if he disagreed with the long course of treatment, he would not fan the flames of a division and tension in the country in a situation which is full of potentialities of social conflict and might end no man knows where. But of course Harold Ickes has no such self-restraint. And so with great self-righteousness he disagreed with everything that the President had done, and when asked what he would do, he said first and foremost the President should fire Dr. Steelman, and that he, Ickes, had told the President last that "John Steelman was in Lewis' corner." [1] I wonder when Harold Ickes' got out of "Lewis' corner," because he certainly spoiled the pitch of things two or three years ago when he aided that smoothy, Abe Fortas, who was then the

---

[1] Dr. John R. Steelman, a top aide of Truman's, at this time was Reconversion Director.

Under Secretary, in yielding to Lewis' terms in disregard of what the other economic and labor agencies of the Government advised. Lloyd Garrison, than whom there is no more just-minded man, who was then with the War Labor Board, told me at the time that Ickes acted in complete defiance of the right of that situation. But at some stage or other there was a break between Lewis and Ickes, because Lewis was also playing with John Steelman and thereby aroused what is so easily aroused in Ickes, his almost morbid jealousy of power and publicity.

Monday, November 25, 1946

Today the Chief delivered his first opinion—it was in the *Tillamooks* case. Evidently he has discarded the views regarding the undesirability of oral opinions, because he read out his views at length in effective anticipation of what he knew was to be Stanley's dissent.

Today the Chief asked to see me and told me that he dined last night with the President and talked about "a certain gentleman" on this Court and India. The President was ready to act on the idea, but he wanted to be sure that the gentleman is serious. Vinson said, "You know there was some talk some time ago that folks were trying to get him off the Court and it is important before any step is taken to know that this is serious business with him and that he is ready to act, and if he is, I think the President is ready to make him happy." I said that all I knew was what Frank Murphy had said to me not only once but thrice, "What they ought to do is to make me Ambassador to India" and gave me his reasons—that he knew the East and the Eastern people trusted him, etc. I then said to the Chief Justice that I had supposed that he had some ideas in view of his experience of how the matter should be dealt with so as to make sure that there was no misunderstanding. He said he had not thought about procedure. He asked me if I would think about it and there the matter was left.

Dean Acheson told me that Jimmy Byrnes has suddenly awakened to what he called the mess in connection with UNESCO, namely, the insistence by us on the candidacy of Francis Biddle for the Directorship and the uncompromising opposition of Great Britain to Francis Biddle. Byrnes has been told that Britain is determined to support Julian Huxley. Jimmy Byrnes said the whole UNESCO business has become inflated to absurd proportions and is likely to do more harm than good when trying to sweep so much into its scope and he said he was going to phone to Francis Biddle to withdraw and avoid the rumpus.

After lunch I found myself alone with Vinson today and I told him how saddened I was by Harold Ickes' broadcast yesterday—I said that to me the times are so agitated and insecure that I thought it was quite undesirable and egotistical of Ickes to be trying to muddy the waters. He had not heard the broadcast of Ickes and I told him that the chief preoccupation of Ickes was to vent his spleen against Steelman. When I told him that Ickes had said that

Steelman was in Lewis' corner Vinson said, "I just wonder when Harold got out of Lewis' corner, because he certainly was in his corner not so long ago." Vinson then went on to say that John Snyder is probably more responsible than any one person for the difficulties in which we find ourselves. "He is not a bad fellow," said the Chief, and when he paused, I said, "but he has very limited horizons." And Vinson said, "That's it. So when he came in with Truman, his old banking associates led him to urge taking off all controls with all the consequences that followed." And then Vinson said, "By God, how that man Prichard called the tune. With that wonderful insight of his he foresaw all this very early and it happened precisely as he foretold. He did not want me to leave the Office of War Mobilization and Reconversion when the President asked me to be Secretary of the Treasury, because Snyder [1] was going to succeed me. But I just could not get the consent of my mind to take that job over to the Treasury. The Secretaryship of the Treasury is a full time job." And I interrupted, "At least," and he echoed, "Yes, at least. But certainly we are in all this mess as Prichard foretold we would be largely because of John Snyder."

The Chief later talked to me about assigning the *Winters v. New York* case, No. 33,[2] involving the constitutionality of the New York statute prohibiting the sale of magazines devoted to crime. Black, Murphy and Rutledge thought the whole statute as interpreted by the Circuit Court of Appeals violated freedom of speech, while Reed and Douglas were for reversal, although they thought the statute as interpreted by the Court of Appeals was not unconstitutional but that there should be a reversal, because the interpretation was *ex post facto* in that the defendant could not have known what it was until after the Circuit Court of Appeals so announced. The Chief first was of that view and then changed it, and I suggested that if he returned to his original view he would then have the assignment and it could then be assigned to someone like Reed who was right on the main issue.

Tuesday, November 26, 1946

Dean spoke this morning of a dinner at Joe Alsop's at which Lord Inverchapel was present. Joe Alsop had just returned from the United Nations

---

[1] John Snyder was an old Missouri crony and political cohort of Truman's. Despite his conservatism, Truman had appointed him Secretary of the Treasury when Vinson left that post to become Chief Justice.

[2] *Winters v. New York*, 333 U. S. 507 (1948).

At the time that Justice Frankfurter made the journal entry regarding this case, it had been twice argued. It was argued before the Court a third time a year later, and the Court, in an opinion by Justice Reed, invalidated as an unconstitutionally vague limitation upon freedom of speech a New York statute prohibiting the distribution of publications devoted to bloodshed and violence. Justice Frankfurter wrote a lengthy dissent, joined by Justices Jackson and Burton. The Court went too far, he contended, in restricting the power of many states that had statutes similar to that invalidated to regulate conduct which the legislatures of those states thought had the effect of inciting crime.

Conference in New York and he said that our people are getting a little tired and eager to wind up affairs. This remark led Inverchapel to break out saying that he knew exactly what is happening, because that has been happening at most of these conferences. The Russians are ready to stay until the cows come home and instead of   [Diary breaks off.]

Saturday, December 14, 1946

Attended Christmas Gridiron Dinner. I was seated between Governor Stassen and Joseph Pulitzer, the owner of the St. Louis *Post-Dispatch*. Stassen confirmed the impression that he gave me on the two other occasions on which I saw him, at both of which he was the speaker. He is, I think, essentially different from the other Republican contenders for the presidency, each of whom was asked to stand up last night—Bricker, Taft, Tom Dewey and Vandenberg. He is very unlike all the other possible Republican contenders, except possibly Vandenberg, but Vandenberg has a good deal of the actor atmosphere about him. Vandenberg is probably more widely read and generally cultivated than Stassen. The latter is very serious, the Scandinavian streak in him is deep, but I think he has a concern for the distressed world. He talked freely, as freely that is as any American public man does, opening up his remarks by saying, "I saw a good many of your friends in Cambridge recently." What in the jargon of the day I might call the over-all impression he left on me was his concern that the Republican party being confident of election will in its policy try to go back to days that are not recoverable and not be adequate to the problems of the changing world. I asked him bluntly whether he thought that Governor Dewey could be stopped from getting the nomination and he said with prompt confidence that he thought he was stopped already—that Dewey was of course way out in the lead and will come to the Convention with great strength, but he thinks he has reached the peak of his strength and will not be able to advance. Stassen is soon going abroad to Great Britain, the continent, the Balkans and, I think, to Russia. He said "I am one of these people who has actually to see and experience in order fully to understand what I read." Altogether, he gave me more direct evidence for my belief that one would have a right to feel [all right] if he were in the White House. I am also convinced that he has not a ghost of a chance of getting there in '48. The Party won't let him. I talked with Joseph Pulitzer about the *Post-Dispatch* and a real free press of which the *Manchester Guardian* and C. P. Snow were to me the best exemplars,   [Diary breaks off.]

(1947)

WRATH AGAINST DOUGLAS

The 1947 Diary describes additional gleanings from Frankfurter's daily walks with Dean Acheson and nostalgic conversations with Adolph Miller about Franklin D. Roosevelt, including Frankfurter's agreement with Miller that an understanding of economics was "not Franklin's forte." We see Frankfurter trying to listen to a lawyer's argument in front of the Bench while Justice Murphy is plying him with reasons why President Truman should appoint him to a choice ambassadorship. There are relaxed entries such as those reporting his calls on retired Chief Justice Charles Evans Hughes and their illuminating gossip about Court personalities in Hughes' time. There is a fascinating account of the discussion among the Brethren when their law clerks asked for permission to invite the Court's black messengers to the clerks' annual Christmas party. Could they do so without entangling the Court, the Justices wondered. Above all, the 1947 entries reflect a preoccupation with Douglas' political ambitions which, as the 1948 presidential election neared, seemed to have become an almost obsessive concern with Frankfurter.

Tuesday, February 4, 1947

Stanley Reed twitted me about my dissent in No. 690, the *Denver, Rio Grande* case.[1] We played back and forth and then followed this colloquy:

[1] *Insurance Group Committee v. Denver & Rio Grande Western Railroad Co.*, 329 U. S. 607 (1947).

The Court in an opinion by Justice Reed again confirmed the reorganization plan for the Denver & Rio Grande, this time by denial of the petition by a group of debtors that the plan be reexamined in the light of the circumstances which had changed since the Interstate Commerce Commission

S. R.   I don't see how you could dissent this time.

F. F.   Stanley, I will tell you that which obviously I could not put in my opinion. You will recall that when the Denver & Rio Grande case was up for the first time, you said at Conference that in order to sustain the plan of reorganization in view of its rejection by the class of general bond-holders, one would have to do "violence" to the statute. That was your phrase, "you would have to do violence to the statute."

S. R.   Yes, I said that, and I still think that one had to do violence to the statute in order to carry out the plan.

F. F.   Well, I don't believe in doing violence to a statute. And since by this decision we had once more to do violence to the statute, because until we affirm what the district court did in this case the plan couldn't be executed, I refuse to be a party to doing such violence to a statute.

Monday, April 7, 1947

Frank Murphy turned to me while we were on the bench today and said, "I see Grady has been named Ambassador to Italy." [1] I assented. The announcement of his appointment had been in the morning papers and I said, "Yes, so I see." Murphy then went on, "While I was well equipped for work in India, since India is not yet free, that weighed with me about going out." He referred to the talk between us some time ago in which he indicated that he would resign from the Court if he were named Ambassador to India. When I subsequently asked him to say without qualification whether he would accept the position if it were offered to him, he said he would accept only if after a year the President would make him Secretary of War! Apparently he completely forgot that condition in now explaining that the reason he said he would decline the offer was because India was not yet free. After a pause, he went on, "If the President were to send me either to Italy or to France, I would leave the Court in June for my work is done and I have written the views for which I stand and there they are in the books. I am thinking of Charley Fahy [2] and what a very good man he would make for the Court and also of the importance

---

hearings were concluded six years earlier. Again Justice Frankfurter dissented. He noted that the President had vetoed a railroad reorganization bill the previous August, not because he disapproved of its purposes, but because he considered it too weak to achieve its stated purposes and that Congress had indicated it would rewrite the bill to meet the President's concerns. The President felt that under the existing Bankruptcy Act control of the railroads could pass from the hands of those concerned with the transportation needs of the areas served by a railroad into the hands of distant banks and insurance companies. The President also wanted the bill to direct a reduction in "grossly excessive interest rates now wasting the funds of the railroads."

[1] Henry F. Grady was a former Assistant Secretary of State.

[2] Instead of being appointed to the Court, Charles Fahy, who had been Solicitor General, became General Counsel to the National Labor Relations Board, and in 1949 was named to the Court of Appeals for the District of Columbia.

of stabilizing the Court." I did not ask him to explain what he meant by "stabilizing" the Court. But he went on, "I wish you would remember this—if I were asked to go either to Italy or France, I would accept without any ifs, ands or buts." He was referring doubtless to the condition on which he would have accepted the invitation to go to India, namely to be made Secretary of War. After a further pause (during which I was trying to listen to the argument), he turned to me again and said, "A little while ago I did not think the President had a chance of reelection, but now I am inclined to think he will be reelected." He then went on to speak deprecatingly of the efforts to run Bill for the Vice-Presidency. "Joe Kennedy is of course heavily behind it and I suppose the President would get $250,000 for the campaign fund if Bill were nominated. What has Bill ever done to identify himself with any real public interest or the promotion of any real public cause?" He continued to speak very disparagingly, as he has often spoken, of Douglas' political manifestations through "Tommy Corcoran" and "those fellows." And then he went on to talk of Joe Kennedy at length, adding, "He once tried to tempt me. Toward the end of my term as Governor of Michigan when there was some talk in the papers that I would become Attorney General, though I knew nothing about it, I was in Washington at the Mayflower on some business and an emissary of Joe Kennedy's came to see me and to say that Joe Kennedy wanted me to take charge of his legal affairs and money was no consideration." He asked me who I supposed was the emissary, and when I said I didn't know, he said it was Arthur Krock.[3] And Murphy said, "I told Krock that I was not interested, that I wanted to give myself to the public service."

Having told Vinson at the time of Murphy's desire to go to India and all that followed, I told Vinson the above conversation after Court adjourned at 4:30 today.

Tuesday, April 8, 1947

While trying to listen to a technical argument, Murphy whispered to me the following on the bench, "This is very confidential, but you are a great friend of Dean Acheson's and I just want you to know that if I were asked to go to Paris I would go at once and I think I could be of great help to the President. I thought you ought to know that in view of your relations to Dean Acheson." I replied that I did not know that Dean Acheson had a thing to do with suggesting appointments of Ambassador and that, at any rate, I did not talk to him about such things.

Friday, April 25, 1947

Visited Chief Justice Hughes and was with him from a quarter of six to a quarter past seven. I had not seen him since January 8th, just before he left for

---

[3] Arthur Krock, the Washington correspondent of the New York *Times*, was one of the mandarins of Washington journalism.

the South. In the meantime on April 11th he had had his eighty-fifth birthday which evidently gave him great joy. He went to New York for a family dinner and they were all there, as he said, apparently happy and healthy—his son Charles, and his two daughters, Mrs. Chauncey Waddell, and Mrs. William Gossett, and twelve grandchildren. He seemed to me extremely vigorous and vital—full of mental alertness, referring with detailed accuracy in the recital of complicated matters and full of vivid interest about the world. When I asked him what he had been reading lately, he said that in Florida he was so busy with visits from his daughters that he had not read much and that since his return so many people have come to see him that he finds it difficult to keep up his reading, adding, "The trouble is I am interested in too many things and try to keep up with them."

When he said, "You would be surprised how many visitors I have had since I have come back," I said, "Yes, I have seen one of them, Professor Charles Fairman of Leland Stanford,[1] who told me of that delicious remark of Justice Miller's which you said was current in explaining the well-known friction between Justice Miller and Justice Bradley,[2] 'The trouble with Bradley is that he does not recognize my intellectual preeminence.'" Hughes got off into more of a discussion about personalities of the Court than has been the case on any other occasion. In fact most of the time was taken up with illuminating and delightful remarks by Hughes regarding the Court before he went on it in 1910 and his own experiences during his first membership on the Court. We found ourselves in entire agreement about Bradley. According to Hughes he was "one of the really great intellects in the history of the Court." He asked me if I had heard, as I had, that Fairman had come upon papers which made it perfectly clear that Bradley had a great deal to do with writing Waite's famous opinion in *Munn v. Illinois*, 94 U. S.[3] He referred to the railroad and corporate ties that Bradley had as a lawyer—perhaps closer corporate ties than any man who went on the Court, certainly before Bradley's time. To which I added that Bradley was a striking disproof of the theory of economic determinism, because he, who by his previous experience would supposedly reflect the bias of financial power, was as free from it as any judge and indeed much more radical than men like Harlan with all his strong popular inclinations.

[1] In 1949 Professor Fairman wrote (2 *Stanford Law Review* 5) "Does the Fourteenth Amendment Incorporate the Bill of Rights? The Original Understanding," in which in the opinion of many scholars he showed conclusively that there had been no consensus in Congress on the point involved.

[2] Justice Samuel F. Miller was appointed to the Court by Lincoln and served from 1862 to 1890. He was one of the Court's outstanding justices. Joseph P. Bradley was named by Grant and served from 1870 to 1892, and is rated by Court-watchers as one of the "near-greats."

[3] Morrison R. Waite was Chief Justice, 1874–1888. *Munn v. Illinois* was the famous Granger case in which Waite ruled that although the Fourteenth Amendment barred illegal government encroachment on private property, it did not forbid the exercise of federal and state power to regulate business "affected with a public interest."

I then told him about the life that is being written of Fuller,[4] and Hughes confirmed what Holmes had told me of his, Holmes' high appreciation of Fuller as Chief. Hughes had the strong impression that Holmes helped Fuller greatly in his work, not that Holmes made any such claim, but Hughes got that impression. Hughes said of the Court in those days—the days of Bradley and Harlan— [5] "It was a brutal Court in its personal relations. I heard that they actually shook fists at one another." He then went on to say that when he came on the Court he looked forward to it with the greatest eagerness. He had got rather tired of politics, etc. and he hoped to find himself in an atmosphere of great serenity with men of marked powers. But he was soon disappointed, because there was something in the atmosphere that was not at all harmonious. He soon discovered that the difficulty was conflicting ambitions for the Chief Justiceship—Fuller having died in the summer of 1910. Harlan, as senior, thought he ought to be the Chief Justice to crown his life's work and White [6] thought he had natural claims to the position, "as indeed he did," said Hughes. White was very unsatisfactory at Conferences, as he would not take a position on most of the cases. But after White was made Chief (he was named on December 12 and took the oath as Chief Justice on December 19,) "everything changed." Hughes said that White was a "very dear man—one of the dearest I have ever known. He was very warm-hearted and most solicitous that the brethren should be as happy as possible." The atmosphere changed the next year when Van Devanter came on the Court to succeed Moody,[7] who, because of illness, had not been sitting for several years, and Lamar succeeded White. "Life was very pleasant," said Hughes, "on the personal side, particularly after Harlan died and Pitney succeeded him." Harlan and Holmes were temperamentally incompatible. At Conference Holmes used to refer to Harlan as "my lion-hearted friend" and Harlan did not like it at all. White was of course a very able man. Everybody liked him and respected his ability, but he completely lacked executive ability and the faculty for conducting the affairs of the Court as Hughes thought they should have been conducted. "Whatever little success I may have achieved when I became Chief Justice, I think it was largely due to the lessons I learned in watching White during the years when I was an associate Justice and seeing how it ought not to be done. I am fond of saying

---

[4] Melvin W. Fuller was appointed Chief Justice by Grover Cleveland and served 1888–1910. A man of conservative views, under him the Court became "a veritable bastion of *laissez faire*." His biography was written by W. L. King (New York, 1950).

[5] John Marshall Harlan, rated as one of the "great" justices, was appointed by President Hayes in 1877 and served until 1911.

[6] Another claimant to the Chief Justiceship had been Hughes himself, who had gone on the Court with a promise from President Taft that he would be so named. Instead Taft promoted Edward D. White, a Confederate veteran, who had been on the Court since 1894.

[7] William H. Moody, 1906–1910; Willis Van Devanter, 1910–1937; Joseph R. Lamar, 1910–1916; Mahlon Pitney, 1912–1922.

that perhaps parents help their children most through their faults, because children hate the faults and failings of their parents and are helped thereby. And so if I had any virtues as Chief Justice they were due to my determination to avoid White's faults. Very often he could not make up his mind and a favorite expression of his was, 'God help us,' as though he counted on God to decide a case. White was a very emotional man and at times he would deliver an extemporaneous oration of an hour's length. I would come home from Conference on Saturday with a strong feeling of frustration. White did not take hold the way that a Chief Justice should in guiding the discussion and taking a position in expounding the matters before the Court." Hughes then told me by way of illustration how he came to write the well-known opinion in the *Minnesota Rate Cases*, 230 U. S.[8] He said aspects of the whole problem of State regulation of intrastate rates had been before the Court, argued in the beginning of the 1910 Term, then ordered for reargument, then reargued in the Spring of 1912. "And we got nowhere and the cases went over for the summer." Hughes said that in order to inform himself, he studied the whole field of commerce regulation by the States and came back in the fall with an elaborate memorandum for his own use which was the substance of a subsequent opinion in the *Minnesota Rate Cases*. Hughes and White had become friends—Hughes said he was "close to him. I don't suppose as close as Holmes, but close to him."

White talked with Hughes about these rate cases and Hughes said that White should have done during the summer what he did—to try to master the field and come before the Conference with definite conclusions for consideration by the Court. He had not done so and when the case came up for consideration by the Conference, White asked Hughes to set forth his views. Hughes did this and then without even taking a vote, White asked Hughes to write up his views for the Conference and that is how the unanimous result was reached, and all but McKenna concurred in the result and joined in Hughes' opinion.

Hughes said that when he became Chief Justice, he recalled vividly his experience under White and resolved to avoid White's failings. As a result he came to the Conferences thoroughly prepared on every case and stated it to the Conference with an expression of his own views so that the subsequent discussion could be directed and not run all over the lot in a diffused inconclusive way.

This account by Hughes of the considerations that governed him as Chief Justice led me to say that I should like to tell him, Hughes, things which I had never supposed I would tell him about himself as Chief Justice as I observed him during the two and a half Terms in which I sat under him. Substantially this is what I said: "The longer I live the more I realize the considerable truth

---

[8] *Minnesota Rate Cases*, 230 U. S. 352 (1912). The Court in sweeping terms had upheld the authority of the states in the absence of federal action to establish intrastate rates.

there is in Henry Ford's statement that history is the bunk, for the reason that such partial or distorted or misunderstood views of happenings gain currency as history. And merely in the interests of truth I should like to say a few things regarding the talk that is going the rounds about Stone as Chief Justice and about you (Hughes) as Chief Justice. It has been so often repeated that it seems to be gaining the authority of undisputed fact that the reason that Conferences were so long on Saturday and sometimes went over to Monday or even Tuesday under Stone was that Stone made possible full and free discussion among the brethren, while Hughes throttled discussion." At this point Hughes laughed heartily and said, "The notion that I could throttle the strong men who were on the Court during my time is funny, even if I had ever thought of doing so, which was the farthest possible from my thought." I went on, "I can testify to that and I have stated it to the few people with whom I felt free to talk, like the Hands. I have said that I never felt the slightest inhibition against expressing my views freely and fully, although in strong opposition to yours, except the inhibition that came from knowing that in your presence I must not make a fool of myself and must be sure that what I was saying was accurate insofar as it dealt with matters in the record or in the Reports, because you were so thoroughly prepared on every case under discussion. And that was true of the other members of the Court. You laid out each case so clearly and so thoroughly that there was very seldom any controversy as to the accuracy or completeness of your statement of the case and the issues at stake. The controversies were canalized by your analysis."

Saturday, October 11, 1947

Conference had previously voted to grant *certiorari* in No. 277, *Bernstein v. Van Heyghen Frères Société Anonyme*.[1] The issue in the case is whether or not the validity of the Nazi confiscation decrees during the period of our diplomatic relations with Nazi Germany can be judicially reexamined in our courts. The question arose by the claim by Bernstein to the ownership of a vessel which by German decree had eventually got into the hands of the respondent. I asked the Conference to reconsider the case in the light of the human implications, if we announce on Monday next that we are going to examine the validity of these Nuernberg laws. I pointed out that scattered all over the world are Jews whose property has been taken and who have lived in anguishing circumstances ever since and to whom announcement that we are going to hear the case will come as refreshing hope. And we ought not to arouse such hopes

---

[1] *Bernstein v. Van Heyghen Frères Société Anonyme*, certiorari denied, 332 U. S. 772 (1947).

Arnold Bernstein, whose ship companies were confiscated before the war by the Nazis because he was a Jew, and, therefore, he contended, they were confiscated illegally, sought to recover $900,000 from Van Heyghen Frères, a Belgian company, which had bought a Bernstein ship after confiscation. Both the district court and the circuit court of appeals had ruled they had no jurisdiction over acts which had taken place in Germany.

unless five members of this Court are now reasonably satisfied that they will reverse the Circuit Court of Appeals. It would add to the agony of these people to give them this hope, and then dash the cup of hope from their lips should the Court then decide to affirm the Circuit Court of Appeals. I cannot imagine that the Court would say that we have judicial power over these decrees, that the Court would not hold that these are political questions and that these German decrees during the period of our peaceful relations with her were a matter of German law to be recognized even if not respected here. As a result of my observations, several members of the Court said they had no doubt they would vote to affirm the decision, but they had not thought about the considerations which I had advanced and on a reconsideration only Douglas and Murphy voted to take the case.

The Chief formally proposed a change in the order of procedure on opinion day whereby motions for admission to the bar would be the first order of business and the reading of opinions would follow. The proposal derived from a request on the part of members of Congress, particularly Senators, who frequently have to wait a good long while for the completion of the oral opinions before presenting their constituents for admission to the bar. Black was for it and so was Reed. When it came to my turn I spoke somewhat at length on the importance of not breaking with a tradition that is as old as the Court, that tradition, particularly in this disordered world, which is a fragile fabric, should be adhered to as one of the great social forces of justice unless change is called for in the interest of the administration of justice. The proposal is not one that is called for in the interest of justice, but merely for the convenience of a few Senators, who, after all, are no busier and no more important than the great Senators of the past who had to wait until the Court was finished with what, after all, is the culmination of its most important task, namely the pronouncement of judgments. I asked the Conference to think twice and thrice before disobeying the injunction, "Remove not the ancient landmarks of thy Fathers." Murphy said he was also opposed. Jackson gave added support to my argument by saying that changes which are not matters of substance had better not be made by people who make so many changes of substance as we do. Leave conservatives, he said, to make such changes. Then Rutledge echoed my sentiments. Burton agreed with the Chief, but expressed himself strongly in favor of written oral opinions. Jackson said that he thought so important a change in the procedure of the Court should be made by formal order and he wanted that done so that he could express dissent from it. I said I felt the same way.

Sunday, October 12, 1947

Bob Jackson phoned to say that he had been thinking some more about the Chief's proposal to change the order of procedure and thought there were some other arguments that were not made. He thought it might be worthwhile to spell them out so that our dissent would appear to be reasoned. He outlined the arguments: Senators are merely pursuing personal business, but there are those who are entitled to have the opinion at the earliest moment, such as representatives of the Government agencies and members of the press who have to meet a deadline. There is also consideration of security in that leaks are rendered more possible the longer the opinions are in the hands of the Clerk for distribution and not actually distributed. I agreed with his arguments and encouraged him to write them out and to circulate his memorandum on Monday.

Herbert Feis called and told of a talk between Lewis Douglas and Dean Acheson the other day in connection with the European situation.[1] He said Douglas was greatly disturbed about the precarious situation of Italian and French conditions and the lack of the sense of urgency on the part of the Government here to meet the situation adequately and in time. Herbert was delighted to find that Lewis Douglas, who in the past had been a theoretical freetrader, rejected the relevance of the so-called Geneva Charter, providing for removal of barriers of free trade in the world, in the present situation. Herb said that it was a besetting sin of Hull to ride a doctrinaire hobby well enough suited for a normal world but not to economic circumstances as abnormal as ours.

Monday, October 13, 1947

Jackson phoned to say that Wiley Rutledge had been to see him to suggest an alternative for the Chief's proposal whereby, in order to save the Senators from waiting until the opinions were announced, motions for admission would not be entertained on Monday. Wiley had asked the Chief to put over the order announcing the change and Jackson said he would for the present not circulate the memorandum which he had written, except to send me a copy. The Chief in the course of the day made various references to "tradition," showing that he had taken hard the opposition to his proposal.

Court met and heard arguments in No. 7, *Morris v. McComb*, No. 14, *Central Greyhound Lines, Inc. v. Mealey*, No. 16, *Priebe & Sons, Inc. v. United States*. Argument started on No. 36, *Sherrer v. Sherrer*.

Tuesday, October 14, 1947

Court met and heard the argument in No. 36, *Sherrer v. Sherrer* finished. Heard argument in No. 37, *Coe v. Coe*. Argument started in Nos. 66, 67 & 68, *Cox v. U. S., Thompson v. U. S., Roisum v. U. S.*

Went to Herb Feis' to see the Alfred Knopfs. Knopf was very lugubrious

---

[1] Herbert Feis was Special Consultant to the Secretary of War. Lewis Douglas was Ambassador to Great Britain. In May and June Acheson and Secretary of State George Marshall had made the landmark speeches that eventuated in the Marshall Plan. The task now was to convert a general proposal into legislation and international agreements.

about the prevailing public taste in books as judged by the best sellers. He illustrated by the very small sale of Trevor-Roper's *The Last Days of Hitler*—something like four thousand—, I having said to Knopf that that was one of the most exciting books I had read in many a year, that there had been a very limited response to it. He said that the public is probably sated with war books and, in any event, the books that obtain a wide response are cheap and well-touted. All this apropos of my remark that Herbert Feis' book about Spain is a book of high scholarship but as exciting as a mystery.[1] It is the kind of book that should be widely read.

We dined at the Bob Jackson's with young Bill and his wife and Frances Watson[2] and Pat Dean,[3] who was part of the Nuernberg prosecution—an Englishman. He was an extremely intelligent young man, whose father is Master of Trinity Hall, Cambridge, who had left the bar for the diplomatic service. Dean said that there was some speculation as to whether Attlee's Government, as now constituted, would survive another year. He thought nothing would happen until the extreme left in Attlee's Government, Bevan, Jennie Lee, and Company, left. In the course of the talk, after one thing or another, Bob Jackson told of circumstances, after Wallace was nominated as Vice President in '40, attending the disclosure of Wallace's silly letters to that woman correspondent in the Eastern cult in which Wallace was interested. As is well known, he had code names for the President and Hull and others in the administration and wrote stuff that would have been embarrassing to F. D. R. because of some of the references regarding the President in some of these letters. They had gotten into the hands of Paul Block[4] and publication was feared. As a matter of fact, not so long ago I heard Anne O'Hare McCormick say that a set was also in the *Times* office and was probably in the hands of other newspapers. Bob told a story that I had also heard from Jim Byrnes to the effect that when the President came back from the West, he called Jim Byrnes, Harry Hopkins and Bob Jackson into conference for a consideration of the problems raised by these letters. The President amusedly said, "Bob, you have the F. B. I. and Edgar Hoover in your shop. Can't they somehow or other discover that Wallace had a love affair with this woman. The American people could understand a romance." And Jimmy Byrnes said, "Can't you find him registered on some hotel blotter with this woman?" The President asked Bob to see Mrs. Wallace and talk to her about the possibility of the letters being published. Jackson went on to say that Mrs. Wallace was a perfect brick about

[1] Herbert Feis, *The Spanish Story* (New York, 1948).

[2] Frances Watson, the attractive widow of General Edwin "Pa" Watson, President Roosevelt's appointments secretary, was an accomplished vocalist and patron of music. She frequently enlisted Frankfurter's help in sponsoring a concert and they occasionally attended concerts together.

[3] Patrick Dean later became Britain's representative at the United Nations and Ambassador to the United States.

[4] Paul Block was the conservative publisher of the Pittsburgh *Post Gazette* and other papers.

it, and said "I told Henry not to write letters to that foolish woman." Jackson then advised her that if the thing should break, she should not be accessible to the press. Block and the Republicans hesitated about publishing them because there was some suggestion about forgery. When Wallace was going around the West making speeches and was asked about these letters he said categorically, "They are forged." That frightened the Republicans and that is where the matter ended.

Wednesday, October 15, 1947

Court met and concluded argument in Nos. 66, 67 & 68. Heard argument in No. 18, *Hunter v. Texas Electric Ry. Co.*, No. 39, *Aero Mayflower Transit Co. v. Bd. of Rd. Commissioners of the State of Montana.*

We went to the National Symphony with Frances Watson.

Thursday, October 16, 1947

At lunch with Adolph Miller [1] last Saturday, he said he wanted to consult me regarding a letter he had had from Grace Tully on behalf of the Franklin Roosevelt Memorial Association, and in order that I might have the matter fully before me he wanted me to read her letter. In substance it stated that they are desirous to have a record from those who had had intimate relations with F. D. R. in public affairs of their recollections of important expressions of views etc. and the evolution of policies during F. D. R.'s Presidency. As an old friend of F. D. R.'s, Miss Tully wrote, she was sure that Adolph Miller could contribute in important ways by putting on paper his recollection of conversations which she knew had taken place between F. D. R. and Adolph M. in regard to economic and financial matters. I told Adolph that Miss Tully's letter opened up a considerable problem and since I had to run off promptly after lunch to return to the conference I would like to come one day in the following week, after Court, and talk the thing out with him—in the meantime I would think about it. Accordingly, I spent the late afternoon with Adolph, canvassing the matter. I told him I appreciated the difficulties of stating briefly important discussions between him and F. D. R. and on the other hand the difficulty of writing at length about these matters without at the same time putting each situation in the total context of F. D. R.'s personality and problems. On the other hand, I thought that history also has its claims and that not merely his, Adolph's, discussions with F. D. R. but his interpretation of them in relation to Adolph's appreciation of F. D. R. in his entirety would furnish important light in the eventual historical judgment of F. D. R. Adolph then told me of two or three rather important talks that he had with F. D. R. in regard to the economic problems that emerged as a result of the depression including an under-

---

[1] Also see entry of November 2, 1946.

standing of the forces that begot the depression. He said that the earliest talk took place in Albany, before F. D. R. came down here, precipitated by F. D. R.'s telling Adolph that he had had a report from Frances Perkins, who was then the Industrial Commissioner for New York, in which she forecast serious difficulties ahead. Adolph said his only disagreement with Miss Perkins' analysis was that it was far too mild, and then explained to F. D. R. why he thought that much more serious breakers [were ahead] than the Government or the people either understood or were ready to face. The essence of the matter was the far-reaching consequences of industrialization by countries that came later in the field than Great Britain, particularly Germany, the conflict of interests that thereby ensued, the relation of this country's economic and political position to these transforming forces and the potential conflict in the world, all of which added up to an interdependence which could only be met adequately by an increase in the freest possible flow of commerce throughout the world. Later on F. D. R. asked Adolph to Hyde Park to talk about things and while there, there came through Colonel House the request from President Hoover to have the President-elect join him in taking economic steps viz à vis Great Britain and forsooth toward an economic conference. Adolph himself helped to draft the reply of F. D. R. leaving the responsibility for all action to the then-President. Adolph then reminded me that after F. D. R. became President and had this Government participate in the London Economic Conference instead of taking what broadly speaking may be called an international economic viewpoint, he reenforced a narrow nationalistic attitude which had begun so disastrously with Hoover's signature of the Smoot-Hawley Tariff Act. I interrupted his recital to say that that of course was the beginning of world deterioration because Smoot-Hawley was followed by the Ottawa agreements and the vicious circle was in full swing. Adolph summarized his feeling about F. D. R.'s attitude towards economic matters by saying "Felix, you know as well as I do that the understanding of economic matters was not Franklin's forte. But temperament and experience, and I think by virtue of his affliction, he was preeminently alive to and concerned with human problems in their obvious human aspects. And the relations that are deemed more or less technical economic questions had little attraction for him. He will live in history, I believe, as a great humanist and of course he also had a kind of cunning interest in politics which with his keen perception about men he so successfully extended to politics on a world stage." I expressed agreement with this analysis but made the further point that while F. D. R. might not act [on] particular views, such as Adolph's, in regard to economics at the time that it was tended, the advice was not lost and he would often put such contemporaneously rejected advice to good use when it fitted in with all the other forces in his mind or feelings that combined to make up judgment. Thus, I pointed out to Adolph, his analysis about economic interdependence and the indispensable need for removing the barriers to a free flow of commerce was not lost on F. D. R. and he later acted on that conviction firmly and effectively. Adolph assented to this and it led me to continue by saying that F. D. R. will be so big in history that he can afford to have Adolph state in his reply to Miss Tully exactly what he stated to me about F. D. R.'s temperamental humanistic gifts, the uncongeniality of mere economic problems, the way he dealt with them and the way he didn't. I left him under the impression that he will do something of the kind though briefly (Adolph has an inhibition that bars writing with any kind of ease and relish).

Friday, October 17, 1947

In our walk down this morning Dean Acheson told me of a visit he paid to Cordell Hull at the Bethesda Hospital. The old gentleman evidently has greatly improved and is full of eagerness about world affairs—eager Dean says to talk about them at great length and apparently reads everything. He talked at length about our relations with Russia and very critically about the way in which we are pursuing our policy. He thinks all this debating and verbal quarreling on almost every point is bad. According to Dean he put it in this colloquial way: "It isn't any use kicking a tough hound around because a tough hound will kick back." Hull dwelt at length apparently on his visit to Moscow and his dealings with the Russians there. Dean said to him "No doubt that was the high-point in cooperative relations with the Russians," but he thought that they had changed their tune since then. Hull agreed with this but apparently implied that he had the great secret of getting friendliness out of the Russians, because when I asked Dean if Hull suggested any constructive action, Dean said that he did not but that he simply was unhappy at the way things were going.

Mr. Reavis who is the law partner of Guido Pantaleoni,[1] came in to fix a date certain for the ceremony by which the Guido Pantaleoni corner, commemorating Guido Pantaleoni, H. L. S. 1923, will be held at Langdell Hall. He said that it would be the desire of all that I should say a few words and I told him that of course I would be honored to do so if that is their wish and we fixed on November

Saturday, October 18, 1947

Conference at which we disposed of the usual petitions for *certiorari* and voted on the following cases argued this week: Nos. 38, 40, 7, 14, 16, 36, 37. The matters that aroused real conflict were the following:

1. No. 300 *Hood v. Texas Co.*[1]—this was an ordinary negligence injury case arising under Texas Law but in the federal courts because of diversity of citizenship. The Court voted to grant and reverse. I protested vigorously against

---

[1] Guido Pantaleoni, a lieutenant colonel with the Office of Strategic Services, was killed in action in Sicily. Justice Frankfurter, Dean Griswold of the Law School, and President Conant spoke at the ceremony.

[1] *Hood v. Texas Co.*, certiorari denied, 332 U. S. 829 (1947).

taking a case which even assuming the Court below was wrong had no other significance than an erroneous decision in an individual case. "Is it really our business," I said, "the business of the Supreme Court of the U.S. to reexamine a record of several hundred pages to see if the trial court should or should not have and if we don't examine the record how can we reverse out of hand. Such action seems so contrary to the duties of this Court and disregard to the conditions under which it should do its business, that I propose to protest in my opinion, setting forth the whole situation." The Chief Justice called attention to the fact that once already this Term after a majority agreed to grant a petition in one of the negligence cases I joined the other in reversing in order to dispense with arguments. To which I replied, "The fact that we keep on doing it shows how wrong I was in acquiescing in the earlier case. We will be sitting here and reversing every negligence case that is brought here by the Circuit Court of Appeals when [a majority] thinks a judgment should have been directed toward the defendant with the result that circuit courts of appeal will gradually get the hint that they should not decide against the plaintiff in a negligence suit, or if they persist, we will be doing precisely that which we would not do." At this point, Jackson took up the discussion with the remark, "Let's be candid about this. It is proposed we reverse the C. C. of A. on this question. Is there any man around this table who has really read the record?" Silence was the only answer he got. And so the matter was left with clear notice from me that I shall write against granting and reversing in this case.

2. No. 50 Misc. *Milch v. United States.*[2] This was a postponed discussion of the motion by General Milch, the Nazi Air Marshal, who was convicted by the Military Tribunal in Germany, erected under our international engagements, for leave to file a petition of *habeas corpus*. The discussion had gone over in the previous week because Burton wanted to inform himself as to the authority of the tribunal which convicted Milch. Also Douglas had not previously participated. The discussion went in the usual order and when it came to my turn I said the all-conclusive reason for denying the motion is that under Article III of the Constitution, we do not have original jurisdiction to review the findings and sentence even of an ordinary court-martial in this country—the courts-martial and military tribunals are not part of the judicial system of the United States and in any event, wholly aside from the unreviewability in my judgment of this military tribunal by any court we have no original jurisdiction and therefore petition should be dismissed. Murphy was of course for granting it, ditto Rutledge, Jackson decided to keep out of it, not because he was at all connected with the tribunal which convicted Milch but because Milch had been examined by him, etc. and he thought it just as well not to

[2] *Milch v. United States*, 332 U. S. 789 (1947).

The Court in a four to four decision refused to intervene in Field Marshal Erhard Milch's life sentence for war crimes. Justice Jackson did not participate. Justices Black, Douglas, Murphy, and Rutledge argued the Court should grant a hearing to determine whether it had authority to review the case. But the other four justices opposed intervention in any form.

participate. Burton said he was first for setting down the case and having the question of jurisdiction argued but after examining into all the documents as to the source of the jurisdiction of the tribunal, he was satisfied to have the petition dismissed because we were without jurisdiction. I forgot to mention Douglas, who said without comment or explanation, that he would deny or dismiss the petition. And so, there were three for hearing the jurisdiction of this Court argued and five for outright dismissal with Jackson not participating. There was some question whether, when three out of eight wished the jurisdictional matter to be heard it was not sufficient to carry the day, but it was assumed that the petition would be denied.

Sunday, October 19, 1947

The usual quiet Sunday at home spent on reading, music, etc. and disposing of a bunch of *certs*.

Monday, October 20, 1947

Continuation of Saturday's conference. Before we got underway on the regular list, Douglas announced that after reconsideration over the weekend, he had changed his mind on the Milch case and would now vote to have the case set down on the question of our jurisdiction, to which he added in a matter of fact voice, "But I don't suppose that my vote alters the conclusion that the case is not to be set down for argument." The Chief promptly said that that made four for having the jurisdictional question argued and he indicated that he thought that that would carry a requirement to set the case down for argument. This precipitated a new issue, namely whether the rule which brings a grant of *certiorari* if four vote for it, as well as entertains an appeal when four vote to note probable jurisdiction, applies to other forms for invoking the jurisdiction of the Court. After a good deal of discussion, both relevant and desultory, a vote was taken that the case was not to be taken even for purpose of hearing the jurisdiction argued with the four voting to entertain the case asking that in the order that went down, their dissent was to be noted, the four being Black, Douglas, Murphy, and Rutledge. There was no doubt at all that it was clearly understood that the order denying the Milch petition would go down with the other orders to be announced by the Chief Justice. This is what happened when we went on the bench at noon.

But long after we took our seat Frank Murphy told me that Rutledge was all stirred upon finding that the order in the Milch case had gone down and that Douglas had stirred up Rutledge so that the latter was going to raise a row about it. This came to me with such a surprise, in view of Douglas' explicit statement that while he had changed his vote, he assumed that that would not change the disposition of the case that I asked Murphy (on the bench) what led him to say that Douglas had stirred up Rutledge. He replied, "I know what I am talking about because Bill sent a note both to Wiley and me saying 'What goes on here? I want to hear the Milch case argued.' " F. M. then went on to say, "It was like a bolt from the blue to me when Bill announced that he had changed his vote in the Milch case. Someone must have applied the heat to him." To which I remarked, "Well he evidently wanted to have it both ways, because while he announced that he had changed his vote to vote to hear the question of jurisdiction argued, he at the same time said that he did not suppose that would change the conclusion of last Saturday that the case would not be heard." To which Murphy replied, "I just want you to know if anyone wants to work up an intrigue against Bob Jackson—for that's what it is—they won't get our support, I mean Wiley's and mine. My vote is an honest vote and so is Wiley's but Bill has stirred up Wiley and says he is going to do what I tried to persuade him he ought not to do and that is to file an opinion protesting against the order that went down." I told him I won't join him, I said what I strongly felt, "Frank, you will be doing a great service to the Court and to Wiley if you dissuade him from writing." Later, Frank told me that Wiley had sent a note to the Chief requesting the calling of a conference for a reconsideration of the whole Milch matter. In the meantime so Murphy told me, Douglas furnished Rutledge with ammunition to establish the proposition that the practise has been to have argument when four vote for it even as to matters other than petitions for *certiorari* and appeals. He referred to the case of *Oklahoma v. Woodring*, 309 U. S. 623, where on a motion for leave to file a bill of complaint four had voted to grant the motion and thereupon the case was set for argument and the motion denied by an equally divided court. And so a conference was called at 4:30 and Rutledge stated that he was surprised to learn that the order in the Milch case denying the application without hearing argument had gone down, and he said he had not understood that such was to be the action taken. The Chief then rehearsed the occurrences of the morning, and asked each member of the Court to state whether he, the C. J., was correct in understanding that that was to be done which was done. Everyone confirmed the correctness of the Chief's understanding except Murphy and Rutledge and they both agreed that he was justified in carrying away the impression that he did, that they may have been inattentive at the time, but Rutledge added with some vigor that the whole incident shows that action by the Court should not be taken in haste and informally. The Court then passed on to the consideration of Rutledge's proposal that the order filed today be recalled and the case set down for argument on the question of our jurisdiction. Black thought it would be a great mistake to do so, if as appears five members of the Court or even four, making a divided court with Jackson not sitting, would find want of jurisdiction. Reed thought it would be a great mistake and I said I cannot imagine anything more calculated to fan the flames of international discord than to have this court take action which would naturally enough be construed by the Russians that even the Supreme Court of the United States is obstructing the denazification program by intervening on behalf of one of the most offensive of Nazi military leaders. Douglas voted against recalling and setting the case down for argument and Murphy too thought it would be a mistake. Rutledge voted yes and Burton also voted no.

Frank Murphy afterwards told me that he hoped I had noted the extraordinary thing of at least two men voting precisely opposite to their conviction in the morning, namely Black and Douglas voting to hear argument but also voting that if four vote that way, it is not necessary to have the case set down for argument. He also said that Bill "tells the Chief one thing and Wiley and me another."

Marion and I dined at the Danish Embassy—the dinner being the occasion at which the Order of the Elephant, the highest honor conferred by the Danish Government was conferred by the Ambassador on Eisenhower in the presence of the Danish Foreign Minister Rasmussen.

Sunday, November 2, 1947

Herbert Swope called up from Long Island on one of his long telephonic visits. He chatted about this and that, including a rather amusing resentment against Walter Lippmann for using the phrase "cold war"—referring to the relations between the United States and Russia—without putting them into quotation marks as though the phrase were his. I said to him, "I duly noted that you tipped off Arthur Krock that the nominal originator of the phrase was Bernie Baruch, and I knew that you were its author." Herbert wasn't content with that and went on to say "Yes, and did you see the editorial—" I stopped and said "Yes, I also saw the editorial in the *Herald-Tribune* duly crediting Bernie with the phrase." Passing from one item of the day to another, Herbert suddenly said, "I suppose you know that your colleague is going to be on Truman's ticket." To which I countered "Since you speak with such authority I am entitled to ask you for your evidence." Beginning with "That's a fair question," he continued, "Ed Flynn was in the other night and I asked him whether it was true that he was backing Jim Forrestal [1] for Vice President. Flynn with a poker face said 'What's the matter with Jim?' 'Well,' I said, 'Hell, Jim Forrestal was a Catholic when he was seventeen, then left the Church, married out of the Church, had children out of the Church, and even though I am told that Spellman is for Jim, I don't think he would help you any.' To which Ed replied 'You couldn't be righter. Of course Jim is out.' I then said 'Well, who is there? I see a lot of Western names mentioned none of whom seems to me very hot.' Whereupon, Ed Flynn said, 'Herbert, who is the fellow who is both radical and conservative, at least seems that way to different people?' To which I replied, 'You mean Bill Douglas.' And Flynn replied, 'Yes and I am for him, I guess he is allright, I don't know much about him.' I said to Ed, 'I don't give a

[1] James Forrestal, after unification of the services, was promoted by President Truman from Secretary of the Navy to Secretary of Defense.

damn who your favorite is. After all, the fellow in the White House will pick his running mate—what matters is what he thinks and not what you think.' Herbert said that Ed Flynn was very categorical in saying, 'I believe Truman wants Douglas.' My next remark was 'Herbert, how much money are you going to put on their election?' 'I will bet on the certainty of their defeat,' was his reply. 'I have been trying to tell people for some time that a heavy swing to the right is under way in the Western world including this country. I have been writing that to Brenden Bracken [2] for some time and he has been insisting that I am a little premature and now comes this heavy conservative swing in England.' " (Today's news announced the loss of more than 600 seats by Labor in the Municipal Election in Great Britain and a corresponding gain by the Conservatives.) Thereupon I said, "Who is it going to be, Herbert, Ike?" "Sure," he promptly replied. "What you may not appreciate, Professor, is that the Republicans will want to win, no matter what. My guess is that Bob Taft will hook up with Bertie McCormick to stop Dewey and there will then come a moment at the Republican Convention when the boys will retire to the sacred precincts of the smoke-filled room and try to agree on the fellow who is sure to win and that is Ike."

Tuesday, November 4, 1947

During the course of the last ten days, Dean Acheson has talked to me several times concerning the means for carrying out the Marshall Plan. State Department people including Bob Lovett, [Under Secretary of State Robert A. Lovett] Budget Bureau officials, Sir Oliver Franks [British Ambassador to Washington] and Dennis Maris (the British representatives who came here in connection with working out the Marshall Plan and the Report of the sixteen Cooperating Governments) and others with whom Dean has had talk on the subject have been told by him that it is vital not to have American authority scattered through several departments or agencies, but to have it concentrated in a single agency like the Lend-Lease Administration exclusively and comprehensively responsible to the President through the Secretary of State. That would not require [the] State Department to be an operating department in the sense that it would have to see to the dispatch and procurement of commodities, etc. etc. any more than the Lend-Lease administration did. State Department would be merely the controlling and deciding agency. This mode of dealing with the problem was also the solution of the Budget Bureau and of the officials technically charged with working out the appropriate agency for the Marshall Plan in the State Department. When the latter said they had difficulty in persuading or being able to persuade probably Marshall and Lovett, Dean told them that it was their business to recommend what they concluded was the

[2] Brendan Bracken, Minister of Information in Churchill's wartime coalition government, was one of Churchill's confidants.

right way to go about the business, leaving considerations of political expediency to political heads, the Secretary and the President.

This morning Dean opened up with the remark "Marshall is a four-engine bomber going only on one engine. I don't know what is the matter with him. He doesn't seem to bring his full force into action." He then went on to tell me that [James E.] Webb, the Director of the Budget Bureau, asked to see him and told him the difficulties which the Budget Bureau is having in getting the scheme of the centralized agency, operating through the State Department, accepted by Marshall. He says the President is all for it, but the President does not want to order Marshall to have such a scheme of administration but would like Marshall himself to appear to want it, and Webb asked Dean how they can persuade Marshall to that view. Dean said the best way is to talk straight from the shoulder very candidly to Marshall and not to try any tack or roundabout way. When Webb agreed that he might talk to Marshall, he replied that he thought that Marshall would have a very smart comeback by saying, "Here you left the State Department, and now you want to tell me how to run it." On the other hand, if Marshall were led to ask him, Dean, he would tell him with complete forthrightness. Webb said that Marshall is somewhat obsessed by the difficulty of finding the proper personnel and Dean said the difficulty is that as Chief of Staff, he knew his material, he would have presented to him a list and would say, "Lt. Colonel Smith is the fellow to make a Brigadier." Webb then asked Dean what he thought of getting together a small group of people with some familiarity of men equipped to run the Marshall Aid agency, keep them together for discussion, if necessary a week, draw up a list of fifty such people and then go to Marshall with it as an available body of administrators. It is no use thought Dean to have Marshall say, "I want somebody like Jack McCloy." He is almost obsessed by his fear of want of available material and the thing to do is to convince him by appropriate process of selection that it is all nonsense. There are such men and here they are.

I said to Dean that the one difficulty is that psychologically Bob Lovett must find it hard probably to talk Dutch to Marshall because he must be still under the old habit of the War Department where Marshall knew more about the things he was dealing with normally than anybody else. It seemed to me humanly awfully hard to have moved Marshall—or rather to have him go— from a field of mastery to a field of novelty. I went on to say that the President's hesitation to put the experience that he has acquired during the last two and a half years at Marshall's disposal now adds a new difficulty to government. I first learned vividly at the Paris Peace Conference that of which I have since become so deeply aware, namely the extent to which subordinates withhold a candid statement of what they believe to be right from their superiors for one reason of prudence or another; now to the relation between Truman and Marshall you have the reverse—the superior, the President of the United States himself, withholds the strength of his views on what he believes to be right because of sensitive regard for his subordinate. Dean smiled and said that that is exactly what is happening.

Tuesday, November 18th, 1974

The Weizmanns came to dinner. He had the apparent debility that comes from being nearly blind. He is soon to have another operation, which, if successful, will give him one eye. Once one got accustomed to it, he seemed in the full vigor of his intellectual powers, with his very special quality of conveying great wisdom through humorous stories. In that respect, as well as in the sane and well-balanced tragic sense that he has of life, he is a sharp reminder of Lincoln. I felt even more vividly than I have in the past, his quality of dealing with a delicate problem by telling a pat story. He spoke with real pain of the change in feeling and sentiment in Great Britain in relation to Palestine from the great days of Balfour, Lloyd George, Smuts, et al. He said that it is mostly Bevin's fault, who is a powerful ignoramus. He recalled what Bevin said of himself at one point, "I am also at the head of the transport workers. I may not be able to organize transport, but I can stop it." And that is what he is trying to do in Palestine, said Weizmann.

Wednesday, November 19th, 1947

Sir B. N. Rau, the framer of the Indian Constitution, came to make a farewell call. The impression I heretofore had of him as a penetrating mind was confirmed and reenforced. He is a man of wide culture and real statesmanlike understanding singularly free in the movemment of his mind. A reference by him to the scheme for working out partition in Palestine led me to ask him whether the expressed hostility of India to a Jewish State would make friendly relations between India and such a Jewish State, if it came to pass, difficult. He promptly said that it would not in the slightest. And he said there would be no reason at all for such hostility, whatever may be the political reasons for India opposing partition now. He then went on to say that Nehru and Weizmann are in correspondence as a result of some observations by Weizmann about the great waste in the use made in India of molasses—a proper use of which might contribute enormously to the food supply of India. Nothing is more important in India, of course, than to open up new food supplies, and the scientific possibilities for improving the food supply of India opened up by Weizmann's Institute in Rehovoth furnish potentialities of friendly relations between India and a Jewish State that would displace any possible theoretical differences. He spoke with great good sense on the whole subject.

Garner Anthony, an old student of mine and former Attorney General of Hawaii, dropped in to say hello. He is a very successful lawyer in Honolulu and I greeted him with, "Anthony, I hope you are not making too much money." And he said, "Don't worry, Sir." I said, "You know, too much money isn't any good." He answered with vehemence, "I can assure you it isn't. In observing some of my clients, I find ample proof of that." Anthony is a man whose observance of the best traditions of the legal profession I should be confident of, and he is also a man of sensitive public spirit. He is very ardent for statehood, and said, "We'll get it too." He said that there is opposition from "our best people," because they are afraid of the racial mixture of our population. Anthony himself said that he has no doubt of their ardent devotion to all that the United States means to us.

Thursday, November 20th, 1947

Worked on cases—Court in session.

Visit from Walter Wilbur, a Law School classmate and an old friend. Wilbur, of an old South Carolinian family, went back to Charleston after graduation from Law School. I asked him what the people of South Carolina are thinking about these days, what are their hopes and fears, etc.? He said that he was sorry to say that they are not thinking about anything, life is at a low ebb, except with one qualification. He said that there is considerable re-thinking of the position of the Negro and a growing liberal outlook in regard to race relations. I remarked that that is thinking about a very important subject, perhaps the most recalcitrant of all our problems. I said I was delighted to hear that there is such a liberal ferment in South Carolina and that it confirmed the impression I had of a growth of a liberal sentiment on the part of the South. I remarked on the difference in students from the South from the time that we were students to recent years and said that I thought it marked an advance and I thought it was very important to give those liberal forces full play and not to make their efforts more difficult by a smug attitude on the part of the Northerners regarding Southern backwardness and Northern righteousness. He felt very strongly that that was so, remarking that the Northerners ought not to play into the hands of the more benighted Southerners.

Alfred Cohn came to dinner, full of talk about the Sydenham Institution. He is down here in connection with plans for the Institution, the essence of which is to make that a greater center of scientific study of the Negro and our environment. He was full of recent experiences, as a result of which he is greatly impressed by the totally different culture among Negroes about which we know so little. He has been seeing a good many Negroes these days, and has been much struck with the courtesy and the kind of deep-rooted wisdom which they manifest, despite the framework of repression of one sort or another within which they have to live.

Thursday, November 20, 1947

Apropos of nothing in particular, as is the case in so many of his remarks to me on the bench, Murphy said, "I think you ought to know that there are people on the Court who are in a quiet, subtle way, trying to poison the Chief against you. They,"—that is the way he always refers to Douglas and Black—

"are doing things that I wouldn't approve of and that I don't do, for I don't ever want to be a party to a feud on the Court. But I thought you ought to know it." I made no comment.

Friday, November 21, 1947

We had for argument cases involving the War Renegotiation Act, and in the course of the arguments there was a reference to the *Bethlehem Steel* case, *United States v. Bethlehem Steel Corp.*, 315 U. S. 289 (1942). (In this litigation the Government claimed in effect that the Bethlehem Steel Corporation took advantage of the Government's necessity of building ships during the last war so as to obtain unconscionable profits.) Murphy said to me, "The *Bethlehem* case first put me wise to Bill Douglas. You remember how at the last minute, as we were on the way to the Courtroom to deliver the opinions in the Bethlehem case, Bill, who had previously been for the *Bethlehem* Company, shifted in a separate opinion, and I held up the reading of the opinion that day." [1] He then went on to talk about Douglas and Black: "You know how highly I think of Justice Roberts. He is a fine man, though I did not agree with him and do not now agree with him about some things. But they (referring to Black and Douglas) really tricked him. They made a fool of him without his knowing it, and then they would come to me and laugh about it. Of course I never said anything to Justice Roberts, because we have to live together on this Court. But I did feel that it was a shame the way they fooled that very nice man."

Saturday, November 22, 1947

Today at Conference we considered at some length negligence cases, sought to be reviewed here on *certiorari*, arising either under the Federal Employers' Liability Act, coming here mostly from State courts, or ordinary negligence suits—usually automobile collisions originating in the federal courts because of the diversity of citizenship between the parties. The taking of these cases raises basic questions as to the function of the Court, that is as to type of case which should occupy its time and energy. In the days of the old Court when the railroad-minded [Pierce] Butler, and others like him, were dominant, the Court would take cases which were decided against the railroads. These

---

[1] In this case Justice Murphy had wanted to file a concurring opinion in order to make a stronger, more direct attack on war profiteering than the majority, because of procedural considerations, was prepared to do. For various reasons, however, he had decided to forego the impulse to preach, but under the stimulus of Justice Douglas's last-minute switch, decided to file a concurrence, and while voting to sustain the contract in order to force Congress to overhaul the procurement system, stated, "I simply cannot in the setting of the defense program today put my imprimatur on a 22½ per cent profit." *Mr. Justice Murphy* by J. Woodford Howard, (Princeton, 1968), pp. 278–279.

were cases which in the main did not involve the formulation of any legal doctrine or the application of the law, but the application of settled legal principles to the myriad diversities in the circumstances of injury on railroads. In my "Business of the Supreme Court," pp. 206—et seq., I said that opinions in these cases "constitute the most copious and futile of the Supreme Court's efforts." After Hughes became Chief Justice, this stream of litigation was dammed, and *certioraris* were denied. After Black came on the Court, he was joined by Douglas, Murphy and later Rutledge, and petitions for *certiorari* in federal employees' and other liability cases again began to be taken, but this time when the decisions below were in favor of the railroad.

Just as Butler brought his railroad slant on to the Court, so Black brought his negligence lawyer, anti-railroad slant to the Court. Since I came on the Court, I have always voted against granting *certiorari*, whether the employees or the railroad was the petitioner, on the theory that at least two courts, and sometimes three, had already dealt with what was ultimately a judgment on the unique circumstances of a particular case. Stone had a sound view of the matter, but Vinson also seems to have brought a keen interest in negligence cases and, in several instances, he voted to grant petitions for *certiorari* in negligence cases. Early this Term, in No. 231 *Thibaut v. Car & General Insurance Corp.*, *certiorari* was granted over my vigorous protest in a case which had gotten into the federal courts solely because of diversity and involved the proper application of Louisiana negligence law, and essentially concerned our consideration here of what took place on a Louisiana highway during a fog. It seemed to me so futile to have a full-dress argument on this that when it was suggested—the petition once having been granted—that there be a reversal out of hand—since five members of the Court were clear there should be a reversal—I joined in such reversal. A few weeks ago another such motor collision case—this time from Texas—came here on petition to review the determination of the Circuit Court of Appeals that there was not sufficient evidence for finding negligence on the part of the defendant, and that therefore the case should not have been allowed to go to the jury. Here the essential and indeed the sole question was the determination whether a truck was on the right or the left side of the road when all the human testimony was one way. Again the majority of the Court, including the Chief, thought the case should be taken and the court below reversed summarily. I then raised a howl and said that to take cases like this one runs counter to the true functions of the Court and that I was going to write on the whole problem of taking these negligence cases simply because we disagree with the lower court in situations that present no general question, no concern of public interest, except insofar as the interest of individual litigants is always a part of the public interest. During all this time we had pending No. 18, *Hunter v. Texas Electric Railway*, another negligence case, but arising out of the Federal Employers' Liability Act, in which a majority of the Court voted to reverse. The case had been assigned to Rutledge, who, after thorough study, came out the other way and with the four of us who had been in dissent, constituted a new majority in deciding against the employee and for the railroad. Black wrote a thundering dissent. I wrote an opinion concurring with Reed on the merits, but protesting at length against the Court's consuming its time with cases that never should be allowed to come here. In the meantime, there were pending before us several other Federal Employers' Liability cases (Nos. 283 and 321) for which there were the usual four for granting, but as to which Black in anger changed his mind in view of the *Hunter* opinion. He said that if the Court was going to have the cases come here and be decided as the *Hunter* case was decided, he was going to vote against bringing it here. Rutledge said then that if we were not going to take these cases, he was going to write against not taking them, particularly in view of my opinion in the *Hunter* case protesting against taking them. And the cases went over from week to week. Wednesday of this week, Rutledge passed me a note to ask whether I would be agreeable to dropping my opinion in *Hunter* if it were just decided without any opinion by anyone and the petitions in all these negligence cases were then denied. I told him that I was entirely agreeable to that disposition, provided it included granting the petition for rehearing which had been filed in the *Thibaut* case (a petition which flagrantly exposed the folly of reversing that case, in view of the law of Louisiana and the facts of the case). Rutledge said his proposal included the *Thibaut* case, which he regarded as the weakest of all cases. Reed talked with me about Rutledge's plan and was very loathe not to read his opinion in the *Hunter* case, which to him seemed a very important contribution to the law of proximate cause. (I had said in my concurring opinion in the Hunter case that the vast mass of opinions on proximate cause constitutes an unedifying chapter in legal history, because the whole concept of proximate cause is rather outmoded and is an effort in most instances to find in a dark room a black cat who isn't there.) At Conference today Rutledge put his plan to the Court, and expressions of agreement were made, resisted, however, by Reed and Murphy. I said I was agreeable to the plan but served notice that *Thibaut* must be part of it. If the reversal in the *Thibaut* case were allowed to stand, I would be compelled to write in protest and set forth the folly of the whole business. I said quietly but sharply that I thought this Court was the last agency of Government that should try to save its face and not admit error, that it was an excellent thing for the country for this Court to acknowledge error when it had made one, as it did in the *Thibaut* case. I said this because there was a good deal of talk around the table about the difficulties of explaining our action in reversing what we had done in the *Thibaut* case. Rutledge said that he agreed that the *Thibaut* case was the weakest in the whole lot and he would have to vote to vacate the judgment and deny the petition. The Chief said that he was one of those who voted to bring up the *Thibaut* case and that while he doesn't often admit that he is wrong once he has taken his position, he is bound to say that "we were wrong" and that he would vote to undo the error. This view prevailed with the result that in the *Hunter* case it was decided to have a summary affirmance of the lower court. The action in the *Thibaut* case was uprooted and in all the other cases the petitions for *certiorari* were denied. So far, so good. It will be interesting to see how long we will appear not to have our time wasted by taking every negligence case.[1]

Tuesday, December 9, 1947

Visited Chief Justice Hughes and was impressed all over again with the unabated vigor of his mind and the range and vividness of his interest in the affairs of the world. No doubt age has taken a toll of strength in that he has less hours of energy than he used to have, but I do not think the quality of his mind or his judgment have abated in the slightest. He speaks with force, he marshals his argument with power and his old habit of precision of detail is evident and when he has occasion to refer to a book or an argument he produces it, he is sure and precise. We talked mostly about foreign affairs and the Russian problem and he was full of concern over an article by Ralph Barton Perry in the December *Atlantic*.[1] Hughes was troubled that so learned and disinterested a thinker as Perry should write something which he thinks is so full of half truths, particularly at a time when it is especially important not to confuse the public mind. I ventured to suggest that one trouble with Perry is that he has never been up against making the necessary adjustments that are the special task of statesmanship. He responded to this remark with great animation saying: "That's it—you have hit the crucial point—not begging your pardon—for though you were a professor for a long time, you managed to deal with the

---

[1] See Introductory essay, pp. 84, 85.

Thibaut v. Car & General Insurance Corp., Ltd., 332 U. S. 751 (1947). Certiorari was granted and the circuit court was reversed in a one-sentence per curiam. A petition for rehearing was granted, the earlier judgment withdrawn, and the circuit court affirmed, Justices Black and Burton dissenting, 338 U. S. 828 (1947). *Hunter v. Texas Electric Railway Co.*, 332 U. S. 827 (1947). The judgment of the Texas Supreme Court was affirmed in a one-sentence per curiam, Justices Black, Douglas, Murphy, and Rutledge dissenting.

In twenty one Terms of Court (1938–1958), wrote Professor Wallace Mendelson, (*Justices Black and Frankfurter: Conflict in the Court* [Chicago, 1961], pp. 22–30), more than sixty Federal Employers Liability Act negligence cases turned on the sufficiency of evidence. Save in one case, Black and Douglas never voted against a workman, and Murphy and Rutledge voted with them until their departure from the Court in 1949. "To put it differently, no four judges are willing to impose the alien chore of negligence litigation upon the Supreme Court for the benefit of the employer. There are four who often do so at the instance of workmen—*over sustained dissent on certiorari grounds*."

[1] "The Logic of Peace" by Ralph Barton Perry, *Atlantic Monthly*, December 1947.

In this article Perry, who was Harvard Professor Emeritus of Philosophy, contended that the United States with one of the weakest communist parties in the world was obsessed with a fear of it. He suspected that this fear was being manipulated in order to keep blacks, workers, and the underprivileged in their places. He feared the United States was embarked upon "a strategy of war," and "since I do not believe that the threat to our security through the spread of communism is either grave or immediate, I would reject the logic of war and follow the logic of peace." The latter required an effort to seek a *modus vivendi* with Soviet Russia, offering her a loan and a ten-year nonaggression pact.

practicalities of life. (I interrupted to say that after all I did not become a professor until I had had eight years of good hard experience at the bar and in Government.) "The trouble with professors is that they do not appreciate, because they have never been confronted with, the thousands of adjustments, as you call them, that have to be made, the people who have to be accommodated, the views that have to be reconciled in the conduct of affairs—and this is a very different thing from solving problems on paper."

December 20, 1947

The Chief raised at conference a matter that evidently had been brewing around here for some days, namely the desire of the law clerks to give a Christmas party and to include among those invited the colored messengers of the various justices and some of the senior colored messengers attached to the Clerk's and the Marshal's office. This is the situation as I understand it which brought the matter to the attention of the Conference.

Last year some of the secretaries initiated a Christmas party in conjunction with the Justices' law clerks as hosts to which the Justices and the various offices of the Court and their secretaries were asked. The proposal to have such a party was again made this year, but the law clerks—some of them, or rather most of them—felt strongly that at least some of the colored employees in the Court should also be asked. It seemed to the law clerks not to do so was not only drawing the color line, but drawing the color line by the Court, or in relation to the Court, charged especially with the duty of not drawing such a color line. This proposal met with opposition among the secretaries—professedly at least—and probably genuinely so as to some—not on the score of racial discrimination but for social reasons as it were—that the messengers are servants, and servants for practical purposes of the secretaries under whose direction they work. These secretarial opponents of the proposal in effect took the position that just as hostesses don't ask their servants to their parties, so they should not be asked at a purely social occasion to ask their messengers. The upshot of the matter was that the secretaries withdrew from the proposed party and the law clerks decided to go on their own as hosts and to invite the Justices' messengers and a few other colored employees. To have the party required of course permission to use a room in the Courthouse appropriate for such a purpose and that required arrangements with the Marshal for such a party. The Marshal declined to give authority for the use of a room if the messengers were to be bidden, without obtaining instructions to that end from the Chief Justice. And this led the Chief Justice to bring the matter up before the Conference to ascertain the wishes or as he said "to get a mandate," from the Court.

As the C. J. started to take up the matter, Douglas left the Conference after whispered conversation with the Chief Justice, saying he had to leave, and he was not present at the discussion that followed.

The Chief put the case in substance as I have given it above and then asked whether the Conference instructs him to tell the Marshal that the law clerks may have the use of the room for their party even though they plan to invite the colored employees. He himself said that whatever one may think about the whole problem, he was for such consent, then calling the Justices in the usual order of seniority, Black said yes, and not another word, Reed also said yes without a word of comment. When I was called upon I said I should like to rephrase the issue, that for me it isn't a question of whether colored people should be allowed to come to a party, but whether if any members of the staff of the Court may use one of the rooms in the Courthouse for a social function either we or the Marshal should have any power of censorship over their guest list. It seemed to me inadmissible or intolerable that we should allow parties to be held in this building that first require those who hold them to submit to us their list of guests, different parties have been held from time to time in this building, as I am informed. For instance, when one of the young women gets married, parties have been held for her in the building, and I should think the sponsors of the party ought not to be required to disclose whom they choose to invite or to have vetos exercised against their guests.

When it came to Jackson's turn, he said he may be sticking his head out but he has different views than those thus far expressed. He thought this whole subject was an explosive one; that the Court is the umpire of great social conflicts in the country and itself went as far as possible to keep out of such conflicts; that he understood that some of the law clerks want to make a demonstration of the matter by holding such a party; that there is a good deal of justice on the part of the girls in not wanting the kind of a party that the boys have insisted upon, and that if we were going to be fair about this business we know damn well that "our hostesses, our wives, don't have our servants, and our messengers, as guests at our parties." He was all against the use of the Courthouse for social purposes, except insofar as any Justice wants to put his own Chambers to any use to which he sees fit. And he would like to have us adopt that rule applicable to the present proposal. That precipitated a considerable discussion, the upshot of which was a result of some further remarks of mine, that I thought there was a great deal to be said not to mix up social problems with essentially Court problems by permitting social functions—other than those for which Justices may be responsible—in this building. I asked that a vote be taken on this, and everybody except Jackson and I voted against Jackson's proposal, the C. J. and Reed feeling it would be very bad to apply it to the present situation. They were afraid of the publicity that might leak. I said there is danger of undesirable publicity no matter what we do, but I thought it was far less hazardous to have such a rule scrupulously and universally observed than for the party to be held and not have every member of the Court attend. Reed said of course he wouldn't attend. I asked him whether he realized the terrible position in which he was placing himself to abstain from going to a party where there are colored people—for so it will be interpreted and is bound to get out—after all the noble utterances of the Court publicly against racial discrimination. He said this is purely a private matter and he can do what he pleases in regard to private parties. I said the very fact that we have been sitting here for nearly an hour discussing the right to hold the party makes it difficult to regard it as purely private. The Court is entangled no matter what way you look at it.

Tuesday, December 30th, 1947

Dean Acheson this morning told me of a call he paid on Cordell Hull, who is at the Bethesda Naval Hospital. He went out to see him with the thought of broaching to him a plan of Dean's to have all the ex-secretaries of State give public support to the Marshall plan—the European Recovery Bill now before Congress. With considerable animation in his face and voice, Dean said, "That old boy Hull has antennae that reach into one's very mind. He must just have surmised what I was going to put to him and he anticipated me by saying, 'Now that my book is finished, I hope before long to be sayin' something that might be helpful in connection with the issues before the world. But I must first gather up my strength and I will get around to it later on, perhaps in April. It might help if I said something.' " Dean quickly picked up the suggestions and said, "It sure would help, the quicker you did it the more it would help." Before he had a chance to become more concrete, Hull broke in with, "Dean, I must first gather my strength before I try to do anything new." And that closed that part of the discussion, because it was perfectly plain, Dean said, that the old man had determined what he was going to do in his own good time. Hull indicated that he would not want to be very specific. "You must put big ideas," Hull told him, "before the people—the idea of Peace, for instance, must be put way in front for the people. Big ideas like Peace are what capture people's minds." (That is evidently what Wallace thinks too and emphasizes, as he did Peace in his last night's speech, counting on the pacifistic feelings of our people.[1] Wallace's problem is not to have that theme drowned by the charges of "communism" against him.)

Hull went on to talk about his book. It is evidently going to be a whale of a book—two fat volumes on thin paper of thousands of pages. He said to Dean that the only American public man who has attempted anything like it is John Quincy Adams, but the latter's effort was "dull" and Adams did not attempt to do his account "in the way in which I have done it." (The book will show "the way in which" Hull did it, but his comments about the writing of American public men show his limited historical learning.)

At lunch today we talked about various cases now waiting decision, and after the others had left, the Chief, Reed and I discussed a number of cases as

---

[1] Henry A. Wallace in Chicago in a speech to the Progressive Citizens of America had announced that he would be a candidate for President on a third-party ticket in 1948. He denounced the Democratic Party as the party of "war and depression" and said the time had come for "a new party to fight these war makers."

to which the Chief thought we were making the wrong decisions, if the vote on the cases stand unchanged. After we came down from lunch, we started to separate and the Chief asked me if I was too busy for a talk and when I went into his room he said, "I have nothing very specific, I just wanted to have some talk with you, and then (with a smile) perhaps we can develop something specific." He went on to talk about *Memphis Natural Gas Co. v. Stone*, No. 94,[2] in which Reed is to write an opinion for the Court to sustain a tax by Mississippi as for a franchise under the pretense of "doing local business" by a utility engaged exclusively in interstate commerce. It is plain from what Reed quite candidly said that he has the greatest difficulty in sustaining such a tax on interstate commerce and can't find good reasons for it and yet wants to force the result. The Chief was deprecating this attitude and made the generalizing remark, "I am very sure that what folks are saying about the Court, what is being written about the Court, both in praise and blame of decisions and members of the Court, really influences decisions of the Court. Now I can honestly say that if criticism has any influence on me at all, it is to stiffen me. I hope it doesn't, but if I am wrong in a decision maybe in time I can be corrected. But if I am criticized for deciding the way I do after giving the matter the best thought I can, it is apt to stiffen me, rather than make me change. Now on the *Memphis* case, I think one of the things that is influencing Stanley is the criticism that so-called liberals have been passing on *Freeman v. Hewitt*, (329 U.S. 249)."

I talked with Stanley Reed about the opinion of Murphy in *Lee v. Mississippi* No. 91.[3] That was a case involving a conviction of a poor devil of a young Negro lad, largely on the basis of a confession by him made under circumstances that the record disclosed to have been coercive. Instead of disposing of it with a few austere strokes within the narrow ground on which we decided the case, in the light of our prior decisions, Murphy made a characteristic harangue, full of sophomoric rhetoric, tasting like rancid butter. Stanley Reed agreed that it was "awful." I went on to say that Wiley agreed that the opinion

---

[2] *Memphis Natural Gas Co. v. Stone*, 335 U. S. 80 (1948).

The Court vote was dispersed. The plurality opinion written by Justice Reed sustaining the Mississippi tax was joined by Justices Douglas and Murphy. Justice Black concurred in the result. Justice Rutledge wrote a separate concurrence. Justice Frankfurter dissented, joined by the Chief Justice and Justices Jackson and Burton. In *Freeman v. Hewitt*, Justice Frankfurter for the Court had upheld the right of the Court to invalidate a state tax under the Commerce Clause, even without supporting legislation by Congress.

[3] *Lee v. Mississippi*, 332 U. S. 742 (1948).

On grounds that Negroes had been excluded from the jury which had convicted a Mississippi Negro of murdering a white man, a unanimous Court, through Justice Black, ordered a new trial. "Murphy commonly walked a stylistic tightrope," wrote his biographer (J. Woodford Howard, *op. cit.* p. 434) "between the jargon of 'justice,' which was stock personal coin, and Black's efforts to peg the Court's intervention on express constitutional rights. Otherwise easy unanimous decisions, such as the *Lee v. Mississippi* confession case, consequently proved to be difficult tasks of linguistic reconciliation in spite of his having a foot in each camp."

was awful, but seems unwilling to realize that the opinion is just a manifestation of a more general situation on the Court whereby various members of the
Court, Murphy, Black and Douglas, each for different reasons, writes not
opinions becoming the great issues that come before the Court and the kind of
dignity that should emanate from the Court, but with an eye, or rather an ear
to the groundlings. It is part and parcel of the Court's failure to be aloof from
the contentions of the day and unconcerned about either praise or blame from
commentators, especially the popular press. Think of a member of this Court
making a speech, as Douglas is tonight, in celebration of the hundredth anniversary of John P. Altgeld. Now I happen to have been for a long time an admirer of Altgeld for his fearlessness and general sympathies as to three matters,
particularly two, which alone give him his place in history. But the two main
ones—his attitude toward the injunction and federal interference in the Pullman strike led by Debs, and his pardoning of the anarchists in the famous
Illinois Anarchist case (see *Spies v. Illinois*, 123, U.S. 121) concern issues that
are actively before this Court, namely the relation of Government to industrial
strife and more particularly the use of the injunction and the reviewing power
of the Court over the conduct of criminal State trials, particularly trials involving or growing out of a clash of opinions. Either a chief speaker at an Altgeld
meeting does nothing about the matters that give him significance, or he
expresses an opinion on issues of a very contentious nature on which he should
be silent, except when expressing opinions in the course of his judicial duties. I
went on to say that there was a good deal to Bob Jackson's clever remark this
morning that the "Court should adjourn until after the election."

At the time I said the above to Reed, I had not seen a column in last
night's evening *Star* entitled "Douglas Steps Forward—Liberal Justice's Address
in Chicago expected to Attract Many from Wallace," by Doris Fleeson, who is
in close relation with Douglas. I referred to this at lunch when I was alone with
the C. J. and Reed and jocularly said to the Chief that I had told Reed that I
thought the Court should adjourn until after election. Both the Chief and Reed
said they had seen the Fleeson column but vouchsafed no other comment.

(1948)

CHURCH AND STATE:
the *McCollum* Decision

Friday, January 16, 1948

I sent this morning's Alsop column on the consideration of Douglas for the Vice-Presidency (herewith annexed) to Stanley Reed with the following note:

S. R.   Friday, Jan. 16/48

Since you read neither the *Washington Post* nor the *N. Y. Herald-Tribune,* you may not have seen this. I think I know the history of the Supreme Court with sufficient intimacy to be confident in saying that never has it been so deeply drawn into the mire of politics as it has been in the last few years. And now we actually have before us litigation in which the law firm of one of the most influential party leaders in selecting the V. P. candidate is heavily interested financially!!

F. F.

to which he replied as follows:

F. F.

Naturally, I agree, as would every man who ever sat on this Court that a Justice should not use his office to advance his political future.

I am sure that neither of the men, whom I have known, Hughes & Roberts—thought they were improperly encouraging politicians to importune them, when they decided cases. Yet they were urged to accept nominations.

For me, Douglas is in their position. He cannot say, "I will not accept." Neither can he denounce the "bosses."

My only reason for hoping that he will not be nominated is that it would be a great loss for him to leave the Bench.

I do read Alsop in the *Post* and the *Herald-Tribune* frequently.

Thanks for both notes of today.

S. R.

My rejoinder was:

1. As to Roberts, I know that he repelled all efforts to allow his name to be used for the Republican nomination for President, both in '44 and '40. He told people who came to see him that under no circumstances would he accept the nomination and he thought it was improper for a member of the Court to leave the Court for a political candidacy.

2. As to Hughes, I know not what preceded his nomination, but I am sure that: (a) he did not have representatives of political bosses come and seek him out; and (b) that there was not a publicity agent, to his knowledge, actively engaged in promoting his candidacy; and (c) that he did not have frequent meetings with friends who were engaged in promoting his candidacy; and (d) he did not have a person with the financial support of Joe Kennedy actively promoting the nomination.

F. F.

Monday, January 19, 1948

Today the decision in *Oyama v. California,*[1] No. 44, dealing with aspects of the California law restricting the holding of agricultural land by Japanese, was handed down. The decision held unconstitutional certain features of the California law insofar as they operated against such land holdings by American-born children of alien parents on the theory that privileges of American citizens were thereby denied by California. The decision did not deal with the main feature of the California law, namely by prohibiting land-holding by Japanese

---

[1] *Oyama v. California,* 332 U. S. 633 (1948).

The Court upheld the right of American minors of Japanese descent to hold land in California. It invalidated a state law escheating lands held indirectly by an alien through a son who was an American citizen, and thus, in the words of Professor Pritchett, began to make amends for its wartime decisions in the Japanese exclusion cases. Chief Justice Vinson wrote for the Court, Black, Douglas, Murphy, and Rutledge concurring, Reed, Burton, and Jackson dissenting. Murphy felt passionately about racial inequality, but Black cautioned him that "softer blows" yielded the same results without displaying ugly facts that enemies abroad could use "to do us harm" (J. Woodson Howard, *op. cit.,* p. 354). It was Frankfurter's view that "the ugly practices of racial discrimination should be dealt with by the eloquence of action, but with austerity of speech" [*ibid.*].

aliens who, in view of our naturalization laws, are themselves ineligible to citizenship. In a series of opinions the old Court had sustained the constitutionality of that decision. Murphy in a long winded soap-boxy attack against racism urged that we overrule these decisions and declare the California land laws unconstitutional. So far as the detailed argumentation of the opinion goes, its statistical data was practically lifted from two articles by Professor McGovney in the California Law Review. Rutledge joined Murphy's opinion. Black told me that with a view to joining Murphy's opinion, he asked Murphy to soften it, but Murphy would not and so Black wrote an opinion taking substantially the line that Murphy did, but in a softer form. Douglas joined Black's opinion. To my great surprise Murphy did not, as he usually does in such cases, deliver his opinion orally. I could feel as I sat next to him on the bench that he was in a great stew about the whole business, and so I asked him why Black and Douglas wrote another opinion, and he replied that it was because he wrote a "powerful opinion" against racism. I said that I could not follow that reasoning. He said that "if you knew all the inside of these opinions it would make you faint." He then went on to say, "Douglas doesn't know that I know, but it is a fact that Bill went to the Chief to get him to have me suppress my dissent. Bill also wrote me a personal note urging me strongly not to publish my dissent. He said that my opinion would be circulated all over Japan and Korea and would play into the hands of the Communists." To which I replied that I did not follow that—"you say he tried to stop you from filing your opinion, because it was against the national interest and yet here he joins in an opinion with Black which says in substance the same thing which you said but in a more diluted form." To which Murphy replied "That is exactly right. But you don't understand some things." To which I rejoined, "You mean that he tried to call you off, but when he didn't succeed, he couldn't politically afford to be less libertarian than you." To which Murphy answered, "That's it exactly," and he added, "If you knew all there was to know about this business you would faint."

Monday, February 2, 1948

Dean Acheson told me this morning that he saw the President on Friday, January 30th, because of a difficulty that arose as to the application of the statute forbidding those holding Government offices from engaging in litigation against the Government in regard to his membership in the Permanent Joint Board on Defense, United States and Canada. He was of the opinion that it would apply and that would prevent not only him, but his partners, from practising law. He resigned, because he concluded that the Code provision would apply and it was arranged that he should see the President in order to secure legislation to allow him to be reappointed and be exempt from the prohibition (a procedure that has often been followed to secure public service as to which the law was not intended to apply, but which in those terms it does). The President said he would send such a request to Congress, but he does not expect them to act on it, because, as Dean quoted the President, "They are not in the mood to do anything for me." Truman said that so far as he was concerned "the meaner they are to me, the better I like it, because the more it helps me." He then referred to the criticism that had been made of him as to the failure to re-appoint Landis to the C. A. B. and his demotion of Eccles [1] from the Chair-manship of the Federal Reserve Board. He said that people talked as though there were a mystery about it. But there is no mystery although he cannot explain—that he couldn't reappoint Landis because he wouldn't have been confirmed, and there is a mess anyhow (Dean didn't explain what the "mess" was). As to Eccles too there was no mystery. The President told Dean that "Eccles double-crossed me three times, and I didn't propose to have him do it again." When Dean told me that, I said, "That's why he gave out a public statement that Eccles has his entire confidence." What Dean told me as to Landis was the first suggestion emanating from any source that Landis was dropped because the President thought he couldn't be reaffirmed. This cer-tainly is contrary to what Vinson said very recently—indeed, the only criticism that has come from Vinson's lips about Truman—that he thought the Landis thing was pretty bad, considering that he, Truman, told Sam Rayburn, who regards himself as Landis' sponsor, two weeks before he was dropped that Landis would be reappointed, and that he told the same thing to Landis a few days before and never gave him any reason thereafter for not reappointing him.

Tuesday, March 9, 1948

For weeks and weeks discussions have been going on in connection with the disposition of the *McCollum* case [1]—the case dealing with the validity of

[1] Marriner S. Eccles believed that he was removed as Chairman because powerful friends of the Giannini banking interests in California—notably Treasury Secretary Snyder and Senator Sheridan Downey—wanted him removed. Eccles felt that Giannini's Transamerica Corporation was a mo-nopolistic branch-bank holding company, inimical to sound banking practices. Henry Morgenthau and Vinson, as Secretaries of the Treasury, had resisted the expansion of Transamerica, but Snyder changed the policy. Eccles had also clashed with Truman and Snyder over his proposal to restrict bank credit as a means of damping down inflation.

[1] *Illinois ex rel. McCollum v. Board of Education*, 333 U. S. 203 (1948).

Justice Black for the Court, with Justices Frankfurter, Rutledge, Jackson, and Burton concurring, and Reed dissenting, invalidated the state's "released time" policy, where public facilities were used for voluntarily requested religious instruction for public school children. Justice Frankfurter in his concurrence, emphasized that "Separation means separation, not something else." In the *Everson* decision [see entry, and footnote, November 20, 1946[Justice Black for a five to four majority upheld a New Jersey law reimbursing parents of parochial school children for transportation costs. There had been sharp dissents in that case by Frankfurter, Jackson, Rutledge, and Burton. The in-tensity of Frankfurter's feelings on the separation issue was indicated by the meeting that he called of the *Everson* dissenters to exchange views on Black's draft opinion in *McCollum*, this in the face of his usual protestations against lobbying and caucusing on the Court. Justice Murphy was bitterly denounced by his co-religionists, including Cardinal Mooney of Detroit, for joining in the *Mc-Collum* decision.

the program regarding religious instruction in the Champaign, Illinois public schools. The vote at the Conference on December 13, 1947, was unanimous for finding unconstitutionality, except that Reed dissented and Murphy passed. The case was assigned for writing to Black who had written the Court's opinion holding constitutional the Jersey bus ordinance. Very quickly Black circulated an opinion in which he referred approvingly to the *Everson* decision. The *Everson* dissenters, Jackson, Rutledge, Burton and myself, consulted as to the position we should take and as Jackson put it, "it would be stultification for us to join Black's opinion." It was accordingly agreed that we should state our grounds for finding the Champaign scheme an infraction of the constitutional requirement of separation of Church from State and the desire was expressed that I try to write such an opinion for the group. Accordingly I did so, and after very few minor suggestions from Rutledge and Burton, to all of which I assented, I secured agreement to my opinion from the other three. Then began efforts on Burton's part to try to get a Court opinion in addition to my opinion on behalf of the four by getting Black to omit every reference to the *Everson* case from his opinion and from mine. Burton is one of these men who thinks you can put evil out of the world by trying to shut your eyes to it. It literally hurts him to have me make a remark that brings to the surface behavior or motives that are not nice or sweet. He hasn't the remotest idea how malignant men like Black and Douglas not only can be, but are. And so he is always trying to cover up differences that lie just beneath the surface on the assumption that thereby you smother them. This trait in him has the best of roots and does not come from any petty or timid quality. There is no man on the bench now who has less pride of opinion—he has the obstinancy that often comes from ignorance or from very limited experience—or more ready to change positions, if his mind can be convinced. And no vanity guards admission to his mind. But he has a kind of a boy scout temperament, as shown by his sympathy with the Buchman movement.

Of course, I would have found it ignominious to find the Champaign released-time program unconstitutional, considering the *Everson* case, without being explicit about the relation between the two cases. But the upshot of these long discussions between Burton and Black and me was that Black took out of his opinion everything except the noble sentiments that Black uttered in the *Everson* opinion, so that Rutledge and Burton could join his opinion and thereby make it a Court opinion. (Poor Burton does not seem to realize that it is a characteristic of Black to utter noble sentiments and depart from them in practice—a tactic of which the *Everson* opinion is a beautiful illustration.)

Throughout these weeks, Murphy stood first on one leg and then on another, and proposed his great solution for all difficulties in the disposition of cases—postponement. But on Saturday, March 6th, when Black's opinion, through the adhesion of Rutledge and Burton had become the Court's opinion, Murphy joined the opinion, announcing, however, that he would also write a little something in addition, but he did not circulate what he was going to write. On Monday, March 8th, the *McCollum* case was announced, but no separate opinion from Murphy.

On the bench today, while a case was being argued, Murphy turned to me and the following colloquy took place—wholly unrelated to anything that preceded:

> F. M.—"Felix, do you know what the Catholic view is regarding the question we decided in the *McCollum* case, because I have not been able to find out.

> F. F.—I don't know any more than you do about it, but I should not suppose that they would have strong feelings in favor of released time.

> F. M.—Well, that is what I think and I was wondering whether you thought that I would be criticized by Catholics for joining in the Court's opinion.

> F. F.—Well, I should think there would be some Catholics who would criticize you, but I think on the whole the Catholics might find comfort in the decision against religious teaching in the public schools, because it would confirm its conviction that the public schools are inherently irreligious or, at all events, it would add strength to their strong desire to have Catholic children go to parochial schools and thereby would add [Diary breaks off here.]

A SIDELIGHT VIEW OF
FELIX FRANKFURTER

At the end of 1951 The Forrestial Diaries, *edited by Walter Millis, were seria-lized in the* Herald-Tribune *and then published in book form. Justice Frank-furter was greatly exercised by some references in the* Diaries *to his alleged behind-the-scenes activities in support of a Jewish state. He sent a letter to Millis setting the record straight from his point of view and asked that when the originals of the Forrestal Diaries were deposited at the Princeton University Library his letter be attached. Although not part of the Frankfurter Diaries, the letter, hitherto unpublished, reads in part like a diary entry and sheds addi-tional light on the line that the Justice drew between proper and improper off-the-bench activities by a Justice of the Supreme Court.*

January 19, 1953.

Dear Mr. Millis:

In the days shortly following the publication of *The Forrestal Diaries* I received a number of inquiries based on statements in the book regarding my alleged intervention on behalf of the establishment of the State of Israel. The letters, both friendly and hostile, drew the natural inference that I had used the prestige of my position to influence the action of the U.N. and of this Govern-ment. Barring a statement of the facts to two intimate friends who were entitled to know the truth, I paid no attention to these inquiries, in conformity with a lifelong practice to try to do my job without having my energy deflected by mis-representations. But in view of the resurgence of virulent anti-Semitism and of the manner in which falsities about me are made to serve wicked purposes that may cause cruelties and death to many innocent people, (see the recent deci-

(345)

sion of the German Federal Constitutional Court in the case of the Sozialis-
tiche Reichspartei (SRP), *Das Urteil des Bundesverfassungsgerichts*, October
23, 1952, p. 70, J. C. B. Mohr [Paul Siebeck] Tübingen), I think in this instance I ought not to indulge the luxury of personal indifference and thus afford
unwarranted ground for the exploiting of misrepresentation.

Before dealing explicitly with the specific items about me in *The Forrestal
Diaries*, let me state my attitude and behavior toward the controversy regarding
Palestine during the period to which these items refer.

I had been an active participant in the Zionist movement from the outbreak of the First World War. When I took my seat on the Supreme Court I
severed all my affiliations with every kind of organization, including social
clubs. This restriction of affiliations broke my active connection with the Zionist movement. This attitude I maintained with what I think may fairly be called
absurd fastidiousness when the establishment of an autonomous Jewish State,
by way of partition of Palestine, became such a lively issue in 1947. (Two incidents, to be referred to later, do not contradict this.) I say that my attitude
may fairly be called absurdly fastidious for this reason. It was common knowledge that President Truman was a supporter of the policy of partition. This was
a matter absolutely unrelated to anything that could be the concern of the
Supreme Court. Certainly one does not cease to be a citizen of the United
States, or become unrelated to issues that make for the well-being of the world
that may never come for adjudication before this Court, by becoming a
member of it. Particularly is this so for one who had the long and deep connection that I had had with the problems of Palestine. And yet, I did more than
abstain from espousing the President's known policy with a view to influencing
friends in and out of this Government. I actually refused to express views in
conformity with the President's, even when solicited to do so.

It so happened that the Chairman of the U.N. Palestine Commission in
1947 was a friend of mine from Harvard days, Dr. Herbert V. Evatt, the
Australian Minister for External Affairs. He came to see me here while the
whole issue was in the balance, and said he was very anxious to have my views.
I told him that as Chairman of the Palestine Commission he was in a quasi-
judicial capacity, (it will be recalled that Dr. Evatt had been a distinguished
Australian judge), and that I did not feel free to talk to him about the merits of
the issue any more than he would talk to me about a case pending before our
Court. The only thing, I added, that I felt free to say to him was that if I had
his responsibility, I would fly to Palestine and get a sense of the situation on the
spot and not rely on the views here of interested parties, however disinterested
they professed to be, because the views even of those who are neither Jew nor
Arab were not really disinterested. He said he had been to Palestine and had
there made a study of the problem. Whereupon I said to him—and I will go to
the stake for the correctness of my memory of the exact words that I used—
"Bert, then I have nothing more to say to you."

My attitude in response to Dr. Evatt's inquiry, my refusal to express a view, even when solicited to do so by so influential a factor in the situation as the Chairman of the U.N. Palestine Commission, is a compendious commentary on second or thirdhand suggestions that I "importuned" anybody or sought to bring "pressure" to bear on anybody.

Let me now deal explicitly with the specific conduct attributed to me in *The Forrestal Diaries.*

I. On pp. 348–349 appears the following:

"At the same dinner Lovett was importuned by Felix Frankfurter on the subject of Palestine and upon his (Lovett's) refusal to enter into discussion Frankfurter became annoyed and Acheson [Dean Acheson, having left the State Department, was at this time in private practice] reported to Lovett afterward that he, the Justice, had been offended. Lovett's conversation was very brief: he said he had had enough of Palestine for a time and did not want to hear of it again."

II. On pp. 357–358 appears the following:

"[At lunch on January 9 Forrestal heard from Loy Henderson more about the 'very great pressure' that 'had been put upon him as well as Mr. Lovett' to get active American solicitation for U.N. votes for the Palestine partition. 'He said Felix Frankfurter and Justice Murphy had both sent messages to the Philippine delegate to the General Assembly strongly urging his vote.' "

I. The first entry is to the effect that I "importuned" Lovett at the Gridiron Dinner on December 13, 1947. It is to be noted that this was two weeks after the crucial decision of the United Nations General Assembly in favor of the partition of Palestine into one Arab and one Jewish State. It is further to be noted that the American Delegation, presumably under instructions from the President through the State Department, voted in favor of that decision. American support was essential to that decision.

At the Gridiron Dinner Lovett and I did meet in the way in which men meet by the merest chance on such an occasion. What took place between us and the only thing which took place, is what follows. As already implied by what I have written, I abstained from any intervention about the Palestine problem, directly or indirectly, with Lovett, who was Undersecretary of State at the time. On the morning of the day that the crucial vote on the issue of partition was to be cast at the United Nation I read an editorial in the New York Herald Tribune which seemed to me so weighty that it stirred in me the feeling that it would be pusillanimous, if not cowardly, on my part—considering my long concern with the problem and my knowledge of its various aspects—not to bring the merits of the editorial to Lovett's attention. Accordingly, I sent him this wire:

"Cambridge, Mass.,
November 29, 1947.

"Dear Bob: Having intimately followed the Palestine problem for more than thirty years and considering the awful probabilities in case of non-action today it would be too finicky to withhold an expression of my conviction that yesterday's editorial in the New York Herald Tribune stated the situation with wisdom and balance. The alternative to acceptance of our policies today is chaos and its consequences which I hardly dare contemplate. Am up here in Cambridge for the dedication of Guido Pantaleoni Memorial. Very sincerely yours.

Felix Frankfurter."

Considering the fact that throughout the war years Lovett and I had warm personal relations, I naturally thought it odd that he should not have acknowledged the telegram. And so, when I bumped into him at the Gridiron Dinner I asked him if he had received my telegram. The substance of his reply—I do not mean to convey his words—was that he had received it but that I might have assumed he knew as much about the subject as I did. My comment was that since I had been concerned with the problem over a much longer period than he had, perhaps I knew a little more about the attitude of some of the State Department officials who were in charge of Palestine than he did and some of these days we might talk about that aspect of it. My recollection is vivid that he indicated that perhaps someday he would talk with me about this. Naturally, the initiative for such a talk was his and from that day to this he has not returned to that subject with me.

If the word "importuned" has any meaning at all, no word less relevantly describes what took place in this chance encounter of about two minutes between Lovett and me at the Gridiron Dinner on December 13th.

II. This entry in the Diaries is a purported communication from Loy Henderson to Forrestal. The short comment to make on it is that I never sent a message by any mode of communication, direct or indirect, to the Philippine Delegate of the Assembly or to any other Delegate. The statement that I did so is an unqualified, unsalvageable untruth. In order that this disavowal leave no distortionable opening, perhaps I ought to add that although Justice Murphy sat next to me on the Bench I never exchanged a word with him about the Palestine issue before the General Assembly and had no knowledge of any communication that he may have sent, if he sent one, to the Philippine Delegate or to any other Philippine personage.

Earlier in this letter I stated that barring two incidents which could not fairly be deemed as such, instead of utilizing my position to bring "pressure" upon, or to "importune", anybody in the Government, directly or indirectly, I did not even exercise the rights of citizenship to do what I legitimately could to further the Presidential policy regarding Palestine. One of these acts I have already narrated, my telegram of November 29th to Lovett. The other was this. Dr. Weizmann was in this country at the time the Palestine issue was before the U.N. He was an old friend of mine; ever since the First World War we had been associated with the Zionist cause, until, on coming to the Court, my activities ceased. Naturally and properly enough, he asked me for an introduction to Secretary Marshall so that he, its undisputed leader, could state the Zionist case to General Marshall directly. I declined to do even that although I was on the friendliest terms with General Marshall. Later, however, I saw a reliable item in the press to the effect that General Marshall had received a visitor on the Palestine problem who, being neither Jew nor Arab, deemed the views submitted to the General to be wholly objective. Being myself convinced of the partial outlook of this visitor, I had qualms of conscience about my finickiness in not asking General Marshall to hear Dr. Weizmann's side. Accordingly, on March 10, 1948, I wrote to Secretary Marshall a letter expressing the hope that he might find time to see Dr. Weizmann. I append herewith copy of my letter and a copy of General Marshall's reply.

I have set forth I believe the totality of all that I did, either directly or indirectly, in regard to our Government's dealing with the Palestine problem in 1947 and 1948—or, for that matter, since.

Having stated the true facts about the statements in the *Diaries* that relate to me, I shall leave it to you to make such use of these corrections as seems appropriate to your standards of historical accuracy. This may take the form of emendations in future editions or reprints of the *Diaries* or lodgment of this letter with the Forrestal Papers so that future historians may draw upon it.

Sincerely yours,
(Signed) Felix Frankfurter

Walter Millis, Esq.,
The New York Herald Tribune,
New York City.

March 10, 1948.

Dear Secretary Marshall:

Having some notion of the burdens you are carrying these days, I should not want to add a featherweight to them. I do not think I do so in venturing to ask you to find time to see Dr. Weizmann.

Dr. Weizmann in himself represents as does no one else the history and the aims of the Jewish Homeland in Palestine. He also happens to be a great man, and, in the estimate of those entitled to judge, a statesman of stature. As you doubtless know, he made very important scientific contributions to the Allied victories in both World Wars.

I venture to ask you to see him, because I am confident it could not but be of help to you in one of the most tangled and anguishing of world problems.

Dr. Weizmann is at the Waldorf-Astoria in New York and is ready to come to Washington at any hour that suits your convenience, either on Thursday or Friday of next week.

With cordial regards,

Very sincerely yours,

(Signed) Felix Frankfurter.

Hon. George C. Marshall.

March 15, 1948.

Dear Frankfurter:

Thank you for your letter of March 10 asking me to see Dr. Weizmann on the Palestine question next Thursday or Friday.

I will be out of the city at that time, making the Charter Day Celebration speech at the University of California. Quite frankly, however, I have found it necessary to forego seeing people on the Palestine matter at this time. There are so many divergent views, nearly all of which are developed in passion and influenced by pressure groups, that I cannot see one without seeing all. I am always glad to receive the views in writing, so that my staff can also benefit.

I suggest that Dr. Weizmann ask Ambassador Austin for an appointment, in New York, and concurrently write to me personally. I believe this would be the most convenient, and at the same time the most logical, manner of having Dr. Weizmann's views considered.

Faithfully yours,

(Signed) George C. Marshall.

Mr. Justice Frankfurter,
The Supreme Court.

Law Clerks for Mr. Justice Frankfurter

Joseph L. Rauh, Jr.	1938–1939
Adrian Fisher	1938–1939
Edward F. Prichard, Jr.	1939
Philip L. Graham	1940
Philip Elman	1941
Stanley Silverberg	1943
Harry K. Mansfield	1944
Philip B. Kurland	1945
Elliot L. Richardson	1945
Louis Henkin	1946
Irving J. Helman	1947
Albert J. Rosenthal	1947
William T. Coleman	1948
Fred N. Fishman	1949
Albert M. Sacks	1949
Hugh H. Calkins	1950
Weaver W. Dunnan	1950
Abram J. Chayes	1951
Vincent L. McKusick	1951
Alexander M. Bickel	1952
Donald T. Trautman	1952
Frank E. A. Sander	1953
James Vorenberg	1953
Matthew G. Herold, Jr.	1954
E. Barrett Prettyman, Jr.	1954
Richard E. Sherwood	1954
Harry H. Wellington	1955
Andrew L. Kaufman	1955–1956
Jerome A. Cohen	1956
J. William Doolittle	1957
John H. Mansfield	1957
Richard N. Goodwin	1958
Howard L. Kalodner	1958
Paul M. Bender	1959
Morton M. Winston	1959
Anthony G. Amsterdam	1960
John D. French	1960
Daniel Mayers	1960
David P. Currie	1961
Roland S. Homet, Jr.	1961
Peter Edelman	1962
David Filvaroff	1962

INDEX